Economic and Soci

CW00349005

This book develops principles of adjudication to facilitate accountability for violations of Economic and Social Rights.

Economic and Social Rights engage with areas relating to social justice and their violation tends to impact on the most vulnerable members of society. Taking the UK as a case study, the book draws on international experience and comparative practice, including progressive reform at the devolved subnational level, that demonstrate the potential reach of Economic and Social Rights when the rights are given legal standing in domestic settings according to their status in international law. The work looks at different models of incorporation of rights into domestic law and sets out existing justiciability mechanisms for their enforcement as well as future models open to development. In so doing the book develops principles of adjudication drawn from deliberative democracy theory that help address some of the critiques of social rights adjudication.

This book will have a global and cross-sectoral appeal to legal practitioners, the judiciary and the civil services, as well as to researchers, academics and students in the fields of human rights law, comparative constitutional law and deliberative democracy theory.

Katie Boyle is Associate Professor in International Human Rights Law at the School of Law, University of Stirling. She has published widely on the justiciability of economic, social and cultural rights and human rights reform during periods of constitutional transition. She was a member of the First Minister's Advisory Group on Human Rights Leadership (Scotland) and previously qualified as a lawyer with the Government Legal Service for Scotland.

Routledge Research in Human Rights Law

Economic and Social Rights Law

Incorporation, Justiciability and Principles of Adjudication

Katie Boyle

Routledge
Taylor & Francis Group

LONDON AND NEW YORK

First published 2020 by Routledge

2 Park Square, Milton Park, Abingdon, Oxon OX14 4RN
605 Third Avenue, New York, NY 10017

Routledge is an imprint of the Taylor & Francis Group, an informa business

First issued in paperback 2022

Publisher's Note

The publisher has gone to great lengths to ensure the quality of this reprint but
points out that some imperfections in the original copies may be apparent.

British Library Cataloguing-in-Publication Data
A catalogue record for this book is available from the British Library

Library of Congress Cataloging-in-Publication Data
A catalog record has been requested for this book

ISBN: 978-1-138-29888-0 (hbk)
ISBN: 978-1-03-233609-1 (pbk)
DOI: 10.4324/9781315098326

Typeset in Galliard
by Integra Software Services Pvt. Ltd.

For James

Contents

Tables and Figures

Table of Cases

Table of Legislation

Tables

Figures

Table of Cases

(*Continued*)

(Cont.)

(Continued)

(Cont.)

(*Continued*)

(Cont.)

European Union Case Law
European Court of Justice, Court of Justice of the European Union

Council of Europe Case Law
European Court of Human Rights

(*Continued*)

(Cont.)

South African Case Law

Colombian Case Law

Irish Case Law

FN v. Minister for Education [1995] 1 IR 409

In re Article 26 and the Health (Amendment) (No.2) Bill [2005] IESC 7

Minister for Posts and Telegraphs v. Paperlink [1984] ILRM 373

Murphy v. Stewart [1973] IR 97

Murtagh Properties v. Cleary [1972] IR 330

O'Carolan v. Minister for Education [2005] IEHC 296

O'Donoghue v. Minister for Health [1996] 2 IR 20 (Ir.)

O'Reilly v Limerick Corporation [1989] ILRM 181

Ryan [1965] IR 313

Sinnott v Minister for Education [2001] 2 IR 545

TD v Minister for Education [2001] 4 IR 259

The State (C) v. Frawley [1976] IR 365

Other

Angela González Carreño Judgment (Spain) 1263/2018 17 July 2018

Angela González Carreño v. Spain, Communication No. 47/20 12, UN Doc. CEDAW/C/58/D/47/2012 (2014)

Awas Tingi v Nicaragua Inter-Am Ct HR, August 31 2001

Canada (Attorney General) v Bedford 2013 SCC 72

Caso Masacre Pland de Sánchez v Guatemala, Reparaciones, Inter-Am Ct. H.R. Series C No.116 (19 Nov. 2004) Eldridge v British Colombia (Attorney General) [1997] 2 SCR 624

European Roma Rights Centre v Bulgaria Complaint No 31/2005, 25 May 2005)

Finnish Society of Social Rights v. Finland, Complaint No. 88/2012, decision on the merits of 9 September 2014

Francis Coralie Mullin v. The Administrator, Union Territory of Delhi, [1981] 2 SCR 516

I.D.G. v Spain, CESCR Communication No. 2/2014, UN Doc. E/C.12/55/D/2/2014 (17 June 2015)

Jaime Efraín Arellano Medina v Ecuador CESCR Communication No. 7/2015, UN Doc. E / C.12 / 63 / D / 7/2015 (14 November 2018)

Kenneth McAlpine v UK, CRPD/C/8/D/6/2011

Klickovic Pasalic and Karanovic v Bosnia and Herzegovina, the Federation of Bosnia and Herzegovina and the Republika Sprska, CH/02/8923, CH/02/8924, CH/02/9364, 10 January 2003

(*Continued*)

Table of Legislation

United Kingdom; Scotland; England and Wales; and Northern Ireland

Acts of Union 1707

Administration of Justice (Language) Act (Ireland) 1737

Apprenticeships, Skills, Children and Learning Act 2009

Borders, Citizenship and Immigration Act 2009

Charities and Trustee Investment (Scotland) Act 2005

Child Poverty Act 2010

Children Act 2004

Children and Young Persons (Wales) Measure 2011

Disability Discrimination Act 1995

Education Act 1944

Employment Equality (Sexual Orientation) (Northern Ireland) Regulations 2003

Equality Act 2006

Equality Act 2010

Equality (Disability) (Northern Ireland) Order 2000

Equality Pay Act (Northern Ireland) 1970

European Communities Act 1972

Fair Employment and Treatment (Northern Ireland) Order 1998

Fair Employment Act 1976

Fair Employment (Northern Ireland) Act 1989

Government of Wales Act 2006

Human Rights Act 1998

Judicature (Northern Ireland) Act 1978

Nationality, Immigration and Asylum Act 2002

(Continued)

(Cont.)

Other

Acknowledgements

This book draws on research spanning more than a decade. I am grateful to a number of funders who have helped support the research underpinning the book: the Department of Foreign Affairs (Ireland); the Economic and Social Research Council (UK); the Scottish Human Rights Commission; the Equality and Human Rights Commission (UK); the Northern Ireland Human Rights Consortium and the Nuffield Foundation (UK).

I am grateful to the support I have received from colleagues at the University of Stirling, the University of Roehampton, the University of Edinburgh, the University of Limerick, the University of Strathclyde and the Government Legal Service for Scotland. I am particularly grateful to those who gave precious guidance and generously went above and beyond, especially Edel Hughes, Stephen Tierney, Aoife Nolan, Rory O'Connell, John McBride, Michele Lamb, Laura Donnellan, Ger Coffey, Eimear Spain, Jennifer Schweppe, Bríd Dunne, Thérèse O'Donnell, Tikus Little, Rowan Cruft, Giles Proctor, Paul Cackette and John Paterson.

A number of colleagues have been instrumental in helping me to develop my ideas. I must thank colleagues in the Economic and Social Rights Academic Network for the UK and Ireland (ESRANUKI) who have generously given constructive feedback throughout the course of the project. In addition I presented papers on the basis of the book at the Society of Legal Scholars conference (University College Dublin) and Socio-Legal Studies Association (University of Lancaster) as well as seminars hosted at the University of Edinburgh, University of Cardiff, the University of Cambridge, the International Institute for the Sociology of Law (ISSL) in Oñati, a workshop hosted by the Scottish Human Rights Commission on incorporation, and two British Council funded visits to Brasília University (Brazil) and Javeriana University (Colombia). I am indebted to participants in these discussions who offered comments on my work in progress. In particular, thanks are due to Kavita Chetty, Alison Hosie, Duncan Wilson, Bruce Adamson, Diego Quiroz, and all those who have worked at the Scottish Human Rights Commission in particular both Alan Miller and Judith Robertson as successive Chairs, Bruce Porter, Aoife Nolan, Rory O'Connell, Paul Hunt, Tobias Lock, Toomas Kotkas, Colm O'Cinneide, Michael Adler, Ben Warwick, Jeff King, Simon Hoffman, Jo Ferrie, Elaine Webster, Leanne Cochrane and Anashri Pillay for being so generous with their time and insight in discussing the subject of this work and giving feedback on draft excerpts. I am grateful to my co-authors (Edel Hughes and Leanne Cochrane) who have generously given me permission to reproduce excerpts from two co-authored articles in the book. In no small part I owe a debt of gratitude to my primary PhD supervisor Edel Hughes who has supported me throughout the course of this research. Likewise, I am indebted to Siobhán Mullally who examined my PhD thesis at the University of Limerick and thereafter generously provided direction to my research and encouraged me to publish what was then the beginnings of this book.

The research that underpins this book benefited tremendously from the opportunity to work hand in hand with many rights-holders, practitioners, researchers and activists. I am indebted to so many who have given their time and expertise to help me better understand the accountability gap in addressing violations of economic and social rights on the ground. I would like to say thank you to Clare MacGillivray, Heather Ford, Juliet Harris, Emma Ritch, Lucy Mulvagh, Kevin Hanratty, Danny Boyle, Mhairi Snowden and Carla Clarke who each champion rights in a truly inspirational way and from whom I have learned a great deal. I have been completely inspired by the work of the Scottish Human Rights Commission which continues to lead on informing the national discourse through a participative model of engagement with those who can often be excluded from rights discourse. It is from my experience in engaging with this work, where I have tried to observe and to listen, that I have learned about those who seek to hold duty-bearers to account every day of their lives without access to the legal means or legal structures to adequately support them. This book is for them.

I owe a great deal of thanks to my colleagues with whom I worked on the First Minister's Advisory Group on Human Rights Leadership, and from whom I learned a great deal, as we addressed our remit on exploring options that seek to improve the everyday lives of the people of Scotland through a renewed human rights framework. I hope that lessons can be learned from this process to enable reform both in Scotland and beyond.

I am so lucky and grateful to have received great support from family and friends. I am especially grateful to Dan and Mary Riordan for their support and kindness over the years.

I want to express my profound gratitude to my parents, Frank and Mary Boyle, for their endless love, support, encouragement and intellectual guidance. It is to them that my brother Danny, my sister Róisín, and I owe everything. It is our gift to pass on to future generations, especially with the arrival of beautiful Oisín to the world.

And lastly, to my dearest husband James Riordan, who continues to fill our home with love, laughter and support. I would not have even considered pursuing my career path nor this body of research had he not encouraged me to do what I love from the moment we met. No part of this would have been possible without him.

1 Principles of ESR Adjudication

The book examines the potential models of incorporation (ways of embedding rights into domestic law) for economic and social rights (ESR) at the national and devolved (subnational) level and the justiciability mechanisms (adjudication by a court) that enable access to effective remedies in court for violations of ESR. In so doing, the book develops principles of ESR adjudication (the building blocks of good practice) and categorises justiciability mechanisms for ESR enforcement at both the national and devolved level.

The book is written with a view to empowering rights-holders and those who support them by setting out routes to remedy for violations of rights and also exploring options for long-term structural change. It is therefore also designed to provide decision makers and those exercising state power with feasible options for progressive human rights reform. It contributes to the academic discourse whilst also engaging with the practicalities of access to justice. The research tells us that there is a significant legal accountability gap in the protection of ESR across the UK jurisdictions and much of the international framework is ignored or rejected unless incorporated.[1] Human rights are conceptually framed in a way that excludes the operation and enforceability of ESR. Indeed, the national political discourse around social rights is dominated by existing domestic human rights structures and our existing domestic human rights structures marginalise ESR to the sidelines[2] – such as forming aspects of civil and political rights, or featuring as part of formal equality.[3] This book re-conceptualises human rights in the UK by bringing in both the devolved and international perspectives. By doing so it becomes clear that the human rights story in the

---

1 Katie Boyle, Models of Incorporation and Justiciability for ESC Rights, Scottish Human Rights Commission (2018), available at www.scottishhumanrights.com/media/1809/models_of_incorporation_escr_vfinal_nov18.pdf
2 For a discussion on this see Paul Hunt, Social Rights Are Human Rights BUT THE UK SYSTEM IS RIGGED, Centre for Welfare Reform (2017) available at www.centreforwelfarereform.org/uploads/attachment/584/social-rights-are-human-rights.pdf
3 Katie Boyle and Edel Hughes, 'Identifying Routes to Remedy for Violations of Economic, Social and Cultural Rights' (2018) 22 *International Journal of Human Rights* 43–69; Katie Boyle, 'The Future of Economic, Social and Cultural Rights in Scotland: Prospects for Meaningful Enforcement' (2019) 23 *Edinburgh Law Review* 110–116.

UK is much broader and much more complex than would first appear. The book makes a contribution to the UK discourse but also provides incorporation models, justiciability mechanisms and principles of adjudication that can apply elsewhere, contributing to the wealth of discourse internationally on best practice for the protection of ESR.

There are two key narratives on ESR at play and each one is engaged throughout the book. The first of which has for some time accepted the legally enforceable status of ESR and has been developing in both discourse and practice in international law and comparatively. The devolved dialogue in Scotland, Wales and in Northern Ireland (during the Bill of Rights process) is now more broadly engaged with the first of these narratives. The second narrative, and the more prominent in the UK national discourse, is that ESR are non-justiciable, cannot legitimately be enforced by a court, contravene parliamentary supremacy and are aspirational in nature. These competing narratives are difficult to reconcile, which in turn frustrates the process of making a contribution to the discourse that is sufficiently advanced to build on the existing research on the former narrative without being completely at odds with the discourse surrounding the latter. This frustration engages with wider debates about political v legal constitutionalism and the fact that different models co-exist concurrently across the UK constitutional framework (with the devolved jurisdictions pertaining to a stronger form of legal constitutionalism).

This introductory chapter contextualises the book in terms of the theory of rights and the status of ESR in the literature and discourse. It deals with arguments for and against the status of ESR as legal rights and so begins by addressing the critical arguments against the exploration of ESR as legally binding rights that can be enforced in court (that they are 'justiciable'). The book is premised on the basis that rights are legally binding and justiciable if the application of the law renders them so (following the positivist approach). This examination is also placed in wider social, economic and cultural contexts in which the questions around justiciability are framed. Critically, the research proposes principles of adjudication that address the critiques of ESR as justiciable rights drawing on constitutional and deliberative democracy theory.

The book proposes the circumstances in which ESR justiciability can be made legitimately possible. As a precursor to this argument, however, it is necessary to briefly address the reasons why ESR should receive any protection at all or whether it is appropriate that they are defended and enforced through the court. The theoretical framework in which the book is based rests on the premise that substantively securing ESR is a good thing for the UK and its constituent parts, and a good thing for society more generally. This position is based on certain assumptions drawn from moral and legal philosophical considerations. It is also based on a theoretical framework in the normative sense drawn from international standards and binding legal obligations sourced from the international legal position.[4] It is not proposed that models of incorporation or justiciability are the only means in which to secure ESR. Rather it is

---

4 International law or international standards can act as a frame of reference for understanding the rule of law value formation in liberal democracies.

proposed that rendering the rights justiciable offers a more comprehensive system of protection that can support other institutional mechanisms as, at the very least, a means of last resort when other mechanisms fail.[5]

Theoretical Objections to ESR

The philosophical account of human rights in both theory and practice traditionally follows a minimalist approach. Generally, this understanding of rights can be explained in terms of right-holders (rights are held by everyone and are universal) claiming rights against addressees (the state and private persons) on the basis of urgent and specific claims of minimum (and progressive) standards that are based on normative values with or without legal recognition.[6] King asserts that there is 'near consensus' amongst philosophers of human rights that ESR are 'real' human rights.[7] Nonetheless, the principal arguments identified in a review of the sceptical perspective (those views that are not within the 'near consensus' category) reveal legitimate concerns in relation to the validity of ESR as viable human right claims in a theoretical and philosophical sense.[8]

---

5 This is supported by the obligation to provide an effective remedy for a violation of an ESR in accordance with international law, discussed in detail in Chapter 2.

6 James W. Nickel, *Making Sense of Human Rights* (2nd ed., Oxford: Blackwell Press, 2007), 9–10. See also, Jeff King, *Judging Social Rights* (Cambridge University Press, 2012), 17–58; Henry Shue, *Basic Rights and Subsistence, Affluence and US Foreign Policy* (2nd ed., Princeton University Press, 1980); Amartya Sen, 'Elements of a Theory of Human Rights' (2004) 32 *Philosophy and Public Affairs* 315; James Griffin, *On Human Rights* (Oxford University Press, 2008); Charles R Beitz, *The Idea of Human Rights* (Oxford University Press, 2009); Marie-Bénédicte Dembour, 'What Are Human Rights? Four Schools of Thoughts' (2010) 32 *Human Rights Quarterly* 1. By moral considerations the book is referring to rights developed through a sense of political morality such as social human rights or citizenship rights that might not necessarily have legal standing. By legal rights the book is referring to rights that are afforded legal status in international law, legislation or constitutions. This distinction reflects that posited by King, at 19.

7 King, ibid. at 22. King states, 'there has been a traditional resistance among philosophers to consider social rights real human rights … however, [t]hese objections have now been dispatched convincingly by what is emerging as a near consensus view among philosophers of human rights that social rights are very much a species of human rights, largely for similar reasons accepted by international lawyers and the UN system much earlier.' See also Michael Freeman, 'Conclusion: Reflections on the Theory and Practice of Economic and Social Rights', in Lanse Minkler (ed.) *The State of Economic and Social Rights* (Cambridge University Press, 2013) 365–386.

8 King and Freeman both systematically repudiate and countenance the arguments posed by human rights sceptics regarding the existence or legitimacy of ESR. For a substantive analysis of the sceptical arguments see the relevant chapters in King ibid. and Freeman, ibid. In brief, they principally address the sceptical approach to enforceable human rights, in particular social rights, as asserted by Maurice Cranston, *What Are Human Rights?* (London: Bodley Head, 1969); Onora O'Neill, 'The Dark Side of Human Rights' (2005) 81 *International Affairs* 427; James Nickel, 'How Human Rights Generate Duties to Provide and Protect' (1993) 15 *Human Rights Quarterly* 77; John Rawls, *The Law of Peoples*, (Cambridge, MA: Harvard University Press, 1991) *inter alia*.

The literature for decades has engaged with dialectic philosophical trajectories entailing the ebb and flow of ESR as legal rights proper. Cranston rejects ESR because they cannot be universal in the same way as civil and political rights. Employee rights, he declares, are not universal because not all humans are employees – how then can this be a universal category? Likewise, Cranston argues that they do not hold the same moral urgency as civil and political rights (CPR), comparing for example the right to paid annual leave compared with the right not to be tortured – ESR and CPR are not on an equal footing.[9] Donnelly rejects these arguments and countenances that not all CPR are universal (such as the right to vote) and some ESR do hold moral urgency (such as the right to food).[10] O'Neill has argued that ESR are not feasible as legally enforceable rights. Drawing on Kant's distinction between perfect obligations and imperfect obligations, O'Neill questions how can right-holders claim obligations to meet claims that have not been allocated to specific obligation-bearers? For example, the right to food entails an imperfect duty dependent on charity or beneficence and the hungry cannot identify who exactly is responsible for feeding them. O'Neill has argued that to proclaim human rights without taking seriously who has to do what to fulfil them is morally irresponsible.[11] Sen has rejected this position in that all human rights can entail aspects of imperfect obligations – this does not mean they are not genuine rights.[12] Thomas Pogge argues that O'Neill is mistaken in assuming a requirement to identify a duty-bearer in order to substantiate a genuine right using the end of slavery as an example of an imperfect obligation with no specific duty-bearer but a right to freedom from slavery is a right nonetheless.[13] Nickel, less dismissive than Cranston or O'Neill, highlights problems of applicability – human rights can only require burdens that are feasible and feasibility is difficult to estimate. ESR, Nickel argues, require institutional mechanisms of implementation.[14] Rawls distinguishes ESR from 'human rights proper' and questions how can ESR be human rights proper when they require specific institutions?[15] This approach is embedded in natural law theory that rights are natural and cannot presuppose specific kinds of institutions, otherwise, they are not rights.[16] This contrasts with Nickel's argument that institutions do not provide the justification of, but

---

9 See Maurice Cranston, *What Are Human Rights?* (London: Bodley Head, 1969).

10 Jack Donnelly, *Universal Rights in Theory and Practice* (2nd ed., Ithaca, NY: Cornell University Press, 2003).

11 Onora O'Neill, n 8.

12 Amartya Sen, 'Human Rights and the Limits of the Law' (2006) 27 *Cardozo Law Review* 2913.

13 Thomas Pogge, 'O'Neill on Rights and Duties' (1992) 43 *Grazer Philosophische Studien* 233.

14 James Nickel, 'How Human Rights Generate Duties to Provide and Protect' (1993) 15 *Human Rights Quarterly* 77.

15 John Rawls, *The Law of Peoples* (Cambridge, MA: Harvard University Press, 1991).

16 John Locke, *Two Treaties of Government* [1689], ed. P. Laslett (Cambridge University Press, 1988).

rather the means of, implementing human rights.[17] Some of these competing theories are evident in recent debates about the democratic legitimacy of relying on adjudication to support ESR enforcement. Gearty and Mantouvalou (discussed further below) debate the legalisation and judicial enforcement of rights. Whilst Gearty highlights the insufficiency of relying on adjudication to fulfil ESR Mantouvalou highlights the importance of embracing it as one means, out of a variety of pathways, required to secure ESR.[18]

These arguments can be categorised into four overarching theoretical objections that require consideration when examining the issue of ESR as legitimate and legally enforceable rights. First, who is responsible for fulfilling ESR, or, who are the duty-bearers as opposed to the rights-holders?[19] Second, through what means can ESR be legitimately enforced, or, what institutional mechanisms are necessary for their fulfilment?[20] Third, who should bear the cost of supporting these institutional mechanisms? In relation to justiciable ESR mechanisms in the UK for example, the burden of paying the considerable cost of fair access to legal justice as it currently stands (in both civil and criminal matters) is a highly contested political issue across the various jurisdictions[21] and the subject of recent case law.[22] And the fourth objection, engages with arguments surrounding 'incompossibility', i.e. that one ESR right may be conceptually, or empirically, incompatible with another.[23]

Addressing the Theoretical Objections

In relation to the first objection, Freeman responds with a positivist answer that states have been identified as the primary bearer of responsibility for ESR in international law.[24] Gauri and Brinks identify a triangular relationship between the

---

17 James Nickel, 'How Human Rights Generate Duties to Provide and Protect' (1993) 15 *Human Rights Quarterly* 77.
18 Conor Gearty and Virginia Mantouvalou, *Debating Social Rights* (Hart, 2011).
19 Onora O'Neill, 'The Dark Side of Human Rights' (2005) 81 *International Affairs* 427.
20 Freeman, n 7 at 375, 'the most searching questions raised for defenders of economic and social human rights by these [sceptical] philosophers are, firstly, O'Neill's requirement that we need to specify who is obliged to what in order to fulfill the rights, and, secondly, Nickel's demand that, for any human rights to be plausible, we must show that their fulfilment is feasible.'
21 Owen Bowcott and Nicola Brown, 'More than Thousand Lawyers Protest Outside Parliament at Legal Aid Cuts', *The Guardian*, 7 March 2014, www.theguardian.com/law/2014/mar/07/lawyers-protest-parliament-legal-aid-cuts; Chris Kilpatrick, 'Lawyers Slam David Ford's Plans to Cut Legal Aid Budget', *The Belfast Telegraph*, 3 March 2014, www.belfasttelegraph.co.uk/news/local-national/northern-ireland/lawyers-slam-david-fords-plan-to-cut-legal-aid-budget-30056365.html; BBC 'Scottish Legal Aid Reform Passed', 29 January 2013, available at www.bbc.com/news/uk-scotland-21245700
22 Unison case the court examined the social minimum with reference to finding the cost of tribunal fees unlawful R (on the application of UNISON) (Appellant) v Lord Chancellor (Respondent) [2017] UKSC 51.
23 On the problem of 'incompossibility' in the theory of rights see Hillel Steiner, *An Essay on Rights* (Oxford: Blackwell, 1994).
24 Freeman, n 7 at 386.

state, the providers and the recipients of ESR.[25] The state (sitting at the top of the triangular hierarchy) owes duties to the recipients of ESR through provision or the allocation of resources, and fulfils duties via the providers through the regulation of how ESR require to be addressed. The providers then owe private obligations to the recipients through a horizontal application of ESR under the regulatory frame-work put in place by the state. Providers can be either private authorities or public bodies depending on how the regulatory framework is managed.[26] The state is pri-marily responsible as the duty-bearer (Freeman) and the operation of a triangular relationship – where private providers can also be engaged in the fulfilment of (and responsible for) duties under the regulatory framework, facilitates a better under-standing of who is responsible for what at any one time (Gauri and Brinks). The state may delegate its responsibility elsewhere by placing obligations on other actors and affording such actors authority and responsibility to fulfil those obliga-tions. Whilst other actors may be held to account for failure to comply with those obligations (under a regulatory framework), the state remains the duty-bearer throughout. In other words, it cannot completely displace its obligations even if it has explicitly delegated that responsibility elsewhere.

In relation to the second objection, there are various different institutional avenues through which the enforcement of ESR can be realised. In the welfare state, for example, there are numerous institutional safeguards to ensure the proper provision of welfare under the relevant welfare legislation. ESR enforce-ment can also be achieved through the avenues of political representation, com-plaints to the ombudsman or through processes such as internal complaint systems, proactive engagement from the regulatory and inspectorate regime,[27] or in tribunal decision-making.[28] These implementation avenues are extremely

---

25 Varun Gauri and Daniel M. Brinks, 'Introduction: The Elements of Legalization and the Tri-angular Shape of Social and Economic Rights', in Gauri and Brinks (eds.), *Courting Social Justice, Judicial Enforcement of Social and Economic Rights in the Developing World* (Cam-bridge University Press, 2008), 11.

26 For example, consider how public authority obligations in relation to health or social care may be provided by private bodies – the regulatory framework ought to encompass the pri-vate obligations owed by the providers to the recipients of health or social care, even although the duties are performed by private bodies that sit outside of the normal vertical relationship between state and individual in the provision of rights. In the context of the book, the justi-ciable mechanisms proposed identify the state as the primary bearer of responsibility and the individual recipient as the primary holder of the right, however, private obligations are also assessed in terms of third party providers where the state has outsourced the obligation.

27 David Barrett, 'The Regulatory Space of Equality and Human Rights Law in Britain: The Role of the Equality and Human Rights Commission' (2019) 39(2) *Legal Studies* 247–265.

28 King, n 6 at 85–95. See also for example some of the more recent developments in this area in relation to mainstreaming ESR through budgetary analysis. See Aoife Nolan et al., *Human Rights and Public Finance: Budgets and the Promotion of Economic and Social Rights* (Hart, 2013); Rory O'Connell et al., *Applying an International Human Rights Framework to State Budget al.locations: Rights and Resources* (Routledge, 2016). This is a multifaceted approach to ESR compatibility and a critical contribution that facilitates a move towards substantive change – within the context of this book it is argued that mechanisms such as this ought to

important in the realisation of ESR. This book is largely concerned with the role of the court and the justiciable enforcement of ESR. However, it is import- ant to note that adjudication is not the first and last answer to ESR enforcement or implementation. The court ought to be available as a means of last resort if all other institutional safeguards fail. The role that the court can play as an important institutional actor is explored in more detail below in tandem with a discussion on the legitimacy of justiciability (i.e. addressing concerns relating to institutional capacity, competence, the separation of powers, the allocation of limited resources and the indeterminacy of ESR). Essentially the research dem- onstrates that compliance with ESR requires the possibility of judicial supervi- sion in order to hold other branches of the state to account – the court being the only institutional body capable of being sufficiently independent to provide the proper review and scrutiny of the actions of the legislature and the execu- tive. The court therefore is indispensable to human rights protections in a functioning democracy but should ideally be a means of last resort.

The third objection relates to access to justice and raises obstacles that are difficult to overcome without a change in the political decisions to reduce the allocation of funds to support legal aid across the UK. The literature demon- strates that a gap in legal aid funding does not necessarily negate ESR being addressed in court as financial and legal support can be sourced from charitable interventions and public interest litigation by rights-orientated lawyers.[29] Nonetheless, the reduction in the availability of legal aid poses several risks to ESR adjudication. First, there is the danger that judicial decisions might redir- ect state resources on a disproportionate basis towards those who are able to fund litigation – exacerbating potential inequalities.[30] Second, the cases that are supported by charitable interventions are dependent on the interests of third parties – meaning the prioritisation of some ESR issues over others with the potential to render the most pressing concerns of the most marginalised furthest from the deliberative court room.[31] The objection to ESR on the ground that the litigation would be too costly equally impacts on CPR, which

be in place before any question of justiciability is engaged with. However, where for example, a procedural requirement is introduced to comply with ESR through budget analysis and this is not adhered to the court would be an appropriate forum to remedy the failure – such as is evident in the framework of the procedural duties under the Equality Act 2010.

29 See, for example, the different approaches employed in India, South Africa, Nigeria and Brazil in Gauri and Brinks (eds.), *Courting Social Justice* (n 25). Public interest litigation is not fre- quently employed in the UK context. This could be because there was until recent times a relatively robust and comprehensive legal aid system in place. However, there is also different rules relating to standing across the various jurisdictions of the UK (see Chapter 5) – public interest litigation was historically illegal in the UK context and, although the English courts began to hear interest group cases, this did not necessarily trickle down to devolved jurisdic- tions. For a discussion on the historical reluctance and a more recent leniency (in England) see Carol Harlow, 'Public Law and Popular Justice' (2002) 65 *The Modern Law Review* 1.

30 Gauri and Brinks, ibid. at 22.

31 Ibid.

are also resource intensive within the judicial system. So this objection relates to the question of whether there is an obligation to enable effective remedies for violations of human rights.

The objection alone does not render ESR outside the realm of legitimate and enforceable rights – it comes down to the same arguments posed by Nickel in response to sceptical arguments on the substance of human rights protection – whether states should facilitate the development of appropriate institutional mechanisms to ensure the implementation of human rights obligations. Without the appropriate provision of legal aid, human rights protection and access to justice, are in a very perilous position, however, it does not render the rights any less real. If anything, the duty to provide an effective remedy encompasses a right to facilitate access to justice, forming an ESR right in itself. There have been significant steps taken by the judiciary in recognition of the right to access justice.[32] Most notably in the recent *UNISON* case that declared prohibitively expensive tribunal fees as unlawful because the fees impeded the constitutional and common law right to access justice.[33]

The fourth theoretical objection is based on the argument that ESR compete against each other or are inherently incompatible based on issues of incompossibility. This objection, similar to that above, impacts on CPR as well as ESR and raises problems for the most uncontroversial human rights.[34] It is not unusual for a court, or other organ of the state, to assess conflicting rights and determine which should take priority in any given situation – for example, the right to freedom of speech of one person may impact on the right to privacy of another and vice-versa. This objection can be addressed through a flexible concept of the principle of indivisibility and applies to ESR in the same manner as that of CPR. This book orientates arguments in favour of substantive rights-based justiciable models. However, it is critical to acknowledge within any substantive system there can be appropriate limitations and safeguards to ensure the appropriate balance between rights can be secured, as can limitations on rights be employed through many of the same mechanisms applied to CPR. It is not proposed that all ESR are absolute and non-derogable. For example, the normative theoretical framework sourced in international law recognises progressive realisation subject to maximum available resources, together with absolute minimum core rights – this reflects Koch's sliding slope of enforcement discussed below in Chapter 2.

In addition to the arguments addressing the sceptical philosophical and theoretical objections, there are also a variety of normative theories that positively support the claims of urgency and priority that ESR demand as legitimate and enforceable human rights. The principle theoretical arguments that justify the protection of human rights (including ESR) are based on the following concepts: that human beings are entitled to a life of dignity and wellbeing

---

32 *R (on the application of UNISON) (Appellant) v Lord Chancellor (Respondent)* [2017] UKSC 51, para.66–87.
33 Ibid.
34 Hillel Steiner, *An Essay on Rights* (Oxford: Blackwell, 1994); Gauri and Brinks, n 25.

(that each person is entitled to minimum standards/threshold of human rights protection)[35]; that human beings are entitled to autonomy (that human rights afford the individual freedom and that the protection of CP and ESR forms an important part of self-determination)[36]; and human beings are entitled to social and political participation in society (that meaningful participation in democracy is dependent on substantive access to at least minimum criteria in CP and ESR protection).[37]

This reasoning aligns with the emerging 'anti-poverty' stream of liberal constitutionalism.[38] The concept that, at the very least, a minimum of ESR protection (as well as CPR) is required in order to fulfil the basic functions of autonomy and that ignoring the socio-economic dimension of citizenship undermines a fully functioning democracy. Indeed, some argue that the human rights framework itself not gone far enough to address systemic inequality and that states

35 Ibid. See also Gauri and Brinks, n 25 – 'a life that achieves the full promise of human dignity requires, among other things, escape from premature death, the resources to withstand debilitating disease, the ability to read and write, and, in general, opportunities and freedoms unavailable in the midst of extreme poverty and deprivation.'

36 Ibid., 23–24. See also: Cécile Fabre, *Social Rights Under the Constitution: Government and the Decent Life* (Oxford University Press, 2001), Chapter 1; Joseph Raz, *The Morality of Freedom* (Oxford University Press, 1986), Chapters 14 and 15. Raz theorises that autonomy (or normative agency) is a prerequisite of freedom and that the exercise of autonomy is dependent on the self-fulfilling creation of an autonomous individual, an 'agent', where the agent's activities are not burdened by worries of mere survival. An autonomy supporting environment requires that agents have capacity, a range of valuable options and are free from coercion and manipulation. See also John Rawls, *A Theory of Justice* (Cambridge, MA: Harvard University Press, 2001). Rawls theory, based on liberal egalitarianism, supports freedom through meaningful choices about the life one chooses to lead – this requires having the capacity to understand political complexities (supported through education) and having health and income security to plan out a meaningful life. This can be supported by constitutionally guaranteeing legally enforceable minimum criteria, John Rawls, *Political Liberalism* (New York: Colombia University Press, 1996), 227–228. This position somewhat differs from the distinction previously asserted by Rawls in relation to 'human rights proper' (n 15) – Rawls' theory develops towards a more substantive based recognition that minimum criteria are essential to social and political participation.

37 King, n 7 at 23. See also arguments supported in theories of social citizenship, civic republicanism and deliberative democracy – ESR are instrumental in, and support, meaningful participation in political decision making. Frank I. Michelman, 'Welfare Rights in a Constitutional Democracy' (1979) 3 *Washington University Law Quarterly* 659; Fabre, ibid., 121–124; David Miller, 'A Human Right to Democracy?' CSSJ Working Papers Series, SJ032 April 2015.

38 See O'Cinneide on the lack of a social dimension in liberal constitutionalism and the emerging anti-poverty dimension in mainstream liberal political theory and Michelman in Colm O'Cinneide 'The constitutionalisation of economic and social rights' and Frank I. Michelman on antipoverty liberalism as an emerging conceptualisation of social democracy, 'Constitutionally Binding Social and Economic Rights as a Compelling Idea: Reciprocating Perturbations in Liberal and Democratic Constitutional Visions' in García et al. (eds.), *Social and Economic Rights in Theory and Practice, Critical Inquiries* (Routledge, 2015), 261–262 and 279–280.

must move beyond minimum criteria if substantive equality is to be achieved.[39] The international human rights framework offers a helpful framework for moving beyond social minimum thresholds. A foundation of ESR protection recognising minimum and progressive thresholds is required to guide the legislature and executive as to human rights compliance. Likewise, both the legislature and the judiciary can build upon this foundation to give greater substance and meaning to rights as epistemic communities responsible for their substantive interpretation.[40]

The adjudication of ESR and the measurement of its success is incredibly complex. There are so many different factors to consider such as accessibility, standing, the degree of protection of the right in law (the domestic law may not in any way meet the standards required in international law for example), the type of review the court might employ, what kind of remedies are available and the degree of compliance post-judgment. There are many problems that social rights adjudication in practice will encounter across these many different factors. For example, Landau provides the example of the development of the *tutela* device under the Colombian constitution as a means of protecting a vital minimum for the most vulnerable to its subsequent misuse serving the health needs of the middle classes.[41] In Brazil, similarly, the allocation of funds in society moved from the poorest to the wealthy when the jurisprudence of the Brazilian courts recognised an immediately enforceable right to the highest attainable health causing greater health inequities as the more privileged and wealthy sought rights enforcement through the court.[42] In India and South Africa, social rights adjudication has engaged with a wide plethora of social rights. However as noted by Kaletski et al., although India and South Africa have strong legal guarantees to the right to food for example, both countries continue to exhibit exceptionally high rates of malnutrition.[43] In fact, in South Africa, where the Constitutional Court has intervened to protect social rights, critics have questioned the genuinely transformative nature of the remedies employed and argued that the jurisprudence has undermined the norm-based

---

39 Samuel Moyn, *Not Enough, Human Rights in an Unequal World* (Harvard University Press, 2018). Moyn's account, whilst helpful in elucidating some of the pitfalls of inadequate legal structures largely concerned with civil and political rights, is misplaced in its understanding of the economic and social rights dimension of the international legal framework and its potential if properly implemented. For a critique see Gráinne de Búrca, 'Shaming Human Rights' (16 August 2018), Forthcoming, *International Journal of Constitutional Law*; NYU School of Law, Public Law Research Paper No. 18–47, available at SSRN: https://ssrn.com/abstract=3233063 or http://dx.doi.org/10.2139/ssrn.3233063

40 Katharine Young, *Constituting Social Rights* (Oxford University Press, 2012), 8.

41 David Landau, 'The Reality of Social Rights Enforcement' (2012) 53 *Harvard International Law Journal* 189.

42 Octavio Luiz Motta Ferraz, 'The Right to Health in the Courts of Brazil: Worsening Health Inequities?' (2009) 11 *Health and Human Rights: An International Journal* 33.

43 Elizabeth Kaletski, Lanse Minkler, Nishith Prakash and Susan Randolph, 'Does Constitutionalizing Economic and Social Rights Promote Their Fulfillment?' (2016) 15(4) *Journal of Human Rights* 433–453 at 456.

foundationalist nature of the Constitution.[44] These issues give rise to problems for social rights adjudication in terms of its democratic legitimacy. At the same time, they by no means undermine it as a means of rights enforcement completely.

The Critiques of ESR Adjudication

To date, the analysis of social rights adjudication has focussed to a large degree on the taxonomy of obligations along the respect-protect-fulfil axis.[45] As the analysis of jurisprudence develops according to the taxonomy of obligations and across jurisdictions so too does the broader understanding of social rights adjudication and new categories and principles emerge.[46] Principles of good practice in ESR jurisprudence can mitigate potential problems building on a theoretical framework for 'democratic legitimacy' in social rights adjudication.[47] Whilst the focus of this book is developing good practice in the context of the UK, the principles of adjudication can act as an assessment framework on a cross-constitutional comparative basis.

Categorising justiciability mechanisms in the book offers new perspectives on the type of enforcement available for ESR whether that be through explicit justiciability enabling provisions or adjudication that occurs under the rubric of something else. In this sense, we can measure both the degree of protection (a taxonomy of obligations) as well as the mechanism through which the rights can be enforced (a taxonomy of justiciability mechanisms). As part of this taxonomy of justiciability mechanisms consideration should also be given to: the sources of law from which social rights adjudication derives, i.e. the means of incorporation (constitutional/legislative/international/common law etc.); the mechanism under which the action can be taken (is it a constitutional

---

44 See, for example, Marius Pieterse, 'Resuscitating Socio-Economic Rights: Constitutional Entitlements to Health Care Services' (2006) 22 *South African Journal on Human Rights* 473; Sandra Liebenberg and Beth Goldblatt, 'The Interrelationship between Equality and Socio-Economic Rights under South African's Transformative Constitution' (2007) 23 *South African Journal of Human Rights* 335; and Christopher Mbazira, 'From Ambivalence to Certainty: Norms and Principles for the Structural Interdict in Socio-Economic Rights Litigation in South Africa' (2008) 24 *South African Journal of Human Rights* 1.

45 Malcolm Langford, 'The Justiciability of Social Rights, From Practice to Theory' in M. Langford (ed.), *Social Rights Jurisprudence, Emerging Trends in International and Comparative Law* (Cambridge University Press, 2008), 12.

46 Langford, ibid. at 13. For example, Nolan et al. identify degrees of enforcement through the tripartite theory to a multitude of varying degrees – from respect, to protect, to fulfil, consideration of progressive realisation and finally non-retrogressive measures, Nolan et al., *The Justiciability of Social and Economic Rights: An Updated Appraisal* (Human Rights Consortium, March 2007). Courtis has expanded this theory to degrees of standard starting with negative, to procedural, through equality and non-discrimination, minimum core arguments, progressive realisation and prohibiting retrogression, Christian Courtis, 'Standards to Make ESR Justiciable: A Summary Explanation' (2009) 2 *Erasmus Law Review* 379.

47 King, n 7.

provision? Or under equality law? Or under the rubric of civil and political rights?); the degree of accessibility (relating to standing/legal aid/victimhood); the type of review (what kind of judicial scrutiny is employed? Is it a weak or strong review?); to what degree is the right enforced (is the duty procedural or substantive? respect-protect-fulfil?); what kind of remedy is available (is it declaratory? Ultra vires? Structural? Supervisory? Participatory?); in what kind of body does the adjudication occur (quasi-court? International court? Domestic constitutional court? – are the decisions binding?); and to what degree is there compliance with the judgment (enforceability post-judgment? Long-term material or symbolic impact?).[48]

In this sense, the way through which social rights can be adjudicated upon can be assessed across the 'adjudication journey' rather than focussing solely on the outcome of judgments. In so doing it is important to contextualise existing jurisprudence within the broader building blocks of ESR adjudication allowing the reader to reflect on the types of cases that do not, or cannot, reach the court room as well as the processes and outcomes associated with the cases that do.

As part of this reflection, principles emerge to counteract some of the long-held and more recently asserted criticisms of social rights adjudication.

Criticism of ESR jurisprudence comes in two distinct waves. The first wave of criticism can be understood as the critique applied before judicially enforceable ESR are introduced in any particular setting – i.e. the very repudiation of ESR as justiciable from the outset. This first critical wave can be sub-categorised as the **'anti-democratic critique'**; the **'indeterminacy critique'** and the **'incapacity critique'**. The second critical wave rejects the justiciability of ESR in a post-adjudication setting and rather than repudiate the justiciable nature of ESR highlights the risks and inefficiencies of relying on ESR adjudication based on the dangers of the court becoming an exercise of elite-driven power. The second critical wave critique is sub-categorised as the **pro-hegemonic critique**. Both critical waves are discussed below.

The first wave **anti-democratic critique** questions whether the court can legitimately interfere in resource dependent policy areas usurping the power of the legislature or executive. So the argument goes, parliament provides sufficient accountability in ensuring the executive abides by human rights obligations at the domestic and international level. Resource allocation by definition 'implicates the interests of nearly everyone [as] we nearly all pay in and take out of the public system'[49] and so the most appropriate decision maker in relation to resource allocation is the representative legislature.[50] The judiciary interfering in the policy matters of the state impinges on the separation of powers and the

---

48 Malcolm Langford, César Rodríguez-Garavito and Julieta Rossi (eds.), *Social Rights Judgments and the Politics of Compliance: Making It Stick* (Cambridge University Press, 2017).

49 King, n 7 at 5.

50 This argument is also closely related to that of polycentricity whereby a holistic understanding of policy implications cannot be something that the judiciary can review on a case-by-case

judiciary should not be able to veto parliamentary decisions. As articulated by Gerard Hogan J.:

> if social and economic rights are made justiciable and are vindicated by the courts, the result will tend to distort the traditional balance of the separation of powers between the judiciary and other branches of government in that more power will flow to the judiciary.[51]

However, CPR are also resource dependent and at times also require the court to intervene as an accountability mechanism. When the court intervenes in civil and political rights determination it does so as an important accountability check on the executive or legislature rather than as a means of usurping the power of other branches of government. One way in which this can occur is to use different types of remedies – some of which may afford larger degrees of deference back to decision makers depending on the circumstances. The court as an intervener in the enforcement of ESR is therefore an important part of a multi-institutional dialogue ensuring accountability rather than a transfer of political power to the judiciary. Ultimately, in a system of parliamentary supremacy, the final decision rests with the central legislature.

A response to anti-democratic critique embraces the democratic legitimacy of courts embracing their role as an important **accountability mechanism**[52] in a multi-institutional dialogue, or ominlogue,[53] given that there are multiple actors *in colloquium* at the same time. King highlights the importance of ESR to social citizenship, and a social minimum, enforceable by the courts as part of a deliberative democracy framework.[54] O'Cinneide similarly identifies strands of constitutional theory that require the legal enforcement of ESR. The first of these strands is a 'legitimation-worthy' constitutional order[55] whereby ESR support autonomous participation in society. The second strand identifies that there should be a social dimension, or 'social principle' embedded in the rule of law through a constitutionalisation of ESR. This would open the door to help ensure ESR are prioritised when weighted against other competing interests.[56] The third identifies that legal enforcement of ESR corresponds with democratic

---

basis. The legislature and executive are the appropriate bodies to deal with those issues that require consideration of a vast number of interconnected variables. Ibid., 5–6.

51 Gerard Hogan, 'Judicial Review and Social and Economic Rights' in William Binchy and Jeremy Sarkin (eds.), *Human Rights, the Citizen and the State: South African and Irish Approaches* (Dublin: Roundhall, Sweet & Maxwell, 2001), 8.

52 Nolan et al., n 46, 15, para.2.2.

53 Rawls, 'Reply to Habermas' (1995) *Journal of Philosophy* 132, 140 as discussed in Rory O'Connell, *Legal Theory in the Crucible of Constitutional Justice* (Dartmouth: Ashgate, 2000).

54 King, n 7 at 27.

55 Frank I. Michelman, 'Socioeconomic Rights in Constitutional Law: Explaining America Away' (2008) 6(3&4) *International Journal of Comparative Constitutional Law* 663–686 at 675.

56 O'Cinneide, n 38 at 270.

principles by ensuring that the politically marginalised groups have a legal mechanism through which their distributive justice claims can be communicated in a manner that compels governments and other duty-bearers to respond to their claims through deliberative (judicial) processes.[57] The principles of deliberative democracy developed here relating to accessibility, participation, deliberation and counter-majoritarianism therefore form important responses to the democratic legitimacy critique in the context of social rights adjudication.

The **indeterminacy critique** of ESR adjudication tells us that ESR are too vague and that their substantive interpretation should not be left to judges. This too is a legitimate concern, however, it is not insurmountable. In the same way that civil and political rights require interpretation, so too do ESR – and in a similar vein, courts can play an important role in giving substance to ESR in the same way that they do with CP rights.[58] This does not require the court to usurp the role of the legislature or executive. If the legislature gives clear instructions to the court on how to interpret rights it can assist in the court fulfilling its role as a guarantor of rights and thus avoiding abdication of this important judicial function.

A response to the indeterminacy critique identifies the role the court must embrace as a body responsible for giving meaning to rights. Young tells us social rights adjudication is nothing more than finding consensus between epistemic communities – including the judiciary – around the meaning of rights.[59] It is in the dialogue between epistemic communities (legislative, executive, judicial) that social rights adjudication can help give meaning to rights, a role that Michelman argues courts should not abdicate.[60] Rather than completely abdicate its role the court must strike the right balance so that it does not 'debase dangerously the entire currency of rights and the rule of law' by failing to engage with the ESR.[61] The principle of deliberation, between institutions and actors at the local, national and supranational level can help the court interpret the substance of ESR by deriving meaning from a number of interpretative sources.

O'Cinneide highlights the importance of embracing both the **procedural and substantive aspects** of this role. Otherwise, the court risks embracing only a hollow form of ESR adjudication that abdicates on enforcing substantive rights when needed:

> At the end of the day, the legitimacy of SER review will depend on the extent to which it succeeds in giving substance to SER whilst integrating their protection into the wider framework of constitutional values...It is only through a close, passionate and reasoned engagement with the

---

57 Ibid.; see also Kathrine G. Young, *Constituting Economic and Social Rights* (Oxford University Press, 2012), 193 and Gauri and Brinks, n 25.
58 Young, ibid. at 30.
59 Young, ibid. at 8.
60 Michelman, n 55 at 683.
61 Ibid.

normative substance of these rights that socially engaged constitutionalism can take root in national legal systems and avoid the hollowed-out fate of its social democratic predecessor.[62]

There is an important component of social rights adjudication that departs from traditional understandings of deliberative democracy in its narrower interpretation. A broader conceptualisation recognises that fairness must account for both procedural and substantive justice – moving from a thin-to-thick conceptualisation of justice. The process principles of accessibility, participation, deliberation and counter-majoritarianism require the court to play a role in giving meaning to rights through legitimate and fair processes. This manifests itself in adjudication that reviews the procedural fairness of decision-making – was it reasonable?/was it proportionate?/has the duty-bearer complied with fair process? On the other hand, there is also a call within deliberative democracy theory itself,[63] and within the wider social rights discourse,[64] that the court when called upon may be required to enforce a substantive threshold (moving from procedural to substantive enforcement). Liebenberg highlights that '[d]espite its pervasiveness in social rights adjudication, the relationship between participatory [as a component of procedural] justice and the substantive dimensions of social rights remains unsettled'.[65] In terms of the principle of fairness, the book proposes both procedural and substantive concepts of fairness must be considered as part of the remit of courts. It may not always be necessary, or appropriate, for the court to enforce a substantive threshold. On the other hand, the more serious the violation, the more necessary for a substantive 'thicker' concept of justice to be developed and enforced. The example seen in the *Hartz IV* case where the judiciary found the process in calculating social security entitlement flawed as well as the substantive level of social security offered highlights the potential of the court to review and determine the procedural fairness of a decision as well as the substantive fairness of the outcome.[66]

---

62 O'Cinneide, n 38 at 274.
63 i.e. provision of the social minimum as the substantive threshold required to participate in society. See the extensive literature cited in King at 26–27. See also Sandra Fredman, 'Adjudication as Accountability' in Nicholas Bamforth and Peter Leyland (eds.), *Accountability in the Contemporary Constitution* (Oxford University Press, 2013), 105.
64 See Anashri Pillay, 'Toward Effective Social and Economic Rights Adjudication: The Role of Meaningful Engagement' (2012) 10(3) *International Journal of Constitutional Law* 732–755; O'Cinneide, n 38 at 274; Langford (2008) n 45, Boyle (this volume); Sandra Fredman, 'Procedure or Principle: The Role of Adjudication in Achieving the Right to Education' (2015) 7 *Constitutional Court Review* 165–199; David Bilchitz, 'Avoidance Remains Avoidance: Is It Desirable in Socio-Economic Rights Cases?' (2015) 5 *Constitutional Court Review* 297.
65 Sandra Liebenberg, 'Participatory Justice in Social Rights Adjudication', (2018) 18(4) *Human Rights Law Review* 623–649.
66 BVerfGE 125, 175 (*Hartz IV*), the German Constitutional Court considered the decision making process to be flawed and that the substantive outcome resulted in a violation of the

Third, **the capacity critique** tells us that courts do not have the capacity to deal with ESR, that there would be a flood of litigation and that judges do not have the expertise to determine the substance ESR or their complex relationship with other areas of governance. The judiciary simply lacks the expertise to decide such matters and it is beyond the institutional capacity of the courts. When the UK Human Rights Act was introduced Edwards firmly rejected the competency of the judiciary in adjudicating on human rights issues calling instead for the principle of due deference to parliament to be firmly established.[67] On socio-economic issues arising in human rights cases he argued that:

> the judiciary are institutionally incompetent to deal with the socio-economic issues that frequently arise in these cases. Not only is adjudication an inappropriate process for assessing complex issues of policy, but the courts also lack the resources and the judiciary the training and expertise to adequately weigh the issues.[68]

However, courts can also help support their capacity by seeking expertise on ESR where needed, including the appointment of *amicus curiae* (a 'friend of the court') if required. In the same way the court can draw on expertise in relation to CP or constitutional matters it can also refer to various sources of law, comparative case law, international guidance as well as domestic experts in order to assist in capacity building when adjudicating ESR. When ESR engage with far-reaching policy considerations the court can ask the legislature or executive to justify its approach, in the same way that it does so in relation to CP rights. The complexity of adjudication in the area of human rights cuts across all different types of rights – it is not unique to the ESR domain. It is important to remember that CPR as well as ESR have core components that may be non-derogable as well as components subject to limitation if justifiable. A more nuanced understanding of the nature of ESR helps contextualise the different ways in which the court can appropriately review ESR compatibility in a democratically legitimate way. A response to this critique would be embed a **theory of justification** to questions of capacity in whatever approach is taken at any time. This approach is facilitated by the principles of deliberation and participation by encouraging engagement with the relevant stakeholders and expertise to inform judicial decision-making.

The second wave of ESR adjudication criticism can be categorised as an ad hoc critique – that adjudication of ESR does not work in practice based on examples of failed attempts. This critique identifies that courts may be inappropriate forums for resolving disputes around ESR and can be distilled as the

---

right to dignity meaning the decision maker had to revisit both process and substantive outcome of the decision. This is discussed in more detail in Chapter 4.

67 Richard Edwards, 'Judicial Deference under the Human Rights Act' (2002) 65 *Modern Law Review* 859, 859.

68 Ibid.

pro-hegemonic critique. The court itself embodies an elite-driven exercise of power that reinforces existing inequalities. The second wave critique claims that social rights adjudication does not help the most vulnerable and does not work in practice.[69] For example, in Brazil an overwhelming number of cases have been filed relating to access to healthcare.[70] Of these cases, over 90% are individuals going to courts for specific benefits, rather than collective suits asking for structural change.[71] Ferraz carried out extensive empirical research with lawyers in Brazil that investigated the reasons for the high number of individual cases seeking individual court orders on access to healthcare.[72] The research suggests that although there are no formal barriers to collective suits lawyers are reluctant to pursue a holistic collective case because the court will be resistant to these types of claims. In a civil law jurisdiction this has meant that those who have been able to afford to raise individual cases have had their right to healthcare secured to the detriment of those who cannot afford (or do not know about) judicial enforcement of ESR.[73] As a result, there has been an increase in health inequities in Brazil.

Gearty makes persuasive arguments against relying on the judicial enforcement of socio-economic rights, the first three of which relate to the first wave of ESR critiques (i.e. that they afford too much power to the courts and so are undemocratic; that they are too vaguely expressed; and the courts are not the correct forum for determining resource allocation and prioritisation – again relating to polycentricity).[74] In addition to this he makes a further case against legalisation by arguing that individual test cases in adversarial proceedings are not equipped to deal with plight of 'thousands of invisible claimants'; that the inappropriateness of the adversarial model to the resolution of broadly framed issues of social rights; that judicialisation offers no follow-up procedure to check whether the decision of the court has been implemented; that seeking 'quick-fixes' through the courts wastes the resources of organisations and institutions seeking to advance social rights when they should be focussing on political change; and finally that there is a danger in empowering a privileged judiciary who will seek to retain the status quo (and concern that the powerful will seek to assert their own social rights as an indirect means of resisting the social rights of others relating to the pro-hegemonic critique).[75]

---

69 See, for example, the key findings by Ferraz, n 42; Octavio Luiz Motta Ferraz, 'Harming the Poor Through Social Rights Litigation: Lessons from Brazil' (2011) 89 *Texas Law Review* 1643; and Landau, n 41 where the court becomes a pro-majoritarian actor upholding the rights of the wealthy to the detriment of the poorer when adjudicating ESR.

70 See Landau, n 41 and Ferraz, n 42.

71 Landau, Ibid.

72 Ferraz, n 42.

73 Landau, n 41 and Ferraz, n 69.

74 Joint Committee of Human Rights, 'A Bill of Rights for the UK?' (Twenty-ninth Report of Session 2007–2008, HL 165, HC 150) para.167.

75 Gearty and Mantouvalou, n 18; Gearty at 56–64.

A response to this critique recognises that the court can also act as an important accountability mechanism and 'institutional voice' for those who are politically disenfranchised.[76] In fact, the courts should take steps to embrace **counter-majoritarian** adjudication.[77] The legal constitutionalisation and adjudication of rights can help support pathways to social justice, among other avenues.[78] In addition, it must be noted that the end result of other avenues may indeed lead to legalisation of ESR – for example, where civil society pressure coalescing with political impetus results in human rights reform that embeds ESR as legal rights (such as evident in Scotland and Wales discussed in Chapter 6). How then should the different branches of power respond to this change? More appropriate remedies are required to help the court embrace this role such as the deployment of structural remedies when systemic issues arise.[79] In a broader social context questions must also be asked about the appointment of judges and the makeup of the judiciary more closely reflecting the diversity of society.[80]

The first and second waves of criticism highlights important issues that require to be addressed, however, these concerns are not insurmountable barriers and should not result in the outright rejection of ESR justiciability or judicial enforcement. Holding firmly to the ESR critiques as evidence of the non-justiciability of rights is now an outdated position.[81] ESR adjudication happens and it can happen in a legitimate way. As such it has become increasingly clear that the outright repudiation of ESR justiciability is based on a false premise from the outset. It has been posited that 'much of the doctrinaire debate about economic, social, and cultural rights throughout the second half of the last century sprang from a legal fiction: that of the separation of human rights into two distinct sets'.[82] This dichotomy and misunderstanding on the legal status of ESR is discussed in more detail in Chapter 2. Importantly, the research tells us

---

76 King, n 7; O'Cinneide, n 38; Nolan et al., n 46; Mantouvalou, ibid.

77 Landau, n 41.

78 Mantouvalou, n 75 and Paul O'Connell, 'Human Rights: Contesting the Displacement Thesis' (2018) 69(1) *Northern Ireland Legal Quarterly* 19–35.

79 Landau, n 41 and César Rodríguez-Garavito and Diana Rodríguez-Franco, *Radical Deprivation on Trial, the Impact of Judicial Activism on Socioeconomic Rights in the Global South* (Cambridge University Press, 2015).

80 For a discussion on the potential of judicial diversity and the associated extensive literature see Rosemary Hunter, 'More than Just a Different Face? Judicial Diversity and Decision-making' (2015) 68(1) *Current Legal Problems* 119–141.

81 This being the case in international law. A blanket refusal to acknowledge the justiciable nature of ESC rights is considered arbitrary by the Committee on Economic, Social and Cultural Rights, UN Committee on Economic, Social and Cultural Rights (CESCR), General Comment No. 9: The domestic application of the Covenant, 3 December 1998, E/C.12/1998/24, para.10.

82 Mónica Feria Tinta, 'Justiciability of Economic, Social, and Cultural Rights in the Inter-American System of Protection of Human Rights: Beyond Traditional Paradigms and Notions' (2007) 29 *Human Rights Quarterly* 431, 432.

Table 1.1 First Wave and Second Wave Critiques and Responses

FIRST WAVE *Pre-jurisprudence criticism*	RESPONSE (safeguards or emerging principles – developing theory addressing concerns)	SECOND WAVE *Post- jurisprudence criticism*
Anti-democratic critique		
ESR entail imperfect obligations (O'Neill 2005)	All rights are imperfect (Sen 2006)	
ESR have no clear duty-bearer (O'Neill 2005)	Does not make it any less of a right (Pogge 1992)	
	Using Gauri and Brink's (2008) triangulation method horizontality helps identify appropriate duty-bearer with state primarily responsible	
ESR are positive and resource dependent	Civil and political rights are resource dependent (Fredman 2010) and contain positive duties (Nolan et al. 2007)	
Breaches separation of powers (Hogan 2001)	Accountability between arms of state – required as part of a multi-institutional approach (King 2012) (Boyle, this volume)	
	There is space for democratic dialogue between institutions (Nolan et al. 2007)	
	Must counteract pro-majoritarian tendency of democracy and protect minority rights (Langford 2009)	
	There can be a strong emphasis on deference to executive and legislature as part of JR process (Young 2012) (King 2012)	
They are not universal and have no moral urgency (Cranston 1969)	Not all CPR are universal (the right to vote) and some ESR do hold moral urgency (the right to food) (Donnelly 2003)	
They are not human rights proper and not required as prerequisite in deliberative democracy (Rawls 1991)	They can constitute what is required for minimum participation in deliberative democracy (Miller 2015)	

(*Continued*)

Table 1.1 (Cont.)

FIRST WAVE *Pre-jurisprudence criticism*	RESPONSE (safeguards or emerging principles – developing theory addressing concerns)	SECOND WAVE *Post- jurisprudence criticism*
	They are prerequisite to facilitate autonomy (Alexy 2002)	
Rights are natural and cannot presuppose specific kinds of institutions (Rawls 1991/Locke 1988)	How can ESR be human rights proper when they require specific institutions? Institutions do not provide the justification of, but rather the means of, implementing human rights (Nickel 1993)	
Polycentric – courts cannot impinge on matters of complex social policy across multiple resource intensive areas (Hogan 2001)	States compelled to justify – accountability model with contextually appropriate remedies (Langford 2008) Judicial incrementalism and reasonableness review can facilitate dealing with complex polycentric issues (King 2012) Adjudication act as important lens to highlight blind spots of a majoritarian system (King 2012) Adjudication can deal with systemic policy problems and transform individual cases into collective case such as 'unconstitutional state of affairs' in Colombia (Landau 2012) (Garavito and Franco 2015)	
Indeterminacy critique ESR are too vague and lack specific content	All rights can be vague – courts must give meaning to rights (Langford 2009) (Young 2012)	
(Cranston 1969) (Feinberg 1973) (O'Neill 2005	Some ESR are precise and some CPR are vague (Nolan et al. 2007) Courts should not abdicate their role in giving meaning to rights (Michelman 2008) Impose corresponding Hohfeldian duties upon the state and other state actors (O'Cinneide 2015)	

(*Continued*)

Table 1.1 (Cont.)

FIRST WAVE *Pre-jurisprudence criticism*	RESPONSE (safeguards or emerging principles – developing theory addressing concerns)	SECOND WAVE *Post- jurisprudence criticism*
Incapacity critique There are insufficient mechanisms to facilitate applicability (Nickel 1993)	More mechanisms must be developed to implement (Nickel 1993)	
Judges should not usurp role of other branches of the state	Judges should not abdicate their role to give meaning to rights (Michelman 2015)	
Potential snowball effect – the floodgate scenario	Manage cases through administrative mechanisms such as collective case or through use of 'test and sist' or collective cases (Boyle and Hughes 2018) (Garavito and Franco 2015)	
Incompossibility (rights clash and impossible to implement them on equal footing) (Steiner 1994)	Rights clash all the time and not all rights are non-derogable (Boyle, this volume) All rights adjudication requires balancing act (Langford 2008) (Alexy 2002)	
Court lacks specialist knowledge	Courts can ask the experts (Nolan et al. 2007) Expertise can assist adjudication (King 2012)	
		SECOND WAVE **Pro-hegemonic critique** **Social rights adjudication does not help the most vulnerable and does not work in practice**
	Constitutionalisation and adjudication can help support pathways to social justice (Mantouvalou 2011)	Politics is more appropriate route to social justice (Gearty 2011)
	Legislation alone has blind spots (King 2012)	
	Not all actors have means of political representation (Nolan et al 2007)	
	More appropriate remedies are required and courts must engage with procedural and substantive components of ESR	Weak review does not help poorest (Landau 2012)

(*Continued*)

Table 1.1 (Cont.)

FIRST WAVE *Pre-jurisprudence* *criticism*	RESPONSE (safeguards or emerging principles – developing theory addressing concerns)	SECOND WAVE *Post- jurisprudence criticism*
	enforcement (O'Cinneide 2015) Pillay 2012) (Fredman 2015)	
	Structural interdicts and positive enforcement of rights when appropriate (Landau 2012)	
	Access to justice must be accessible and affordable (Boyle, this volume)	Courts tend to act as pro- majoritarian actors favouring wealthier classes (Landau 2012) (Ferraz 2009)
	Courts must defend those who are most disadvantaged and politically marginalised (Nolan et al. 2007)	
	Courts need to develop coun- ter- majoritarian judicial approach including the use of structural interdicts to deal with systemic issues (Landau 2012) (Boyle, this volume)	
	Institutional capacity of courts revisited – tendency to deal with individual instead of col- lective. In Brazil the civil law jurisdiction created a disproportionate tendency towards individual claims with- out precedent or collective sys- temic response (Landau 2012)	Social rights adjudication is causing health inequities in Brazil (Ferraz 2009)

that is not 'whether' but 'how' to judicially enforce ESR that is the question that remains to be addressed.[83]

Principles of ESR Adjudication

Clearly, there are aspects of ESR justiciability that are problematic. How then, can ESR justiciability occur in a democratically legitimate way and what are the

---

83 Mark Tushnet, 'A Response to David Landau' (2013) Opinio Juris, available at http://opinio juris.org/2012/01/23/hilj_tushnet-responds-to-landau/As; O'Cinneide (2015) also points out – the questions of whether and how to enforce ESR are closely linked n 38 at 273.

basic principles of ESR adjudication that require to be taken into account when considering the role of the court as a guarantor of ESR?

One possibility relies on the distinction between weak and strong forms of judicial review, discussed by Tushnet.[84] Weak-form systems of judicial review hold out the 'promise of reducing the tension between judicial review and democratic self-governance' by ensuring deference to the other branches of government on issues engaging with ESR.[85] Weaker review includes mechanisms such as reasonableness review[86]; an interpretative mandate[87]; non-binding declarations of incompatibility[88] and a 'dialogic' mode of review.[89] Strong-review systems on the other hand see a more intense tension between judicial enforcement of constitutional limitations and democratic self-government.[90] A strong-review approach means judicially enforceable constitutional provisions even in cases where there is reasonable disagreement about interpretation.[91] A strong-review approach recognises ESR as justiciable, immediately enforceable and on a par with CPR.[92] Under Tushnet's weak v strong form judicial review courts can either lean towards usurping the elected branches of government thus risking the democratic legitimacy of their role, or, they can lean towards rejecting the justiciability of ESR all together abdicating their democratically legitimate role of giving meaning to rights and holding the other branches of government accountable.[93] Tushnet suggests that courts must adopt and adapt to a more nuanced form of weak review for ESR therefore overcoming the democratic legitimacy critique by applying tentative weak-form remedies before engaging in stronger interventions where necessary.[94]

Garavito and Franco develop Tushnet's dyad by introducing an intermediate category: a 'moderate rights' approach.[95] Under a moderate-rights approach the court can recognise the reviewability, justiciability and enforceability of ESR but strike the appropriate 'democratic legitimacy' balance by issuing moderate remedies when a violation occurs. They argue that strong remedies require precise,

---

84 Mark Tushnet, *'Weak Courts, Strong Rights': Judicial Review and Social Welfare Rights in Comparative Constitutional Law* (Oxford: Princeton University Press, 2008), 23.
85 Ibid.
86 Ibid.
87 Including the interpretative approach used under section 3 of the Human Rights Act 1998, Tushnet, ibid. at 25.
88 Including the declaration under section 4 of the Human Rights Act 1998, Tushnet, ibid. at 29.
89 including constitutional provisions such as the override (section 1) and notwithstanding (section 33) clauses in the Canadian constitution, Tushnet, ibid. at 31.
90 Tushnet, ibid. at 22.
91 This is particularly apparent in the US constitutional setting where under a strong-review model there is little recourse when the courts interpret the Constitution reasonably but in the reasonable alternative view of a majority (of people), mistakenly. Tushnet, ibid. at 2922.
92 Garavito and Franco, n 79 at 10.
93 Sandra Liebenberg and Katherine Young, 'Adjudicating Social and Economic Rights: Can Democratic Experimentalism Help?' 237–258 at 239; and O'Cinneide, n 38 at 274; and Frank I. Michelman, at 287 in Helena Garcia et al., n 38.
94 Tushnet, n 84 at 238.
95 Garavito and Franco, n 79 at 10.

outcome-orientated orders whereas weak remedies tend to leave implementation back in the hands of government agencies.[96] Moderate remedies on the other hand, can outline procedures and broad goals, as well as criteria and deadlines for assessing progress whilst at the same time leave decisions on means and policies to government.[97] This approach can see the deployment of multiple forms of remedies at once including the various models developed by Landau: individual-level affirmative relief, negative injunctions, weak-form review, to structural injunctions.[98] A multidimensional approach to remedies in and of themselves may help provide some answers to the challenges faced by relying on a weak-form model of review that enters into inter-institutional dialogue without providing any substantive underpinning to ESR. This approach is discussed below as the hybrid approach (employing both procedural and substantive elements).

Young develops a typology of review employed by courts when assessing ESR claims: deferential review (placing the decision back onto the elected branches); managerial review (where the court assumes direct responsibility for the substantive component of ESR adjudication); peremptory review (where the court registers its superiority in demanding and controlling an immediate response); experimentalist review (where the court encourages a participative element by including relevant stakeholders in seeking a solution) and conversational review (where the court engages in interbranch dialogue to resolve the determination of ESR).[99] The typology of review does not in itself identify a preferential approach in terms of the strength or weakness of any one mechanism. Rather, as Young highlights, the judicial review deployed when approaching how to enforce any one right in the particular circumstances at hand is multidimensional.[100] The typology of review is there as a heuristic device for understanding the variety of approaches the court may take at any one time. The various approaches available to the court therefore align with a flexible approach to both degree of review as well as to the type of remedy employed. In a similar sense, the principles of adjudication here can be engaged to different degrees depending on the circumstances. Rather than set thresholds they highlight significant points for consideration on the adjudication journey (like building blocks for ESR that can be deployed in different ways to different degrees).

At the national level in the UK human rights adjudication falls within the weak-form review model. Yet at the same time, at the devolved level a strong-form human rights review prevails. Declarations of incompatibility under the Human Rights Act 1998 can be contrasted with ultra vires remedies and strike down powers of the court under each of the devolved frameworks. Rather than align the UK or human rights adjudication under a strong or weak form of adjudication it is clear that both strong and weak review co-exist, with different remedies and forms of compliance engaged

---

96 Ibid.
97 Ibid.
98 Landau, n 41.
99 Young, n 57 at 142.
100 Young, ibid. at 143.

in some form or another at any one time. At times it may be necessary for a court to adopt a strong review and remedy with an outcome-orientated order. At other times it may be more appropriate for a court to adopt a deferential approach and refer the matter back to the legislature/executive. Despite the insistent reluctance of the UK to accept the justiciability of ESR the judicial framework is very well placed to take steps to develop an innovative approach to remedies for ESR violations and as discussed in Chapter 5 adjudication of ESR already occurs every day in practice across the UK but it is piecemeal, incremental and often under the rubric of something else.[101]

The principles of adjudication developed here are not proposed on the basis of strength or weakness. Nor are they proposed as a measurement tool as such or purely heuristic. They are proposed as principles of good practice that counteract the multiple critiques of social rights discussed above, whilst at the same time requiring a degree of flexibility in their application at any given time. They are principally derived from deliberative democracy theory and form part of a multi-institutional theoretical framework where responsibility for ESR, and human rights more broadly, are the responsibility of the legislature, executive and judiciary where each must pertain to a substantive normative standard (either set out in the constitution or derived from international law). In this sense, the judiciary must be equipped with flexible principles to respond to its constitutional role as a deliberative accountability mechanism. For example, whilst at times a substantive peremptory review might be called for and a strong form of remedy deployed, at other times a deferential approach will be required and a conversational or participative experimentalist review should be undertaken. The principles capture the 'adjudication journey' and can be **flexibly** deployed under weak, moderate or strong interventionist approaches by the court, and at times an innovative approach will be required where multiple remedies are issued to deal with different aspects of a case.

The following principles of good practice are therefore intended for consideration across the ESR adjudication journey as important building blocks to be deployed using flexibility to respond to the particular circumstances:

Principle of Accessibility

The first principle is based on accessibility and requires questioning whether access to justice affordable/accessible? Are there barriers to accessing justice because of legal aid or standing? This could include consideration of whether the standing test should be expanded for public interest litigation[102] and for collective cases in addition to whether the legal aid rules have been sufficiently adapted to account for ESR cases. Likewise, enabling access to that structure is paramount for the proper administration of justice. Problems relating to legal aid are significant in the UK context. For example, in England and Wales the introduction of the Legal Aid,

---

101 Boyle and Hughes, n 3.
102 See *Christian Institute v Others* [2015] CSIH 64, para.43–44 – standing established on EU law grounds but not under s100 of Scotland Act as charities could not meet victim test.

Sentencing and Punishment of Offenders Act 2012 ('LASPO') in April 2013 has seen the provision of legal aid decimated. The legislation removed access to legal aid significantly in social welfare areas and only facilitated potential support for breach of a Convention right.[103] This has serious implications for access to justice and the principle of accessibility in relation to social rights jurisprudence. The Legal Aid Board has, for example, refused legal aid to homeless people to challenge the criminalisation of homelessness and in response has defended its actions by indicating that such litigation could be funded through 'crowd fund sources'.[104]

Importantly, access to justice consists of both procedural and substantive claims. Whilst the literature often identifies problems around legal aid, standing and representation there is more scope to reflect on how our substantive conception of justice impacts on accessibility (if for example, civil claims engaging with ESR are not taken sufficiently serious).[105] The principles developed here move beyond a mapping of access to justice to include a substantive component that reflects on how a 'fairer distribution of rights' may be primary to justice.[106] In other words, in addition to procedural access to justice the principle of accessibility read together with the other principles must also revisit the structure and substance of the definition of 'justice' in and of itself in any particular setting. A broader conceptualisation and legal structure that includes ESR will be better prepared for addressing violations and enabling effective remedies.

Principle of Participation

Does adjudication facilitate the participation of those most impacted, especially the most marginalised? Are multi-party and structural cases facilitated when dealing with systemic problems? Do courts have the institutional capacity and procedures to respond to systemic societal problems? Are rights-holders able to participate in legal processes in which they are engaged and are they able to meaningfully engage in the outcome of those processes (including the remedies offered)? This principle is closely linked with the deliberative quality of adjudication and the counter-majoritarian principle in enabling the court to act as an institutional voice for the marginalised. As

---

103 Public Law Project, Top Legal Aid and Access to Justice Cases. Available at https://public lawproject.org.uk/wp-content/uploads/2018/08/Top-legal-aid-and-access-to-justice-cases-of-recent-years.pdf

104 Sarah Marsh and Patrick Greenfield, 'Legal Aid Agency Taken to Court for Refusing to Help Rough Sleepers', *The Guardian*, 23 October 2018, available at www.theguardian.com/society/2018/oct/23/legal-aid-agency-taken-to-court-for-refusing-to-help-rough-sleepers

105 See, for example, the claims and counter-claims to Lord Sumption's remarks around civil legal aid as a non-essential component of justice, Mark Elliot, 'Civil Legal Aid as a Constitutional Imperative: A Response to Lord Sumption', *Public Law for Everyone*, 28 November 2018, available at https://publiclawforeveryone.com/2018/11/28/civil-legal-aid-as-a-constitutional-imperative-a-response-to-lord-sumption/

106 Roderick MacDonald, 'Access to Civil Justice' in Peter Cane and Herbert M. Kritzer (eds.), *The Oxford Handbook of Empirical Legal Research* (Oxford University Press, 2010), 492–521 at 502.

highlighted by Liebenberg, participation in decisions is an important aspect of the maxim *audi alteram partem* (hear the other side).[107] It recognises the importance of ensuring people have an opportunity to participate in decisions that will affect them and an opportunity to influence the outcome of those decisions.[108] The UN Special Rapporteur (UNSR) on Housing includes participation as a key principle that must be enabled to ensure access to justice is secured. As part of this principle, the UNSR highlights the importance of participation 'in all stages of rights claims and in the implementation of remedies'.[109] In other words, all decisions around ESR should include rights-holders, including the designing and implementing of strategies and programmes. Where genuine participation has not occurred then the court must intervene to facilitate meaningful engagement with both the legal process as well as the remedies offered.[110] Genuine participation requires proactive steps to ensure systemic barriers are removed whether they be physical, economic, social or cultural.[111] Further, different persons will have different needs and so participation should reflect those requirements with particular regard to barriers faced by women, children, disabled persons, racial and ethnic minorities, migrants, among other minority groups.

Whilst participation is a key component of access to justice it is not sufficient on its own to ensure substantive enforcement of rights. Participation and meaningful engagement in the adjudication process in South Africa, for example, has come under criticism for failing to give substance to rights.[112] The principle of fairness goes some way to address this gap by encouraging participation through fair processes, as well as substantive enforcement through stronger review and remedies where appropriate (in those cases demanding stronger intervention). Ultimately, the principle of participation is about facilitating access to procedural as well as substantive justice.

Principle of Deliberation

Does the court engage in dialogic methods? Is there deliberation between institutions/across jurisdictions/with key stakeholders? Does the court seek to ensure its practice is informed, inclusive, participatory and transformative or exercising deference where appropriate? There is a substantial body of literature that encourages 'dialogue'

---

107 Liebenberg, n 65.
108 Ibid., citing Hoexter, *Administrative Law in South Africa* (2nd ed., 2012) 363.
109 UN Special Rapporteur, Access to justice for the right to housing Report of the Special Rapporteur on adequate housing as a component of the right to an adequate standard of living, and on the right to nondiscrimination in this context, 15 January 2019, A/HRC/40/61.
110 Sandra Liebenberg, 'Remedial Principles and Meaningful Engagement in Education Rights Disputes' (2016) 19 *Potchefstroom Electronic Law Journal* 1–43 at 5–6.
111 Ibid., para.49. See also General Recommendation No. 33 (2015) on women's access to justice, para. 3; and Committee on Economic, Social and Cultural Rights, general comment No. 16 (2005) on the equal right of men and women to the enjoyment of all economic, social and cultural rights, paras. 21 and 38.
112 Anashri Pillay, 'Toward Effective Social and Economic Rights Adjudication: The Role of Meaningful Engagement' (2012) 10(3) *International Journal of Constitutional Law* 732–755.

between the legislature and executive.[113] Indeed, the literature indicates that the UK already operates within a dialogic model through the existing human rights framework. As alluded to in *Miller* and argued by Eleftheriadis, the UK constitution is a 'matter of law, open to legal deliberation and reasoning to be determined by the legislature, the executive and the courts working together'.[114] By way of example, when the court issues a declaration of incompatibility under section 4 of the Human Rights Act it is inviting the legislature to revisit an incompatible provision in a deferential way and under a dialogic model. Deliberative adjudication can include weak-form judicial review when appropriate where courts may take a deferential approach and refer a matter back to the legislature[115] and strong review, where appropriate, that can include substantive review and outcome-oriented orders, including the use of specific implement.

Deliberation should occur horizontally across institutions and vertically between the local and supranational level. This approach engages with the principles of participation when facilitating deliberation of those impacted by court decisions. For example, a form of deliberation might include facilitating the role of an intervener, where a human rights institution might intervene on behalf of a group impacted. Likewise public interest litigation can fulfil the role of a bottom-up approach to deliberation where systemic issues are brought before the court by key interest groups. Deliberation can include an upwards form of dialogue with supranational and international actors, including in dialogue with UN bodies (and in response to their outputs) and regional and international courts (and in response to their judgments) and an internal and local form of dialogue with domestic and devolved institutions. It does not imply a direct line of communication but a dialectic and dialogic engagement that is alive to the continuous development of social rights adjudication. In its simplest form, this would see the court using other forms of social rights determination as interpretative sources to help inform its own approach where appropriate.

Principle of Fairness (Process and Substance)

Does adjudication ensure compliance with fair procedures? Does adjudication move beyond procedural review where appropriate? Is adjudication informed by substantive standards (with reference to international human rights law)? Are courts giving meaning to rights? Does the substance of the decision respect the dignity of the applicant? Are remedies employed to ensure substantive change for violations of ESR, or, alternatively, is the deference to parliament/executive on the substance justified? A critique of

---

113 For discussion see, Sandra Fredman, 'From Dialogue to Deliberation: Human Rights Adjudication and Prisoners' Rights to Vote' in Murray Hunt et al. (eds.), *Parliaments and Human Rights: Redressing the Democratic Deficit* 152–156 (Hart Publishing, 2015), 296–297; Alison Young, *Democratic Dialogue* (Oxford University Press, 2017); Murray Hunt, 'Reshaping Constitutionalism' in John Morison et al. (eds.), *Judges, Transitions and Human Rights* (Oxford University Press, 2007), 468 at 470.

114 Pavlos Eleftheriadis, 'Two Doctrines of the Unwritten Constitution' (2017) 13 *European Constitutional Law Review* 525–550 at 549.

115 Tushnet, n 84 at 23.

'democratic experimentalism' highlights the normative weakness of relying on process of deliberation and participation alone in the determination of rights.[116] Courts must also abide by substantive and normative benchmarks, whether domestically or internationally conceived, in the determination of rights. This could include the development of judicial review that considers whether the decision itself is fair based on an independent examination of the evidence. Whilst this type of review is in its infancy[117] there is potential for courts to develop review that takes into consideration the fairness of substantive outcomes in terms of rights compliance. In other words, over and above reviewing the decision-making process or the power (*vires*) to make the decision, is the outcome itself compliant with ESR? Courts may therefore adopt a hybrid approach that looks at the fairness of process and the substance of the decision/outcome.

Sometimes it may be that a violation of a right requires an outcome-orientated substantive remedy and a deferential remedy for different parts of the same judgment. For example, a violation of the right to adequate housing might require an order compelling a government body to provide adequate housing for a litigant, whilst at the same time issuing a deferential declaration regarding the reasonableness of the government's overarching housing strategy and a supervisory order which allows the court to revisit the reasonableness of the policy at a future date – giving the government an opportunity to revisit the flawed housing strategy. This hybrid approach was evident in the *Hartz IV* litigation when the German Constitutional Court declared a social security policy unfit for purpose (unreasonable) and also issued a substantive decision on what was required to make it reasonable (that the policy should ensure a social minimum that protects human dignity).[118] A mixture of different types of review and remedies can be used under a 'hybrid' form of social rights adjudication.

Expanding Grounds for Review

ESR can be adjudicated upon each of the grounds of review in the same way as CP rights. Grounds of review tend to be classified under a threefold division:[119] **illegality (unlawfulness), irrationality (unreasonableness) and procedural impropriety (unfairness).** Depending on whether the ground is procedural (procedural

---

116 Sandra Leibenberg and Katherine G. Young, 'Adjudication Social and Economic Rights, Can Democratic Experminteralism Help?' in Helena Alviar García et al. (eds.), *Social and Economic Rights in Theory and Practice, Critical Inquiries* (Routledge, 2015), 237–257 at 248.

117 For a discussion of the development of evidence-based judicial review in cases engaging with systemic unfairness see Joe Tomlinson and Katy Sheridan, 'Judicial Review, Evidence, and Systemic Unfairness in the UK' IACL-AIDC Blog (3 September 2018) available at https://blog-iacl-aidc.org/blog/2018/9/3/judicial-review-evidence-and-systemic-unfairness-in-the-uk. Courts may well start to develop substantive-based review of outcomes moving beyond an assessment of vires in and of itself. See, for example, the court's approach to tribunal fees in which they considered evidence on what constituted a social minimum based on criteria set by academics and the *Joseph Rowntree Foundation: R (UNISON) v Lord Chancellor* [2017] UKSC 51.

118 *Hartz IV*, n 66.

119 *Council of Civil Service Unions v Minister for the Civil Service (The GCHQ case)* [1985] AC 374, [1985] ICR 14.

Table 1.2 Grounds of Review

Ground of review	What does this mean?	What kind of review might be employed?
Illegality	Was the decision lawful?	A court will look at whether the decision is within the power of the decision maker or whether it is *ultra vires* (outwith the power of the decision maker). This is a substantive form of review that goes beyond looking at fair process
Irrationality	Was the decision reasonable?	A court will look at the decision-making process and assess whether the outcome of the process was reasonable (rational)
Procedural Impropriety	Did the decision maker follow the correct procedural rules when making the decision?	The court will look at the fairness of the decision-making process and the type of review will be concerned with the procedural aspects of the decision

impropriety) or substantive (unlawful/unreasonable) will determine what type of review the court will apply. The grounds for review are not intended to be exhaustive or mutually exclusive.[120] This means, for example that a case could be examined on the grounds that it is potentially unlawful, unreasonable and unfair, as well as on other potential grounds that might emerge in the future.

Intensity of Review

Depending on the grounds for review the court can employ different types of review in the determination of ESR including reasonableness, proportionality, procedural fairness and even anxious scrutiny. Each of the types of review can vary in intensity. Likewise, sometimes various forms of review can be used at the same time, including both procedural and substantive aspects. There is scope for the court to continue to develop the intensity of review in different types of cases. Courts could, for example, develop review techniques that also examine the fairness of the outcome of a decision and its compatibility with rights similar to the approach adopted in the *Hartz IV* case in Germany.[121] This type of review, whilst in its infancy in the UK, is evident in cases such as *UNISON*,[122] where the court considered evidence on what constituted a social minimum when considering the fairness of tribunal fees, or in the case of *RF* where the court considered the lack of empirical evidence to justify a policy unlawful.[123] This type of review is categorised below as substantive fairness.[124]

---

120   *Wheeler v Leicester City Council* [1985] UKHL 6 (25 July 1985).
121   *Hartz IV*, n 66.
122   *R (UNISON) v Lord Chancellor* [2017] UKSC 51.
123   *RF v Secretary of State for Work And Pensions* [2017] EWHC 3375 (Admin).
124   See Joe Tomlinson and Katy Sheridan, 'Judicial Review, Evidence, and Systemic Unfairness in the UK' IACL-AIDC Blog n 116.

Table 1.3 Intensity of Review

Intensity of review	Definition – what must the judiciary ask itself?
Reasonableness	Was the decision-making process reasonable and rational? If not, would no other sensible person applying logic have arrived at the same outcome? (This is the UK threshold; more expansive forms of reasonableness are discussed below)
Proportionality	In the context of human rights, was the decision the most proportionate way to achieve a legitimate aim when balancing out the alternatives and taking into account the necessity of the action?
Procedural Fairness	Did the decision-making process follow due process, was it fair? Were all of the decision-making procedures followed correctly?
Anxious Scrutiny[125]	In the context of fundamental rights decisions, does the particular area and severity of the decision merit the judiciary taking a closer look at the substantive and procedural aspects of the case?
Substantive Fairness[126]	Over and above whether the process was fair, was the decision itself fair based on an independent examination of the evidence? Whilst this type of review is in its infancy[127] there is potential for courts to develop review that takes into consideration the fairness of substantive outcomes in terms of rights compliance. In other words, over and above reviewing the decision-making process or the power (*vires*) to make the decision, is the outcome itself compliant with ESR?

In relation to ESR it is particularly important to be aware of the difference between different types of review such as procedural review or more substantive

125 Anxious scrutiny is employed in asylum cases where the court has held that only the highest standards of fariness will suffice, *Secretary of State for the Home Department v. Sittampalam Thirukumar, Jordan Benjamin, Raja Cumarasuriya and Navaratnam Pathmakumar*, [1989] Imm AR 402, United Kingdom: Court of Appeal (England and Wales), 9 March 1989; *Kerrouche v Secretary of State for the Home Department* [1997] Imm. A.R. 610. In the case of *Pham (Appellant) v Secretary of State for the Home Department (Respondent)* 2015 UKSC 19, the court noted that the tests of anxious scrutiny and proportionality may produce very similar results (the tests are not the same but when engaging with fundamental rights the tests may reach the same outcome).

126 As per Lord Steyn, 'the rule of law in its wider sense has procedural and substantive effect' *Secretary of State for the Home Department, Ex Parte Pierson, R v.* [1997] UKHL 37. Whilst in this case the issue in question was the *vires* of the decision of the Home Secretary to retrospectively increase a tariff (a power the court decided he did not have) there is potential scope for the court to move beyond this assessment to consider the substantive outcome of decisions (and whether the decision itself is fair – or complies with ESR). In other words, the courts may begin to develop review of the outcome of the decision based on an independent examination of the evidence. See FN below and the UNISON case where the court examined evidence in establishing what constituted a social minimum, *R (UNISON) v Lord Chancellor* [2017] UKSC 51. This type of review would be required to assess components of ESC compatibility, particularly on an assessment of the minimum core. The *Hartz IV* case is a comparative example where the court assesses both the procedure and the substantive outcome of the decision.

127 For a discussion of the development of evidence-based judicial review in cases engaging with systemic unfairness see J Tomlinson and K Sheridan, n 116. Courts may well start to develop

review assessing the reasonableness of a decision, proportionality analysis or establishing the substantive fairness of a decision. For example, if an applicant claims that the decision maker has failed to comply with due process, they can seek a remedy on the grounds of procedural impropriety. This type of action could include whether or not a decision maker has had regard to all relevant factors. For example, if a decision maker is under a statutory duty to have due regard to an outcome this is a right to a process (similar to the approach under section 149 of the Equality Act or the Children and Young Persons (Wales) Measure 2011 implementing UNCRC as a relevant factor in decision-making). If the decision maker has had due regard as part of the decision-making process then the requirement (the duty) will be fulfilled even if this results in no substantive change to the outcome in favour of the rights-holder.[128] The duty is concerned with the lawfulness of the process and not the lawfulness or the adequacy of the outcome.[129]

Reasonableness review can take on different connotations depending on the jurisdiction. In the UK an applicant can seek judicial review on grounds of reasonableness and the court will assess the applicant's case based on whether or not the policy or decision relating to the provision of the right is 'reasonable'. The threshold for unreasonableness is high in jurisprudence across the UK. Based on the well-developed *Wednesbury* reasonableness test an action (or omission) must be 'so outrageous and in defiance of logic…that no sensible person who had applied his mind to the question … could have arrived at it'.[130] This degree of review means that the onus of proving 'unreasonableness' rests with the applicant and that the court requires a high degree of 'irrationality' to find a matter unreasonable. Whilst this works well in relation to some areas of human rights law it may not be suitable or appropriate for all alleged human rights violations. For example, there is a difference in challenging whether or not a long-term policy is fit for purpose or the immediate need of someone who is living in absolute destitution. The latter may compel a more interventionist approach than the former.

An expanded form of reasonableness review has been the type of review employed in South Africa.[131] In the context of ESR, it has been understood as a right to a reasonable policy (p) to access a right (x).[132] In other words, the court assesses the policy or strategy seeking to achieve the right [p(x)] rather

substantive-based review of outcomes moving beyond an assessment of vires in and of itself. See, for example, the court's approach to tribunal fees in which they considered evidence on what constituted a social minimum based on criteria set by academics and the Joseph Rowntree Foundation: *R (UNISON) v Lord Chancellor* [2017] UKSC 51.

128 There is no jurisprudence on the Welsh Measure, however, the court's approach to the due regard duty is evident in a number of cases under the Equality Act 2010 (discussed in Chapter 5).

129 *MA & Ors, R (on the application of) v The Secretary of State for Work and Pensions* [2014] EWCA Civ 13 (21 February 2014) para.92.

130 *Council of Civil Service Unions and Others v Minister for the Civil Service* [1985] AC 374.

131 For example, see the reasonableness test as applied in *Government of the Republic of South Africa v Grootboom* 2001 (1) SA 46 (CC).

132 Amartya Sen, 'The Right Not to be Hungry' in Philip Alston et al. (eds.), *The Right to Food* (The Hague: Martinus Nijhoff, 1984), 70.

than outcome [(x)]. In the case of *Grootboom*, the court assessed the reasonableness of the housing policy in South Africa and determined that the state had not gone far enough in providing housing for those in desperate need thus acting unreasonably.[133] The outcome was that the state was required to revisit its housing strategy (this did not provide an immediately enforceable right to housing for Mrs Grootboom). Sometimes remedies may have no immediate material impact that results in transformative change for a particular applicant, but the longer-term symbolism of the court's interjection will create the space for broader societal change and there are still substantive components to this approach (i.e. the longer-term outcome of a revised housing strategy).[134]

This broader approach to reasonableness facilitates a more substantive, or thicker, conception of justice than purely procedural review. South African jurisprudence has developed reasonable review that encompasses substantive standards. These standards include reviewing the reasonableness of state action by assessing whether the approach adopted to realise ESR is coherent, balanced, flexible, comprehensive, workable and non-discriminatory[135] as well as whether there has been meaningful engagement in the decision-making process.[136] In addition, it compels states to adopt measures that have taken into account the most marginalised groups and prioritise grave situations or situations of serious risk (invoking theories of prioritisation).[137] Importantly, the UK test of *Wednesbury* reasonableness falls significantly short of these broader substantive 'reasonable' standards as conceived of in the South African approach.

The development of proportionality analysis has been an important development in UK jurisprudence in the wake of the European Convention on Human Rights (ECHR) litigation and arguably now performs a role as both a common law ground of review[138] as well as potentially imposing a greater intensity of review when it is invoked.[139] Once a prima facie breach of a right has been found, proportionality, in its most widely conceived theoretical exposition[140] asks whether the infringement pursues a legitimate aim?; second, was the measure necessary (was there no alternative, less restrictive approach)?; third, on balance, do the benefits outweigh the costs

---

133　*Grootboom*, n 131.

134　Garavito and Franco, n 79 at 19–21.

135　Katharine G. Young, 'Proportionality, Reasonableness, and Economic and Social Rights' in Vicki Jackson and Mark Tushnet (eds.), *Proportionality, New Frontiers and New Challenges* (Cambridge University Press, 2017), 248–273 at 254.

136　Anashri Pillay, 'Toward Effective Social and Economic Rights Adjudication: The Role of Meaningful Engagement' (2012) 10(3) *International Journal of Constitutional Law* 732–755.

137　Young, n 135 at 269.

138　Meaning it can be applied in cases engaging with fundamental rights beyond ECHR jurisprudence.

139　See *R v Secretary of State for the Home Department, ex parte Daly* [2001] UKHL 26 and *Pham v Secretary of State for the Home Department* [2015] UKSC 19.

140　The UK approach is still rather reticent to the broadest interpretation of proportionality. See obiter dicta *Pham* ibid. as per Lord Mance para.95–97.

imposed on the rights-holder?[141] Nonetheless, even with more substantive review on the grounds of reasonableness or proportionality the violation of a right might not necessarily be addressed. This relates to the fact that not all rights are immediately enforceable (they are derogable) and the enforcement of rights of different persons will no doubt require a balancing act. The question remains, are there some circumstances where a more interventionist approach around substantive enforcement might be required – such as for example, when the violation breaches the dignity of the applicant,[142] where the breach causes conditions to fall below a minimum core/social minimum,[143] or where there is a breach of a peremptory threshold as set out in statute (see the discussion below).

A more interventionist approach might rest on a challenge to the standard of provision of an ESR on the grounds that it is manifestly unfair based on one of the grounds identified (dignity/minimum/peremptory). So rather than focussing purely on procedural justice, reasonableness or proportionality, asking the court to assess the fairness of the actual substantive outcome. In in the *Hartz IV* case, the German Constitutional Court assessed whether the substantive outcome of a policy as well as the process leading to the outcome was substantively fair.[144] The court adopted a hybrid approach to judicial review where they assessed the decision-making process as well as the fairness of the outcome. The court found that the process was flawed, and that the outcome of that process was unfair. The more substantive degree of review meant that the public body had to revisit the process as well as the outcome in order to comply with the court's decision. This is a more absolutist approach.

In terms of developing ESR adjudication courts in the UK will require to move beyond the traditional reasonableness review and develop other means of assessing human rights compliance. For example, this could manifest as a more thorough form of reasonableness review beyond 'irrationality' to encompass more substantive elements, including aspects of proportionality. Based on the South African approach the UN CESCR has for example developed reasonableness as a test that takes into consideration the following factors:

- The extent to which the measures taken were deliberate, concrete and targeted towards the fulfilment of economic, social and cultural rights.
- Whether discretion was exercised in a non-discriminatory and non-arbitrary manner.
- Whether resource allocation is in accordance with international human rights standards.

---

141 Young, n 135 at 257. See also Alexy (the original proponent of the proportionality model of review). Robert Alexy, *A Theory of Constitutional Rights* (Oxford University Press, 2002).
142 As seen in Colombian jurisprudence around mínimo vital – discussed in more detail in Chapter 4.
143 Ibid., see also the example of German jurisprudence including *Hartz IV*, n 66.
144 *Hartz IV*, ibid.

- Whether the State party adopts the option that least restricts Covenant rights.
- Whether the steps were taken within a reasonable timeframe.
- Whether the precarious situation of disadvantaged and marginalised individuals or groups has been addressed.
- Whether policies have prioritised grave situations or situations of risk.
- Whether decision-making is transparent and participatory.[145]

Similar consideration could be given for example to tests of proportionality, aspects of which are evident in the expansive reasonableness test above, and which allow a court to weigh up the different considerations a public body has had regard to in making a determination. Again, this approach may not take into account whether or not the substantive outcome is unfair. Sometimes this type of review is the most appropriate but again, if the situation relates for example to a non-derogable component proportionality may not be enough. These different considerations all relate to what degree courts might enforce rights along the respect, protect, fulfil analogy.

The process v substance dimension of social rights adjudication remains to a large degree unsettled in the literature and practice. Here I propose that there are two approaches where the substance of rights must feature more prominently in the adjudication of the court. The first approach is when the violation is so obvious and severe as to directly impact on the applicant's dignity and meaningful enjoyment of the minimum level of rights, the *dignity or social minimum threshold*.[146] In this instance, the court must intervene with a substantive enforcement and outcome-orientated order. The second approach is for the court to be more proactive in responding to instructions placed upon the decision maker by the legislature, *the peremptory threshold*. For example, if the legislature instructs the decision maker to have 'due regard' to an outcome, or to implement a policy that seeks to achieve the outcome, then the peremptory threshold is not met as no substantive outcome is anticipated or guaranteed. Whereas, if the legislature instructs the decision maker to establish and meet a person's need in the provision of a right then the peremptory threshold is met because the legislature anticipated and guaranteed a substantive outcome. When the assessment of need is carried out this should materialise, or crystallise, into a duty to fulfil or realise

---

145 Bruce Porter, Rethinking Progressive Realisation, Social Rights Advocacy Centre (2015) at 6 and United Nations Committee on Economic, Social and Cultural Rights, *An Evaluation of the Obligation to Take Steps to the 'Maximum of Available Resources' under an Optional Protocol to the Covenant*, UNCESCROR, 38th Sess, UN Doc E/C.12/2007/1, (2007); Malcolm Langford, 'Closing the Gap? – An Introduction to the Optional Protocol to the International Covenant on Economic, Social and Cultural Rights' (2009) 27(1) *Nordic Journal of Human Rights* 2; General comment No. 3 (1990) on the nature of States parties' obligations, para. 2; UNSR on Housing, Access to Justice Report, n 109, para.25–27.

146 See Fredman, n 64 . For a discussion on human dignity as a principle of human rights adjudication see Conor Gearty, *Principles of Human Rights Adjudication* (Oxford University Press, 2005).

the particular right meaning a substantive outcome is enforceable by the court.[147] In other words, the court should be prepared to enforce a substantive outcome when the decision maker fails to follow the instructions placed upon it by the legislature to do so.

Counter-majoritarian Principle

Is adjudication elite-driven? Has the court taken steps to review the holistic implications? Has the court considered whether the judgment will further marginalise vulnerable groups? If ESR are engaged, is the person/group impacted by the violation excluded from influencing change in a pro-majoritarian political system?

Table 1.4 Classification of Innovative Approach to Procedural v Substantive Remedies[148]

Type of right	Weak	Moderate	Strong
	Right to a fair process (for ex. due regard)	*Right to a policy (not necessarily a substantive outcome)*	*Right to an outcome*
Nature of duty (or obligation)	Duty-bearer must implement process (for ex. have due regard as part of decision-making process)	Duty-bearer must implement policy to realise right (for ex. establish national strategy to fulfil a right)	Duty-bearer must realise right – through process or policy or other means – resulting in a substantive outcome
Intensity of review	**Due process (Procedural fairness)**	**Reasonableness/ Proportionality (Irrationality +)**	**Illegality (Substantive fairness)**
What the courts might consider	Process-based – was the process followed? Deference to Parliament/Government to remedy incompatible legislation/action/omission	Was the policy reasonable? Was the interference proportionate? Decisions on means and policies left to government	Was the decision fair? (vires and substance) Apply a threshold to measure compliance

(*Continued*)

147 See the judicial commentary on crystallisation of duties in *McGregor v South Lanarkshire Council* 2001 SC 502. Examples of statutory needs assessment can be found in s37(1) of the Children and Families Act or s12A Social Care (Scotland) Act 1968.
148 This table is developed from the remedy typology developed by Tushnet n 84 and expanded upon by Garavito and Franco, n 79 at 10. See Chapters 4, 5 and 6 for further discussions on the cases mentioned.

Table 1.4 (Cont.)

Type of right	Weak Right to a fair process (for ex. due regard)	Moderate Right to a policy (not necessarily a substantive outcome)	Strong Right to an outcome
Type of remedy	**Revisit the process**	**Revisit the policy**	**Revisit the outcome**
Type of Enforcement	Deference to Parliament/Government to remedy incompatible legislation/action/omission Compliance left to discretion of decision makers	Court can outline procedures and broad goals Criteria and deadlines for assessing progress Decisions on means and policies left to government	Ultra vires declarations/Outcome-orientated orders, including outcome-orientated structural interdicts in multi-party cases
Examples in practice[149]	Due regard duty under the Equality Act 2010 – PSED requires that the decision maker has due regard to equality of outcomes but does not include duty to ensure equality of outcomes Declaration of incompatibility – *Hirst* case (no change in law – parliament could choose to ignore)	Ultra vires declaration in *Napier* (damages awarded which led to Scottish Government addressing the issue in a substantive sense – a broad goal had been inadvertently set – the symbolic nature of the deferential judgment resulted in material change) Reasonableness judgment in *Grootboom* (right to a reasonable housing strategy not an immediate right to a house)	Statutory framework where assessment of needs crystallises into duty to provide (see s37(1) of the Children and Families Act 2014 or s12A Social Care (Scotland) Act 1968) *Hartz IV* (hybrid remedy – right to a reasonable process and the right to an outcome to meet threshold of dignity) Structural interdict Colombia (*T025* structural interdict including revised policy/budget and outcome for internally displaced persons) Structural interdict in Argentina (*Agüero* – budget, plan, outcome for housing)
Type of Defence	We took it into consideration	Our existing policy is reasonable and/or proportionate	We do not have enough resources to achieve x[150]

---

149 The cases mentioned here are discussed in more detail in Chapter 4, 5 and 6.

150 This defence may not be insufficient in terms of fulfilling a statutory obligation see, for example, *MacGregor v South Lanarkshire Council* 2001 SC 502 and *R v Gloucestershire County Council (Ex p Barry)* [1997] AC 584.

Where persons or groups are politically marginalised Landau has argued that the court can become an important institutional voice for those who cannot seek recourse through pro-majoritarian politics.[151] Deliberative models of adjudication must take into account the potential unequal bargaining power of participants. The danger is that the inherent inequality between the parties in ESR adjudication can undermine inclusive deliberation unless genuine agency is facilitated for the marginalised.[152] For example, costly litigation can exclude those who cannot afford litigation and adversarial litigation can exacerbate structural inequalities. This can create a 'disenfranchisement effect' where the experience of poverty prohibits genuine participation in deliberative processes, including adjudication.[153] The danger of the court acting as a pro-hegemonic exercise of power can be balanced through facilitating structural remedies to deal with systemic problems.[154] This will only work if other principles are adhered to, including the need to ensure access to justice is affordable and accessible.

The Colombian Constitutional Court has heard and decided 'structural' cases where it considers whether an 'unconstitutional set of affairs' requires to be remedied.[155] Usually this will involve multiple applicants (collective cases) and will allow the court to review whether the state can remedy a systemic problem engaging multiple stakeholders and multiple defendants.

These types of structural cases tend to:

(1) affect a large number of people who allege a violation of their rights, either directly or through organisations that litigate the cause;
(2) implicate multiple government agencies found to be responsible for pervasive public policy failures that contribute to such rights violations; and
(3) involve structural injunctive remedies, i.e., enforcement orders whereby courts instruct various government agencies to take coordinated actions to protect the entire affected population and not just the specific complainants in the case.[156]

If structural issues arise in relation to ESR it would not be beyond the reach of the legislature, executive and judiciary to work together to remedy the matter.[157]

---

151 Landau, n 41. See also Mantouvalou in Gearty and Mantouvalou n 75.
152 Leidenberg and Young, n 93 at 251.
153 Ibid.
154 Landau, n 41.
155 For an in-depth discussion on this see César Rodríguez-Garavito, 'Beyond the Courtroom: The Impact of Judicial Activism on Socioeconomic Rights in Latin America' (2011) 89 *Texas Law Review* 1669–1698.
156 Ibid. at 1671.
157 Such as the response by the executive and legislature to introduce emergency legislation to deal with the fall out of systemic human rights violations following the Cadder judmgment. See *Cadder v Her Majesty's Advocate (Scotland)* [2010] UKSC 43 (26 October 2010) and the Criminal Procedure (Legal Assistance, Detention and Appeals) (Scotland) Act 2010.

For example, if a systemic problem arises in relation to human rights protection then there could be a role for the court to supervise whether the legislature and/or executive could take steps to remedy this through a form of structural injunction. Landau argues that addressing violations of social rights through a structural approach to remedies facilitates a form of social rights adjudication that positively impacts on the lives of poorer citizens and prioritises the most vulnerable.[158]

Remedial Principle

Are the remedies appropriate and are they effective? Are they procedural or substantive in nature? Are they deferential where appropriate and outcome-orientated where appropriate? Are they participative and are there sufficient monitoring mechanisms to ensure compliance? Are structural remedies used where appropriate?[159] The approach to remedies requires a much broader and deeper understanding as to how the court can respond in a dialogic manner whilst also protecting the most vulnerable and those most in need with outcome-orientated orders when appropriate. Garavito claims that this approach to adjudication works best when courts clearly affirm the justiciability of the right in question (strong rights); leave the policy decisions to the elected branches of power whilst laying out a clear roadmap for measuring progress (moderate remedies); and actively monitor the implementation of the court's orders through participatory mechanisms like public hearings, progress reports and follow-up decisions (strong monitoring).[160]

In addition, courts must also balance this principle with the principle of substantive fairness and intervene with stronger outcome-orientated remedies where appropriate (employing the social minimum or peremptory thresholds). A flexible approach to adjudication and to the principles of adjudication enables courts to weigh up the most appropriate remedy in any given context. This means developing remedies to meet the most urgent of needs in serious violations as well as remedies that respond to broader claims around progressive realisation, revenue generation and allocation, as well as national strategies to fulfil rights.

Ultimately courts should have a constellation of remedies readily available to them. What is remedially appropriate in any given case will be dependent on a number of factors (number of applicants, degree of interference with the right, complexity of resource allocation, number of defendants, fairness of the outcome and so on). The overriding principle must be that the remedy adopted in any given case is 'effective in protecting and vindicating

---

158 Landau, n 41 at 189–247. See also Mantouvalou in Conor Gearty and Virginia Mantouvalou, *Debating Social Rights* (Hart, 2011).

159 For a discussion on the different types of remedies available for social rights see Malcolm Langford, César Rodríguez-Garavito and Julieta Rossi (eds.), *Social Rights Judgments and the Politics of Compliance: Making It Stick* (Cambridge University Press, 2017) and Boyle, n 1.

160 Rodríguez-Garavito, n 138 at 1692.

the rights at issue and responsive to the circumstances at hand'.[161] As Porter identifies:

> there is no universally preferred social rights remedial and enforcement strategy. Social rights claimants do not always aspire to achieve broader structural change or transformative effect. If a claimant requires only a correction to an existing entitlement system in order to secure housing, food or healthcare, perhaps qualifying for an already existing benefit, the most effective and appropriate remedy may be one of immediate application, applying to a single entitlement, identifying a single respondent government [agency]. In other cases [...] claimants may undertake litigation with clearly transformative aims, identifying multiple entitlements and respondents and demanding the implementation of ongoing strategies with meaningful engagement and stakeholders. It is important to ensure that range of remedial and enforcement strategies are employed and effective enforcement is in place in all cases.[162]

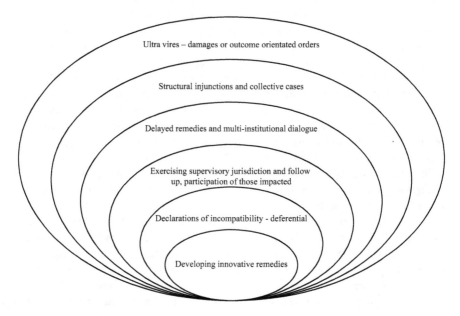

Ultra vires – damages or outcome orientated orders

Structural injunctions and collective cases

Delayed remedies and multi-institutional dialogue

Exercising supervisory jurisdiction and follow up, participation of those impacted

Declarations of incompatibility - deferential

Developing innovative remedies

Figure 1.1 Developing Innovative Remedies

161 Bruce Porter, 'Canada: Systemic Claims and Remedial Diversity', in Malcolm Langford et al. (eds.), n 48 201–254 at 204.
162 Ibid., 205–206.

The legal definition of what constitutes an effective remedy in international law is discussed in the next chapter.

Some Key Definitions

For the purposes of the book, it may be helpful to clarify some key definitions. The rights referred to as 'economic and social rights' (or ESR) refer to the broad category of rights enunciated in international law such as the right to education, the right to the enjoyment of the highest attainable standard of physical and mental health, labour rights, the right to an adequate standard of living, the right to adequate housing, the right to social security, amongst others.[163] The definition of incorporation adopted is the domestication of international norms coupled with access to an effective remedy for a violation. Sometimes incorporation can be direct – such as through direct reference to an international treaty.[164] Sometimes incorporation can be indirect, such as through the constitutionalisation or legalisation of a right mirroring an international normative standard implicitly but not explicitly. And sometimes incorporation of a right can be sectoral, where for example the right to adequate housing is

---

163 Examples of economic rights include labour rights, examples of social rights include the right to education, the right to adequate housing, the right to health, the right to freedom from destitution and so on. ESR more broadly protect vulnerable groups such as those with disabilities, children, the elderly, minority communities or those who are unemployed. The rights protected in international law fall under treaties such as the International Covenant on Economic, Social and Cultural Rights 1966, UN General Assembly resolution 2200A (XXI) of 16 December 1966, United Nations, Treaty Series, vol. 993, p. 3; the European Social Charter (Revised) 1996, Council of Europe, ETS 163; the Convention on the Rights of the Child 1989, UN General Assembly, resolution 44/25 of 20 November 1989, United Nations, Treaty Series, vol. 1577, p. 3; the Convention on the Elimination of Discrimination Against Women 1979, UN General Assembly resolution 34/180 of 18 December 1979, United Nations, Treaty Series, vol. 1249, p. 13; the Convention on the Elimination of Racial Discrimination 1965, United Nations General Assembly resolution 2106 (XX) of 21 December 1965 United Nations, Treaty Series, vol. 660, p. 195; and the Convention on the Rights of Persons with Disabilities 2006, United Nations General Assembly resolution A/RES/61/106 of 24 January 2007, 76th plenary meeting; issued in GAOR, 61st sess., Suppl. no. 49. 'Annex: Convention on the Rights of Persons with Disabilities': pp. 2–29. 'Economic, social and cultural rights' sometimes referred to as simply 'economic and social rights' (as they are in this book), or socio-economic rights. Cultural rights, *per se*, can engage with a very different normative and conceptual debates relating to minority rights, rights to cultural identity, the meaning of 'culture', multicultural citizenship and so forth (see, for example, Siobhán Mullally, *Gender, Culture and Human Rights: Reclaiming Universalism,* (Hart 2006) . It is not within the ambit of this book to draw on this wider engagement in the literature relating to cultural rights. However, the book recognises the indivisibility of all rights and that, whilst sub-categories may exist and are important to recognise, the categorisation of 'economic, social and cultural rights' can be synonymous with 'economic and social rights', 'socio-economic rights' or simply 'social rights'.

164 See, for example, the constitution of Argentina (Article 25) or the Norwegian Human Rights Act 1999.

provided for under housing legislation, or the right to social security under social security legislation. Essentially domestic incorporation of international norms, be that direct, implicit or sectoral, should be both derived from and inspired by the international legal framework and should at all times be coupled with an effective remedy for a violation of a right.[165] Forms of legal integration that do not facilitate access to a remedy for a violation of a right cannot amount to incorporation but should be defined as a means of implementation, rather than incorporation.

The term justiciability refers to the adjudication of a right by a court.[166] It is important to note that justiciability does not necessarily mean, or equate to, full compliance or enforcement of a right. Some justiciability mechanisms may be weaker than others depending upon how the right, and associated duties, are formulated in law and how willing the court is to engage with enforcement in any given context. Nonetheless, as discussed in more detail in Chapter 2, justiciability can be either (or both) a means of implementation along a scale of enforcement and an important accountability mechanism that ensures either partial or full compliance. Justiciability itself can therefore be measured on a scale between weak enforcement and strong enforcement. The book looks at different models of incorporation and justiciability across this spectrum contextualised within the principles of adjudication discussed above.

---

165 Katie Boyle, Models of Incorporation and Justiciability of Economic, Social and Cultural Rights, Scottish Human Rights Commission, (2018) at 14. See also UN Committee on Economic, Social and Cultural Rights (CESCR), *General Comment No. 19: The right to social security (Art. 9 of the Covenant)*, 4 February 2008, E/C.12/GC/19. Para.77–80; UN General Assembly, *Basic Principles and Guidelines on the Right to a Remedy and Reparation for Victims of Gross Violations of International Human Rights Law and Serious Violations of International Humanitarian Law: resolution/adopted by the General Assembly*, 21 March 2006, A/RES/60/147. See also UN Committee on Economic, Social and Cultural Rights (CESCR), General Comment No. 9: The domestic application of the Covenant, 3 December 1998, E/C.12/1998/24, para.4.

166 See, for example, the definition provided by Dennis and Stewart, 'Among scholars and non-governmental advocates, the term 'justiciability' seems to be used most often to refer merely to the existence of a mechanism or procedure to resolve alleged violation of the rights in question. In this view, rights (or disputes about rights) are justiciable when there is a mechanism capable of adjudicating them, and non-justiciable when one is lacking.' Michael Dennis and David Stewart, 'Justiciability of Economic, Social, and Cultural Rights: Should There Be an International Complaints Mechanism to Adjudicate the Rights to Food, Water, Housing, and Health?' (2004) 98 *The American Journal of International Law* 462; or by Arambulo, 'Justiciability of a human rights means that a court of law or another type of supervisory body deems the right concerned to be amenable to judicial scrutiny', Kitty Arambulo, *Strengthening the Supervision of the International Covenant on Economic, Social and Cultural Rights: Theoretical and Procedural Aspects* (Hart Intersentia, 1999), 16–18; or by Craven, '[T]he justiciability of a particular issue depends, not on the quality of the decision, but rather on the authority of the body to make the decision.', Mathew Craven, *The International Covenant on Economic, Social, and Cultural Rights, A Perspective on Its Development* (Clarendon Press and OUP, 1995), 102.

Structure of the Book

This book is divided into six chapters, each focussing on aspect of how ESR can be better embedded in our legal systems in a way that can facilitate an approach to ESR adjudication based on flexible principles of good practice derived from deliberative democracy theory. As this chapter highlights, ESR and their judicial enforcement remain contested in the UK discourse, and yet the discourse and practice has moved on both internationally and comparatively, meaning an ESR accountability gap has emerged. The principles of adjudication set out in this chapter seek to contribute to the international discourse whilst offering a new lens through which to view ESR in the UK context specifically. They address the first and second critical waves of ESR justiciability (i.e. the anti-democratic critique; the indeterminacy critique; the capacity critique; and the pro-hegemonic critique). The principles include: the accessibility principle; the participation principle; the principle of deliberation; the principle of fairness; the counter-majoritarian principle and the remedial principle. They frame the discussion throughout the following five chapters.

The second chapter looks at the status of ESR in international law arguing that recourse to an effective (judicial) remedy now forms part of state obligations to progressively realise ESR. Chapter 2 revisits the original separation of human rights that occurred during the development of the International Bill of Rights and explains how this bifurcation of rights into different categories (civil and political v economic, social and cultural) has been misunderstood resulting in a false dichotomy of rights. The legal position now acknowledges that access to justice in and of itself is a right, and this includes the need to develop effective remedies for violations of all human rights. Responding to this need requires innovation and imagination if legal systems are to be properly equipped to ensure access to effective remedies.

The third chapter focusses on the regional human rights frameworks as they apply regionally and in the UK. In particular the chapter sets out how EU law and the treaties associated with the Council of Europe, in particular the ECHR, form important pillars of the UK constitution. Both of these regional systems protect ESR to different degrees, and both of the European frameworks are at risk of being lost as part of regressive human rights reform in the domestic sphere. This chapter sets out the particular risks to human rights as a result of Brexit and the UK's fluctuating position in relation to retaining or repealing the Human Rights Act 1998 (thus risking the status of the ECHR and protection of human rights in domestic law). It also sets out the potential of regional mechanisms not yet fully explored, including the revised European Social Charter and the work of the European Committee of Social Rights.

Chapter 4 addresses the constitutional resistance to human rights in the UK and places this discussion within a wider comparative context drawing from models of constitutionalism that favour both parliamentary and judicial supremacy. The chapter explains that the UK exists in a state of flux between different models of constitutionalism (legal v political; framework v process) and that the devolved lens completely reframes the way in which rights can be understood as forming a substantive component of the rule of law. Chapter 4 looks at different models of constitutionalism and how states seek to holistically (or not) address human rights, including ESR, in their constitutional arrangements.

The fifth chapter sets out the ways in which ESR adjudication occurs. The 'justiciability mechanisms' are framed as models and assessed with reference to the principles of adjudication. The justiciability mechanisms include the type of adjudication that already occurs (under the statutory framework broadly speaking; under equality law; through the dynamic interpretation of CPR; and as part of common law incorporation of international human rights law) as well as future mechanisms – i.e. how the justiciability of ESR might occur in the future (recourse to an international or regional ESR complaints mechanism; and/or a renewed constitutional framework through an Economic and Social Rights Act or codified constitution).

This chapter explores the definition of 'incorporation' proposing that incorporation can take on many different forms, crucially however, it requires the creation of rights coupled with effective remedies meaning weaker models of implementation, whilst helpful, are not the same as incorporation of rights. Justiciability can at times be a means of implementation (it can facilitate the enforcement of rights) without necessarily ensuring full compliance. It also has the potential to be an accountability mechanism – the stronger the model of incorporation, the more scope there is for accountability. The book orientates models of justiciability and incorporation towards a multi-institutional constitutional model. This model is the best means of ensuring access to justice for ESR (and CPR) and recognises that the legislature, executive and judiciary each have a role to play in upholding human rights.

The sixth chapter sets out the means through which ESR are developing in the devolved frameworks of Wales, Northern Ireland and Scotland. The book highlights that there is no universal human rights and equality framework that applies across the UK and that the trajectories of the devolved regions have completely transformed the way in which human rights are framed. Chapter 6 highlights the significant steps already taken by the devolved legislatures with respect to implementing and observing international human rights law such as through the Children and Young Persons (Wales) Measure 2011; the Social Security (Scotland) Act 2018; the recommendations of the Northern Ireland Human Rights Commission for a (now suspended) Bill of Rights for Northern Ireland; and the recommendations of the First Minister's Advisory Group on Human Rights Leadership in Scotland on the incorporation of economic, social, cultural and environmental rights into Scots law.

Overall, the book seeks to offer ways forward for ESR according to the principles of adjudication and the particular justiciability mechanisms available under different forms of incorporation (constitutionalisation) of rights. In particular it gives practical examples of how the legislature, executive and judiciary can act as guarantors of rights and proposes that the court must act as an accountability mechanism, and a means of last resort, should other institutional mechanisms fail. In so doing, it seeks to propel the national discourse beyond discussions around regressive human rights reform and presents pathways to better protect ESR both within the UK and beyond.

2 ESR in International Law

Justiciability and Remedies

The duty to progressively achieve ESR entails that states must take steps to the maximum available resources to achieve the rights without delay. Here, I examine the historical context of the duty to progressively achieve and how the development of the framework now includes a requirement to enable access to an effective judicial remedy, at least as a means of last resort, when a state fails to comply with its obligations.[1] It is important to note the distinction between duties of implementation, compliance and the requirement for accountability. The duty to implement rights can occur through the development of laws, regulations, judicial and quasi-judicial decisions, policies, plans, programs, projects, practices, and other interventions or initiatives that are designed to ensure the realisation of human rights'.[2] The duty to comply with human rights, on the other hand, is about conformity to rules.[3] States might implement international human rights law without being in full compliance. Human rights therefore require both implementation and compliance.[4] Accountability mechanisms should address the gap when implementation falls short of compliance.

Justiciability or adjudication of rights can be characterised as a means of implementation, through judicial decision making.[5] At the same time, it can also be characterised as an accountability mechanism when other implementation mechanisms fail to adhere to a common human rights framework – and so

1 Basic Principles and Guidelines on the Right to a Remedy and Reparation of Victims of Gross Violations of International Human Rights and Serious Violations of International Humanitarian Law, UN General Assembly Resolution, Basic Principles and Guidelines on the Right to a Remedy and Reparation for Victims of Gross Violations of International Human Rights Law and Serious Violations of International Humanitarian Law: resolution/adopted by the General Assembly, 21 March 2006, A/RES/60/147.
2 Paul Hunt, 'Configuring the UN Human Rights System in the "Era of Implementation": Mainland and Archipelago' (2017) 39 *Human Rights Quarterly* 489–538 at 495.
3 Jana von Stein, 'The Engines of Compliance', in Jeffrey L. Dunoff and Mark A. Pollack (eds.), *Interdisciplinary Perspectives on International Law and International Relations: The State of the Art* (2013), 477 and 493.
4 Hunt, n 2 at 496.
5 Ibid.

is about taking steps to ensure compliance.[6] Justiciability in and of itself does not guarantee full compliance with ESR as set out in international law. This book argues that accountability is required for a violation when implementation is insufficient to meet the threshold of compliance, and that, ultimately, an effective remedy should be available in court for a violation of a right as a means of last resort (once all other accountability mechanisms are exhausted). Deconstructing the nature of state obligations in international law can help illuminate the different degrees of implementation (respect/protect/fulfil and minimum core) and what role the court can play in upholding them. The chapter therefore looks at what constitutes an effective remedy as well as examining the nature of rights: the principle of indivisibility, the false dichotomy of rights (and its misunderstood historical origin), as well as the different taxonomies of enforcement.

Universal Indivisibility

According to the Universal Declaration of Human Rights, all human rights are equal and inalienable:[7] civil, political, economic, social and cultural rights are indivisible in nature.[8] Yet, historically there has been a dichotomy of rights between civil and political on the one hand, and economic, social and cultural on the other. In an analysis of the *travaux préparatoires* to the founding international treaties on human rights: the Universal Declaration of Human Rights (UDHR) 1948,[9] the International Covenant on Civil and Political Rights (ICCPR) 1966[10] and the International Covenant on Economic, Social and Cultural Rights (ICESCR) 1966,[11] it becomes clear that the principle of indivisibility was pivotal to the intended application of human rights.

---

6 Sandra Fredman, 'Adjudication as Accountability' in Nicholas Bamforth and Peter Leyland (eds.), *Accountability in the Contemporary Constitution* (OUP, 2013), 118.
7 Preamble to the Universal Declaration of Human Rights, United Nations General Assembly resolution 217 A (III) of 10 December 1948, 'Whereas recognition of the inherent dignity and of the equal and inalienable rights of all members of the human family is the foundation of freedom, justice and peace in the world.'
8 The World Conference on Human Rights, Vienna Declaration and Program of Action, UN GAOR, Word Conference on Human Rights, 48th Session, 22d plen. Mtg., UNDoc.A/CONF.157/24, PART I, 23.
9 Universal Declaration of Human Rights 1948 n 7. Hereinafter the 'UDHR', or simply 'the Declaration'.
10 UN General Assembly, International Covenant on Civil and Political Rights, resolution 2200A (XXI) of 16 December 1966, United Nations, Treaty Series, vol. 999, p. 171. Hereinafter the 'ICCPR'.
11 International Covenant on Economic, Social and Cultural Rights 1966, UN General Assembly resolution 2200A (XXI) of 16 December 1966, United Nations, Treaty Series, vol. 993, p. 3. Hereinafter the 'ICESCR'. The UDHR, ICCPR and the ICESCR are collectively known as the International Bill of Rights.

The concept of indivisibility is based on the idea that civil, political, economic, social and cultural rights are equal – that each right is dependent on the enforcement of the other and that each right is mutually important for the substantive enjoyment of the others. This principle is apparent throughout the drafting of the UDHR and was reaffirmed in the Vienna Declaration 1993:

> The World Conference on Human Rights reaffirms the solemn commitment of all states to fulfil their obligations to promote universal respect for, and observance and protection of, all human rights and fundamental freedoms for all in accordance with the Charter of the United Nations, other instruments relating to human rights, and international law. The universal nature of these rights and freedoms is beyond question ... [a]ll human rights are universal, indivisible and interdependent and interrelated. The international community must treat human rights globally in a fair and equal manner, on the same footing, and with the same emphasis.[12]

The principle of indivisibility gives rise to an obligation to protect all human rights on an equal footing.[13]

The Human Rights Misconception

The Point of Bifurcation in 1948

Human rights suffer from a deep misunderstanding in relation to their legal status based upon the separation of civil and political rights, on the one hand, and economic, social and cultural rights on the other into two different branches. They are often referred to as first and second generation with the latter perceived as of lesser status than the former (and a third generation relating to collective rights following suit).[14] This categorisation is an unhelpful

---

12 The Vienna Declaration, n 8 at 23. For an account of the historical development of the principle of indivisibility see Daniel Whelan, *Indivisible Human Rights: A History* (University of Pennsylvania Press, 2010). Whelan clarifies that the term 'indivisible' did not arise until the drafting of the International Covenants and that the quadripartite terminology that all human rights are universal, indivisible, interdependent and interrelated was introduced by the Vienna Declaration. For the purposes of this book the author discusses the principle of indivisibility as an emerging concept evident in the preparatory work to the UDHR.
13 Manfred Nowak, *UN Covenant on Civil and Political Rights, CCPR Commentary* (2nd ed., NP Engel, 2005) 'it is today recognised that all human rights are equal, indivisible and interdependent' at 20.
14 Karel Vasak, 'Pour une troisième génération des droits de l'homme', in Christophe Swinarski (ed.), *Studies and Essays on International Humanitarian Law and Red Cross Principles in Honour of Jean Pictet* (1984) at 837; Karel Vasak, Les différentes catégories des droits de l'homme, in André Lapeyre, François de Tinguy and Karel Vasak (eds.), *Les Dimensions universelles des droits de l'homme. Vol. I.* (1991).

analogy – it is problematic in its legal grounding as well as in its historical association with competing narratives of human rights relative to different social, cultural and experiential foundations (Western/liberal, Soviet/socialist and Third World).[15] The historical separation of two different branches of rights is referred to as the 'bifurcation' of rights. The point of bifurcation is often cited as having originated in the competing ideologies of the parties to the Covenants.[16] The means through which ESC rights could be implemented certainly shaped the drafting of Article 2(1) of the ICESCR which contains weaker enforcement measures. However, the original point of bifurcation occurred during the drafting of the UDHR. The theory that the dichotomy was a result of an attempt to undermine the status of ESR is actually a misconception. Whilst it is clear that the eventual bifurcation and competing approaches to enforceability framed the drafting of two separate Covenants, the original separation of rights was designed to reinforce the status of ESR. This is articulated in the *travaux préparatoires* to the UDHR.

The question of proclaiming a right without sanction was discussed at length. The Soviet representative to the Economic and Social Council in 1948, Mr. Pavlov, crystallised this point when he stated that proclaiming a right without guaranteeing observance was futile:

> [t]he old democracy was too formal. It proclaimed certain rights but did not guarantee observance. The Soviet Union would always be in favour of full implementation. If the means to exercise a right were not specified, the fact of proclaiming that right had no great value.[17]

This statement ignited a debate over how ESR should be enumerated in the UDHR. Their inclusion *per se* was not disputed, rather, it was how to include them that fuelled the debate. The French representative, Mr. Cassin pushed to explicitly enumerate ESR in order to reflect a changing tide in human rights'

---

15 For a counter-argument to the dominant narrative see Jack Donnelly, 'Third Generation Rights', in Catherine Brölmann, René Lefeber and Marjoleine Zieck (eds.), *Peoples and Minorities in International Law* (1993) 119.

16 See, for example, Scott who submits that 'the bifurcation of what is now thought of as the two grand categories of human rights ... had yet to occur at the time of the UDHR's adoption. These categories were progeny of the UDHR and, later created through [the] two instruments' Craig Scott, 'Reaching beyond (without Abandoning) the Category of Economic, Social and Cultural Rights' (1999) 21 *Human Rights Quarterly* 633, at 633. See also Mathew Craven, *The International Covenant on Economic, Social, and Cultural Rights, A Perspective on Its Development* (Clarendon Press and OUP, 1995), 9 and Nowak, n 13 at 22–23 – the point of bifurcation is normally assigned to the political and ideological differences between East and West (discussed below), however, this is a simplification of the division into separate covenants and that in any event, the point of bifurcation actually occurred at an earlier stage during the drafting of the UDHR.

17 E/CN.4/SR65 1948, ECOSOC, Commission on Human Rights, Third Session, 65th mtg. (Mr. Pavlov).

universality.[18] The Lebanese representative stated that, 'it was not enough to enumerate economic and social rights but that society itself should be of such a nature as to ensure observance'.[19]

The underlying political ideologies firmly accepted the inclusion of ESR. The French representative argued that the inclusion of a separate article for economic and social rights was necessary in order to secure their full implementation.[20] The Lebanese representative and the Yugoslav representative feared, 'the adoption of the French proposal would mean that economic and social rights, the importance of which none could deny, would be given preferential treatment over other rights of equal importance'.[21] It was argued that a prefatory article was required in order to highlight the importance of ESR as these rights would be less well known.

The original wording of Article 22 UDHR was proposed by the French representative in the following terms:

> 'Everyone as a member of society has the economic, social and cultural rights enumerated below, whose fulfilment should be made possible in every state separately or by international collaboration'.[22]

The UK representative did not agree with the inclusion of 'should be made possible' as this gave rise to an obligation to implement that was not enumerated in respect of the other rights. This, he argued, would give economic, social and cultural rights priority over civil and political rights:

> To introduce into a covering article on social and economic rights the question of the method of applying those rights gave them priority ... It would be unfortunate were such an important text to give priority to [ESR] rights, thus placing them before all others .... Such details which were justified in the Covenant should not appear in the Declaration. In a question of such importance the Commission should proceed circumspectly, and should avoid giving the impression that the fulfilment of social and economic rights was more important than that of the other human rights.[23]

The separate enumeration of economic and social rights was not debated on the basis that they were lesser rights but that their explicit inclusion might undermine the principle of indivisibility by relegating civil and political rights to

---

18 E/CN.4/SR67 1948, ECOSOC, Commission on Human Rights, Third Session, 67th mtg. (Mr. Cassin).
19 E/CN.4/SR65 1948 n 17, at 3 (Mr. Malik, Lebanon).
20 E/CN.4/SR72 1948, ECOSOC Commission on Human Rights, Third Session, 72nd mtg.
21 Ibid. at 4–5 (Mr. Malik Lebanon) – the UK representative (Mr. Wilson) agreed with this statement at 6.
22 E/CN.4/SR67 1948, n 18 at 2.
23 E/CN.4/SR71 1948, ECOSOC, Commission on Human Rights, Third Session, 71st mtg. (Mr. Wilson) at 4.

a lesser status. On 24 June 1948, the Commission, by ten votes to six, approved the idea of having a separate article for economic and social rights rather than a single article covering all the rights in the declaration – this vote resulted in Article 22 of the UDHR:

> Everyone, as a member of society, has the right to social security and is entitled to realisation, through national effort and international co-operation and in accordance with the organization and resources of each state, of the economic, social and cultural rights indispensable for his dignity and the free development of his personality.
>
> (UDHR 1948 Article 22)

The French representative, Mr. Cassin offered a useful insight to the intentions of the parties in securing the explicit recognition of ESR:

> [N]ow that the Commission had approved the articles dealing with economic and social rights, the general situation was clearer. It was plain for instance that the Commission should follow the example to be found in all constitutions adopted in recent years and should treat those rights separately from the rights of the individual. Economic and Social rights, in order to be fully realised, required the material assistance to be furnished by the state – a practical difference which the Declaration could not ignore.[24]

There is no provision which specifically refers to 'civil and political rights' in the UDHR as they are implicit (along with economic and social rights) within the articles of the treaty. Whilst the preamble affirms the inalienability of all rights, the inclusion of Article 22 demonstrates that the parties wished to strengthen the enforcement of ESR rather than deviate from the principle of indivisibility. This is the point upon which the original bifurcation occurred, and, viewed in light of the *travaux préparatoires,* it is clear that the substantive realisation of economic and social rights was the fundamental intention of the parties.

From Declaration to Implementation

The draft Declaration of Human Rights was placed on the agenda of the third session (21 September to 12 December 1948) of the General Assembly and on 10 December 1948 the General Assembly adopted and proclaimed the Universal Declaration of Human Rights as 'a common standard of achievement for all peoples and all nations'.[25] Concurrently, the General Assembly requested the Economic and Social Council ('the Council') to ask the Human Rights Commission ('the Commission' – a sub-committee of the Council) to prepare a draft

---

24 E/CN.4/SR72 1948 n 20 (Mr. Cassin) at 4.
25 Preamble to the UDHR.

covenant on human rights and measures of implementation with a view to examining the wider possibility of a right to petition.[26] As such, the Declaration was to be followed by an International Covenant that would not only 'declare' universal rights, but would provide mechanisms for implementation and legal redress. It was during the consideration of the subsequent Covenant that the second point of bifurcation occurred, embedding the dichotomy and leading to the adoption of two separate treaties rather than an all-encompassing binding Covenant. In its initial deliberations[27] the Commission created a draft Covenant which focused primarily on civil and political rights, with a view to expanding inclusion of other rights through subsequent treaties. The Council considered the draft Covenant on 9 August 1950 and by way of resolution[28] requested the General Assembly to make a policy decision on whether economic, social and cultural rights should also be included within the draft Covenant.

On 4 December 1950, the General Assembly considered the Council's position and determined that the Covenant should be 'drawn up in the spirit and based on the principles of the Universal Declaration of Human Rights'.[29] The position of the General Assembly was explicitly clear on the inclusion of ESR within the draft Covenant, reaffirming the inalienability of all human rights and declaring:

> [T]he Universal Declaration regards man as a person, to whom civic and political freedoms as well as economic, social and cultural rights indubitably belong ... [T]he enjoyment of civic and political freedoms and of economic, social and cultural rights are interconnected and interdependent [and] when deprived of economic, social and cultural rights, man does not represent the human person whom the Universal Declaration regards as the ideal of the free man.[30]

The decision of the General Assembly unsurprisingly was to 'include in the Covenant of Human Rights ... a clear expression of economic, social and cultural rights in a manner which relates them to the civic and political freedoms proclaimed by the draft Covenant'.[31] This mandate was again put to the Commission tasked with drafting the Covenant. The Commission produced a Memorandum[32] 'discussing certain problems raised' by the inclusion of ESR, in particular, submitting that 'the economic and social development of different countries may have a bearing on the implementation of economic, social and

---

26 GA Res. 217 (III), 10 December 1948.
27 Official Records ECOSOC, Ninth Session, Supplement No. 10.
28 ECOSOC Res. 303 (XI), 9 August 1950.
29 GA Res. 421E (V), 4 December 1950.
30 Ibid.
31 Ibid. para.7(a).
32 E/CN.4/529 Memorandum of Secretary General, Commission on Human Rights, Seventh Session, Agenda item 3, 29 March 1951.

cultural rights'.[33] The Commission considered evidence from the United Nations Educational Scientific and Cultural Organisation (UNESCO) and from the International Labour Organisation (ILO), amongst others. There was a clear recognition by many representatives, on hearing this evidence, that the inclusion of ESR was a *sine qua non*, of the substantive enjoyment of CPR:

> [I]t was stressed by many representatives that the enjoyment of economic, social and cultural rights was a prerequisite for that of civic and political freedoms, that it would be an anachronism in the twentieth century to provide for the protection of one without the other, and that such an omission would deeply disappoint the public and would leave the principles of the Universal Declaration, according to which man's rights were conceived of as an integrated whole, only incompletely reflected in the covenant.[34]

This relationship of indivisibility between the two sets of rights was further examined by the Commission in order to explore its particular idiosyncrasies. For example, the right to life was said to depend upon the guarantee of health, work and education; the prohibition of slavery was dependent on the protection of the right to work and to receive sufficient payment to maintain an adequate standard of living; and the right to vote dependent on the right to education. This relationship rested on the premise that, 'only men who were economically and socially free and had been educated to exercise their own judgment would be capable of maintaining civic freedom and of governing themselves by democratic processes'.[35]

During this stage of the proceedings there was no lack of consensus on the symbiotic nature of rights and the importance of the principle of indivisibility. Clearly, the problem faced by the Commission in the inclusion of ESR was not a lack of support, as the momentum was there to enumerate. Nonetheless, the impetus to enumerate the rights in one single covenant was lacking. At the Commission's seventh session (1951), India proposed that the Assembly be asked to reconsider enumerating in a single treaty as 'economic, social and cultural rights, though equally fundamental and therefore important, formed a separate category of rights from that of civil and political rights, in that they were not justiciable rights and that the method of their implementation was, therefore different.'[36] And so, the degree of implementation and method by which it was to be achieved was argued as requiring separate treaties to cater for separate enforcement measures. The debate regarding implementation of the two different categories of rights therefore precipitated the lack of consensus.

---

33 Ibid. E/CN.4/529, n 32 para.50.
34 Ibid. E/CN.4/529, n 32 para.9.
35 Ibid. E/CN.4/529, n 32 para.12.
36 UN DOCE/1992 (1951) Commission on Human Rights, Report of the Seventh Session, 13 UN ESCOR, Supplement 9 at 15, para.67.

Underpinning the debate on ESR inclusion was the qualification contained in Article 22 UDHR that ESR can only be guaranteed 'in accordance with the organisation and resources of each state'.[37] The relevance of the differing stages reached in the economic and social development of different countries became the deciding factor in recommending two covenants. It was considered that since all states are not at the same stage of economic and social development that it would be unrealistic to expect all states to accept the same standards within the field of economic and social rights. As a result, and amidst much contestation, the Council approached the General Assembly for a second time, requesting that the previous policy decision be reconsidered.[38] On 5 February 1952, the General Assembly directed the Council to produce two separate Covenants, one to contain civil and political rights and the other to contain economic, social and cultural rights.[39] These were to be implemented concurrently with an emphasis on the principle of indivisibility.[40]

The Shift of the Bifurcation Axis – The 'Progressive Achievement' Debate

The original bifurcation, manifested in Article 22 UDHR, sought to reinforce ESR rather than undermine them. Nonetheless, as apparent in the dichotomy which still persists today, the bifurcation axis shifted during the drafting of the International Covenants. The enforceability dichotomy is encapsulated by the two competing enforcement provisions of the International Covenants. Article 2(3)(b) of the International Covenant on Civil and Political Rights obligates states to:

> [E]nsure that any person claiming a remedy shall have his right thereto determined by competent judicial, administrative or legislative authorities, or by any other competent authority provided for by the legal system of the state, and to develop the possibilities of judicial remedy.
>
> (ICCPR 1966, n 10)

This clearly brings remedies within the realm of judicial enforcement. Conversely, Article 2(1) of the International Covenant on Economic, Social and Cultural Rights stipulates:

> Each State Party to the present Covenant undertakes to take steps, individually and through international assistance and co-operation, especially economic and technical, to the maximum of its available resources, with a view

---

37 E/CN.4/529 n 32 para.49.
38 ECOSOC Res. 384 XIII, 29 August 1951.
39 GA Res. 543 VI, 5 February 1952.
40 Ibid.

to *achieving progressively* the full realization of the rights recognized in the present Covenant by all appropriate means, including particularly the adoption of legislative measures.

(emphasis added) (ICESCR 1966)

Here, the question of justiciability is a discretionary one and therein lies the pivotal point upon which the misconception is based and from which the human rights' dichotomy emerged. The failure to enumerate in a single covenant was not based on an abandonment of the indivisibility principle, but was based on a lack of consensus on implementation according to the particular historical context.

These irreconcilable approaches to enforcement have been understood as resting upon the premise that some states viewed all rights as equal and immediately enforceable (USSR and socialist bloc) and others viewed economic social and cultural rights as aspirational and subject to 'progressive achievement' (Western states). This has been the dominant narrative on the historical development of the UDHR and subsequent covenants.[41] As Craven explains:

> the reason for making a distinction between first and second generation rights could be more accurately put down to the ideological conflict between East and West pursued in the arena of human rights during the drafting of the Covenants. The Soviet states, on the one hand, championed the cause of economic, social and cultural rights, which they associated with the aims of the socialist society. Western states, on the other hand, asserted the priority of civil and political rights as being the foundation of liberty and democracy in the free world.[42]

However, the 'East v West' narrative, has been challenged in the literature as scholars revisit the historical context, in which Western support, and in particular US support was much stronger for ESR than the dominant narrative suggests.[43] Indeed, Whelan and Donnelly concluded that the 'myth of Western opposition' was both 'ludicrous' and 'revisionist history of the worst kind'.[44] They cite the growth of Western welfare states and the post-war economic order, such as Roosevelt's Four Freedoms (including freedom from want) and the 1944 'Economic Bill of Rights' as indicative of US support for progression on economic, social and cultural rights.[45] This challenge to the dominant

---

41 Sally-Anne Way, 'The Myth and Mystery of US History on Economic, Social, and Cultural Rights: The 1947 United States Suggestions for Articles to Be Incorporated in an International Bill of Rights', (2014) 36 *Human Rights Quarterly* 869–897 at 869.

42 Craven, n 16 at 9.

43 Way, n 41 at 870 and Daniel J. Whelan and Jack Donnelly, 'The West, Economic and Social Rights, and the Global Human Rights Regime: Setting the Record Straight', (2007) 29 *Human Rights Quarterly* 908 at 910.

44 Whelan and Donnelly, ibid.

45 See discussion in Way n 41 and Whelan and Donnelly n 43, see also Daniel Whelan, *Indivisible Human Rights* (University of Pennsylvania Press, 2010) at 11–31.

narrative is not without its critiques,[46] however, empirical research conducted by Way into the US contribution to the UDHR reveals the original position in the drafting of the treaty reflects support for the inclusion of ESR as was apparent in the preparatory work to the UDHR.[47] This aligns with the contribution of this book, that the original CP v ESR bifurcation occurred in the drafting of the UDHR to strengthen the importance of ESR. Way argues that, at the very least on a positivist reading of the rhetorical and official position, the US demonstrated more than fleeting support for the 'inclusion of economic, social and cultural rights in an aspiration if not legally binding covenant'.[48] The UK, she argues, took a more conservative view on the inclusion of ESR but supported a legally binding treaty.[49]

The dominant historical narrative saw the development of an erroneous positive and negative alignment of CP v ESR enforcement.[50] Civil and political rights were perceived as negative in that they required governments to abstain from infringement, were cost-free and immediately enforceable. Economic, social and cultural rights were perceived as positive in that they required active intervention on behalf of states, were resource-intensive and purely aspirational. This position has since been debunked. The original point of bifurcation was an attempt to reinforce the equal status of all human rights (Article 22). The bifurcation axis then shifted to the 'progressive realisation' debate during the drafting of the Covenants. The positive v negative dichotomy of rights historically led to a clear alignment of justiciable and non-justiciable rights that does not accurately reflect the legal status of each of the categories. This separation, or dichotomy, has permeated the development of human rights law from its inception and the categorisation of rights misrepresents the original intentions of the parties to the UDHR.[51] As Craven submits:

> The fact of separation has since been used as evidence of the inherent opposition of the two categories of rights. In particular, it has led to a perpetuation of

---

46 Susan L. Kang, 'The Unsettled Relationship of Economic and Social Rights and the West: A Response to Whelan and Donnelly', (2009) 31 *Human Rights Quarterly* 1006, 1007; Alex Kirkup and Tony Evans, 'The Myth of Western Opposition to Economic, Social, and Cultural Rights?: A Reply to Whelan and Donnelly', (2009) 31 *Human Rights Quarterly* 221, 222.

47 Way n 41 cites the 1947 US paper that proposes CPESC rights for the UDHR, 'United States Suggestions for Articles to be Incorporated in an International Bill of Rights' (US Suggestions), *Report of the Drafting Committee on an International Bill of Human Rights to the Commission on Human Rights,* U.N. ESCOR, Comm'n on Hum. Rts., 1st Sess., Annex C, at 41–47, U.N. Doc. E/CN.4/21 (1947).

48 Way, n 41 at 873.

49 Way, n 41 at 877.

50 Alston et al., 'The Nature and Scope of States Parties' Obligations under the International Covenant on Economic, Social and Cultural Rights' (1987) 9 *Human Rights Quarterly* 156 at 159.

51 The dichotomy is apparent in the development of the regional mechanisms under the Council of Europe and European Union for example, as discussed below.

excessively monolithic views as to the nature, history, and philosophical concep- tion of each group of rights and has contributed to the idea that economic, social and cultural rights are in reality a distinct and separate group of human rights. Of greater concern, however, is that despite the clear intention not to imply any notion of relative value by the act of separating the Covenants, it has nevertheless reinforced claims as to the hierarchical ascendance of civil and political rights. Although within the UN there is now almost universal acceptance of the theoret- ical 'indivisible and interdependent' nature of the two sets of rights, the reality in practice is that economic, social, and cultural rights remain largely ignored.[52]

The reluctance of obligated states to ensure judicial enforcement is indicative of CP v ESR; negative v positive; legal v political; and justiciable v non-justiciable antinomies.[53] These positions are now outdated – and to a great extent considered to be remnants of a 'legal fiction'.[54] In other words, the international legal commu- nity, and international law, has long since moved on from the negative v positive cat- egorisation of rights. New categories emerged and as concepts around the meaning of rights have developed, so too have the means of implementation expanded, includ- ing the right to an effective remedy for a violation of ESR now forming a component of ESR obligations in international law.[55]

The Minimum Core – An Absolute or Relative Standard?

The minimum core concept emerged following the Limburg Principles (1986) that 'each [ESC] right must … give rise to a minimum entitlement, in the absence of which a State party is in violation of its obligations'.[56] This led to the development of minimum core obligations (MCO) in the progressive realisa- tion of ESR.. The UN Committee responsible for observing implementation of ICESCR indicated that where a:

> State party in which any significant number of individuals is deprived of essential foodstuffs, of essential primary health care, of basic shelter and

---

52 Craven, n 16 at 9.
53 There are several other antinomies that can be derived from this misconception such as resource intensive v cost free; progressive v immediate; vague v precise; and political v non-political. Each of these antinomies can misrepresent the status of, or obligations attached to ESR based on a positive v negative categorisation. Scott, n 16 at 833.
54 Mónica Feria Tinta, 'Justiciability of Economic, Social, and Cultural Rights in the Inter- American System of Protection of Human Rights: Beyond Traditional Paradigms and Notions' (2007) 29 *Human Rights Quarterly* 431 at 432.
55 UN Guiding Principles n 1 and UN Committee on Economic, Social and Cultural Rights (CESCR), General Comment No. 9: The domestic application of the Covenant, 3 Decem- ber 1998, E/C.12/1998/24. The following sections explore the nature of the duty to progres- sively achieve ESR as well as the right to an effective remedy for a violation.
56 Philip Alston, 'Out of the Abyss: The Challenges Confronting the New UN Committee on Economic, Social and Cultural Rights', (1987) 9 *Human Rights Quarterly* 352.

housing, or of the most basic forms of education [then the State party] is, prima facie, failing to discharge its obligations under the Covenant. If the Covenant were to be read in such a way as not to establish such a minimum core obligation, it would be largely deprived of its raison d'être.

(CESCR General Comment 3)

The indeterminacy of what constitutes an MCO has not been resolved in the literature. Young, for example, argues for a relative standard[57] whereas others, more concerned with immediate survival of the most marginalised demand the recognition of an absolute non-negotiable MCO that enables survival and basic dignity.[58] Forman et al. conclude that the minimum core suffers from a multitude of problems relating to its conceptualisation asking is it:

> core fixed or moveable, non-derogable or restrictable, universal or country-specific? Is its function to guarantee specified bundles of the most essential … facilities, goods and services, or it is to require governments to act reasonably to progressively realize these minimal … entitlements? Is the concept legitimate in terms of international law? And what are acceptable methods to further develop the content of these entitlements and duties?[59]

In practice, the UN legal position has been to place the onus on state's themselves to determine what actually constitutes an MCO in any given context dependent on a number of variables such as the right in question, the resources available, the measures taken and the prevailing social, economic, cultural, climatic, ecological and other conditions the Committee on Economic Social and Cultural Rights ([CESCR] General Comment 12 right to food).[60]

The 'minimum core' is legally binding and most likely non-derogable (meaning states cannot justify non-compliance).[61] However, as discussed above, what it actually means in practice is not necessarily always clear. Some of the UN General Comments elaborate on what is required to meet a minimum core

---

57 Katharine Young, *The Minimum Core of Economic and Social Rights: A Concept in Search of Content* (Yale Journal of International Law, 2008).

58 David Bilchitz, 'Towards a Reasonable Approach to the Minimum Core: Laying the Foundations for Future Socio-Economic Rights Jurisprudence' (2003) 19 *South African Journal on Human Rights* 15.

59 Lisa Forman, Luljeta Caraoshi, Audrey R. Chapman and Everaldo Lamprea, 'Conceptualising Minimum Core Obligations under the Right to Health: How Should We Define and Implement the "Morality of the Depths"' (2016) 20(4) *The International Journal of Human Rights* 531–548 at 531.

60 UN Committee on Economic, Social and Cultural Rights (CESCR), General Comment No. 12: The Right to Adequate Food (Art. 11 of the Covenant), 12 May 1999, E/C.12/1999/5 para.7.

61 For a full and comprehensive discussion on the nature of the minimum core obligation in international law see Amrei Müller, 'Limitations to and Derogations from Economic, Social and Cultural Rights' (2009) 9 *Human Rights Law Review* 557 at 654.

threshold in relation to a particular right.[62] One of the most expansive interpretations is contained in the CESCR General Comment 14 (right to health) in which the Committee gives an interpretative list with normative thresholds including:

- access to health facilities, goods and services on a non-discriminatory basis, especially for vulnerable or marginalised groups;
- access to the minimum essential food which is nutritionally adequate and safe, to ensure freedom from hunger to everyone;
- access to basic shelter, housing and sanitation, and an adequate supply of safe and potable water;
- access to essential drugs, as from time to time defined under the WHO Action Programme on Essential Drugs;
- the equitable distribution of all health facilities, goods and services;
- implementation of a national public health strategy and plan of action, *inter alia*.[63]

This approach seeks to identify obligations of conduct and outcome-orientated results[64] in meeting the MCO of right to health whilst still allowing significant discretion to the state to substantive interpretation and means of provision. In addition, the Committee stresses that a State party cannot, under any circumstances whatsoever, justify its non-compliance with the MCO, which is

---

62 UN Committee on Economic, Social and Cultural Rights (CESCR), General Comment No. 13: The Right to Education (Art. 13 of the Covenant), 8 December 1999, E/C.12/1999/10, para.57; UN Committee on Economic, Social and Cultural Rights (CESCR), General Comment No. 14: The Right to the Highest Attainable Standard of Health (Art. 12 of the Covenant), 11 August 2000, E/C.12/2000/4; UN Committee on Economic, Social and Cultural Rights (CESCR), General Comment No. 15: The Right to Water (Arts. 11 and 12 of the Covenant), 20 January 2003, E/C.12/2002/11 para.37; UN Committee on Economic, Social and Cultural Rights (CESCR), General Comment No. 17: The Right of Everyone to Benefit from the Protection of the Moral and Material Interests Resulting from any Scientific, Literary or Artistic Production of Which He or She is the Author (Art. 15, Para. 1 (c) of the Covenant), 12 January 2006, E/C.12/GC/17 para.39; UN Committee on Economic, Social and Cultural Rights (CESCR), General Comment No. 18: The Right to Work (Art. 6 of the Covenant), 6 February 2006, E/C.12/GC/18, para.31; UN Committee on Economic, Social and Cultural Rights (CESCR), General Comment No. 19: The right to social security (Art. 9 of the Covenant), 4 February 2008, E/C.12/GC/19, para.59.
63 General Comment 14 ibid. para.43.
64 Forman et al., n 59 at 538. Although the authors also note that the approach under General Comment 14 n 62 may have been designed for pragmatism as alluded to by Paul Hunt as Special Rapporteur, UN Committee on Economic, Social and Cultural Rights, Twenty-Second Session, Summary Record of the 10th Meeting Held at the Palais Wilson, Geneva, UN Doc. E/C.12/2000/SR.10, 4 May 2000, para. 27. (In a previous comment on education the committee had struggled with how to incorporate core content, eventually taking 'the pragmatic approach of defining not the core content but the core obligations incumbent upon States parties', an approach it had decided to adopt in the general comment on health) Forman et al., n 59 at 537.

non-derogable.[65] A similar approach is taken in General Comment 15 (2003) where the MCO is declared non-derogable.[66] However, in General Comments 19 (2008) and 17 (2006) the Committee oscillates to a lesser obligation where the State may justify non-compliance if it can attribute its failure to meet the MCO threshold to a lack of available resources by demonstrating that every effort has been made to use all the resources at its disposal in an effort to satisfy as a matter of priority its minimum obligations.[67] In General Comment 19, the Committee stipulates that a minimum right to social security should entail essential health care, basic shelter and housing, water and sanitation, foodstuffs and the most basic forms of education.[68] If there is not enough resources to achieve this minimum the Committee suggests consultation on meeting a core group of 'social risks and contingencies' within the state's capacity.[69] Across these different approaches there is an underlying suggestion that there is indeed a minimum core relative to the state's maximum available resources in addition to an absolute non-derogable minimum that applies despite a state's available resources. The former threshold will adjust on a scale depending on the prevailing circumstances and the latter performs a permanent and absolute baseline from which departure can never be justified.

In terms of how states can demonstrate achieving the MCO, the means through which to achieve the standards and what they mean in practice in any given context are to a significant degree left to the state's discretion based on an interpretation of the normative elaboration set out in the various General Comments.[70] The nature of the obligation to realise the minimum core can therefore be more easily assessed by reviewing whether the state has taken all necessary measures in order to ensure a basic minimum relative to the country's wealth as well as employing an objective normative threshold as to an immediately enforceable absolute minimum core. This is the 'conduct-based' approach. Chapman argues for the conduct-based approach as the most feasible, where conduct-orientated core obligations in the respect, protect and fulfil categories help states understand their immediate obligations.[71] Chapman argues against an approach based primarily on obligations of result given the absence of reliable data for most countries, the absence of means to carefully measure progress and

---

65 General Comment 14 n 62 para.47.
66 General Comment 15 n 62 para.40.
67 General Comment 19 n 62 para.60.; General Comment 17 n 62 para.41.
68 General Comment 19 n 62 para.59(a).
69 General Comment 19 n 62 para.59(b).
70 UN Committee on Economic, Social and Cultural Rights (CESCR), General Comment No.3: The Nature of States Parties' Obligations (Art. 2, Para. 1, of the Covenant), 14 December 1990, E/1991/23 'each State party must decide for itself which means are the most appropriate under the circumstances' para.4.
71 Audrey R. Chapman, 'Core Obligations Related to the Right to Health', in Audrey Chapman and Sage Russell (eds.), *Core Obligations: Building a Framework for Economic, Social and Cultural Rights* (Antwerp: Intersentia, 2002), 185–215.

the potential impossibility of incorporating all measures necessary to achieve particular health outcomes into a minimum applicable to all countries.[72]

Young has highlighted there has been a tendency towards developing, or calling for the development of, indicators and measurement frameworks though which to assess minimum cores and progressive achievement.[73] However, there is, as Young points out, a 'chicken-and-egg' aspect to this argument. Whilst there is an important relationship between underlying norms that guide the formulation of indicators and their adherence to rights, 'what is needed to guide this assessment may be a more open formulation of rights, rather than the fixed and narrow parameters of a substantive minimum core or other minimalist doctrine'.[74]

Ultimately, the more vague the content, obligation or expected outcome the more difficult it will be to assess compliance with the minimum core, or the progressive achievement, of ESR. As argued by Forman et al., further development of the core concept requires going 'considerably beyond the status quo to develop each constituent component of entitlements, content and duties'.[75] This is based on Shue's concern, that without spelling out the duties, one has not really spelled out the rights, and spelling out the substance of rights is essential to defining their entitlements.[76] States acting in good faith must therefore meet the requirements explicitly identified in international law in relation to the minimum core (the absolute measures) whilst also going further in defining and giving substance to the concept of a minimum core relative to the prevailing social, economic, cultural, climatic, ecological and other conditions present in the state (the relative measures). Judges can also play a role in giving definition and substance to rights where states fail to do so (acting as an accountability mechanism and addressing the indeterminacy critique). Ultimately, whilst states must take steps to meet minimum core obligations this does not detract from the broader obligations to progressively achieve rights to the state's maximum available resources. In this sense, whilst recognising the non-derogable nature of immediate core obligations, states must move beyond the minimum thresholds without delay. In other words, the minimum core marks only the basic starting point of a much larger ESR picture.

From Dichotomy, to Trichotomy, to a Multitude of Standards

Fredman cites a helpful analogy in consideration of the negative (cost-free) v positive (resource-intensive) divide with reference to the right to a fair trial.[77]

---

72 Ibid.
73 Young, n 57 at 93.
74 Ibid.
75 Forman et al., n 59 at 543.
76 Henry Shue, *Basic Rights: Subsistence, Affluence and US Foreign Policy*, (2nd ed., Princeton, NJ: Princeton University Press, 1996), ix and 15.
77 Sandra Fredman, 'New Horizons: Incorporating Socio-Economic Rights in a British Bill of Rights' (2010) April *Public Law* 297 at 301.

This involves trial within a reasonable time and access to legal aid – a civil right which is cost intensive. Similarly, some ESR are cost-free and negative in nature such as the right not to be evicted, or the right to join a trade union. Rather than frame the human rights binary within the positive v negative dichotomy, Asbjørn Eide developed a tripartite typology[78] which perceives the realisation of human rights through a duty to (i) respect; (ii) protect and; (iii) fulfil:

> The obligation *to respect* requires the state, and thereby all its organs and agents, to abstain from doing anything that violates the integrity of the individual or infringes on her or his freedom, including the freedom to use the material resources available to that individual in the way she or he finds to satisfy basic need. The obligation *to protect* requires from the state and its agents the measures necessary to prevent other individuals or groups from violating the integrity, freedom of action or other human rights of the individual – including the prevention of infringements of his or her material resources. The obligation *to fulfil* requires the state to take the measures necessary to ensure for each person within its jurisdiction opportunities to obtain satisfaction of those needs, recognized in the human rights instruments, which cannot be secured by personal efforts.[79] (emphasis added)

The tripartite typology is applicable to all human rights and allows ESR to hold parity with CPR through a process of 'realisation'. Koch argues that ESR undergo 'waves of duties' at varying degrees and that a gradual slope in increasing standard will lead to the eventual enforcement of all human rights (each right must undergo the tripartite process at varying degrees). Koch contends that states rely on the positive v negative dichotomy to undermine the incorporation of ESR treaties into domestic legislation.[80] This paradigmatic shift in perspective helps to reframe 'progressive achievement' as a gradual change from recognition to full enforcement and remains respectful of the indivisibility principle. The trichotomy of rights through the tripartite theory offered by Eide played a significant role in the interpretation of Article 2 by the CESCR. In General Comment 12 on the right to adequate food the CESCR stated that, '[t]he right to adequate food, like any other human right, imposes three types or levels of obligations on states parties: the obligation to respect, to protect and to fulfil'.[81]

This development parallels the international shift towards alternatives to the positive v negative dichotomy. The South African Constitution, for example, employs a 'quodchotomy'[82] of duties: to respect, protect, promote and fulfil

---

78 Asbjørn Eide, 'Realization of Social and Economic Rights and the Minimum Threshold Approach' (1989) 10 *Human Rights Law Journal* 35.

79 Ibid. at 37.

80 Ida Koch, 'Dichotomies, Trichotomies or Waves of Duties' (2005) 5 *Human Rights Law Review* 81 at 101.

81 CESCR General Comment 12 n 60 at para.15.

82 The term *quodchotomy* is used to describe a four-fold application of rights, see Koch (n 80).

ESR.[83] In relation to the duties of transnational companies, John Ruggie reframed the application of human rights to a 'respect, protect and remedy' formation arguing that this would help address the human rights deficit for governments and private corporations alike.[84] Nolan et al. identify degrees of enforcement through the tripartite theory to a multitude of varying degrees – from respect, to protect, to fulfil, consideration of progressive realisation and finally non-retrogressive measures.[85] Courtis expanded this theory to degrees of standard starting with negative, to procedural, through equality and non-discrimination, minimum core arguments, progressive realisation and prohibiting retrogression.[86] The literature has therefore tended to examine the area of ESR justiciability on an axis measuring the varying degrees (or the standard) of ESR protection/enforcement. This examination is critical in providing an understanding of how ESR can be enforced from negative enforcement (i.e. a duty not to interfere), to minimal enforcement (i.e. a duty to protect a minimum non-derogable core), to substantive enforcement (i.e. a positive duty on the state to ensure substantive fulfilment) with various levels being identified along the standard threshold axis.

However, whilst rejecting the positive v negative dichotomy, critics of the tripartite typology (respect; protect; fulfil), or the categorisation of models according to standard of enforcement (moving from negative to substantive at varying degrees with a minimum core obligation), highlight that this approach also does not adequately reflect the complex nature of the fulfilment of human rights obligations. In developing the theory, Koch contends that it is difficult to place obligations on an upwards scale moving between different levels and that a slope is of realisation is a more apt analogy:

> As an abstract construct the tripartite typology has advantages and situations to which the typology applies without difficulties can be easily imagined ... However, the typology seems to lose some of its applicability when one has to decide what it takes in a concrete situation for a state party to comply with its human rights obligations. Many situations cannot be dealt with exclusively by means of one of the three levels of tripartite obligations, and some are so complex that they require efforts that fall within all three levels, respect, protection and fulfilment. The relevant level is unidentifiable and the conception of human rights obligations as a ladder one climbs step by step is not very much to the point. The adequate metaphor would rather be a slope, not divided into levels, as the obligation imperceptibly increases for each tiny little movement

---

83 Constitution of the Republic of South Africa 1996, Art.7(2).

84 Human Rights Council, John Ruggie 'Respect, Protect and Remedy: A Framework for Business and Human Rights' 7 April 2008, A/HRC/8/5.

85 Nolan et al., *The Justiciability of Social and Economic Rights: An Updated Appraisal* (Human Rights Consortium, March 2007).

86 Christian Courtis, 'Standards to Make ESR Justiciable: A Summary Explanation' (2009) 2 *Erasmus Law Review* 379.

uphill ... The CESCR's choices of categories in its General Comments probably reflect these difficulties, and one may totally agree that the picture is blurred. However, if one wants to have it both ways – i.e. insist on making use of the typology and at the same time accept a blurred picture – one has to face the possibility that the typology loses some of its applicability as an analytical tool.[87]

Shue has also warned against the 'frozen abstraction' of the tripartite typology that was never intended to occupy the same rigid conceptual space previously held by 'negative rights' and 'positive rights'.[88] Nickel argues that the varying degrees of protection are dependent on a move from minimal implementation mechanisms through to 'high quality implementation' measures, including remedies for non-compliance.[89] Implementation is the vehicle and realisation and full compliance is the end goal.

The focus on fulfilment through standards of realisation does not necessarily present the full picture. The literature indicates that there is a need to develop this theory further. Scott warned against the categorisation of rights against abstract legal concepts (and the failure to recognise that human experience rarely confines itself to neat categories).[90] Nickel feared that an oversimplification of indivisibility would undermine the need for the development of high quality implementation mechanisms that would lead to eventual substantive realisation. Shue has indicated that the tripartite typology risks occupying the same rigid categorisation that the positive v negative dichotomy perpetuated. Koch has asked whether it is time to 'to throw typologies overboard – be they trichotomous, quadruple or quintuple – and focus on what it takes to provide proper human rights protection'.[91] Looking at the different ways that ESR justiciability occurs, or can occur (the justiciability models discussed in Chapter 5), helps offer a new way of categorising ESR, and hence contributes to a better understanding of enforcement/under-enforcement. This contribution effectively offers a new axis through which to measure the enforcement of ESR – each mechanism can be measured against a multitude of varying degrees then contextualised within principles of adjudication. In this sense, the contribution of the mechanisms deepens the review.

---

87 Koch, n 80 at 92–93.
88 Shue, n 76 at 160, as cited in Koch, n 80 at 103.
89 Nickel argues that 'A right is fully implemented or has high quality implementation when all of the major threats to the right have been adequately blocked or neutralized through actions such as gaining recognition and compliance with the right's associated moral and legal duties, providing protections and other services, and providing legal and other remedies for noncompliance with the right. Realization is the end and implementation is the means.' James Nickel, 'Rethinking Indivisibility: Towards a Theory of Supporting Relations between Human Rights' (2008) 30 *Human Rights Quarterly* 984 at 992.
90 Craig Scott, 'Reaching beyond (without Abandoning) the Category of Economic, Social and Cultural Rights' (1999) 21 *Human Rights Quarterly* 633, 636.
91 Koch, n 60 at 103.

So what does this mean in practice? Courts must respond to the claim before them whether that be a violation of a minimum core threshold or progressive realisation and whether the offending act or omission relates to the duty to respect (the state's duty to abstain from interfering with the right); the duty to protect (the state's duty to stop others from interfering with the right); or the duty to fulfil (the state's duty to take steps to realise a right). Each of these duties can require different types of review and different remedies for a violation.

The Right to an Effective Remedy in International Human Rights Law

The nature of state obligations under the ICESCR depends upon the interpretation of 'progressive achievement' of the full realisation of the rights to the maximum available resources contained in the Covenant, in other words, '[t]he concept of progressive achievement is in many ways the linchpin of the whole Covenant. Upon its meaning turns the nature of state obligations'.[92]

The preparatory work to the Covenant indicates that Article 2(1) was binding on states but that there was no obligation to achieve the objective through judicial remedies, although this mechanism was not explicitly excluded. The application of the law of treaties in international law requires states to perform their duties in good faith according to the principle of *pacta sunt servanda* enshrined in Article 26 of the Vienna Convention on the Law of Treaties 1969 (the 'Vienna Convention').[93] As justiciability did not form part of the agreement reached in the drafting of the Covenant a state which meets its obligations in good faith and chooses not to offer judicial remedies cannot be in breach of *pacta sunt servanda*. However, the state must fulfil its obligations nonetheless, and the *bona fide* fulfilment of obligations contained in the ICESCR depends on the interpretation of the phrase to 'achieve progressively'.

The concept of 'progressive achievement' was included in the text of Article 2 in recognition of the fact that some of the rights in the treaty could not be implemented immediately. It was a contentious solution to the question of enforceability around which there was little consensus. The meaning of the concept was debated during the drafting process as the Soviet representative feared that the word 'progressively' 'would render the Commission's work meaningless'.[94] Whilst it was generally accepted that not all rights were immediately enforceable (due to the availability of resources, or lack thereof, along with inept societal structures), there was also a recognition that these rights must be pursued, without respite, to the maximum available resources of the state.[95]

---

92 Alston et al., n 50 at 172.
93 United Nations, *Vienna Convention on the Law of Treaties*, 23 May 1969, United Nations, Treaty Series, vol. 1155 at 331.
94 E/CN.4/SR.271 (1952), 8 U.N. ESCOR C.4, 271st mtg. (Mr Morozov, U.S.S.R.) at 8.
95 E/CN.4/SR.233 (1951), 7 U.N. ESCOR C.4, 233rd mtg. (Mr Azmi Bey, Egypt) at 8.

There was a suggestion that the more liberal and developed democracies ought to allow the developing nations a chance to catch up without breaching the Covenant. However, there was also a concern that developed countries would, at a later stage, cite the weakness of the clause as a means of enforcement evasion, as the Lebanese representative noted:

> [This] provides an excuse for states which were unwilling to act as quickly as they were able in achieving the realization of rights to which effect could be given at once. The covenant was a legal text, and the possibility of bad faith must therefore be taken into account ... the deletion of "progressively" was desirable as that expression added nothing and might be interpreted as discouraging immediate implementation even in cases where such implementation was possible, because a state would be able to say it was only bound to implement the rights in the Covenant progressively.[96]

Whilst judicial remedies were not foreseen at the drafting stage, the Committee has since stipulated that the duty to 'progressively achieve' now demands that the original flexibility of Article 2(1) coexists with the obligation to provide remedies to an aggrieved individual:

> But this flexibility coexists with the obligation upon each state party to use all the means at its disposal to give effect to the rights recognized in the Covenant. In this respect, the fundamental requirements of international human rights law must be borne in mind. Thus the Covenant norms must be recognized in appropriate ways within the domestic legal order, appropriate means of redress, or remedies, must be available to any aggrieved individual or group, and appropriate means of ensuring governmental accountability must be put in place.[97]

This would suggest that where no such remedies are available the state is not in compliance with its international obligations.

The UN Basic Principles and Guidelines on the Right to a Remedy and Reparation for Victims of Gross Violations of International Human Rights Law and Serious Violations of International Humanitarian Law provides that states must ensure that their domestic law is consistent with their international obligations (including customary law). This obligation includes making available adequate, effective, prompt and appropriate remedies, including reparation for violations of civil, political, economic, social and cultural rights.[98] The international legal position asserts that 'where there is a right, there is a remedy' based on the

---

96 E/CN.4/SR.271 n 94 (Mr. Azkoul, Lebanon) at 5.
97 CESCR General comment 9. (General Comments) 3 December 1998, E/C.12/1998/24.
98 Basic Principles and Guidelines on the Right to a Remedy n 1.

principle of *ubi ius ibi remedium*.[99] The Maastricht Guidelines on violations of economic, social and cultural rights recommend that the right to an effective remedy encompasses violations of ESR as well as CPR. The Guidelines assert that any person or group that is subject to violation of an ESR right should have access to effective judicial or other appropriate remedies at both international and national levels.[100] The international position makes clear that remedies for violations of ESR ought to be available at the domestic level, and that this should include access to justiciable remedies.

What does this mean in the domestic context? The UK position is out of step with international law requirements. The prevailing view reflected captured in the Green Paper[101] that was prepared by the 2005–2010 UK administration on a proposed UK-wide Bill of Rights and Responsibilities. The government clearly stipulated that it:

> does not consider a general model of directly legally enforceable rights or responsibilities to be the most appropriate. In terms of economic, social and cultural rights, for example, this may not be the best mechanism for ensuring fair provision for society as a whole.[102]

The government at the time indicated its commitment to the protection of ESR but did not consider the court as the most appropriate mechanism for achieving this. Instead, it was argued that 'Parliament remains the most appropriate forum for making politically sensitive decisions on resource allocation'.[103] The argument advanced by successive UK Governments in so far as ESR are concerned is that they have already been largely implemented through domestic legislation and do not require entrenchment through an inflexible Bill of Rights.[104] The Green Paper on a Bill of Rights outlined the history of the social

---

99 The formulation of this principle was first established in 1928 by the Permanent Court of International Justice in the *Chorzów* Factory case where the court held that reparations ought to 'wipe out all the consequences of the illegal act and re-establish the situation which would, in all probability, have existed if that act had not been committed'. Chorzów Factory, 1928 P.C.I.J. (ser. A) No. 17, at 47. The International Law Commission's draft articles on state responsibility require states to make reparations for wrongful acts (G.A. Res. 56/83, Annex art. 30 and 31, U.N. Doc. A/RES/56/83/Annex (28 January 2002)) reflecting the principle first formulated in Chorzów. This area of law is concerned with state responsibility between states rather than between state and individual, however, it is increasingly applying to the area of international human rights regarding the relationship between state and individual and to wrongful acts committed against the international community, Dinah Shelton, *Remedies in International Human Rights Law* (Oxford University Press, 1999), Chapter 2.

100 The Maastricht Guidelines on Violations of Economic, Social and Cultural Rights, Maastricht, 22–26 January 1997, (1998) 20 *Human Rights Quarterly* 691, para.23.

101 Ministry of Justice, *Rights and Responsibilities: Developing our Constitutional Framework* Cm 7577 (March 2009), Cm.7577 (Green Paper).

102 Ibid., 10, para.3 Executive Summary.

103 Ibid. para.3.12; see also para.4.27.

104 Ibid.

welfare system in the UK citing the enactment of the Education Act 1944 and the National Health Service Act 1948 as examples of this. In successive reporting procedures to the UN, the UK Government continues to defend this position stating that implementation of the Covenant is achieved through legislation and administrative measures, which in turns ensures fulfilment of its obligations under the Covenant.[105]

Whilst these mechanisms may implement some rights to some degree they have fallen short of normative standards in international law and do not facilitate access to an effective remedy as an accountability mechanism. This has been clarified by the UN Committee on Economic, Social and Cultural Rights (CESCR), which continues to urge the UK to fulfil its international obligations by ensuring the rights are made justiciable, making it clear that domestic justiciable remedies form part of the obligations under ICESCR:

> The committee urges the state party [the UK] to ensure that the Covenant is given full legal effect in its domestic law, that the Covenant rights are made justiciable, and that effective remedies are available for victims of all violations of economic, social and cultural rights. The Committee reiterates its recommendation that, irrespective of the system through which international law is incorporated in the domestic legal order (monism or dualism), following ratification of an international instrument, the state party is under a legal obligation to comply with such an instrument and to give it full effect in its domestic legal order.[106]

The UN CESCR has noted with concern that despite the adoption of a wide range of laws with regard to ESR the Covenant has not been incorporated into the domestic legal order and therefore cannot be directly invoked before the courts.[107] These concerns continue to be reiterated and the UN CESCR has noted that the failure of the state to incorporate ICESCR may 'restrict access to effective legal remedies' for violations of ESR.[108]

The UK position continues to be at odds with the position of the Committee. In discussing the domestic application of the Covenant, the Committee has made clear that only in exceptional circumstances will derogation from judicial

---

105 Committee on Economic, Social and Cultural Rights Consideration of reports submitted by States parties under articles 16 and 17 of the International Covenant on Economic, Social and Cultural Rights Sixth periodic reports of States parties due in 2014 E/C.12/GBR/6, 25 September 2014, para.11.

106 Concluding observations of the UNCSECR's Forty-second session, 4 – 22 May 2009 Consideration of reports submitted by States parties under articles 16 and 17 of the International Covenant on Economic, Social and Cultural Rights, United Kingdom of Great Britain and Northern Ireland, the Crown Dependencies and the Oversee dependencies, 12 June 2009, E/C.12/GBR/CO/5, at para.13.

107 Ibid. para.13.

108 UN CESCR, Concluding observations on the sixth periodic report of the United Kingdom of Great Britain and Northern Ireland, 14 July 2016, E/C.12/GBR/CO/6, at para.5.

remedies be accepted.[109] This is supported by the acknowledgment that an individual must have access to an effective remedy in international law.[110] The Committee has stated that these assertions are supported by two overarching principles of international law:

> Questions relating to the domestic application of the Covenant must be considered in the light of two principles of international law. The first, as reflected in article 27 of the Vienna Convention on the Law of Treaties, is that "[A] party may not invoke the provisions of its internal law as justification for its failure to perform a treaty". In other words, states should modify the domestic legal order as necessary in order to give effect to their treaty obligations. The second principle is reflected in article 8 of the Universal Declaration of Human Rights, according to which "Everyone has the right to an effective remedy by the competent national tribunals for acts violating the fundamental rights granted him by the constitution or by law" ... a state party seeking to justify its failure to provide any domestic legal remedies for violations of economic, social and cultural rights would need to show either that such remedies are not "appropriate means" within the terms of article 2, paragraph 1, of the International Covenant on Economic, Social and Cultural Rights or that, in view of the other means used, they are unnecessary. It will be difficult to show this and the Committee considers that, in many cases, the other means used could be rendered ineffective if they are not reinforced or complemented by judicial remedies.[111]

The Committee suggests that the domestic protection of economic, social and cultural rights should be given effect to using the same mechanisms for civil and political rights and that there would need to be a compelling justification to derogate from this general rule:

> The need to ensure justiciability ... is relevant when determining the best way to give domestic legal effect to the Covenant rights. Second, account should be taken of the means which have proved to be most effective in the country concerned in ensuring the protection of other human rights. Where the means used to give effect to the Covenant on Economic, Social and Cultural Rights differ significantly from those used in relation to other human rights treaties, there should be a compelling justification for this, taking account of the fact that the formulations used in the Covenant are, to a considerable extent, comparable to those used in treaties dealing with civil and political rights.[112]

---

109 General Comment 9 n 97.
110 Ibid. General Comment 9 n 97.
111 Ibid. General Comment 9 n 97 para.3.
112 Ibid. General Comment 9 n 97 para.7.

Judicial remedies are often cited as a *sine qua non* (a prerequisite) of the success-ful application of a right in international law.[113] Many argue that without judi-cial sanction, a right is without merit.[114] A blanket refusal to acknowledge the justiciable nature of the rights is considered arbitrary:

> The adoption of a rigid classification of economic, social and cultural rights which puts them, by definition, beyond the reach of the courts would thus be arbitrary and incompatible with the principle that the two sets of human rights are indivisible and interdependent. It would also drastically curtail the capacity of the courts to protect the rights of the most vulnerable and dis-advantaged groups in society.[115]

The International Commission of Jurists has also called for legitimate justiciable mechanisms to be explored with a view to bridging the gap between the justicia-bility of civil and political rights and ESR.[116] Tinta concludes that according to the rules of international law, any violation of a primary rule, including those concerning ESR, should be open to an effective remedy, including judicial remedies.[117] It is through the principle of indivisibility that judicial remedies are inevitably opened to violations of ESR. Just as states can be liable for violations of CPR, so too can they be liable for violations of ESR. Mechanisms for protect-ing human rights that reflect the indivisibility principle are enshrined in the Maastricht Guidelines on Violations of Economic, Social and Cultural Rights:

> It is now undisputed that all human rights are indivisible, interdependent, interrelated and of equal importance for human dignity. Therefore, states are as responsible for violations of economic, social and cultural rights as they are for violations of civil and political rights ... As is the case with civil and political rights, both individuals and groups can be victims of violations of economic, social and cultural rights.[118]

According to the international legal position and an ever-increasing body of litera-ture, the capability of vindicating ESR before the courts is of paramount import-ance in a democratic society committed to the domestic protection of international human rights obligations according to the principle of indivisibility.

---

113 For example, Article 2(3) of the ICCPR provides for an effective remedy determined by judicial, administrative or legislative authorities.
114 Alston et al., n 50.; Hans Kelsen, *Pure Theory of Law* (1967) at 125–126; Vierdag, 'The Legal Nature of the Rights Granted by the International Covenant on Economic, Social and Cultural Rights' (1968) 9 *Netherlands Yearbook of International Law* 69.
115 General Comment 9 n 97 para.10.
116 International Commission of Jurists, *Courts and the Legal Enforcement of Economic, Social and Cultural Rights, Comparative Experiences of Justiciability*, (Geneva: International Com-mission of Jurists, 2008).
117 Tinta, n 54 at 442.
118 The Maastricht Guidelines on Violations of Economic, Social and Cultural Rights, n 100 at 4.

What Constitutes an Effective Remedy?

The concept of an effective legal remedy is derived from Article 8 of the UDHR which states that 'everyone has the right to an effective remedy by the competent national tribunals for acts violating the fundamental rights granted him by the constitution or by law'.[119] The UDHR, as noted earlier, did not distinguish between civil and political rights and economic, social and cultural rights – the initial bifurcation occurred to bolster the strength of ESR and the later separation of rights into binary categories (misconstrued as affording a lesser status to ESR) was to occur later with the enactment of the two Covenants. Thus Article 8 can be considered as applying to *all* fundamental rights.

Two separate concepts are inherent in the idea of remedies:

> [i]n the first sense, remedies are the processes by which arguable claims of human rights violations are heard and decided, whether by courts, administrative agencies, or other competent bodies. The second notion of remedies refers to the outcome of the proceedings, the relief afforded the successful claimant.[120]

In considering the purpose of remedies we can identify those that are applicable to both of these concepts. Shelton, for example, emphasises the potential for remedies to provide compensatory or remedial justice; to play a part in condemnation of the violation or retribution; as a form of deterrence; and as playing a part in restorative justice or reconciliation.[121] Remedies, of course, can take many forms but the importance of a *legal* remedy for violations of human rights is emphasised by Shelton:

> [m]ost legal systems today recognize the importance of safeguarding the rights of access to independent bodies that can afford a fair hearing to claimants who assert an arguable claim that their rights have been infringed. Indeed, many writers include the element of enforceability in their definition of legal rights, because the notion of rights entails a correlative duty on the part of others to act or refrain from acting for the benefit of the rights-holder. Unless a duty is somehow enforced, it risks being seen as a voluntary obligation that can be fulfilled or ignored at will.[122]

This question of enforceability is of particular relevance to the debate on ESR. In the UK a clear gap emerges. What happens if the state fails to ensure ESR are implemented according to international law? In other words, if the administrative and legislative mechanisms fail how can the state be held to account?

---

119 Universal Declaration of Human Rights, UN General Assembly Resolution 217(A) III, 10 December 1948.
120 Shelton, n 99 at 7 (footnotes omitted).
121 Ibid. at 10–15.
122 Ibid. at 8 (footnotes omitted).

The right to an effective remedy in UK law is somewhat contested. Despite both international and regional obligations to provide one, an effective remedy is not always available at the domestic level. The international position is enshrined in Article 8 of the UDHR which in and of itself is not directly enforceable in the domestic regime. Regional human rights frameworks that the UK is party to reflect the international standards required for an effective remedy. Article 13 of the ECHR is based on Article 8 UDHR and Article 47 of the EU Charter of Fundamental Rights draws its inspiration from Articles 6 and 13 of the ECHR and goes somewhat further than Article 6 in its scope of protection.

Article 13 of the ECHR, modelled on Article 8 UDHR, outlines the right to an effective remedy. It provides:

'Everyone whose rights and freedoms as set forth in this Convention are violated shall have an effective remedy before a national authority notwithstanding that the violation has been committed by persons acting in an official capacity'.

The 'Guide to good practice in respect of domestic remedies' published by the Council of Europe in 2013, emphasises the fundamental importance of Article 13 underlying the Convention's human rights protection system and notes that Convention requires that a remedy 'be such as to allow the competent domestic authorities both to deal with the substance of the relevant Convention complaint and to grant appropriate relief'.[123] The jurisprudence of the Court has confirmed that a remedy will only be considered 'effective' (for the purposes of Article 13) if it is available and sufficient and it must be sufficiently certain both in theory and in practice.[124] A remedy must be effective in practice as well as in law,[125] having regard to the individual circumstances of the case. The Convention system does not prescribe any particular form of remedy and, as the good practice guide highlights, States parties to the Convention have a margin of discretion in how to comply with their obligation.[126] However, 'the nature of the right at stake has implications for the type of remedy the State is required to provide'.[127]

---

123 'Guide to good practice in respect of domestic remedies', adopted by the Committee of Ministers on 18 September 2013, at 7 and 12. Available at https://edoc.coe.int/en/european-convention-on-human-rights/6608-guide-to-good-practice-in-respect-of-domestic-remedies.html

124 *McFarlane v. Ireland*, App. No. 31333/06, 10 September 2010, paragraph 114; *Riccardi Pizzati v. Italy*, App. No. 62361/00, Grand Chamber judgment of 29 March 2006, paragraph 38.

125 *El-Masri v. 'the former Yugoslav Republic of Macedonia'*, App. No. 39630/09, 13 December 2012, paragraph 255; *Kudła v. Poland*, App. No. 30210/96, judgment of 26 October 2000, paragraph 152.

126 'Guide to good practice in respect of domestic remedies', adopted by the Committee of Ministers on 18 September 2013, at 12. Available at https://edoc.coe.int/en/european-convention-on-human-rights/6608-guide-to-good-practice-in-respect-of-domestic-remedies.html

127 Ibid., per *Budayeva and Others v. Russia*, App. No. 15339/02 etc., judgment of 20 March 2008, paragraphs 190–191.

Article 13 ECHR has not been incorporated into domestic UK law under the Human Rights Act 1998 and the declaration of incompatibility under Section 4 of the HRA is not deemed to meet the threshold of an effective remedy under Article 13. In the case of *Burden*[128] the Grand Chamber of the ECtHR found that the applicants did not have to pursue their claim within the domestic courts if the only possible remedy available is a declaration of incompatibility under the HRA (as part of the admissibility requirement to exhaust domestic remedies under Article 35 ECHR). The court found that remedies must be sufficiently certain, in practice as well as in theory, failing which they will lack the requisite accessibility and effectiveness.[129] The declaration of incompatibility does not meet the threshold of an effective remedy according to Strasbourg jurisprudence. The court alludes to the potential for such a declaration to amount to an effective remedy but only at a 'future date' if UK Government Ministers develop a 'long-standing and established practice' of giving effect to the courts' declarations of incompatibility by remedying the incompatible legislation.[130]

Article 47 of the EU Charter of Fundamental Rights provides protection to a much broader form of effective remedy at the domestic level than Articles 6, 13 and 35 ECHR.[131] However, whilst the protection afforded is far reaching it is limited in so far as it is only engaged when falling within the scope of EU law. For example, when examining the lawfulness of employment tribunal fees the Supreme Court found that prohibitively expensive fees precluded the opportunity to access to an effective remedy. The fees imposed limitations on the exercise of EU rights in a disproportionate way and were deemed unlawful under EU law.[132] Under the proposed terms of the UK's exit from the EU Article 47 will no longer be operable to the same degree meaning the strength of this route as an effective remedy is lost.[133] Although, in this particular case, the judiciary also derived the remedy from the common law right to access justice.[134]

The concept of remedies for rights violations is very much interlinked with that of justiciability. As noted earlier, the idea that ESR are non-justiciable has now been debunked, both in theory and in practice and only appears today

---

128 Burden v UK Application No 13378/05, Judgment, 12 December 2006.

129 Ibid., at para.36.

130 Ibid., at para.36.

131 The jurisprudence of the CJEU has developed the right to an effective remedy under Art. 47, EUCFR, through cases such as *DEB* ECJ 22 December 2010, Case C-279/09, *Alassini* ECJ 18 March 2010, Case C-317–320/08, and *Pfleiderer* ECJ 14 June 2011, Case C-360/09. In the case of *DEB* the court affirmed that Article 47 should be read in line with Article 6 and 13 of the ECHR.

132 *R (on the application of UNISON) (Appellant) v Lord Chancellor (Respondent)* [2017] UKSC 51, para.116–117.

133 Alison Young, '*Benkharbouche* and the Future of Disapplication', U.K. Const. L. Blog (24 October 2017), available at https://ukconstitutionallaw.org/2017/10/24/alison-young-benkharbouche-and-the-future-of-disapplication/

134 UNISON n 132, para.64.

'as a quiet echo from the past'.[135] Interestingly, in response to the concluding observation of the Committee on Economic, Social and Cultural rights urging the UK 'to consider signing and ratifying the Optional Protocol to the Covenant', the government noted that it:

> considers that protection for ICESCR-based rights is already afforded by domestic law, including under the Human Rights Act 1998 and the Equality Act 2010; individuals *may therefore seek remedies* in UK courts or tribunals if they feel that their rights have been breached.[136]

Though clearly avoiding the issue presented by the Committee, this could also be interpreted as tacit acceptance of (if not support for) the domestic justiciability of ESR.[137] Domestic justiciability has been embraced in numerous other jurisdictions that have taken on the challenge of enforcing ESR, which as Roach highlights, does involve a re-think of our traditional concepts of remedies:

> [t]he challenge of enforcing ESC rights may require some re-thinking of the traditional idea that remedies must be immediate and track the contours of the right and the violation, and that the courts can order one shot remedies that achieve corrective justice.[138]

Shelton argues that although the 'remedies for cases involving socio-economic rights will often be classical remedies, such as compensation and declarations of wrongdoing, more often general and structural remedies will be necessary'.[139] This is not a novel legal dilemma Shelton notes.[140] And Roach expands on this:

---

135 See Martin Scheinin 'Justiciability and Indivisibility of Human Rights' in John Squires, Malcolm Langford, Bret Thiele (eds.), *The Road to a Remedy: Current Issues in the Litigation of Economic, Social and Cultural Rights* (University of New South Wales Press, 2005), 17–26 at 17. Scheinin notes that '[t]he old counter-argument related to the alleged "different nature" of these rights, as compared to more traditional human rights generally described as civil and political rights, is perhaps not yet dead and buried but nevertheless appears today as a quiet echo from the past. The shift [is] towards a general recognition of the principle of the justiciability of ESC rights – which is something far less than asserting that ESC rights are generally justiciable ... '

136 United Nations International Covenant on Economic, Social and Cultural Rights, United Kingdom, British Overseas Territories, Crown Dependencies 6th periodic report, 2014, para. 89, page 36. Available at www.justice.gov.uk/downloads/human-rights/ICESCR-sixth-periodic-report.pdf (emphasis added).

137 Katie Boyle and Edel Hughes, 'Identifying Routes to Remedy for Violations of Economic, Social and Cultural Rights' (2018) 22 *International Journal of Human Rights* 43–69.

138 Kent Roach, 'Crafting Remedies for Violations of Economic, Social and Cultural Rights' in John Squires et al. (eds.), n 135 at 111–126 at 111.

139 Dinah Shelton, 'Remedies and Reparation', M. Langford et al. (eds.), *Global Justice, State Duties, The Extraterritorial Scope of Economic, Social and Cultural Rights in International Law* (Cambridge University Press, 2013), 367–390 at 380.

140 Ibid.

An over simplified understanding of the remedies for civil and political rights as simple corrective remedies that have no distributive effects is a barrier to effective remedies for socio-economic rights. Many traditional political and civil rights require complex dialogic relief with distributional implications to be effective. Once this is recognised then the remedial process that is required to enforce socio-economic rights will appear much less anomalous, albeit no less complex.[141]

An innovative approach to remedies is required to fully embrace the potential of ESR adjudication. This includes exploring new ways of facilitating access to justice (accessibility principle); enabling participation for the most vulnerable through collective complaints processes where appropriate (participation principle); and enabling remedies that move beyond deferential orders to collective and structural injunctions dealing with systemic problems (the remedial principle). Each of the above is discussed in turn below under the effectiveness of existing and potential future justiciability mechanisms.

Conclusion

The international position clearly provides a framework in which domestic justiciable remedies ought to be made available. Indeed, the right to access justice and recourse to an effective judicial remedy (at least as a means of last resort) now forms part of states obligations under international law.

The original intention of the parties to the UDHR has been historically misunderstood. The bifurcation of rights into distinct categories was based on a misconception. According to the preparatory work to the International Bill of Rights the original point of bifurcation occurred before the drafting of the UDHR as the result of the intention of the parties to reaffirm the importance of ESR. This separation then became associated with a hierarchy of rights according to their positive or negative nature. This categorisation of rights is misconstrued as civil, political, economic, social and cultural rights all contain negative and positive aspects. The status of ESR at the international and domestic level has been subject to an unhelpful categorisation following the negative v positive dichotomy – a now completely outdated position. The literature and the legal framework are developing towards a more coherent vision of human rights based on the principle of indivisibility with minimum core and progressive obligations. The Committee on Economic, Social and Cultural Rights has advised that the duty to progressively realise ESR ought now to accommodate judicial

---

141 Kent Roach, 'The Challenges of Crafting Remedies for Violations of Economic, Social and Cultural Rights' in M. Langford (ed.), *Social Rights Jurisprudence: Emerging Trends in International and Comparative Law* (Cambridge University Press, 2008), 46–58 at 58.

remedies if a violation occurs – i.e. if states fail to progressively achieve the full realisation of ESR within the maximum available resources without delay and in good faith. This means that mechanisms ought to be developed to adjudicate ESR in a way that accommodates the teleological move towards human rights protection according to the principle of indivisibility.

3 The Jurisdictional Hierarchy as Pillars of the UK Constitution
The Regional Framework

The Regional Framework

The UK is a party to numerous international human rights treaties. It is a member of the Council of Europe (CoE) and, until its imminent departure, a member state of the European Union (EU), each of which impose different human rights obligations. Whilst the dualist system renders international treaties beyond the competence of the courts unless incorporated through domestic legislation, the UK's membership of the CoE and the EU creates a regional framework of human rights application that does engage with enforceable rights at the domestic level (both national and devolved). The regional legal frameworks have acted as important pillars of the UK constitution in this respect. These obligations are subject to change within the context of the UK leaving the European Union ('Brexit') and the potential repeal of the Human Rights Act 1998[1] and so the structure of the human rights constitutional framework in the UK is also in flux.

Under the terms of the Human Rights Act 1998, the ECHR (an instrument of the CoE) is partially incorporated into the domestic legal system meaning individuals can rely on ECHR protection in the domestic courts. The relationship between the UK and EU is defined according to competences in which Member States of the EU have agreed to be bound through the development of the treaties. Under the Lisbon Treaty, the EU Charter of Fundamental Rights now forms part of the EU legal order and has partial engagement at the domestic level within the scope of EU law. Supplementary to this, the Treaty of the European Union (TEU) also provided for the accession of the EU to the ECHR.

Through the operation of devolution the UK Parliament at Westminster has transferred competences to the Northern Ireland Assembly, the Scottish Parliament and the Welsh Assembly. In addition, the competence of the devolved jurisdictions is limited with reference to the European pillars of the UK constitution. For example, the Scotland Act 1998 requires compliance with the ECHR and

---

1 The Conservative manifesto pledge in 2015 included repeal of the Human Rights Act 1998 and reiterated this promise in 2017 but with a temporary delay until EU departure was concluded (Conservative Party Manifesto 2015 at 73 followed by Conservative Manifesto 2017 at 37).

EU law granting rights-derived from these systems constitutional status within the devolved settlement. Section 29(d) of the Scotland Act limits the competence of the Scottish Parliament in so far as any Act passed that is incompatible with Convention rights or EU law is not law (the Courts can declare said Acts void with immediate effect). Section 101 of the Scotland Act compels the reading of Acts of the Scottish Parliament to be read as narrowly as is required to be within devolved competence and any act by the Scottish Ministers is deemed *ultra vires* if it is in breach of ECHR of EU law (section 57). Similar provisions constitute the devolved settlements in Northern Ireland[2] and Wales.[3]

This means that both the ECHR and EU law hold constitutional status within the devolved context. In fact, the ECHR in particular takes on a stronger constitutional footing at the devolved level than at the national level. Each of these jurisdictional hierarchies (from regional to national to devolved) require clarification insofar as they relate to economic and social rights (ESR).

The Council of Europe

The ECHR was drafted shortly after the UDHR and was in many respects part of a dialectic process – in a sense a reaction to the UDHR and a precursor to the International Covenants, each being influenced by the development of the other.[4] In 1949, the Consultative Assembly of the CoE recommended to the Committee of Ministers that a European Convention be drafted enshrining the rights recognised in the Declaration and to have a separate complaints mechanism to afford substantive enforcement.[5]

---

2 See Northern Ireland Act 1998, s.6(1)(c) (legislative competence); s.24(1)(c) (Ministerial competence); s.83 (interpretation of Acts of the Assembly).
3 See Government of Wales Act s.81(1) (Ministerial competence); s.94(6)(c) (legislative competence); s.154 (interpretation of Acts of the Assembly).
4 For a discussion on the dialectic relationship between the UDHR, the ECHR and the ICCPR see Manfred Nowak, *UN Covenant on Civil and Political Rights, CCPR Commentary* (2nd ed., NP Engel, 2005), XXII–XXIII. Nowak explains that the UN Human Rights Commission started work on a human rights convention at the same time as the ECHR was being drafted by the CoE. The CoE relied in part on the HR Commission's drafts – however the work was delayed within the HR Commission and in the meantime the ECHR was completed. Thereafter the Western states sought to model the UN Convention on the 1950 ECHR model as 'its reach was to be limited to liberal rights directed against undue state interference and directly enforceable before courts' – (the opposing view of the socialist states was that a Convention should reflect interdependency but enforcement ought to be left exclusively within the sovereignty of the individual states parties). Of course, this binary narrative has been challenged elsewhere as discussed by Daniel J. Whelan and Jack Donnelly, 'The West, Economic and Social Rights, and the Global Human Rights Regime: Setting the Record Straight' (2007) 29 *Human Rights Quarterly* 908 at 910.
5 Recommendation 3 (Doc. 108), Human Rights and Fundamental Freedoms, 8 September 1949, available at http://assembly.coe.int/nw/xml/XRef/Xref-XML2HTML-en.asp?fileid=51&lang=en

The ECHR does not reflect the principle of indivisibility enunciated in the UDHR and largely protects civil and political rights and not economic, social or cultural rights (with some limited exceptions to this, such as a limited right to education). The reluctance to enumerate for the full body of human rights recognised in the UDHR was based on a concern instigated by the UK representative that the UDHR lacked clarity and precision as to the nature of the obligations Member States would be under and to the limitations that could be imposed on rights:

> The United Kingdom Government attached great importance to the conclu-
> sion of a Convention relating to human rights by the states represented on the
> Council of Europe, but that it was essential to proceed on the right lines. In
> the Universal Declaration of Human Rights and Fundamental Freedoms there
> was set out a number of ideals which had not and were not intended to have
> any legal effect. That had been fully recognized in the discussions which had
> taken place at Lake Success, and for that reason the Commission on Human
> Rights was drawing up a Draft Covenant intended to be legally binding on the
> parties thereto. In the view of the United Kingdom Government, an essential
> prerequisite to any Convention on the subject of human rights was the precise
> definition of the rights to be safeguarded and the permitted limitations to
> those rights. It was necessary that these definitions should be in legislative
> form so as to make it quite clear what was the nature and extent of the obliga-
> tions to be assumed by the states party to the proposed Convention.[6]

During the drafting process, there were two potential treaty templates under consideration. The first option was based on a universal and indivisible approach using the
UDHR format as a template. The second was proposed by the UK Government as an
alternative to the UDHR. This was a more clearly defined instrument but with
a narrower scope in terms of inclusion of rights and their universality (coupled with
a complaints mechanism). The second proposal was adopted by the CoE. This was to
be an interim solution before being able to adopt an indivisible approach:

> Certainly, professional freedoms and social rights, which have themselves an
> intrinsic value, must also, in the future, be defined and protected. Everyone
> will, however, understand that it is necessary to begin at the beginning and to
> guarantee political democracy in the European Union and then to co-ordinate
> our economies, before undertaking the generalisation of social democracy.[7]

The Council of Europe later produced the European Social Charter (ESC) to
provide for the rights not protected in the Convention (i.e. ESR). Williams has
been critical of the approach adopted by the Council of Europe in separating

---

6 Preliminary Draft Report of the Committee of Experts to the Committee of Ministers (24 February 1950), ECHR Travaux Préparatoires, Art 1, Cour (77) 9-EN1290551.
7 Council of Europe, Seventeenth Sitting, 7 September 1949, Presentation of Report No. 77,
   (Mr Teitgen) at 1144.

rights into categories that undermine the principle of indivisibility and, as a result, reaffirming the dichotomous misconception surrounding the status of rights:

> From this perspective there is a clear failing in the ECHR regime. The Convention is overwhelmingly focused on civil and political rights. Although the Council of Europe has presided over the development of a European Social Charter, extremely detailed in its identification of economic and social rights deemed essential "to improve the standard of living and to promote the social well-being' of the Contracting Parties" populations, there is a clear acceptance that the ECHR is partial in its human rights scope. Indeed, the revised version of the Social Charter produced in 1996 accepted the need "to preserve the indivisible nature of all human rights, be they civil, political, economic, social or cultural and, on the other hand" through refreshing its content. There was therefore explicit recognition that the ECHR provided a restricted approach to human rights which had to be remedied through another instrument. The fact that the Social Charter does not allow access to a court to pronounce with the gravitas of the ECtHR, has also meant that there persists a direct challenge to the accepted indivisibility principle overseen by the ECHR.[8]

Aligning the protection of human rights to separate treaties in the Council of Europe perpetuates the dichotomy of rights. Furthermore, the complaints mechanism provided for under the European Social Charter does not, in the view of Williams, provide the same level of protection as the mechanism available under the Convention. In any event, the UK is not party to the Additional Protocol[9] enabling an application to the European Social Committee, nor has it ratified the revised Charter.[10] The function of the European Social Charter at the domestic level enables a monitoring system in relation to ESR in the UK. The monitoring system is governed by the submission of reports by the UK Government to the European Social Committee who then considers the reports and issues conclusions as to whether the UK is in conformity with the particular rights under consideration according to a four-year cycle where rights are considered under one of four separate thematic headings on an annual basis.[11] For example, in 2010 the European Committee of Social Rights examined the state's obligations in relation

---

8 Andrew Williams, 'The European Convention on Human Rights, the EU and the UK: Confronting a Heresy' (2013) 24 *European Journal of International Law* 1157 at 1172.

9 Council of Europe, *Additional Protocol to the European Social Charter providing for a System of Collective Complaints*, 9 November 1995, ETS 158.

10 Council of Europe, European Social Charter (Revised), 3 May 1996, ETS 163.

11 This reporting system was introduced by a decision of the Committee of Ministers in 2006, European Social Charter, Governmental Committee of the European Social Charter, New system for the presentation of reports on the application of the European Social Charter, Proposal of the Governmental Committee, 963rd meeting, 3 May 2006, Item 4.2 CM(2006)53. The thematic areas are: Group 1 (employment, training and equal opportunities), Group 2 (Health, social security and social protection), Group 3 (Labour rights), Group 4 (Children, families, migrants).

to the rights associated with employment, training and equal opportunities (the right to adequate standard of living etc.).[12] The Committee concluded that the UK was not in conformity with ten out of the thirteen related articles.[13] In 2013, the Committee found the minimum level of incapacity benefit, the state pension and job-seeker's allowance to be manifestly inadequate and in breach of Article 12 of the Charter (the right to social security).[14] In 2017, the Committee found that the level set for incapacity benefit, employment seekers allowance and statutory sick pay to be inadequate.[15] The reporting procedure facilitates an awareness of the status of the rights protected in the European Social Charter at the domestic level, however, the failure to adopt the Additional Protocol removes the option of accessing a remedy for a breach. The potential and efficacy of the European Social Charter as a route to remedy is explored further in Chapter 5.

Without domestic enforcement mechanisms for the European Social Charter there is an ESR accountability gap in the breadth of rights protected under the CoE system. In relation to the potential of the ECHR to fill this gap, the Commission, and latterly the European Court of Human Rights (ECtHR), has taken a somewhat teleological approach to interpretation indicative of the principle of indivisibility.[16] The approach adopted by the ECtHR in *Tyrer v UK*, in which it was stated that the Convention must be viewed as 'a living instrument which must be interpreted in the light of present day conditions',[17] has shaped the interpretative process. The ECtHR has adjudicated on socio-economic issues and furthermore has extended the interpretation of civil and political rights to include protection of ESR.[18] In some such cases the ECtHR has indicated its reluctance

---

12 European Social Charter, European Committee of Social Rights, Conclusions XIX-3 (2010), (UNITED KINGDOM), Articles 2, 4, 5 and 6 of the Charter, December 2010.

13 Articles 2§2, public holidays with pay; 2§3, annual holidays with pay; 2§4, Reduced working hours or additional holidays in dangerous or unhealthy occupations; 2§5, weekly rest period; 4§1, decent remuneration (The Committee concludes the minimum wage is manifestly unfair.); 4§2 increased remuneration for overtime worked; 4§4, reasonable notice of termination of employment; 5 right to organise; 6§2, right to bargain collective; 6§4.collective action.

14 European Social Charter, European Committee of Social Rights, Conclusions XX-2 (2013), (GREAT BRITAIN) Articles 3, 11, 12, 13 and 14 of the 1961 Charter, January 2014. In association with the other rights under the thematic review 'Health, social security and social protection' the Committee concluded 11 incidences of conformity in relation Articles 3§1, 3§2, 3§3, 11§1, 11§2, 11§3, 13§1, 13§2, 13§3, 14§1 and 14§2 and one incidence of non-conformity under Article 12§1.

15 European Social Charter, European Committee of Social Rights, Conclusions XXI-2 (2017), (GREAT BRITAIN) January 2018.

16 Smith argues that the greatest success of the Convention can be attributed in part to the pioneering work of the Commission and Court in its jurisprudence – 'Teleological and dynamic interpretative techniques have facilitated the evolution of rights and freedoms in concert with changing norms of society'. Rhona Smith, *Textbook on International Human Rights* (5th ed., Oxford University Press, 2012), 98.

17 *Tyrer v United Kingdom* (1978), 2 EHRR 1, Ser A, No. 26 at para.31.

18 Whilst it is not within the remit of the book to examine each of these cases, the following examples indicate the increasing number of cases before the ECtHR expanding the protection

to interfere in the realm of policy matters. Thus in the case of *Chapman* the ECtHR stated 'Whether the state provides funds to enable everyone to have a home is a matter for political not judicial decision.'[19] On the other hand, the ECtHR has also aligned the jurisprudence to the indivisibility principle and stipulated that, '[w]hile the Convention sets forth what are essentially civil and political rights, many of them have implications of a social or economic nature ... [T]he mere fact that an interpretation of the Convention may extend into the sphere of social and economic rights should not be a decisive factor against such an interpretation; there is no water-tight division separating that sphere from the field covered by the Convention'.[20] An example would be the interpretation of Article 8 (right to private and family life) to include the right to protection of property on cultural grounds in the case of nomadic travellers (*Connors*)[21] There are currently 188 judgments of the ECtHR directly referencing 'economic, social and cultural rights' and this is on an upward trend, with 177 of the 188 decisions occurring from 2005 onwards.[22] It is not unusual for the court to now reference the International Covenant on Economic, Social and Cultural Rights as a means of interpretation, together with other relevant international treaties.[23] ICESCR performs, at the very least, an important interpretative role.

Smith and Koch concur that the Commission and the Court has therefore played an evolutionary role in human rights protection through a teleological

and enforcement of ESR – indicative of the indivisibility principle: Paposhvili v. Belgium, 41738/10 [2016] ECHR 1113, 13 December 2016 (*asylum seeker – right to health – procedures to prohibit removal if Art 3 engaged*); Dybeku v. Albania, Application no. 41153/06, 18 December 2007 (*right to health – prisoners rights*); Khamidov v. Russia, Application no. 72118/01, 2 June 2008 (*housing rights – property rights*); Airey v. Ireland, 32 Eur Ct HR Ser A (1979): [1979] 2 E.H.R.R. 305 (*Economic development and poverty – equality and non-discrimination – women's rights*); Belgian Linguistic Case (Nos. 1 & 2) (No.1) (1967), Series A, No.5 (1979–1980) 1 EHRR 241 (No.2) (1968), Series A, No.6 (1979–1980) 1 EHRR 252 (*Education Rights – civil and political rights – equality and non-discrimination*); López Ostra v. Spain, Series A, No 303-C; (1995) 20 EHHR 277 (*Environmental rights – housing rights – positive obligations*); Botta v. Italy (1998) 26 EHRR 241 (*people with disabilities – obligation to provide – positive obligations*); Selçuk and Asker v. Turkey, (1998) 26 EHRR 477 (*Housing rights – property rights – forced evictions – inhuman treatment*); Akkus v. Turkey, App. no. 00019263/92, Judgment 24 June 1997. (*Property rights – compensation*).

19 *Chapman v United Kingdom* (2001) 33 E.H.R.R. 18 ECtHR para.99.

20 *Airey* v. *Ireland* 32 Eur Ct HR Ser A (1979): [1979] 2 E.H.R.R. 305, para 26.

21 *Connors* v. *United Kingdom*, (European Court of Human Rights, Application no. 66746/01, 27 May 2004), para. 95. The Court noted that, 'the eviction of the applicant and his family from the local authority site was not attended by the requisite procedural safeguards, namely the requirement to establish proper justification for the serious interference with his rights and consequently cannot be regarded as justified by a "pressing social need" or proportionate to the legitimate aim being pursued. There has, accordingly, been a violation of Article 8 of the Convention'.

22 Search of HUDOC database 30 January 2019, available at https://hudoc.echr.coe.int/eng

23 See, for example, *Yordanova and Others v Bulgaria,* Application no. 25446/06, 12 April 2012 and *Winterstein and Others v France,* Application No. 27013/07, 17 October 2013.

approach to interpretation.[24] Whilst there is scope to move beyond the dichotomous approach to human rights within the Council of Europe through the jurisprudence of the ECtHR, Williams also points out that there is only so much the court can do:

> it would be expecting too much to rely on the jurisprudence of any court to cure what was a theoretically defective constituting text. Indeed, any court which attempted to do so could be admonished for its lack of respect for the internationally negotiated text *and* have its judgments questioned on the basis of an unjustified activism that arguably contradicts the authorizing instrument. That would put in jeopardy the whole mantle of legitimacy placed on the Convention.[25]

So whilst recognising that ESR are enforceable at the supranational, national and devolved level as a result of the jurisprudence of the ECtHR, it is also critical to acknowledge that there are systemic limitations to this approach:

> The Convention's textual architecture denied a sense of coherence through the concept of human dignity (or any other explicit idea) to underpin and thus realize universalism as promoted by the UDHR. None of the rights in themselves or as a disparate collection offer that cohering concept. Rather, they are arbitrarily disaggregated in conception, something which might be ameliorated through judicial interpretation but can never be resolved.[26]

The system operating under the CoE is aligned to the binary application of rights. There is a degree of intersectionality between the binary application and the principle of indivisibility through the jurisprudence of the ECtHR. However, there are also barriers and impediments in place to a full realisation of human rights according to the principle of indivisibility as a direct result of the inherent limitations of the dichotomous approach (most evident in the separation of civil and political rights (CPR) and ESR into two distinct treaties with two distinct complaints mechanisms).

European Union

The framework of rights under the European Union offers a potentially more robust system of protection more closely aligned with the principle of indivisibility. This section outlines the operational framework of EU law and examines the position of ESR and ESR justiciability under the renewed constitutional

---

24 Smith, n 16 at 98 and Ida Koch, 'Economic, Social and Cultural Rights as Components in Civil and Political Rights: A Hermeneutic Perspective' (2006) 10 *The International Journal of Human Rights*, 405, 410. *Tyrer v UK* (1978), 2 EHRR 1, Ser A, No. 26 at para. 31.
25 Williams, n 8 at 1173.
26 Williams, ibid. at 1166.

framework of the EU legal order. In a national referendum, on 23 June 2016, 51.9% of the electorate voted to leave the European Union.[27] As the UK prepares to leave the European Union the status of EU law will change at the domestic level. This section captures the existing relationship between the UK and the EU law and explains the potential impact of the UK exiting the EU in relation to human rights, in particular ESR.

Whilst the European Communities Act 1972 remains in force section 2(1) provides that all rights, powers, liabilities, obligations and restrictions created by or arising under EU treaties are recognisable and given effect to in UK law. Section 3 of the 1972 Act ensures that courts in the UK are bound by decisions of the Court of Justice of the European Union (CJEU). The primacy of EU law is further entrenched under section 2(4) which ensures any legislation passed after the entry into force of the 1972 Act should be construed and given effect to in accordance with EU law. This hierarchical relationship reflects the doctrine of the supremacy of EU law as developed by the CJEU.[28] This requires the national courts to disapply primary legislation of the UK Parliament that is inconsistent with EU law[29] and the jurisprudence of the CJEU affords individuals the right to rely on EU law in the domestic court under the principle of direct effect.[30] The primacy of EU law is further entrenched under the terms of devolution.[31]

Fundamental rights have formed part of the EU legal order from as early as 1969.[32] Trstenjak and Beysen contend that the adjudication of rights by the CJEU (then the European Court of Justice) developed in reaction to the constitutionalisation of rights in Germany whereby the CJEU was reluctant to assign the assessment of EU compatibility with fundamental constitutional rights to a national adjudicator, preferring to assume this role itself.[33] As the jurisprudence of the CJEU

---

27 The Electoral Commission, 'EU Referendum Results', available at www.electoralcommission. org.uk/find-information-by-subject/elections-and-referendums/past-elections-and-referendums/eu-referendum/electorate-and-count-information. The electorate in England voted to leave with 53.2% vote and Wales with 51.7% vote; whereas, Scotland voted to remain with 62% vote and Northern Ireland to remain with 55.7% vote.

28 See *Costa v Enel* [1964] ECR 585 (6/64) whereby the Court of Justice held that EU law supersedes national law and Van *Gend en Loos v Nederlandse Administratie der Belastingen* (1963) Case 26/62 where the court held that EU law operates with direct effect in national courts of Member States.

29 *Factortame (No 1)* [1990] 2 AC 85; *Factortame (No 2)* [1991] 1 AC 603 and *R v Secretary of State for Transport, ex p. Equal Opportunities Commission* [1995] 1 AC 1.

30 Van *Gend en Loos* n 28.

31 Section 6 of the Northern Ireland Act 1998 limits the legislative competence of the Northern Ireland Assembly in so far as any provision of an Act will be *ultra vires* if it is incompatible with EU law and section 24 provides that any Minister of the Northern Ireland Department is also bound to comply with EU law. *C.f.* Sections 29 and 57 of the Scotland Act 1998 respectively and ss.94 and 81 of Government of Wales Act 2006 respectively.

32 *Stauder v City of Ulm* (29/69) [1969] E.C.R. 419; [1970] C.M.L.R. 112.

33 This was in reaction to citizens in Germany being able to seek review of legislation based on constitutional rights – the CJEU had originally resisted review of EU legislation based on compatibility with fundamental rights but did not want to risk the legality of EU law being

developed, so too did the recognition of human rights as 'general principles' of EU law.[34] International human rights treaties were to serve as a source for these general principles as was the national constitutional traditions of Member States.[35] This body of jurisprudence was by no means restricted to the binary application of rights entrenched in the Council of Europe system and some ESR form part of the 'general principles' of EU law. As Williams asserts, 'the development of social policy internally and identification of economic and social rights for promotion externally point to an institutional appreciation of indivisibility within the EU that simply transcends the limitations of the Convention. The CJEU's jurisprudence also indicates a willingness to see matters of equality and solidarity as human rights matters worthy of protection as well as being justiciable. It is plausible to suggest therefore that indivisibility is a working normative principle applicable in the EU context, one which is not shared by the ECHR in its constitution.'[36]

The indivisibility approach is now explicitly evident in the EU legal order since the entry into force of the Lisbon Treaty with its three constituent parts: the Treaty of the European Union (TEU),[37] the Treaty on the Functioning of the European Union (TFEU)[38] and the European Charter of Fundamental Rights (the Charter).[39] Article 6(2) TEU confirms the continuing relevance of fundamental rights as general principles of Union law[40] and Article 6(1) of the

---

reviewed within the German constitutional court at a national level based on compatibility with constitutional norms that ensured fundamental rights – for a brief account of the history see Verica Trstenjak and Erwin Beysen, 'The Growing Overlap of Fundamental Freedoms and Fundamental Rights in the Case-Law of the CJEU' (2013) 38 *European Law Review* 293, 303: the court had resisted fundamental rights review in *Stork & Cie v High Authority of the European Coal and Steel Community* (1/58) [1959] E.C.R 19 at 26; and in *Präsident Ruhrkohlen-Verkaufsgesellschaft v High Authority* (36, 37, 38 and 40/59) [1960] E.C.R. 424 at 438–439. However, in view of the ongoing debate in the German doctrine and the accompanying threat of a national judicial review of EU actions on the basis of provisions of national constitutional law, the CJEU changed its position in *Stauder v City of Ulm* (29/69) [1969] E.C.R. 419; [1970] C.M.L.R. 112. See P.J.G. Kapteyn, "Een zich van zijn rechten bewuste bijstandstrekker en de aankoop van goedkope Europese boterbergboter" in Thomas Beukers and Herman Van Harten (eds.), *Hetrecht van de Europese Unie in 50 klassieke arresten* (Den Haag: Boom Juridische Uitgevers, 2010), 38 as cited in Trstenjak and Beysen, at 303.

34 Tawhida Ahmed and Israel de Jesús Butler, 'The European Union and Human Rights: An International Law Perspective' (2006) 17 *European Journal of International Law* 771, 774.

35 *Nold v Commission Case* 4/73 [1974] ECR 491.

36 Williams, n 8 at 1172.

37 European Union, *Treaty of Lisbon Amending the Treaty on European Union and the Treaty Establishing the European Community*, 13 December 2007, 2007/C 306/01.

38 European Union, *Consolidated version of the Treaty on the Functioning of the European Union*, 26 October 2012, 2012/C 326/47.

39 European Union: Council of the European Union, *Charter of Fundamental Rights of the European Union (2007/C 303/01)*, 14 December 2007, C 303/1.

40 'The Union shall respect fundamental rights, as guaranteed by the European Convention for the Protection of Human Rights and Fundamental Freedoms signed in Rome on 4 November 1950 and as they result from the constitutional traditions common to the Member States, as general principles of Community law'. Art 6(2) TEU.

TEU incorporates the EU Charter of Fundamental Rights into the EU legal order as a matter of primary law holding the same status as the TEU and the TFEU. Article 6(3) of the TEU also provides that the EU shall accede to the ECHR and negotiations on this culminated in a draft accession agreement.[41] The draft accession agreement was deemed unfit for purpose by the CJEU and EU accession to the ECHR is on hold until such time as a future accession agreement is reached.[42] Polakiewicz has argued that this gap ought to be closed as soon as possible as there is a growing need for legal certainty, coherence and consistency between the two legal orders.[43]

The Charter articulates many of the same rights contained in the ECHR with additional protection afforded to ESR. However, there are several barriers in place to extending the ESR protected in the Charter to the jurisdiction of either the supranational or national court. The application of the Charter is limited in two respects: first, in relation to its general application and, second, in relation to the specific application of ESR. Each is discussed in turn below.

First, in relation to the general application of the Charter, Article 6(1) of the TEU and Article 51(2) of the Charter clarify that there is no extension of EU competence and that the Charter cannot lead to extended competences of the EU to act or legislate in new areas, including ESR. Second, the Charter only applies at a domestic level when the Member States are implementing Union law (Article 51 (1)). Whilst this has been granted a broad interpretation as a requirement of Member States' action to be 'within the scope of EU law',[44] it is still limited to the specific areas of EU competence.

Allan Rosas, judge at the CJEU, addressed concerns raised in the literature and in practice of the practicability of these limitations by reiterating what he

---

41 Draft Agreement on Accession of the European Union to the Convention for the Protection of Human Rights and Fundamental Freedoms (The text of the draft accession agreement, its explanatory report as well as related instruments are annexed to the report from the last negotiation meeting between the CDDH ad hoc negotiation group and the *European Commission on the accession of the EU to the ECHR (3–5 April 2013)* was agreed at negotiators' level on 5 April 2013, available at www.coe.int/t/dghl/standardsetting/hrpolicy/Accession/Meeting_reports_en.asp

42 Opinion 2/13 of the Court (Full Court) of 18 December 2014 ECLI:EU:C:2014:2454.

43 Jörg Polakiewicz, 'EU Law and the ECHR: Will the European Union's Accession Square the Circle?' (2013) 6 *European Human Rights Law Review* 592; Polakiewicz raises concerns regarding jurisprudence of the CJEU that undermines the status of the ECHR in the EU legal order under the the Bosphorus presumption – this amounts to 'an acknowledgement of the fact that the European Union ... is not bound by the ECHR' (*Bosphorus Hava Yollari Turizm v Ireland [GC]*, no.45036/98, ECHR 2005-VI). In the event of accession, it may result in double standards. If this is not clarified in the accession agreement then the principle of subsidiarity (now enshrined in protocol open to signature following the Brighton declaration – Protocol No.15 to the ECHR art.1, http://conventions.coe.int/Treaty/en/Treaties/Html/213.html>) through the margin of appreciation might facilitate a continuation of the Bosphorus presumption post accession meaning different levels of obligations between member states and the EU as a legal entity.

44 *Åkerberg Fransson*, Case C-617/10, ECLI:EU:C:2013:105.

describes as an already existing Union norm.[45] Article 6(1) TEU together with Article 51(1) EU merely enumerate the principles of EU law already established in jurisprudence of the CJEU prior to the enactment of the Charter in so far as EU fundamental rights should be protected when 'implementing' EU law at both the EU and national level.[46] Implementation, he argues, relates to applicability, so when a Union norm is sufficiently relevant to the outcome of a case (*in concreto* as opposed to *in abstracto*), this opens the door for an application of the Charter provisions as well.

Second, in relation to the specific limitation of ESR, there is an unusual distinction between rights v principles. During the drafting of the Charter the UK Government expressed concern as to the incorporation of economic and social rights in the Charter[47] (Denmark also expressed reservations).[48] In order to overcome this reluctance, the Convention on the Future of Europe (responsible for drafting the Charter) added a paragraph to Article 52 reiterating a distinction between 'rights' and 'principles' in the Charter. There is no definition of the rights v principles distinction in the text of the Charter other than to clarify that rights are justiciable, and principles are the responsibility of the legislature and executive with limited justiciability:

> [t]he provisions of this Charter which contain principles may be implemented by legislative and executive acts taken by Institutions and bodies of the Union, and by acts of Member States when they are implementing Union law, in the exercise of their respective powers. They shall be judicially cognisable only in the interpretation of such acts and in the ruling on their legality.[49]

As to what constitutes rights or principles, there is no clear definition on content either. The explanatory notes state that articles 25 (rights of the elderly),

---

45 Allan Rosas, 'When Is the EU Charter Applicable at National Level?' (2012) 19(4) *Jurisprudencija: Mokslo darbu žurnalas* 1269–1288.

46 In the case of *Wachauf* the court confirmed that Union fundamental rights 'are also binding on the Member States when they implement Community rules' Case 5/88 *Wachauf* [1989] ECR 2607, para.19. See also for example: Case C-60/00 *Carpenter* [2002] ECR I-6279, para.37–40; Case C-117/01 *KB* [2004] ECR I-541, paras 30–34. Rosas contrasts the approaches taken in these cases with that of *Kremzov*, where the court held that the the situation did not 'establish a sufficient connection with Community law to justify the application of Community provisions', Case C-299/95 *Kremzov* [1997] ECR I-2405, para.16.

47 Diamond Ashiagbor, 'Economic and Social Rights in the European Charter of Fundamental Rights' (2004) 1 *European Human Rights Law Review* 62, 71. Ashiagbor states that the UK Government's representative on the Convention which drafted the Charter fought hardest for the inclusion of a horizontal clause distinguishing rights and principles.

48 L. Burgorgue-Larsen, 'L'article II-112', in L. Burgorgue-Larsen et al. (eds.), *Traité établissant une Constitution pour l'Europe. L'architecture constitutionnelle, Partie II – La Charte des droits fondamentaux de l'Union, Commentaire article par article* (Bruylant, 2005), 683, as cited in Kohen Lenaerts, 'Exploring the Limits of the EU Charter of Fundamental Rights' (2012) 8 *European Constitutional Law Review* 375, 399.

49 Article 52(2).

36 (access to services of general economic interest) and 37 (environmental protection) are examples of principles and that articles 23 (equality between men and women), 33 (family and professional life) and 34 (social security and social assistance) are illustrative of provisions that contain rights and principles. Further, the explanations to Art 35 (healthcare) and 38 (consumer protection) say that these are principles. Lenaerts identified early on that the interpretation of the Charter will fall to the CJEU when an issue in relation to rights v principles arises.[50] Barnard suspected that the court may well draw the line along the positive v negative dichotomy in order to maintain a coherent interpretation across Member States (in line with the distinction drawn under Protocol 30 as discussed below).[51] On the other hand, Ashiagbor questions whether ESR contained in the Charter 'can simply be rendered non-justiciable' when they have been capable of judicial or quasi-judicial interpretation and

50 Lenaerts, n 48 at 400. The Charter has extended the protection of ESR under an indivisible interpretation of CPR. See, for example, the following cases: *J. Mc. B. v L. E., Case C-400/10 5 October 2010* (father's rights of custody relating to family rights [Art 7] and the best interests of the child [Art 24.2]); *M. M. v Minister for Justice, Equality and Law Reform, C-277/11, 22 November 2012* (greater procedural protection for those seeking asylum [Art 41 Right to good administration]); Joined Cases C-411/10 and C-493/10 *N.S.* and *M.E.* ibid. (held: Article 3(2) of Council Regulation (EC) No 343/2003 of 18 February 2003 falls within the scope of EU law and indivisible approach to those seeking asylum in EU, removal to another member state and the right to freedom from inhuman and degrading treatment [Art 3 ECHR and Art 4 EU Charter]), 'Article 4 of the Charter of Fundamental Rights of the European Union must be interpreted as meaning that the Member States, including the national courts, may not transfer an asylum seeker to the "Member State responsible" within the meaning of Regulation No 343/2003 where they cannot be unaware that systemic deficiencies in the asylum procedure and in the reception conditions of asylum seekers in that Member State amount to substantial grounds for believing that the asylum seeker would face a real risk of being subjected to inhuman or degrading treatment within the meaning of that provision'. At para.106. EU fundamental rights also extend the protection of ESR under Article 21 of the Charter in relation to non-discrimination. For example, there is a series of case law dealing with equal treatment of migrants (discrimination on grounds of nationality within freedom of movement and EU citizenship framework) and access to social protections. See: *Martinez Salla*, Case C-85/96 (child raising allowance); *Grezelczyk* Case C-184/99 (student social assistance); *Trojani* Case C-456/02 (access to minimum social assistance); and *Förster* Case C-158/07 (student maintenance grant). ESR adjudication under the rubric of something else is considered in more detail in the final chapter addressing the various models of justiciability mechanisms. More recently there has been the development of ESR protection under the rubric of EU citizenship and the protection of fundamental rights in relation to reunification of the family – see: *Zambrano* Case C-34/09; *McCarthy* Case C-434/09; and *Dereci* Case C-256/11. It is crucial to note that the rights v principles distinction and directly justiciable ESR under the Charter have not yet been extended beyond the rights already recognised in EU law prior to the adoption of the Lisbon Treaty.

51 Catherine Barnard, 'The EU Charter of Fundamental Rights: Happy 10th Birthday?' (2011) 24 *European Union Studies Association Review* 5. See also the *Melloni* case in which the CJEU limited the application of more stringent fair trial safeguards at the national level in order to reflect a universal approach in the operation of the European Arrest Warrant as an area fully regulated by EU law, *Melloni* C-399/11, 26 February 2013.

application in the past, especially as many such rights 'originate in Community social law or the [European Social Charter]'.[52]

The domestic application of the Charter in the UK was initially contested under the terms of Protocol 30[53] to the Charter, whereby the UK[54] sought to diminish the applicability of the Charter by rendering the Charter rights contained in Title IV (Solidarity) as non-justiciable.[55] The rights contained in Title IV of the Charter relate to ESR such as labour rights,[56] the right to social security[57] and the right to adequate healthcare.[58] This distinction mirrors the positive v negative dichotomy that undermines the principle of indivisibility. Jurisprudence of the CJEU has found that Protocol 30 did not relieve the UK of obligations in relation to the application of the Charter at the national level when considering an aspect of EU law under Article 1(1)[59] nor does it prevent the EU defining the extent of EU rights contained in the Charter. However, the operation of Article 1(2) of the Protocol, that seeks to limit the justiciability of ESR under Title IV, was not clarified in case law.

The Treaty on the Functioning of the European Union[60] introduced a three-tier system of competences between the EU and Member States: exclusive competences,[61] shared competences[62] and supporting competences.[63] Social policy is amongst the competences that Member States and the institutions of the EU have agreed to share responsibility.[64] Responsibility for meeting social policy objectives is shared with Member States, however, only in so far as the EU has not exercised its competence (meaning a presumption in favour of the EU as opposed to national fulfilment of the policy).[65]

The EU has now initiated the process of recognising a European Pillar of Social Rights.[66] This is based on a commitment to meet the objectives to promote

---

52 Ashiagbor, n 47 at 71.
53 Protocol (No 30) on the Application of the Charter of the Fundamental Rights of the European Union to Poland and to the United Kingdom annexed to the TEU and the TFEU.
54 And Poland.
55 Article 1(2) Protocol 30 to Charter of Fundamental Rights and Freedoms.
56 Articles 27–32.
57 Article 34.
58 Article 35.
59 Joined Cases C-411/10 and C-493/10 *N.S.* and *M.E.*, judgment of 21 December 2011, 'Article 1(1) of Protocol (No 30) explains Article 51 of the Charter with regard to the scope thereof and does not intend to exempt the Republic of Poland or the United Kingdom from the obligation to comply with the provisions of the Charter or to prevent a court of one of those Member States from ensuring compliance with those provisions' at para.120.
60 European Union, Consolidated version of the Treaty on the Functioning of the European Union, 26 October 2012, 2012/C 326/47 (n 154).
61 Article 3 TFEU.
62 Article 4 TFEU.
63 Article 6 TFEU.
64 Article 4(2)(b) TFEU.
65 Article 2(1) TFEU.
66 European Commission, Commission Recommendation of 26 April 2017 on the European Pillar of Social Rights, Brussels, 26 April 2017 C(2017) 2600 final.

employment, improve living and working conditions and to harmonise proper social protection based on the fundamental rights set out in the European Social Charter and the EU Charter of Fundamental Rights.[67] On announcing the policy then President Junker stated:

> Today we commit ourselves to a set of 20 principles and rights. From the right to fair wages to the right to health care; from lifelong learning, a better work-life balance and gender equality to minimum income: with the European Pillar of Social Rights, the EU stands up for the rights of its citizens in a fast-changing world.[68]

The initial implementation of the policy does not, in itself, give rise to justiciable ESR. It does however articulate what is clearly considered to be within the competency of the EU legal order, and this in turn renders the associated ESR within the competency of the CJEU. The rights and principles identified and developed as part of the Social Pillar may give rise to further enforceable rights as defined in the Charter or developed under the general principles of EU law over time.[69]

The Implications of Brexit[70]

So what are the human rights implications of Brexit? In the *Miller* case, the Supreme Court emphasised the centrality of rights to the process of Brexit – finding that the triggering of Article 50 by notifying withdrawal from the EU would result in a fundamental change in the constitutional arrangements of the United Kingdom.[71] This fundamental change occurs because the process of exiting the EU results in the loss of rights and remedies deriving from EU law.[72]

At the time of writing, the UK has not yet agreed a way forward internally on what type of Brexit it seeks to undertake. The choices before it allow for three potential outcomes: leaving on the terms of the negotiated draft EU Withdrawal

---

67 Ibid. para.3 citing Article 151 TFEU.
68 President Juncker on the proclamation of the European Pillar of Social Rights, 17 November 2017, available at https://ec.europa.eu/commission/priorities/deeper-and-fairer-economic-and-monetary-union/european-pillar-social-rights_en#documents
69 Koen Lenaerts and Jose A. Gutiérrez-Fons, 'The Constitutional Allocation of Powers and General Principles of EU Law' (2010) 47(6) *Common Market Law Review* 1629–1669.
70 This section is derived from Katie Boyle and Leanne Cochrane 'The Complexities of Human Rights and Constitutional Reform in the United Kingdom: Brexit and a Delayed Bill of Rights: Informing the Process' (2018) 16(1) *Journal of Human Rights* 23–46 and I am grateful to the *Northwestern Journal of Human Rights* and my co-author Leanne Cochrane for permission to reproduce this excerpt.
71 *R (Miller) v Secretary of State for Exiting the European Union*, [2017] UKSC 5, [2017] 2 W. L.R. 583 at para.78–81.
72 Ibid. at 80.

Agreement and then subsequent agreements, seeking to extend the transition either indefinitely or for a specified period of time (delaying full departure from the EU legal framework), or leaving the EU without a deal and facing a hard Brexit at the end of the transition period. Each of these approaches present different rights regimes internally for the UK. Retaining the status quo under the transition arrangements either indefinitely or for a specified period retains many of the rights derived from EU law both domestically, with many of the the same rights and remedies including recourse to the CJEU. Leaving with a future trade deal requires a two-stage process, first the transition period and then a future relationship framework (as yet unknown). The transition period as negotiated under the EU Withdrawal Agreement seeks to retain some aspects of rights (labour and environmental rights) and remedies (see Article 4 on the ability of UK courts to disapply primary legislation incompatible with EU law), and the Protocol for Northern Ireland seeks to ensure non-regression on rights and equality for Northern Ireland. The third scenario entails reaching the end of the transition period and leaving without a deal in which case the EU (Withdrawal) Act 2018 retains aspects of EU law (subject to future repeal/erosion), does not retain the Charter[73] and emasculates the general principles, which can no longer serve as a cause of action.[74]

On close inspection, we can see that the impact is serious for human rights protections in the UK with the inevitable loss of rights and remedies derived from the much broader EU framework. In particular the rights at risk include equality provisions,[75] the right to a fair trial in both civil and criminal matters as well as the right to an effective remedy,[76] and social rights as they may develop under the solidarity framework.[77] Furthermore, the existing rights of non-UK EU citizens living and working in the UK who were not part of the EU referendum plebiscite now feature as a 'bargaining chip' in the post-referendum

---

73 Section 5(4) EU (Withdrawal) Act 208.
74 The general principles are no longer a cause of action (Schedule 1 para.3(1)) save a limited three year exemption period (Schedule 8 para.39(5)).
75 UK equality law derives significantly from the EU legal framework, including the general treaty provision.
76 The jurisprudence of the CJEU on remedies and Art. 47, EU Charter of Fundamental Rights, through cases such as, Judgment of 22 December 2010, Case C-279/09 '*DEB*' (OJ 2010 C 55, p. 9), Judgment of 18 March 2010 Case C-317-320/08, '*Alassini*', (OJ 2010 C 134, pp. 3–4) and Judgment of 14 June 2011 Case C-360/09, '*Pfleiderer*' (OJ 2011 C 232, pp. 5–6). The original jurisprudence of the CJEU on remedies started from the principle of national procedural autonomy with limited harmonisation. This was true subject to the principles of 'effectiveness' (national law should not make it virtually impossible to bring an EU law) and 'equivalence' (national law should not treat the EU claim any less favourably than a claim brought under national law). In the *DEB* case, the CJEU started a shift from the traditional approach towards a focus on Art. 47. In *Alassini*, the CJEU applied both approaches, ie. the principles of 'effectiveness' and 'equivalence' first and then after that, Art. 47. The nature of the jurisprudence and the tests applied under Art. 47 are different from the traditional approach to remedies. In *Pfleiderer*, the CJEU had the opportunity to apply Art. 47 but choose not to – again reflecting an oscillating jurisprudence.
77 The EU Charter of Fundamental Rights will not be incorporated into UK law post-Brexit (section 5 EU (Withdrawal) Act 2018.

negotiations.[78] As noted by Lock, the biggest threat to human rights as a result of Brexit is that withdrawal from the EU framework opens the door to human rights regression in all of the areas of EU competence.[79] There is a major threat to ESR not currently protected by the ECHR, in particular labour rights and socio-economic rights not yet fully developed (from the yet untapped potential of the EU Charter). The potential loss of rights is further exacerbated by the loss of the associated remedies under EU law.[80] Initially, the UK Government promised to maintain a degree of legal certainty for UK citizens on departure of the EU by ensuring that pre-Brexit EU law would remain in force in the UK, where practicable, until such a time as it can be individually reviewed and potentially repealed.[81] For example, the Government's White Paper had explicitly promised to protect and enhance EU-derived workers' rights and the draft EU Withdrawal Agreement contains provisions seeking to protect worker's rights.[82] The loss of the broad body of EU law post-transition period (in the event of a deal), or in the event of a hard Brexit (without a deal), however has much further reaching consequences than employment rights and even with a 'deal' some rights and remedies will be irrevocably lost at the domestic level.

EU rights continue to be in a state of constant flux. In fact, the ambit of the rights and remedies which were incorporated into domestic law under section 2 of the 1972 Act varies with the UK's obligations 'from time to time' under the treaties.[83] Their interpretation relies significantly on the jurisprudence of the CJEU. As discussed above, this comes as no surprise given, for example, the

---

78 Ruvi Zeigler, Logically Flawed, Morally Indefensible: EU Citizens in the UK Are Bargaining Chips, Brexit Blog LSE (16 February 2017), available at http://blogs.lse.ac.uk/brexit/2017/02/16/logically-flawed-morally-indefensible-eu-citizens-in-the-uk-are-bargaining-chips/

79 Tobias Lock, 'Human Rights Law in the UK after Brexit', Nov Supp (Brexit Special Extra Issue 2017) *Public Law* 117, 118.

80 Katie Boyle and Leanne Cochrane, *Brexit and a British Bill of Rights: Four Scenarios for Human Rights* and The UK in a Changing Europe Explainer, 17 May 2016, available at https://ukandeu.ac.uk/explainers/brexit-and-a-british-bill-of-rights-four-scenarios-for-human-rights/ and Katie Boyle and Leanne Cochrane, 'Rights Derived from EU Law: Informing the Referendum Process', U.K. Const. L. Blog (13 April 2016), available at https://ukconstitutionallaw.org/2016/04/13/katie-boyle-and-leanne-cochrane-rights-derived-from-eu-law-informing-the-referendum-process/

81 UK Government, The United Kingdom's exit from and new partnership with the European Union (Cm 9417), available at www.gov.uk/government/uploads/system/uploads/attachment_data/file/589191/The_United_Kingdoms_exit_from_and_partnership_with_the_EU_Web.pdf at 1.1.

82 Ibid. and Draft Agreement on the withdrawal of the United Kingdom of Great Britain and Northern Ireland from the European Union and the European Atomic Energy Community, as agreed at negotiators' level on 14 November 2018, TF50 (2018) 55 – Commission to EU27, Article 24 (Rights of Workers) protected for duration of transition period and Protocol Annex 4 Article 2 (non-regression on environmental protection – applies during transition and post-transition) and Article 4 (non-regression on labour rights – applies post transition).

83 Ibid. at 76; European Communities Act 1972, section 2.

absence of clearly defined rights, as opposed to principles, in the Charter.[84] Relying on courts to give meaning to rights is not unusual practice and it would seem this ad hoc formation of rights through the jurisprudence of the CJEU and national courts was perhaps deliberate if not unavoidable.[85] De Vries has indeed argued that the court's interpretation of the Charter may be 'generating its own meaning' for rights.[86] The UK Government has established a consistent line in negotiations to 'bring an end' to the jurisdiction of the CJEU in Britain post-Brexit[87] and that the EU Charter of Fundamental Rights is not to be incorporated into UK law.[88] The President of the UK Supreme Court has called on Parliament 'to be very clear' in explaining what UK judges are to do with decisions of the CJEU, or any other EU topic, after Brexit indicating that the then EU (Withdrawal) Bill, as it was then, was not fit for purpose.[89]

The lack of attention to the implications for rights protection in the referendum has arguably undermined the requirements of an informed and deliberative referendum process.[90] The discourse did not engage with the vast potential consequences of Brexit on the UK constitutional framework – particularly in relation to the implications for human rights protection.[91]

Prior to the referendum Leanne Cochrane and I noted four areas of major concern in the post-Brexit rights landscape: the loss of citizenship rights; the loss of rights derived from general principles of EU law; the loss of rights derived from EU treaties including the loss of rights derived from the EU Charter of Fundamental Rights; and the loss of rights derived from regulations and directives which engage with human rights either directly or indirectly.[92] Rights

---

84 Lenaerts, n 48 at 375.

85 Ibid. at 399.

86 Sybe de Vries, 'The Protection of Fundamental Rights within Europe's Internal Market after Lisbon – An Endeavour for More Harmony' in Sybe de Vries et al. (eds.), *The Protection of Fundamental Rights in the EU after Lisbon* (Hart, 2013), 71 and 73.

87 Tobias Lock, 'A Role for the ECJ after Brexit?' *European Futures Forum*, 3 July 2017, available at www.europeanfutures.ed.ac.uk/article-4872: citing the Theresa May Lancaster House speech where she promised to 'bring an end to the jurisdiction of the European Court of Justice in Britain'.

88 Department for Exiting the European Union, Legislating for the United Kingdom's withdrawal from the European Union, 2.25 (March 2017).

89 Clive Coleman, *UK judges need clarity after Brexit – Lord Neuberger*, BBC news, 8 August 2017, www.bbc.co.uk/news/uk-40855526 .

90 Boyle and Cochrane, *Brexit and a British Bill of Rights: Four Scenarios for Human Rights* and *Rights Derived from EU Law: Informing the Referendum Process* n 80.

91 See e.g. Sionaidh Douglas-Scott, 'What Happens to "Acquired Rights" in the Event of a Brexit?' U.K. Const. L. Blog, 16 May 2016, available at https://ukconstitutionallaw.org/2016/05/16/sionaidh-douglas-scott-what-happens-to-acquired-rights-in-the-event-of-a-brexit/; Piet Eeckhout, 'The Real Record of the EU Charter of Fundamental Rights', U.K. Const. L. Blog, 6 May 2016, available at https://ukconstitutionallaw.org/2016/05/06/piet-eeckhout-the-real-record-of-the-eu-charter-of-fundamental-rights/

92 For further discussion of these various categories see Boyle and Cochrane, *Rights Derived from EU Law: Informing the Referendum Process* n 80.

deriving from regulations include, for example, rights engaging with the coord-ination of national security systems[93] and the corresponding right to social security.[94] Rights deriving from directives include, by way of example, directives on child sexual abuse,[95] trafficking in human beings,[96] data protection,[97] gender equality in employment[98] and racial equality.[99] The EU Withdrawal Act seeks to retain aspects of EU law and although directives are not directly transposed (section 7(1)), the domestic legislation implementing them can continue to apply. Nonetheless, Parliament will be able to modify retained implementing legislation in ways that would have been inconsistent with (the intentions of) the original directive giving rise to it.[100]

Furthermore, Brexit means that the remedies currently available under EU law for breach of an EU right will also no longer be available in the UK. Remedies include the disapplication of primary law (although note the distinction made in Article 4 of the Withdrawal Agreement).[101] This is a much stronger remedy than available under the Human Rights Act for a violation of an ECHR right.[102] For example, in the *Benkarbouche* case, Ms Benkarbouche and Ms Janah were employed by the Sudanese and Libyan embassies in London. They were dismissed and brought claims against the embassies for unfair dismissal, failure to pay the national minimum wage and breach of the Working Time Regulations 1998. Ms Jannah also claimed racial discrimination and harassment. The embassies sought to claim immunity under the State Immunity Act 1961 – primary legislation which seeks to exclude foreign embassies from domestic rules regarding employment. The Court of Appeal in England[103] (later confirmed by the Supreme Court)[104] found that,

---

93 For example, Regulation (EC) 883/2004 of the European Parliament and of the Council (29 April 2004), on the coordination of national security systems falling within the frame-work of free movement of persons and contributing towards improving their standard of living and conditions of employment.

94 Article 34 of the EU Charter of Fundamental Rights.

95 Directive 2011/92/EU of the European Parliament and of the Council (13 December 2011).

96 Directive 2011/36/EU of the European Parliament and of the Council (5 April 2011).

97 Directive 95/46/EC of the European Parliament and of the Council (24 October 1995).

98 Directive 2006/54/EC of the European Parliament and of the Council (5 July 2006).

99 Council Directive 2000/43/EC (29 June 2000).

100 Graham Cowie, House of Commons Briefing Paper, The status of 'retained EU Law', Number 08375, 30 July 2018.

101 See *R v. Secretary of State for Transport, ex p. Factortame (No 2)* [1991] 1 AC 603 at 658–659, [1990] 3 W.L.R. 818 (appeal taken from Eng. & Wales, reference made to E.C. J.); *Benkharbouche v. Secretary of State for Foreign and Commonwealth Affairs* [2017] UKSC 62, 78, [2017] 3 WLR 957 (on appeal from Eng. & Wales); and *Google Inc v. Vidal-Hall* [2015] EWCA Civ 311, [2016] Q.B. 1003.

102 See '*Hirst*' discussed below – the strongest remedy available under the HRA for an incom-patible primary legislation is a declaration of incompatibility which has no impact on the operative provision.

103 *Benkarbouche v. Embassy of Sudan* [2015] EWCA Civ 33.

104 *Benkharbouche v Secretary of State for Foreign and Commonwealth Affairs* [2017] UKSC 62 (18 October 2017).

amongst other issues, there had been a breach of the Working Time Regulations and anti-discrimination law which fell within the scope of EU law.[105] The UK State Immunity Act 1961 was disapplied in order to grant the applicants an effective remedy.[106] This form of domestication of supranational law allowed the court to offer the most robust remedy available in the UK whereby the court was able to quash primary legislation that breached the rights of the applicants. Without a deal, this type of remedy will be lost on the UK's departure from the EU under the terms of the EU Withdrawal Act and will be a major loss in terms of access to an effective remedy in the domestic context. Under the proposed deal, Article 4 of the draft Withdrawal Agreement envisages that the UK courts will retain the power to disapply some domestic legislation that is incompatible with EU law within the scope of that agreement. These multiple layers of law, or potentially incompatible or competing regimes, make the UK's departure from the EU all the more complex – which, in turn, risks undermining the integrity of the rule of law.

Disentangling the UK from the EU framework whilst also dealing with potential changes to the partially incorporated nature of the European Convention of Human Rights under the Human Rights Act 1998 is an incredibly problematic (if not careless) path for the UK to take without adequate safeguards in place. During the referendum process it became increasingly difficult to ensure that voters had access to the necessary information for an informed vote and this in turn may have had a significant detrimental impact on the deliberative quality of the constitutional referendum process in and of itself.[107] The revelations emerging in relation to Cambridge Analytica and widespread manipulation in both the US election and the UK EU referendum raise serious concerns about whether the electorate had been misinformed, particularly around the impact on rights, to the extent that an informed vote was significantly impeded.[108] There is also a lack of clarity in post-vote negotiation process. It is entirely unclear what kind of post-Brexit rights landscape might exist and whether the UK will indeed continue to protect existing rights and if so to what extent. Inevitably some rights and remedies will be lost irrevocably – others may be protected in the immediate aftermath but could be eroded over time. There will be no obligation on subsequent administrations to retain the same level of protection that the current government might guarantee, unless negotiated as part of a trade agreement. Given the nature of the UK constitution and Parliament's prerogative to repeal this opens the door to regressive measures on fundamental rights across the board.

---

105 See also *Google Inc v. Vidal-Hall* [2015] EWCA Civ 311 for a similar remedy in the disapplication of primary UK law contrary to EU law.

106 Note that the court also employed Article 47 of the Charter and the right to an effective remedy.

107 Boyle and Cochrane, *Brexit and a British Bill of Rights: Four Scenarios for Human Rights* and *Rights Derived from EU Law: Informing the Referendum Process* n 80.

108 Carole Cadwalladr, 'The Cambridge Analytica Files', *The Guardian*, 18 March 2018, available at www.theguardian.com/news/2018/mar/17/data-war-whistleblower-christopher-wylie-faceook-nix-bannon-trump

There is no provision made for the vast array of EU-derived rights in the EU (Withdrawal) Act 2018 and the use of (or abuse of) delegated legislation risks undermining parliamentary oversight even further.[109] The UK constitution facilitates a form of legislation which allows Parliament to pass primary legislation which thereafter enables secondary legislation to be passed by the executive without the need to go through full parliamentary scrutiny. These delegated powers, also known as Henry VIII powers, can undermine parliamentary scrutiny of potential changes to the human rights regime. As mentioned above, the EU (Withdrawal) Act 2018 does not preserve the Charter[110] and emasculates the general principles.[111] Whilst the EU (Withdrawal) Act 2018 places the Human Rights Act 1998 outside the remit of delegated legislation[112] the vast array of rights derived from other sources of EU law is not guaranteed by this exemption. Notably the same exemption is not applied to the Equality Act 2010 which largely implements the EU equality related directives and directly impacts on socio-economic rights.

Nonetheless, the EU human rights framework will most likely retain continuing relevance. As part of the negotiation process the EU may seek to ensure that any future agreement with the UK does not compromise its own human rights standards. This has often formed a prerequisite of negotiation with third country agreements with other countries outside of the EU.[113] It may form part of a prerequisite for future trade negotiations.[114] In the meantime, it has formed a component of the Political Declaration (a commitment to respect the ECHR framework) and the Withdrawal Agreement (where partial rights protection extends in to UK law, to EU citizens in the UK and comes with a commitment of non-diminution of rights in Northern Ireland). Whilst the general ambivalence towards social rights in the EU is noted[115] there is also a need to reflect on the fact the Charter places civil and political rights on the same footing as economic and social rights – even if this equality is more 'apparent than real'.[116] That is not to say the direction of the court may change in the future – particularly with the

---

109 See the evidence session to House of Lords Constitutional Committee, 1 February 2017, available at http://parliamentlive.tv/event/index/75194d6a-b303-436b-8bd8-e4b1dec58b3f
110 Section 5(4).
111 The general principles are no longer a cause of action (Schedule 1 para.3(1)) save a limited three year exemption period (Schedule 8 para.39(5)).
112 Ss.8, 9, Schedule 2 para.12 of the EU (Withdrawal) Act.
113 Lorand Bartels, Human Rights and Democracy Clauses in the EU's International Agreements (European Parliament 2005), available at www.europarl.europa.eu/meetdocs/2004_2009/documents/nt/584/584520/584520en.pdf
114 Joint Committee on Human Rights, the Human Rights Implications of Brexit (2016) HL 88, 9, HC 695 at 9.
115 As discussed by Catherine Barnard, 'The Silence of the Charter: Social Rights and the Court of Justice' in Sybe de Vries et al. (eds.), *The EU Charter of Fundamental Rights as a Binding Instrument – Five Years Old and Growing* (Hart Publishing, 2015), 173.
116 Ibid.

introduction of the EU Social Rights Pillar. The EU may therefore have a role to play in guiding the direction of the UK in terms of upholding existing rights and remedies in so far as it is possible to do so.

The position of the UK signals to the international arena a disregard (if not, a careless approach) towards EU and national citizenship in terms of the domestic enforcement of rights and ensuring their continuation. This position undermines the UK on the global stage as concessions are made to assuage nationalist demands at the expense of global relationships. The UK has been subject to scrutiny by UN bodies concerned about the hate-filled political rhetoric leading the domestic charge against minority groups, which, resulted in a spike in hate crimes around the referendum.[117] In the literature Crawford has highlighted the emerging global trends of states retreating from the global sphere by withdrawing from international treaties such as in the case of Brexit, the US withdrawal from the Paris Agreement and South Africa's purported withdrawal from the Rome Statute.[118] These emerging trends speak to the fragility of international law and the backlash against globalisation.[119] Nonetheless, as Crawford identifies, withdrawal, or a retreat from supranational mechanisms still requires a role for a supranational dispute resolution.[120] In the case of Brexit the rejection of the jurisdiction of the CJEU 'will have to be replaced by something because there will continue to be a collection of rights and regimes that exist to govern relations between the EU and the UK.'[121] The EU Withdrawal Agreement provides recourse to an arbitration mechanism, for example. In this sense, there is simply no way of fully retreating as an actor on the global stage. The UK will continue to be subject to rules and regulations governing its relationship with the EU regardless of what demands are placed domestically.

The conclusion therefore is that the picture is much more complex than a simple repeal and replace scheme. The danger is that the current trajectory risks sleepwalking into a human rights legal deficit with many EU rights swept away with inadvertent measures or deliberate erosion. Much of the Brexit process has overlooked the potential impact that such a loss will have on those rights-holders who are no longer able to seek a remedy for a breach of EU-derived human rights law when this source of law has for decades provided

---

117 UN Doc. CERD/C/GBR/CO/21-23 (2016), at para 15. The UN Committee on the Elimination of Racial Discrimination raised concerns about the spike in hate crimes associated with the referendum noting that the referendum campaign was marked by 'divisive, anti-immigrant and xenophobic rhetoric', and that many politicians and prominent political figures not only failed to condemn such rhetoric, but also created and entrenched prejudices, thereby emboldening individuals to carry out acts of intimidation and hate towards ethnic or ethno-religious minority communities and people who are visibly different.

118 James Crawford, 'The Current Political Discourse Concerning International Law' (2018) 22(1) *Modern Law Review* 1.

119 Ibid. Crawford at 2. See also, e.g. Richard Haass, *A World in Disarray: American Foreign Policy and the Crisis of the Older Order* (Penguin, 2017).

120 Crawford, n 118 at 17.

121 Ibid. Crawford, n 118 at 17.

a constitutional pillar of a domestic rights regime. This is a constitution in transition without the appropriate safeguards.

Repeal of the Human Rights Act 1998

Political and academic discussion on repeal of the Human Rights Act has been notably more muted since the UK Westminster election of June 2017. In 2015 the Cameron Government, elected with a majority, achieved a political mandate for its pledge to 'scrap the [Human Rights Act 1998] and introduce a British Bill of Rights.'[122] Theresa May, a long-time critique of the Act and the European Convention on Human Rights, readily inherited this commitment, and until early 2017 consultation proposals toward that end were awaited.[123] According to the Conservative Party's 2017 Manifesto, which preceded the snap election in June, the UK Government no longer intend to repeal or replace the Human Rights Act 'while the process of Brexit is underway' but promise to 'consider [the] human rights legal framework when the process of leaving the EU concludes'.[124] The political declaration between the UK and EU as part of Brexit negotiations at the very least saw a commitment to the shared values of human rights and fundamental freedom and the UK's commitment to the ECHR.[125]

Whilst this turn of events explains the recent reduction in discussion concerning the potential repeal of the Human Rights Act, criticism of the Act remains an issue of immediate concern. The negativity and oscillation as to the UK's human rights legal framework gives the impression, rightly or wrongly, of a Government intent on undermining the current level of human rights protection. In the very least it is stifling progress as civil society organisations redirect their efforts to maintaining the status quo as opposed to re-imagining a more progressive legal framework.

A core discourse underpinning the proposed repeal of the Human Rights Act is the repatriation of sovereignty (discussed further below as relating to the constitutional resistance to rights in the UK). It is, in fact, an often celebrated

---

122 The Conservative Party Manifesto 2015, at 73. See also, Conservatives, *Protecting Human Rights in the UK – The Conservatives' Proposals For Changing Britain's Human Rights Laws* (2014), available at www.conservatives.com/~/media/files/downloadable%20files/human_rights.pdf

123 See, former Justice Secretary Liz Truss interview, Radio 4, 22 August 2016. It first appeared the proposal to repeal the Human Rights Act would receive a temporary stay in January 2017. See, comments of Sir Oliver Heald, Justice Minister, HC Deb, 24 January 2017, Vol 620, Col 153.

124 The Conservative and Unionist Party Manifesto 2017, at 37.

125 Outline of the Political Declaration Setting Out the Framework for the Future Relationship between the European Union and the United Kingdom, 14 November 2018, available at https://assets.publishing.service.gov.uk/government/uploads/system/uploads/attachment_data/file/756378/14_November_Outline_Political_Declaration_on_the_Future_Relationship.pdf

aspect of the Human Rights Act that it accords structural respect to parliamentary sovereignty, and in turn the will of the UK electorate as expressed through representative democracy. The effort to respect parliamentary sovereignty manifests in particular in how the statute deals with legislation through sections 3 and 4 of the Act.

Section 3 of the Human Rights Act requires courts to interpret legislation in 'so far as it is possible to do so' in a manner compatible with European Convention rights. Where this is not deemed possible, section 4 provides that the courts (High Court and above) can make a 'declaration of incompatibility' between UK primary legislation and the Convention. As such, the legal validity of the primary legislation remains intact, unlike with secondary legislation, which the courts may strike down. This model of rights protection applied by the Act is commonly conceived as a hybrid which sits somewhere between a model which rests all the powers of adjudication in the courts with one where the legislature has the final say on rights matters.[126]

The most detailed account of the criticisms levelled against the Human Rights Act remain to be found in the February 2016 evidence delivered by the then Justice Secretary Michael Gove to the House of Lords EU Committee Inquiry on the proposed repeal and introduction of a new British Bill of Rights.[127] Based on this evidence which contains relatively minor alterations, along with the Minister's comment that human rights have developed 'a bad name in the public square' due to associations with claims by 'unmeritorious individuals' and with 'foreign intervention' on British courts,[128] the EU Committee rightly concluded that the motivations behind repealing the Human Rights Act were directed at ensuring human rights had a greater national identity rather than increasing human rights protection in the UK. The Committee expressed its lack of clarity as to 'why a British Bill of Rights was really necessary', nor was it clear how a British Bill of Rights would address the Justice Secretary's concerns any more than the Human Rights Act.[129]

---

126 The approach of the Act has been said to sit between the political constitutionalism/legal constitutionalism dichotomy and has been called a 'parliamentary bill of rights', 'statutory bill of rights', 'weak-form judicial review' as well as the 'new commonwealth model of constitutionalism'. See, for respective examples, Janet Hiebert and James B. Kelly, *Parliamentary Bills of Rights: The Experiences of New Zealand and the United Kingdom* (Cambridge University Press, 2015); James Allan, 'Statutory Bills of Rights: You Read Words In, You Read Words Out, You Take Parliament's Clear Intention and You Shake It All About – Doin' the Sankey Hanky Panky', in Tom Campbell et al. (eds.), *The Legal Protection of Human Rights: Sceptical Essays* (Oxford University Press, 2011) 108–127; Jeremy Waldron, *Political Theory* (Harvard University Press, 2016); Stephen Gardbaum, *The New Commonwealth Model of Constitutionalism: Theory and Practice* (Cambridge University Press, 2013).

127 For a summary of the Gove evidence, see House of Lords EU Committee, House Of Lords EU Committee, The UK, The EU and a British Bill Of Rights, 2016, HL 139, 46, ch. 3.

128 See Michael Gove evidence, EU Committee, Inquiry into 'The Potential Impact on EU Law of Repealing Human Rights Act', 2 February 2016, Q 79–90.

129 House of Lords EU Committee n 127, at 46 and 49.

Considering the enormity, both in symbolic and constitutional terms, of the action of repealing the Human Rights Act, it might be stressed just how minor the Government's expressed concerns were. The substantive changes suggested by Gove involve three possible clarifications to the law as it stands. First, it was proposed that a British Bill of Rights would ensure that the jurisprudence of the ECtHR is advisory only. Section 2 of the Human Rights Act presently requires that domestic courts 'take into account' relevant Strasbourg jurisprudence and opinion. This requirement was interpreted in 2004 by the House of Lords as a 'mirror' principle: meaning that section 2 was to be read as having placed a 'duty [on] national courts [...] to keep pace with the Strasbourg jurisprudence as it evolves over time: no more, but certainly no less'.[130] The domestic courts have, however, since distanced their approach from this position, interpreting section 2 as instead requiring something more akin to *consideration* of the Strasbourg position.[131] When queried therefore by the Committee on the continuing relevance of this suggestion, the then Justice Secretary expressed a desire to avoid future courts returning to the 'mirror' interpretation.

The second substantive change proposed was a specific derogation from Convention rights in times of war. Derogations from Convention rights are already permitted under Article 15 of the Convention with the proviso that it is 'to the extent strictly required by the exigencies of the situation' and with a blanket prohibition on derogating from certain articles such as those prohibiting torture and slavery. Based on both prior and subsequent Government statements, the underlying desire to derogate is focused on British troops in overseas combat zones and is derived from concerns over the application of extraterritoriality to the Convention by Strasbourg.[132] Yet it is difficult to understand how what has since been espoused as a formal 'presumption to derogate' from the European Convention in times of war, relates or affects the current operation of Article 15.[133] Indeed,

---

130 *R v Special Adjudicator ex p Ullah* [2004] UKHL 26 at 20, [2004] 2 A.C. 323 (appeal taken from Eng. & Wales).

131 For an overview, see Brice Dickson, *Human Rights and the United Kingdom Supreme Court* (Oxford University Press, 2013), 39–43.

132 See, Conservatives (2014) n 122 at 7; Ministry of Defence, 'Government to Protect Armed Forces from Persistent Legal Claims in Future Overseas Operations', *Press Release*, 4 October 2016, available at www.gov.uk/government/news/government-to-protect-armed-forces-from-persistent-legal-claims-in-future-overseas-operations. Note however that Gove's evidence drew potential parallels with the French Government's Convention derogations in the aftermath of the Bataclan tragedy occurring on French soil. For information on that derogation see, Press Release, Council of Europe Secretary General, 25 November 2015, available at www.coe.int/en/web/secretary-general/news-2015/. Article 15(2) ECHR however states: 'No derogation from Article 2, except in respect of deaths resulting from lawful acts of war, or from Articles 3, 4 (paragraph 1) and 7 shall be made under this provision'.

133 Ibid. (Ministry of Defence). Evidence submitted to the Joint Committee on Human Rights Inquiry in 2017 into the proposed derogation can be located at here, www.parliament.uk/business/committees/committees-a-z/joint-select/human-rights-committee/inquiries/parliament-2015/government-proposed-echr-derogation-16-17/

in October 2016 the UK Government formally announced its intention with the qualification that this is 'if possible in the circumstances that exist at that time'.[134] The final substantive clarification expressed in evidence concerned a proposed adjustment of the balance accorded to the qualified rights. This meant, for example, placing more emphasis on freedom of expression than the right to privacy; such modifications were referred to as 'glosses' and said to better mimic the difference in approach between the UK and continental jurisdictions.[135]

Though the headline of the Justice Secretary's evidence was on giving more control to British courts vis-à-vis the Strasbourg court, a significant, if not predominant feature of the proposals, is on giving more control to Parliament.[136] Yet despite a number of earlier creative interpretations under section 3,[137] the practice of the domestic courts is generally considered to be respectful of the doctrine of parliamentary sovereignty. In Dickson's comprehensive review of the UK Supreme Court he refers for example, to the 'sense' that the judiciary prefer to issue incompatibility declarations which do not change the law over section 3 compatible interpretations which would directly contradict the wording of the legislation.[138] On a whole, the judiciary is cognisant of the democratic arguments and so deferential to the views of the legislature. A more curious observation is that Parliament has not, on a whole, been challenging the judicial determination on rights. Since the Human Rights Act came into force in October 2000 until the end of July 2017, the UK Government reports 25 final (i.e. not the subject of further judicial proceedings) declarations of incompatibility issued by UK courts. As of July 2017, of these 25, 20 have been remedied or are in the process of remedy, whilst five are under consideration as to how to remedy.[139] One reason for such a high uptake of judicial recommendations could be the force behind the 'ultimately binding nature' of the Convention, and the availability of the ECtHR as an alternative forum for remedy.[140] Another reason could be the simple fact that the issues raised by the incompatibility declarations relate to matters not initially considered in the development of the legislation and were a result of 'blind spots' in the legislative process (discussed in more detail below).

---

134 Ibid. (Ministry of Defence).
135 House of Lords EU Committee n 127 ch. 3.
136 See e.g. Conservatives (2014) n 122 at 4 (also 6).
137 For a common example, see *Ghaidan* v *Godwin-Mendoza*, [2004] UKHL 30; [2004] 2 AC 557, which gave tenancy rights to unmarried gay couples despite the legislation applying only to married couples.
138 Dickson, n 131 at 376–377. Nor do domestic courts commonly strike down secondary legislation.
139 Ministry of Justice, Responding to Human Rights judgments: Report to the Joint Committee on Human Rights on the Government's response to Human Rights judgments 2016–2017, Annex A (December 2017, Cm 9535), available at www.gov.uk/government/uploads/system/uploads/attachment_data/file/669445/responding__to_human_rights_judgments_2016-17.pdf
140 See, Mark Elliott, 'Beyond the European Convention: Human Rights and the Common Law' (2015) 68 *Current Legal Problems* 85, 111.

One somewhat infamous declaration of incompatibility that had, until recently, remained outstanding with little agreement between the UK Parliament and both the domestic and the ECtHR, concerned the blanket ban on prisoner voting under section 3 of the Representation of the People Act 1983. In *Hirst*[141] the ECtHR determined a blanket ban on prisoner voting rights to be incompatible with the right to vote as protected by Article 3 of Protocol 1 of the Convention. The UK courts have likewise issued a declaration of incompatibility in a series of cases under section 4 of the Human Rights Act.[142] After over a decade of delay, the UK Government has only recently come to an arrangement that the Council of Europe has accepted as addressing the incompatibility. In a fairly limited expansion of voting rights, prisoners under home detention curfew and certain prisoners back in the community on license should soon be able to vote.[143] The prisoner voting issue, which is likely to resolve with the reality of an increase of approximately 100 additional prisoners with voting rights on any given day,[144] portrays a legislature with the capacity to hold a position in opposition to judicial rights rulings should it feel compelled to do so.

The UK Government's Human Rights Act proposals appear then to be directed at increasing parliamentary control of human rights. Yet the above discussion understands the Human Rights Act as structurally respectful of parliamentary sovereignty and in practical terms notes the strength of Parliament should it choose to defy international courts.[145]

Conclusion

Whilst the regional mechanisms offer some form of protection at a domestic level, there are inherent limitations in the structure of both frameworks in adequately addressing ESR in accordance with the principle of indivisibility. Despite their shortcomings, however, they have played important pillars of the UK constitution, essentially providing a constitutional rights framework for citizens beyond the very limited rights available under the common law system together with an uncodified constitution. Brexit presents as hugely problematic for rights protection and the significance of the loss of the Charter and the general principles of EU law creates a seismic gap in the rights and remedies available when violations of rights occur. Likewise, the to and fro on repeal of the Human Rights Act 1998 and seeking to further disassociate with European derived rights frameworks creates a national picture of increasing regression on rights protection.

---

141 *Hirst v the United Kingdom* (No 2) [2005] ECHR 681.
142 See e.g. *Smith v Scott*, [2007] CSIH 9.
143 Ministry of Justice (Cm 9535) n 139 at 44 (Annex A).
144 HC Deb, 30 January 2018, Written Question 124158.
145 For a further discussion and the additional argument that a repeal of the Human Rights Act as proposed will actually 'increase foreign engagement with British "sovereignty" not diminish it' due to the continuing availability of taking a case directly to the Strasbourg court, see Conor Gearty, *On Fantasy Island* (Oxford University Press, 2016) 191.

Ultimately, the regressive processes of Brexit and potential repeal of the Human Rights Act create a rights discourse at the UK level which exhausts civil society in debates on retention of the status quo rather than progressive reform. This discourse has a chilling effect in terms of addressing rights not currently covered by the ECHR, EU law or the common law. In turn, the discourse at the national level sits separately to discussions on rights reform at the devolved level. In the end, this has seen diverging trajectories emerge across the UK where rights protection, enjoyment and enforcement measure differently depending on where you live. There is no coherent or universal human rights framework at play across the UK jurisdictions.

4 The Constitutional Resistance to Human Rights

The UK in a Comparative Context

This chapter examines the particular constitutional framework applicable in the UK and the historical reluctance to afford ESR justiciable status. This examination reveals that competing conceptualisations of constitutionalism exist in the UK and that this directly impacts on the devolved regions where commitments to human rights are undermined at the national level. This examination is also placed within a broader analysis of other constitutional models and ESR adjudication in practice in order to set out examples of what is constitutionally and judicially possible in the context of ESR justiciability. Whilst there is no panacea, the chapter concludes by demonstrating that ESR justiciability is possible, it happens elsewhere and it can occur with appropriate safeguards to ensure the separation of powers remains intact. The UK can learn from alternative models both comparatively (other countries) and domestically (devolved jurisdictions). Critically, this chapter questions whether or not the current constitutional arrangements in the UK are fit for purpose.

Constitutional Protection of Fundamental Rights

The UK constitution is uncodified. Dicey delivered the orthodox exposition on the principle of parliamentary sovereignty when he defined it to mean that Parliament has 'the right to make or unmake any law whatever; and further, that no person or body is recognised by the law [...] as having the right to override or set aside the legislation of Parliament'.[1] Traditionally, protection of fundamental rights in the UK was assigned to rights protected in legislation or through those developed in the common law. Prior to the enactment of the Human Rights Act 1998 the courts had developed a plethora of quasi-constitutional rights.[2]

---

1 Albert Venn Dicey, *An Introduction to the Study of the Law of the Constitution* (10th ed., Macmillan, 1965), 40.
2 'the common law was more and more inclined to give autonomous recognition to the notion of constitutional rights' R (Beeson) v Dorset County Council [2002] EWCA Civ 1812 [2003] UKHRR 353 [at 18].

The common law has also traditionally afforded legislative supremacy to Parliament,[3] meaning that where a provision of legislation derogated from a [quasi-constitutional] right the legislation would take precedence in accordance with the doctrine of parliamentary sovereignty. This constitutional theoretical framework is based on a Diceyan view of foundational sovereignty. Murray Hunt has elaborated on this concept in distinguishing two polarised frameworks through which sovereignty can be understood. The first adheres to legal positivism and is described by Hunt as amounting to a democratic positivist perspective – 'viewing a formalistic notion of the separation of powers and romantic attachment to the idea of parliamentary sovereignty'[4] (i.e. the Diceyan view). The second is identified as liberal constitutionalism, which supports a more prominent role for the judiciary and the 'priority of fundamental rights and the sovereignty of court'.[5] This dichotomy engages with competing concepts of constitutionalism in the UK at the devolved and national level (legal v political). Both polarised frameworks paradoxically co-exist in the UK constitution, with either approach being cited by the judiciary to justify a decision.[6] Since the EU referendum Douglas-Scott has identified a third competing concept at play, that of popular sovereignty.[7] Matters are complicated further by the co-existence of competing narratives of constitutionalism in itself in addition to the polarised concepts of sovereignty. The UK constitution, Loughlin concludes, is in crisis.[8] The EU referendum has brought this to the fore with Gordon arguing that the referendum on EU membership directly challenged the British style of constitutionalism.[9] And against the backdrop of contemporary constitutionalism (and its fluctuating state) we can see what Loughlin determined was the rejection of not one, but multiple forms of the constitution.[10]

Feldman has highlighted opposing concepts of constitutionalism as falling into two major categories. The first is placed in a process model, whereby

---

3 *R v Lord Chancellor, ex p Witham* [1998] QB 575, 581E, per Laws J.
4 Murray Hunt, 'Reshaping Constitutionalism' in John Morison et al. (eds.), *Judges, Transitions and Human Rights* (Oxford University Press, 2007), 468.
5 Ibid.
6 Ibid., 468–469, see dicta of Lord Hoffman for example adopting different approaches in *Secretary of State for the Home Department, Ex Parte Simms Secretary of State for the Home Department, Ex Parte O'Brien*, R v [1999] UKHL 33; [2000] 2 AC 115; [1999] 3 All ER 400; [1999] 3 WLR 328 (8 July 1999) and *Secretary of State for the Home Department v Rehman* [2001] UKHL 47.
7 Sionaidh Douglas-Scott, 'Brexit, Article 50 and the Contested Constitution' (2016) 79 *Modern Law Review* 1019–1040.
8 Martin Loughlin, 'The End of Avoidance: Martin Loughlin on the UK's Constitutional Crisis' *London Review of Books*, 28 July 2016.
9 Michael Gordon, 'Brexit: A Challenge for the UK Constitution, of the UK Constitution?' (2016) 12 *European Constitutional Law Review* 409–444.
10 Loughlin, n 8 argues that the EU referendum is a challenge to a Hobbesian tradition of Queen in Parliament, a rejection of cosmopolitan constitutionalism and the globalisation of a market-orientated constitution and a challenge to the unique and separate constitutional identities of both Scotland (as a devolved entity seeking independence) and Northern Ireland (as a devolved entity subject to an international peace agreement).

constitutional legitimacy is ensured through democratic processes and this in turn engenders legitimacy. The second is placed within a framework model, whereby legitimacy is ensured through the state conforming to a framework that places limitations on all actors exercising state authority, these limitations are generally concerned with a pre-negotiated, pre-committed set of norms – including recognition of human rights norms.[11] The first of these concepts aligns with political constitutionalism and the latter with legal constitutionalism.

Combining Hunt and Feldman's models of sovereignty and constitutionalism it could be said that the UK falls within a democratic positivist process model. Pre-devolution Craig described the constitutional arrangement in the UK as a 'unitary, self-correcting democracy'[12] in so far as legitimacy is ensured through democratic processes (as opposed to pre-committed limitations) and parliamentary sovereignty is afforded unlimited discretion without having to abide by a framework of limitations. However, with the implementation of devolution a new form of constitutional arrangement has emerged that is quite different. In Northern Ireland for example, the peace agreement, subject to approval by the *demos* through the exercise of direct democracy (i.e. approved by referendum), places limitations on the constitutional framework. Morison and Lynch have argued that the Northern Ireland settlement therefore sits outside of the Westminster model of democracy as the settlement is conditioned by a pre-commitment to non-negotiable fundamental norms such as equality and human rights.[13] Both Wales and Scotland also pertain to a framework of limitations. The devolved constitutional arrangements follow a framework model (pertaining to a foundation) and at the UK level the constitution follows a process model (pertaining to fair processes). This can cause constitutional incoherence when engaging with models of rights enforcement.

Traditionally, the notion of sovereignty in the UK has pertained to an English understanding of the concept.[14] This notion is conceptualised in accordance with

---

11 Feldman cites the example of *Grundgesetz* or Basic Norm of the 1949 Constitution for the Federal Republic of Germany and the Constitution of Bosnia and Herzegovina, Article X.2 of which provides 'Human Rights and Fundamental Freedoms. No amendment to this Constitution may eliminate or diminish any of the rights and freedoms referred to in Article II of this Constitution or alter the present paragraph' creating a framework in which fundamental human rights norms are foundational, non-derogable and beyond the reach of retrogressive legislative measures. In other words, they hold constitutional status. David Feldman, 'Constitutionalism, Deliberative Democracy and Human Rights' in John Morison et al. (eds.), n 4 at 447–453.

12 Paul Craig, *Public Law and Democracy in the United Kingdom and the United States of America* (Oxford University Press, 1991), Chapter 2.

13 John Morison and Marie Lynch, 'Litigating the Agreement: Towards a New Judicial Constitutionalism for the UK from Northern Ireland', in John Morison et al. (eds.), n 4 at 142.

14 See, for example, the competing sovereign ideologies emerging between Scotland and England based on inherently different understandings of sovereignty – The applicability of the English concept of sovereignty in Scotland was challenged in *MacCormick v Lord Advocate* 1953 SC 396 where the Lord President held that 'the principle of unlimited sovereignty of Parliament is a distinctively English principle and has no counterpart in Scottish constitutional law.' See also *Gibson v Lord Advocate* 1975 SC 136 and *Jackson v Attorney General*, [2005] 3 WLR 733.

the strictest interpretation of the doctrine of parliamentary sovereignty resting on the concept of the 'Queen in Parliament'. As per Lord Scott in *R (Hooper)*, '[t]here are not, under English domestic law, any fundamental constitutional rights that are immune from legislative change'.[15] There is an emerging theoretical tension in the UK between parliamentary and judicial 'supremacists'.[16] In accordance with each of the constitutional models proposed above, the role of the judiciary differs according to the role conferred on it – i.e. either responsible for ensuring fair process under the process model (political constitutionalism), or, responsible for ensuring fundamental norms, in accordance with the framework model (legal constitutionalism). The Westminster model is process-based and the democratic positivist narrative means that Parliament remains 'the supreme law-giver in our constitutional arrangements and is therefore the final arbiter of the meaning of ... rights, and can exercise its sovereignty by defining what those rights mean in particular contexts'.[17] As Ekins submits:

> [t]he traditional account of the Westminster constitution ... is that Parliament has substantively unlimited legislative power, and no person or body can dispute the legal validity of its enactments. The rule is the foundation of legal reasoning and enables identification of law without moral reasoning. Within this paradigm, it is illegitimate for judges to use principles of political morality to undermine the authority of Parliament. If this traditional account is true then the argument for judicial supremacy, which is directly inconsistent with the Westminster constitution's rule of recognition, cannot succeed as a legal argument'.[18]

The alternative theory is founded on the constitutional recognition of fundamental rights (i.e. Feldman's framework model). The liberal constitutionalist views the courts as the final arbiter on whether a right is being violated as they are the 'guardians of inviolability into which public authorities cannot step'.[19] Rather than view judicial supremacy as imposing or usurping the sovereignty of Parliament, the case for a substantive rights-based conception of the rule of law binds both the legislature and the judiciary to a set of fundamental principles from which neither can derogate unless justified. This model requires compliance with substantive norms, as well as fair processes.

The Westminster model most certainly falls within the confines of the parliamentary supremacy paradigm and, without a written constitution or Bill of Rights offering justiciable remedies, will most likely there remain. Indeed, post-EU

---

15 *R (Hooper) v Secretary of State for Work and Pensions* [2005] UKHL 29 [2005] 1 WLR 1681 at [92].

16 Richard Ekins, 'Judicial Supremacy and the Rule of Law' (2003) Jan *Law Quarterly Review* 119, 127.

17 Hunt, n 4 at 468.

18 Ekins, n 16 at 135.

19 Hunt, n 4 at 469.

referendum the threat of a third constitutional model emerges in what is now perceived as an executive driven formation of the rule of law evident in the sweeping
powers afforded to the executive under the EU Withdrawal Act and the extra-
ordinary exercise of prerogative power to prorogue (suspend) Parliament
unlawfully.[20]

Even the strictest interpretation of the rule of law and the doctrine of parliamentary supremacy cannot ignore that certain limitations are already placed on the sovereignty of parliament in the UK in relation to human rights protections (even if
these limitations were self-imposed). Turning first to the role of human rights, the
Human Rights Act 1998 at the very least allows for the courts, including
a supranational court, to determine whether Acts of the UK Parliament are incompatible with the ECHR (although the declaration has no effect on the operation of
the legislation). The *Hirst*[21] case, discussed above, is an example where there has
been a clear determination that a blanket ban on prisoner voting contravenes Article 3 Protocol 1 of the Convention. This facilitates an acknowledgement that the
Representation of the People's Act 1983 was incompatible but there was no substantive change in the application of the law as a result (i.e. parliamentary supremacy prevails until parliament changes the law). In an unusual twist, the UK
Government sought to address the judgment through administrative measures to
allow those released on a temporary licence to vote and suggested that these measures would be 'the best approach to credibly, effectively and swiftly address the
Hirst group of cases'.[22] The Committee of Ministers responsible for supervising
execution of ECHR judgments, has since noted its satisfaction at this result given
the reluctance of parliament to produce broader legislative change and the wide
margin of appreciation in the area.[23] Turning second to the role of EU law, until
the UK departs fully from the EU legal order then the doctrine of parliamentary
supremacy may continue to be subject to the primacy of EU law as evident in Article
4 of the Withdrawal Agreement. The case of *Factortame*[24] is indicative of how
domestic legislation can cease to have effect if it is incompatible with EU law. This is
a much stronger remedy than the declaration of incompatibility available under the
Human Rights Act 1998. There is therefore a precedent within the constitutional
makeup of the UK to limit parliamentary supremacy, or to limit the sovereignty of

---

20 See Stephen Tierney, 'The Legislative Supremacy of Government', U.K. Const. L. Blog
   (3 July 2018), available at https://ukconstitutionallaw.org/ on the former, and *Miller,
   R (on the application of) v The Prime Minister* [2019] UKSC 41 (24 September 2019) in
   relation to the latter.
21 *Hirst v the United Kingdom* (No 2) [2005] ECHR 681.
22 UK Action Plan November 2017, Communication from the United Kingdom concerning
   the case of Hirst (No. 2) v. the United Kingdom (Application No. 74025/01), para.10.
23 Council of Ministers and Secretariat of the Council of Ministers, 1302nd meeting,
   5–7 December 2017 (DH), Human rights H46-39 *Hirst No. 2 group v the United Kingdom*
   (Application No. 74025/01), Supervision of the execution of the European Court's
   judgments, CM/Notes/1302/H46-39. Note, the administrative changes apply to England
   and Wales. Scotland and Northern Ireland will require separate measures.
24 *Factortame (No 2)* [1991] 1 AC 603, 658–659.

parliament, to some extent, even if only temporarily.[25] This type of limitation can be understood as a 'self-regulatory' mechanism that can be repealed at a later date.

Hunt has noted that the constitutional flux between democratic positivism and liberal constitutionalism means that the UK lacks an overarching coherent vision of democratic constitutionalism and that this stagnates a proper understanding of what constitutional arrangements currently exist, or ought to exist. In this respect, Hunt points out that 'so long as we are dependent on crude notions of sovereignty and authority for our underlying conceptions of law and legality, our public law will remain condemned to this perpetual lurching between democratic positivism and liberal constitutionalism'.[26] Hence, the status of human rights is very difficult to determine definitively as there is no tangible backdrop that applies across the UK in the same way. Even the enforceability of the ECHR through the Human Rights Act 1998 and the Scotland Act 1998 takes on different forms depending on the primary or subordinate nature of the legislature (i.e. Westminster v devolved legislature).

Statutes of a 'Constitutional Nature'

The status of statutes of a 'constitutional nature' are exempt from the doctrine of implied repeal whereby any amendment to the nature of the rights in the statute can only be altered by explicit unambiguous words of the later statute. As per Lord Justice Laws, in the case of *Thoburn v Sunderland City Council*:[27]

> In the present state of its maturity the common law has come to recognise that there exist rights which should properly be classified as constitutional or fundamental [...] And from this a further insight follows. We should recognise a hierarchy of Acts of Parliament: as it were "ordinary" statutes and "constitutional" statutes. The two categories must be distinguished on a principled basis. In my opinion a constitutional statute is one which (a) conditions the legal relationship between citizen and state in some general, overarching manner, or (b) enlarges or diminishes the scope of what we would now regard as fundamental constitutional rights. (a) and (b) are of necessity closely related: it is difficult to think of an instance of (a) that is not also an instance of (b).[28]

---

25 See also *Costa v. ENEL* (1964) Case 6/64 '... the Members states have limited their sovereign rights and thus have created a body of law which binds both their nationals and themselves.' para.3; and *Van Gend en Loos v Nederlandse Administratie der Belastingen* (1963) Case 26/62 'the Community constitutes a new legal order of international law for the benefit of which the states have limited their sovereign rights, albeit within limited fields and the subjects of which comprise not only the Member States but also their nationals.' para.3.

26 Hunt, n 4 at 469.

27 *Thoburn v Sunderland City Council* [2002] QB 151.

28 Ibid. at 62.

Laws LJ identified the Magna Carta, the Bill of Rights 1689, the Acts of Union 1707, the Reform Acts, the Human Rights Act 1998, the Scotland Act 1998, the Government of Wales Act 1998 and the European Communities Act 1972 as constitutional statutes. The Northern Ireland Act 1998 also falls within the constitutional statute category, even more so because of its political framework, whereby its provisions enacted obligations set forth in the peace agreement. In *Robinson v Secretary of State for Northern Ireland*,[29] the House of Lords ruled that the Northern Ireland Act is a 'constitutional statute' that should be interpreted 'purposively and generously' in order to support its constitutional nature.[30] The recognition of constitutional statutes is being gradually recrafted into a more general focus on 'constitutional principle(s)'[31] or the 'constitutional character' of a particular provision.[32]

The reluctance or resistance to acknowledge fundamental, or constitutional rights, in the UK is firmly placed against the backdrop of parliamentary sovereignty and the doctrine of implied repeal – i.e. that no parliament can bind its successor. However, there is a growing school of thought that recognises the role of fundamental rights in reaffirming democratic legitimacy in a modern democracy (Feldman's framework model and Hunt's liberal constitutionalism). Koch and Vedsted-Hansen argue for a concept of democratic legitimacy complemented by human rights protections:

> this line of reasoning is based on a qualified concept of democracy which perceives democratic legitimacy as not exclusively stemming from popular support and majoritarian decision-making, but also including the protection of individual and collective rights and freedoms, not least those of minorities and political opponents of the ruling majority. Thus, defending human rights as a conceptual element of democracy is logically connected to the foundation of international human rights law as norms and principles

---

29 *Robinson v Secretary of State for Northern Ireland* [2002] UKHL 32.

30 Adam Tomkins has argued that the judiciary are moving away from the definition of constitutional statutes in recent jurisprudence such as *Imperial Tobacco* [2012] UKSC 61 (in relation to the Scotland Act 1998) and the *Welsh Byelaws* case referred by the Attorney General [2012] UKSC 53 (in relation to the Government of Wales Act 2006). Tomkins notes however, that even although the Supreme Court is arguably moving away from the constitutional status of such Acts as being different to any other Act of the UK Parliament, the political context of the Northern Ireland Act affords a more generous interpretation in favour of a constitutional statute. For further discussion see Adam Tomkins, *The emergence of a devolution jurisprudence?* March 2013, available at http://britgovcon.wordpress.com/

31 *R (HS2 Action Alliance Ltd) v Secretary of State for Transport*, [2014] UKSC 3, at 79, [2014] 1 W.L.R. 324 (appeal taken from Eng. & Wales).

32 *R (Miller) v Secretary of State for Exiting the European Union*, [2017] UKSC 5, [2017] 2 W. L.R., at 67. See also, Lord Neuberger's reluctance to comment on whether the Government of Wales Act 2006 should be approached as a constitutional enactment in the reference *Local Government Byelaws (Wales) Bill 2012 – Reference* [2012] UKSC 53 at 69, [2013] 1 A.C. 792 (AG reference under section 112 of the Government of Wales Act 2006).

restraining the sovereign powers of governments and legislatures, based on the tragic experience of those holding domestic powers.[33]

International human rights law can act as a normative frame of reference, and/or legally binding, framework that can provide constitutional stability to domestic states lacking in fundamental human rights protection. An unwritten constitution, or a constitution that does not fully provide protection for constitutional or fundamental rights, renders the protection of human rights in a precarious position. This is the current position in the UK. The application of international norms therefore become all the more important. Bingham has argued that that fundamental human rights must feature in a substantive and 'thick' conception of the rule of law in the UK.[34]

So how can the competing perspectives on sovereignty, constitutionalism and the role of the judiciary be reconciled given the wide discrepancies across the UK on how each of these pillars of democracy are understood? It is proposed that the deliberative democracy model can assist in understanding how this process might work. For example, Sunstein has argued for a liberal constitutionalist framework model through a deliberative democracy paradigm.[35] Under this model, judges play an important role in facilitating deliberation as part of an overall democratic process that opens the deliberative process to the public. Feldman explains that this model operates through control of the people, or *demos* (vested in elected representatives who exercise control on their behalf) who participate as a body of politically active citizens engaged with a responsive legislature and executive, accompanied by the time and space for dialogue (between institutions and within institutions) during which deliberation can occur.[36] Tierney submits that this can occur at both the micro or macro level.[37] Deliberative democracy at the micro level would include mechanisms such as referendums – a direct exercise of sovereignty, whereas deliberative democracy at the macro level, or elite deliberative democracy, operates between institutions (between the court, parliament and executive). Hunt has argued for a 'culture of justification' to permeate the democratic dialogue between the legislature, the executive and the judiciary.[38] In this sense creating an opportunity to transparently scrutinise human rights compliance within a deliberative democracy framework. Through a culture of justification the court can act as a forum where

---

33 Ida Elisabeth Koch and Jens Vedsted-Hansen, 'International Human Rights and National Legislatures – Conflict or Balance?' (2006) 75 *Nordic Journal of International Law* 3.

34 Tom Bingham, *The Rule of Law* (Penguin Books, 2011), Chapter 7. Note however, wider criticisms that a fully substantive approach to the rule of law 'rob[s] the concept of any function which is independent of the theory of justice which imbues such an account of law', Paul Craig, 'Formal and Substantive Conceptions of the Rule of Law: An Analytical Framework' (1997) Autumn *Public Law* 467 at 487.

35 Cass Sunstein, *Designing Democracy: What Constitutions Do* (Oxford and New York: Oxford University Press, 2001).

36 Feldman, n 11 at 458.

37 Stephen Tierney, *Constitutional Republicanism* (Oxford University Press, 2012), 3–4.

38 Hunt, n 4 at 470.

actions are justified if an alleged human rights breach occurs. Extending this deliberative framework to ESR would facilitate a democratically accountable judicial mechanism that opens scrutiny of ESR compliance to the public and allows the state the opportunity to justify any alleged interference.

ESR Constitutionalisation in Practice

The question of whether to constitutionalise or incorporate human rights, or ESR more specifically, has been the subject of constitutional debates beyond the context of UK.[39] Other common law jurisdictions with uncodified constitutions have constitutionalised human rights, such as Canada[40] and New Zealand.[41] The Constitutional Advisory Panel in New Zealand recommended exploring the possibility of extending human rights protection by constitutionalising ESR and granting the courts power to assess legislative compliance with the rights[42] and the jurisprudence of the Canadian Supreme Court has in some cases extended the protection of human rights to unenumerated ESR under the Constitution's equality provision.[43] States with codified constitutions have also enshrined, or are considering enshrining, ESR. The Finnish Constitution[44] which came into force in 2000 strengthened the protection of ESR subject to potential judicial review if the state fails to comply – scarcely exercised in practice.[45] The Constitutional Convention in Ireland voted in favour (85% of the

---

39 For a fuller discussion on the different constitutional movements, constitutional enumeration of ESR and ESR constitutional adjudication see Jeff King, *Judging Social Rights* (Cambridge University Press, 2011) and Malcolm Langford, 'Domestic Adjudication and Economic, Social and Cultural Rights: A Socio-Legal Review' (2009) 6 *International Journal on Human Rights* 11. The 1917 Mexican Constitution pioneered ESR constitutionalisation and preceded the Weimar Constitution of 1919. Globally countries undergoing processes of constitutional transition have embraced ESR dimensions ever since.

40 For example, the Canadian model that is based on the Westminster system without a codified constitution but with a constitutional statute, the Constitution Act 1982, which defines the Constitution and incorporates the Charter of Rights and Fundamental Freedoms into the Constitution (this Charter has since been interpreted to extend protection to some ESR under the rubric of the equality provision).

41 New Zealand follows a similar model to the UK through the enactment of a human rights statute subject to parliamentary repeal, the Bill of Rights Act 1990 (NZBORA) and the New Zealand Human Rights Act 1993.

42 Report on a Conversation; He Kōtuinga Kōrero mō, Te Kaupapa Ture o Aotearoa,' November 2013, available at www.ourconstitution.org.nz/store/doc/FR_Full_Report.pdf – the government has since indicated to the UN CESCR that it has no intention to implement this recommendation at this time, Committee on Economic, Social and Cultural Rights, Fourth periodic report submitted by New Zealand under articles 16 and 17 of the Covenant, due in 2017, 6 October 2017, E/C.12/NZL/4.

43 See, for example, *Eldridge v British Columbia (Attorney General)* [1997] 2 SCR 624 (requiring interpretation services in hospitals for the hearing impaired).

44 The Constitution of Finland, 11 June 1999, 731/1999, see in particular Article 19 the right to social security.

45 Kaarlo Tuori, 'Rights Democracy and Local Self-governance: Social Rights in the Constitution of Finland' (2007) 13 *Juridica International* 70–73.

Convention) of strengthening the protection of ESR in the Irish Constitution.[46] The Constitutional Convention in Ireland was a citizen-based initiative that considered potential constitutional change in Ireland. Its membership consisted of 66 randomly selected citizens, 33 politicians from both Houses of the Oireachtas and the Northern Ireland Assembly and an independent chair. The Convention voted in favour of inserting a new provision in the Constitution 'that the state shall progressively realise ESR, subject to maximum available resources and that this duty is cognisable by the Courts'.[47] In Norway the Parliament passed legislation that incorporated the International Covenant on Economic, Social and Cultural Rights, the UN Convention on the Rights of the Child, the International Covenant on Civil and Political Rights, the European Convention of Human Rights and the UN Convention on the Elimination of All Forms of Discrimination Against Women into domestic law under the Human Rights Act 1999. The international treaties will prevail when in conflict with domestic law. These movements are indicative of a general constitutional trend where ESR feature more prominently in constitutional renewal processes across many different legal systems.[48]

The difficulty faced in creating justiciable constitutional rights begins at the constitutional drafting stage when the separation of powers between the legislative, executive and judicial organs of the state requires elaboration within the constitution itself. There are numerous models upon which a constitution can be based. Tuori has placed constitutional models on a scale moving from parliamentary supremacy to judicial supremacy, with hybrid models as potential solutions in between these dichotomous approaches.[49] Creating constitutional ESR

---

46 As part of this recommendation there was strong support for the better protection of rights relating to housing (84% in favour); social security (78%); essential health care (87%); rights of people with disabilities (90%); linguistic and cultural rights (75%); and rights covered in the International Covenant on Economic, Social and Cultural Rights (80%), Constitutional Convention Press Release 23 February 2014, 'Constitutional Convention votes in favour of reforming economic, social and cultural rights in the Constitution, 85 % of members say Constitution should be amended to strengthen the protection of Economic, Social and Cultural rights', available at www.constitution.ie/AttachmentDownload.ashx?mid=adc4c56a-a09c-e311-a7ce-005056a32ee4

47 Ibid. The author made representations to the Constitutional Convention on the inclusion of ESR in the Irish Constitution: Katie Boyle, 'An Explanation of the Legal Arguments for the Inclusion of Economic, Social and Cultural Rights in the Constitution', August 2013, available at www.constitution.ie/SubmissionDetails.aspx?sid=8e2111f2-5e03-e311-a5a0-005056a32ee4 . See also Katie Boyle, 'Economic, Social and Cultural Rights – Why the Constitution?', *Human Rights in Ireland*, February 2014, available at http://humanrights.ie/constitution-of-ireland/economic-social-and-cultural-rights-in-ireland-why-the-constitution/ and Katie Boyle, 'Economic, Social and Cultural Rights in Ireland: Models of Constitutionalisation' (2015) 3(1) *Irish Community Development Law Journal* 33–48.

48 For a historical contextualisation of this trend see Colm O'Cinneide, 'The Constitutionalisation of Social and Economic Rights' in Helena Garcia et al. (eds.), *Social and Economic Rights in Theory and Practice, Critical Inquiries* (Routledge, 2015), 258–277 at 268 .

49 Tuori identifies the German model as the archetypal model of judicial supremacy and the UK model as the archetypal model of parliamentary supremacy. The Finnish model he argues is a hybrid model seeking to balance parliamentary and judicial authority through an *ex ante*

can be further complicated by the risk of what Tuori sees as the potential politicisation of adjudication and the potential juridification of politics, with too much power being assigned to the judiciary on matters that relate to the allocation of limited resources at the state's disposal and potential over-prescriptive constitutional provisions that essentially remove political decisions from the legislature that have already been determined at the constitutional level:

> [ESR] can easily be interpreted as symptoms of an excessive constitutionalisation of the legal order and of a development toward the so-called judicial state. Such a development involves – in a rather paradoxical way – the risk of both a politicisation of adjudication and a juridification of politics: a politicisation of adjudication in the sense that courts take a position on issues of a political nature that should be left to the domain of political decision-making in the Parliament and the government and a juridification of politics in the sense that legislative activities are increasingly seen as a specification and implementation of decisions already made at the constitutional level.[50]

There are, of course, risks associated with constitutionalising ESR and so those states that have undergone the process have attempted to introduce safeguards to ensure that constitutional adjudication does not usurp the powers of the executive or the legislature unless it is justifiable to do so. Constitutional models that incorporate ESR tend to lean towards either legislative or judicial supremacy in a balancing act.

Parliamentary Model

In Finland, there is a hybrid constitutional model in place with safeguards ensured through ex ante (pre-legislative) parliamentary scrutiny of potential legislation and potential ex post (post-legislative) judicial review of enacted legislation as a means of last resort.[51] The Constitutional Law Committee of Parliament in Finland performs ex ante review of legislation prior to enactment. The Committee consists of Members of Parliament, however, its decisions are largely based on the deliberations of constitutional experts from whom the committee seeks evidence.[52] What is more, the reports of the Committee tend to be legally, rather than politically, focused.[53] The decision of the Committee on the

---

legislative scrutiny process and a *ex post* judicial scrutiny mechanism as a means of last resort, Kaarlo Tuori, 'Chapter 18, Judicial Constitutional Review as a Last Resort' in Tom Campbell et al. (eds.), *The Legal Protection of Human Rights: Sceptical Essays* (Oxford University Press, 2011), 365–392.

50 Tuori, n 45 at 71.

51 Tuori, n 49 at 365. I am also grateful to Toomas Kotkas, Professor of Jurisprudence and Social Law at the University of Eastern Finland, for his generosity in explaining how the Finnish system operates over the course of our discussions. Any errors remain my own.

52 Ibid. at 380.

53 Ibid.

compatibility of legislation with constitutional rights, including ESR, is binding on Parliament.[54] The ex ante review of a bill secures a strong degree of constitutional compatibility *in abstracto* following which, the court is authorised to remedy any conflict with the Constitution on a case-by-case basis if a contradiction arises.[55] The ex post judicial review of incompatible legislation takes on a relatively weak form of judicial review in the Finnish system.[56]

The responsibility for enforcing constitutional ESR is directed at the legislature: the right to citizenship (Article 5); the right to equality before the law (Article 6); educational rights (Article 16); the right to language and culture (Article 17); the right to work (Article 18) and the right to social security (Article 19) must all be given effect to through subsequent legislation.[57] The constitutional mandate to fulfil the ESR obligations is therefore directly addressed to the legislature. In this sense, the constitution imposes a mandatory obligation on the legislature to legislate for the protection and fulfilment of ESR. This model is therefore consonant with the doctrine of parliamentary supremacy but with the caveat that if the legislature fails to meet its constitutional obligations the court can intervene. In Finland, the ability of the court to intervene is a relatively new construct introduced with the change in constitution in 2000. In Sweden, a similar pre-enactment preview process is in place. Thomas Bull has argued that this type of ex ante review of legislation through the Parliamentary system makes it difficult (although not impossible) to legislate in a way that infringes fundamental rights.[58] Notably, judicial recourse in Sweden, Finland and Denmark has not been employed frequently as a form of constitutional review.[59] This, Hirschl and Rosevear argue, demonstrates that a long-standing tradition of constitutional rights and judicial review is not a necessary condition for high levels of human development.[60] Nonetheless – the *ex ante* review of legislation at least provides a rights-affirmative framework in which legislation is passed.

---

54 Ibid.
55 The primacy of the Constitution is protected under section 106 which stipulates that 'if in a matter being tried by a court of law, the application of an Act would be in evident conflict with the Constitution, the court of law shall give primacy to the provision in the Constitution'. However, Tuori also points out that, similar to the operation of the section 33 Canadian declaration (the 'notwithstanding' clause), the Finnish Parliament can enact a 'statute of exception' whereby a bill which the Committee has found to be unconstitutional can still be enacted under the qualified procedure required for amending the Constitution, Tuori, ibid. at 381.
56 Juha Lavapuro, Tuomas Ojanen and Martin Scheinin, 'Rights-based Constitutionalism in Finland and the Development of Pluralist Constitutional Review' (2011) 9(2) *International Journal of Constitutional Law* 505–531. Lavapuro et al. point out that the travaux préparatoires to section 106 acknowledges only a limited role for the court in reviewing the constitutionality of legislation.
57 The constitutional provisions stipulate that rights will be guaranteed by being 'provided by an Act'.
58 Thomas Bull, 'Judges without a Court – Judicial Preview in Sweden' in Campbell et al. (eds.), n 49 at 393.
59 Ran Hirschl and Evan Rosevear, 'Constitutional Law Meets Comparative Politics: Socioeconomic Rights and Political Realities' in Campbell et al. (eds.), n 49 at 213.
60 Ibid.

In the UK parliament the Joint Committee on Human Rights (JCHR) can assess proposed legislation for its compatibility with human rights.[61] Within the UK Parliamentary system the JCHR considers the compatibility of legislation with international human rights, including ESR, along the respect, protect, fulfil axis.[62] The JCHR scrutinises legislation before enactment in terms of human rights compatibility and make recommendations to parliament on its conclusions. The recommendations of the JCHR are not binding on the legislature and so the work of the committee acts as a review system differing from the Finish model. What is more, there is no constitutional footing for ESR, meaning the assessment of legislative provisions against compatibility with ICESCR for example is informative, but by no means necessarily persuasive, given the constitutional reluctance to acknowledge ESR as legal rights.[63] Because the recommendations of the JCHR are not binding on the UK Parliament any ex ante review of legislation does not impact on the passing of legislation, other than as a means of informing the process.

On the justiciability of ESR the JCHR has recommended partial judicial recognition in line with the obligation to progressively achieve the rights, however, there has been no transformation of the role of the judiciary based on this recommendation.[64] Whilst the JCHR has been able to make some incremental changes in informing the consideration of legislation by Parliament in relation to human rights, it lacks status to some extent as it does not share the same relationship with the UK Parliament as for example the Finnish Committee shares with the Finnish Parliament. For example, in the passing of the Welfare Reform Act 2012 the JCHR raised significant concerns about the impact on vulnerable groups, disproportionate discrimination and the infringement of ESR.[65] The consequent adjudication in the Supreme Court revealed similar

---

61 For a discussion on the role of the Joint Committee on Human Rights in the UK Parliament see Murray Hunt, 'Enhancing Parliament's Role in Relation to Economic and Social Rights' (2010) 3 *European Human Rights Law Review* 242. See also David Feldman, 'Can and Should Parliament Protect Human Rights?' (2004) 10 *European Public Law* 635 at 642. This is also reflected in the Cabinet Office's Guide to Making Legislation (May 2009) which advises departments that: 'The JCHR may also ask about compliance with any international human rights instrument which the United Kingdom has ratified; it does not regard itself as limited to the ECHR' at para.12.32.

62 Hunt, ibid. at 242.

63 As discussed earlier in this chapter.

64 Hunt, n 61 at 244 in the context of the Bill of Rights debate the committee did not accept that ESR were inherently non-justiciable and recommended that they be subject to review on grounds of reasonableness and non-discrimination, 'Any such measure should recognise the limits of the courts' institutional competence in relation to rights that are progressively realised, and should limit judicial scrutiny to grounds of reasonableness and non-discrimination' JCHR Committee Report, The International Covenant on Economic, Social and Cultural Rights, HL Paper No.183 (Session 2003–04) para.73.

65 House of Lords, House of Commons, Joint Committee on Human Rights Report, Legislative Scrutiny of Welfare Reform Bill, 12 December 2011, HL233, HC 1704, available at www.publications.parliament.uk/pa/jt201012/jtselect/jtrights/233/233.pdf

concerns.[66] Neither the JCHR nor the court were able to oblige Parliament to revisit a more proportionate means of achieving welfare reform in accordance with international ESR standards.

Perhaps the legitimacy of the Finnish model is reinforced by the constitutional recognition of human rights, including ESR, from the outset, meaning to ignore the Committee's recommendations would be to risk acting *ultra vires* the constitution. The work of the JCHR on the other hand, can be more easily dismissed in the UK Parliamentary system where parliamentary supremacy prevails. In this sense the JCHR is viewed more as a 'thorn in the side' of the legislature,[67] rather than a form of ex ante constitutional deliberation engendering legitimacy in the legislative process.

It is also worth noting that the JCHR's role is limited to Acts of the UK Parliament. There is limited monitoring of secondary legislation in the devolved legislatures in this respect. In Wales, the Equality, Local Government and Communities Committee includes a commitment to scrutinise, *inter alia*, equality and human rights but without explicit mention of ESR. In Scotland, an Equality and Human Rights Committee (EHRiC) has recently extended its remit to include human rights review – however there is currently no specific focus for the Committee to consider compliance with ESR as a matter of course. In 2018, the EHRiC took significant steps to consider how to enhance the parliament's role as a guarantor of human rights and its recommendations are discussed in more detail below (in Chapter 6).[68] There is no Committee in the Northern Ireland Assembly with a specific duty to review compliance with human rights. Paragraph 11 of Strand One of the Belfast (Good Friday) Agreement provides that the Assembly could appoint a special Committee 'to examine and report on whether a measure or proposal for legislation is in conformity with equality requirements, including the ECHR/Bill of Rights'.[69] This special type of Ad Hoc Committee has only been established once during the lifetime of the Northern Ireland Assembly in connection with the passage of the Westminster-based Welfare Reform Bill.[70] Without specific committees to consider compatibility with ESR on an

---

66 See dissenting opinions the benefit cap case in *R (on the application of SG and others (previously JS and others)) v Secretary of State for Work and Pensions* [2015] UKSC 16.
67 For a brief discussion on this tenuous relationship see Colin Muray, 'The UK Parliament's Joint Committee on Human Rights: Life from beyond the (Political) Grave?' *Human Rights in Ireland* (5 July 2010), available at http://humanrights.ie/civil-liberties/the-uk-parliaments-joint-committee-on-human-rights-life-from-beyond-the-political-grave/
68 Human Rights and the Scottish Parliament Inquiry 2018, available at www.parliament.scot/parliamentarybusiness/CurrentCommittees/106453.aspx
69 The procedure for setting up and operating such a special Committee (an Ad Hoc Committee on Conformity with Equality Requirements) is provided for by Standing Order 35.
70 The Ad-Hoc Committee found that there were no specific breaches of equality or human rights. The report of the committee was not approved by the Assembly following a debate on the committee's findings. See: Report on whether the Provisions of the Welfare Reform Bill are in Conformity with the Requirements for Equality and Observance of Human Rights, 21 January 2013, available at www.niassembly.gov.uk/globalassets/documents/ad-hoc-welfare-reform-committee/report/nia921115.pdf

ongoing basis each of the devolved legislatures operate without robust ESR constitutional safeguards in place. There is no mechanism for ex ante or ex post review of ESR compatibility of devolved legislation as a matter of course.

Judicial Model

The South African Constitution 1996[71] enshrined ESR in a number of ways and is indicative of a constitutional model that supports judicial intervention.[72] In terms of ESR adjudication, the South African example has been developed by a cautious judiciary that has employed a theory of deference or judicial restraint in order to try and strike a balance in the separation of powers and with the objective of ensuring that concerns relating to polycentricity and the allocation of budgetary resources are adequately addressed within the confines of the court's jurisprudence.[73] This approach has been both welcomed and criticised concurrently in the literature. Those who welcome the cautious approach argue that the judiciary has succeeded in striking the correct balance.[74] Sunstein has suggested that the deferential standard of review in socio-economic rights cases is 'novel and exceedingly promising' and 'respectful of democratic prerogatives and of the limited nature of public resources, while also requiring special deliberative attention to those whose minimal needs are not being met'.[75] Those critical of the approach suggest that the judiciary has been over-cautious and failed to secure any substantive content of the rights protected in the Constitution, undermining the foundational and norm-based nature of the Constitution and, as a result, failing to realise the transformative potential of the Constitution envisaged as part of the transitional framework.[76] Pieterse has argued that if the court's jurisprudence:

---

71 Statutes of the Republic of South Africa – Constitutional Law, Constitution of the Republic of South Africa, No.108 of 1996.

72 Section 23 deals with labour relations; section 24 provides for environmental rights; section 26 provides for the right to adequate housing; section 27 provides for the right of access to health care, food, water and social security; and section 28 provides absolute rights in relation to children; section 29 provides for a right to education; section 30 protects the right to language and culture; section 31 provides for the right to enjoy and maintain cultural, linguistic and religious community membership.

73 Dennis Davis, 'Adjudicating the Socio-Economic Rights in the South African Constitution: Towards "Deference Lite"?' (2006) 22 *South African Journal of Human Rights* 301.

74 See, for example, King, n 39 at 116, Cass Sunstein, 'Social and Economic Rights – Lessons from South Africa' (2001) 12 *Constitutional Forum* 123 and Mark Kende, 'The South African Constitutional Court's Embrace of Socio-Economic Rights. A Comparative Perspective' (2003) 6 *Chapman Law Review* 137.

75 Sunstein, n 35 at 221, 234, 237 .

76 See, for example, Marius Pieterse, 'Resuscitating Socio-Economic Rights: Constitutional Entitlements to Health Care Services' (2006) 22 *South African Journal on Human Rights* 473; Sandra Liebenberg and Beth Goldblatt, 'The Interrelationship between Equality and Socio-Economic Rights under South African's Transformative Constitution' (2007) 23 *South African Journal of Human Rights* 335; and Christopher Mbazira, 'From Ambivalence to

is to have any tangible significance for socio-economic rights' beneficiaries, the Constitutional Court needs to reverse its stance against the recognition of individually enforceable claims and to ground the affirmative remedies it awards in socio-economic rights cases in a purposive understanding of the entitlements entailed by the rights in question.[77]

These varying approaches mirror the discussion in Chapter 1 on the weak v strong review and remedies employed by courts and as noted previously Garavito and Franco persuasively argue that even weak and moderate remedies can have long-term symbolic and material impact beyond the judgments themselves.[78] This is a view echoed by Porter in relation to remedies employed in Canada and the value of dialogic models of engagement.[79]

The South African model is a mixture of substantive rights recognition, together with safeguards and limitation clauses contained in the constitution. Rights are also afforded protection to different degrees along the respect, protect, promote, fulfil axis.[80] Some rights are afforded non-derogable status, such as rights relating to children.[81] Other rights are considered to be subject to progressive realisation such as the right to access adequate housing and the right to access healthcare, food, water and social security.[82] There is a general limitation clause under section 36 whereby rights may be limited if reasonable and justifiable in an open and democratic society.

The primacy of the Constitution is protected under section 172 whereby a court must declare that any law or conduct that is inconsistent with the Constitution is invalid and may make any order that is just and equitable in the circumstances. The declaration has no effect in law until it is confirmed by the Constitutional

---

Certainty: Norms and Principles for the Structural Interdict in Socio-Economic Rights Litigation in South Africa' (2008) 24 *South African Journal of Human Rights* 1.

77 Pieterse, ibid. at 490.

78 For a full discussion on this see Chapter 1 and César Rodríguez-Garavito and Diana Rodríguez-Franco, *Radical Deprivation on Trial, the Impact of Judicial Activism on Socioeconomic Rights in the Global South* (Cambridge University Press, 2015), 17–21.

79 Bruce Porter, 'Canada: Systemic Claims and Remedial Diversity' in Malcolm Langford, César Rodríguez-Garavito and Julieta Rossi (eds.), *Social Rights Judgments and the Politics of Compliance, Making It Stick* (Cambridge University Press, 2017), 201–254.

80 Section 7 of the Constitution.

81 Such as the right to be protected from maltreatment, neglect, abuse or degradation; and the right to be protected from exploitative labour practices (section 28(1)(d) and (e)). See section 37(5)(c) for a table listing non-derogable rights in the Constitution. For a discussion on the rights of the child (particularly girls' ESR) in the South African Constitution see Ann Skelton, 'Girls' Socio-Economic Rights in South Africa' [2010] 26 *South African Journal of Human Rights* 141.

82 For example, section 26 of the South African Constitution provides for the right to have access to adequate housing and section 27 provides for the right to have access to health care, food, water and social security. The constitution further provides that the state must take reasonable legislative and other measures, within its available resources, to achieve the progressive realisation of each of these rights (Sections 26(2) and 27(2) respectively).

Court (so where a lower court makes an order the final decision on validity rests with the Constitutional Court). It is open to the lower courts to enforce an interim remedy pending the confirmation of the declaration by the Constitutional Court (section 172(2)(b)). The declaration of invalidity can be limited as to its retrospective effect (section 172(1)(b)(i)). Furthermore, similar to the 'delayed remedy' employed by the Canadian Supreme Court,[83] section 172(1)(b)(ii) provides that judges may make an order suspending the declaration of invalidity for any period and on any conditions, to allow the competent authority to rectify the defect. This framework affords a great deal of flexibility to the court in how best to develop jurisprudence and potential remedies for violations within the parameters of its constitutional authority. The options of remedial action are open ended (the court may make any order that is 'just and equitable') and at the same time the impact of the orders can be controlled temporally (with the option to limit the retrospective effect of a declaration, suspend the prospective application in the immediate future and seek to apply interim measures in the meantime).

The great difficulty in affording flexibility in this respect relates to how the judiciary in South Africa should approach the degree of protection that ought to be afforded to those rights that are subject to progressive realisation within the states available resources on a case-by-case basis. Does the constitutional recognition of ESR in this way confer authority on the court to interfere in relation to how state resources are allocated? And, if so, is this interference workable in practice without a politicisation of adjudication?

This concern essentially relates to the argument that such a constitutional power invites the judiciary to engage in issues of a high policy nature, and offer remedies that will simply shift around money within the respective department rather than increase overall funding.[84] There is the risk that adjudication will lead to the development of ESR constitutional norms on a case-by-case basis, potentially drawing public funds from one policy area to another without a holistic approach to resource allocation.[85] In relation to this risk, King argues

---

83 See, for example, the delayed remedy employed in *Canada (Attorney General) v Bedford* 2013 SCC 72 in which the Supreme Court suspended the declaration of invalidity under section 52(1) of Canada's Constitution Act 1982 for one year to allow Parliament sufficient time to avoid an eventual regulatory void. This case concerned the legality of prohibitions on sex workers that the court found violated the safety and security of prostitutes – the difficulty with the delayed remedy route places those at risk to remain in a state of violation during the interim period in which the declaration of invalidity is suspended. For a discussion on this case and the constitutional impact of delayed remedies see: Robert Leckey, 'Suspended Declarations of Invalidity and the Rule of Law' U.K. Const. L. Blog (12 March 2014), available at http://ukconstitutionallaw.org/

84 King, n 39 at 3.

85 This could, for example, lead to the allocation of funds from the poorest in society to the wealthy. See, for example, the jurisprudence of the Brazilian courts that recognised an immediately enforceable right to the highest attainable health causing greater health inequities as the more privileged and wealthy, Octavio Luiz Motta Ferraz, 'The Right to Health in the Courts of Brazil: Worsening Health Inequities?' (2009) 11 *Health and Human Rights: An International Journal* 33.

that it is possible 'to develop a theory of adjudication that gives us good reason to believe that when paying Paul, we are not always robbing Peter to do it'.[86]

King develops a theory of adjudication based on judicial restraint and incrementalism as a viable solution to ESR constitutionalisation and adjudication. Judicial restraint, he argues can be managed through the consideration of four principles that should temper the incremental development of jurisprudence: democratic legitimacy;[87] polycentricity;[88] expertise;[89] and flexibility.[90] By incrementalism, King argues that the principles of restraint will require only a very small departure from the status quo as the common law develops on an incremental basis – when dealing with issues of significant macro-policy (large scale polycentric issues), there ought to be, according to King, a significant degree of administrative and/or legislative flexibility by way of response to any judgment.[91] King has identified South Africa as a constitutional model that provides an exemplary solution to this theory of adjudication.[92]

ESR Adjudication in Practice

Whilst no state's practice is a panacea, lessons can be learned from the growing legalisation of ESR through legislation, constitutionalisation, international complaints mechanisms and ESR jurisprudence. This section reflects on social rights adjudication

---

86 King, n 39 at 56.
87 King argues that a just democracy depends on the guarantee of social human rights – 'in any such democracy that guarantee is delivered through a legislative programme of social rights, administered by a responsible executive and buttressed by the existence of legal accountability [through constitutional adjudication]' King, ibid. at 187. Democratic legitimacy requires that the court respects a presumption in favour of legislative authority and steps in to correct limitations in the legislative process on a substantive basis for vulnerable groups and on a procedural, deferential basis in relation to other cases.
88 Some issues require the comprehension of a vast number of interconnected variables in order to understand the likely consequences of any change to policy. King argues that resource allocation is at the nationwide level a polycentric activity and that the judiciary must be aware of the potential adjudication of polycentric issues relating to budget allocation that may have drastic consequences for other areas of policy. In order to overcome objections to this principle the courts must have regard to the judicial mandate afforded to them, the degree of polycentricity, access to information, relative competency of the courts and its alternatives and the flexibility of the remedy or possibility for revisitation, King, ibid. at 210.
89 King argues that the courts must have regard, and potentially exercise deference in relation to issues of expertise outwith the competence of the courts. However, this must be balanced with an open approach to judicial review and accountability in order to uncover a failure of expertise or a procedural injustice.
90 In this regard courts should give weight to flexibility in the course of social rights adjudication in terms of flexibility in the process of interpretation (leaving the option open for future development of a precedent) and flexibility in the remedies offered (preferring for example deferential remedies as opposed to structural remedies that should be employed only as a means of last resort).
91 King, ibid. at 9.
92 King, ibid. at 116.

in practice in a number of different contexts under a variety of different constitutional models. This is by no means intended as a comprehensive review but gives a very brief insight into the wealth of international and comparative ESR jurisprudence that has developed in recent decades. The literature is rich with discussions on existing ESR jurisprudence and scholars continue to critique emerging case law some of which is engaged with in the following sections.

South Africa

The jurisprudence of the Constitutional Court of South Africa employs reasonableness as the means through which to assess constitutional compatibility as initially set out in the *Grootboom*[93] case. This case related to an application made under sections 26 and 28 of the Constitution in relation to the right to access adequate housing and the rights of children to shelter respectively. Mrs Grootboom and 899 others had been living in appalling circumstances in an informal settlement. They then illegally occupied nearby private land designated for low-cost housing and were forcibly evicted. Their shacks were bulldozed and burnt, and their possessions destroyed. Following an interim order issued by the High Court in favour of Mrs Grootboom and the other respondents the state lodged an appeal with the Constitutional Court. A further intermediary solution was sought between the parties, however, the state failed to adhere to the agreed terms. An urgent application was thereafter made to the Constitutional Court and the court made a declaratory order. The order required the state to act to meet the obligation imposed upon it by section 26(2) of the Constitution (the progressive realisation of the right to housing). This included the obligation to devise, fund, implement and supervise measures to provide relief to those in desperate need. The court assigned responsibility to the Human Rights Commission under section 184 of the Constitution to monitor compliance with the declaratory order.

In the unanimous judgment issued by Justice Yacoob the court reaffirmed the justiciable nature of ESR as enshrined in the Constitution and confirmed in the Certification Judgment.[94] The court identified that the difficulty in giving substance to the ESR in the constitution related to how best to enforce the rights in any given case:

> Socio-economic rights are expressly included in the Bill of Rights; they cannot be said to exist on paper only. Section 7(2) of the Constitution requires the state "to respect, protect, promote and fulfill the rights in the Bill of Rights" and the courts are constitutionally bound to ensure that they are protected and

---

93 *Government of the Republic of South Africa v Grootboom* 2001 (1) SA 46 (CC).

94 The certification case challenged the justiciability of ESR enshrined in the Constitution. The court held that ESR hold the same positive and negative qualities that civil and political rights have and 'the fact that socio-economic rights will almost inevitably give rise to [budgetary] implications does not seem to us to be a bar to their justiciability. At the very minimum, socio-economic rights can be negatively protected from improper invasion.' *Ex Parte Chairperson of the Constitutional Assembly: In Re Certification of the Constitution of the Republic of South Africa*, 1996 (4) SA 744; 1996 (10) BCLR 1253 (CC) para.78.

fulfilled. The question is therefore not whether socio-economic rights are justiciable under our Constitution, but how to enforce them in a given case. This is a very difficult issue which must be carefully explored on a case-by-case basis.[95]

The court made some distinctions as to the extent of protection offered under the text of the constitution. The provisions of the Constitution dealing with the progressive realisation of rights were textually different to the more extensive protection afforded in international law under ICESCR.[96] As a result, the court rejected the argument posed by the amici curiae[97] that the court ought to follow the recommendations of the Committee on Economic Social and Cultural Rights under paragraph 4 of General Comment No. 3 as a guide to interpretation in so far as ESR contain an inherent non-derogable minimum core.[98]

Instead, the court held that the real question before the court was whether the measures taken by the state to realise the right to access adequate housing were reasonable.[99] Despite some laudable legislative and administrative measures in place to address the national housing situation the court considered that the state had not sufficiently addressed their obligations in respect of those who were in desperate need.[100] They held that there was nothing in the constitution that conferred an immediate right upon the respondents[101] and the court emphasised that, under the prevailing circumstances in relation to the plight of housing in South Africa, that it would be very difficult for the state to progressively achieve access to housing on a nationwide scale and certainly impossible to achieve this as an immediately enforceable universal right (nor did the constitution confer such a right).

Nonetheless, it was held that the constitutional obligation to progressively achieve the right must be complied with, and the courts must enforce it, in accordance with the availability of resources and in a reasonable manner. As Justice Yacoobs stated:

> I am conscious that it is an extremely difficult task for the state to meet these obligations in the conditions that prevail in our country. This is recognised by the Constitution which expressly provides that the state is not obliged to go beyond available resources or to realise these rights immediately. I stress

---

95 *Grootboom* n 93 para.20.
96 *Grootboom* n 93 para.28.
97 The Human Rights Commission and the Community Law Centre of the University of the Western Cape were admitted as amici curiae to the case.
98 The court described the minimum core as 'the floor beneath which the conduct of the state must not drop if there is to be compliance with the obligation' at para 31 and rejected this concept as forming part of the obligation under the constitution at *Grootboom*, n 93 para.32–33.
99 Ibid. para.33. The court did not rule out the possibility of litigation based on a minimum core argument but emphasised that establishing a minimum core would be difficult, and even where appropriate, would require sufficient information on the needs and the opportunities for the enjoyment of the right in any given context.
100 Ibid. para.66.
101 Ibid. para.95.

however, that despite all these qualifications, these are rights, and the Constitution obliges the state to give effect to them. This is an obligation that courts can, and in appropriate circumstances, must enforce.[102]

The judgment in *Grootboom* set out the reasonableness test as the standard of review in ESR adjudication. In this case, the state had not gone far enough to meet the needs of those in desperate need, and, as a result had acted unreasonably.

In terms of the lessons that can be learned from this judicial approach, at the very least, it demonstrates that procedural review of ESR can contribute to the alleviation of ESR violations in a state emerging from conflict and deeply entrenched inequality and exclusion. On the other hand, it arguably demonstrates a failure to achieve any substantive change for those upon whose behalf the case was taken. Mrs Grootboom was reported to have died 'homeless and penniless' some eight years after the declaratory order was made.[103] Justice Cameron of the Constitutional Court submits that Mrs Grootboom's death is a 'humbling reminder to those in the business of law and of constitutional rhetoric that our craft has limits'.[104] The reason why the decision of the court did not result in a transformative societal impact may arguably be identified in the types of remedies offered as opposed to the standard of review.[105]

The case demonstrates a reluctance to impose additional policy burdens on the state[106] whilst still trying to uphold the role of the judiciary in overseeing compliance with the constitution. Deference and judicial restraint are central to the judgment itself and to the form of remedy. The choice of remedy employed (a declaratory order) was indicative of the court's reluctance to engage in a supervisory role over the implementation of the order.[107] Mbazira has argued for the use of a structural interdict as a more appropriate form of remedy in the South African context in order to realise substantive change.[108] The structural

---

102 Ibid. para.92.
103 See Pearlie Joubert, 'Grootboom Dies Homeless and Penniless', *Mail and Guardian*, 8 August 2008, available at http://mg.co.za/article/2008-08-08-grootboom-dies-homeless-and-penniless
104 Edwin Cameron, 'What Can You Do with Rights?', Law Commission of England and Wales, The Fourth Leslie Scarman Lecture, 25 January 2012, para.30, available at http://lawcommission.justice.gov.uk/docs/Scarman_2012_Justice_Cameron_What_you_can_do_with_rights.pdf
105 According to Mbaziro, one of the key problems with the South African system is the failure of the court to enforce meaningful remedies following a judgment in favour of the claimant – he argues too much deference is afforded to state authorities to comply in good faith and there is not enough accountability post judgment, Mbazira, n 76.
106 Davis, n 73 at 304.
107 Preferring instead to allocate this responsibility to the Human Rights Commission. See also Davis, ibid. at 304.
108 Ibid. and also Christopher Mbazira, 'You Are the "Weakest Link" in Realising Socio-Economic Rights: Goodbye, Strategies for Effective Implementation of Court Orders in South Africa', Socio-Economic Rights Project, Community Law Centre, University of the Western Cape (2008).

interdict facilitates a role for the court in supervising compliance with the judgment rather than deferring compliance to the legislature or executive without any mechanisms for accountability for non-compliance.[109] This form of remedy, he argues, can act as a tool of dialogue between courts and the executive without usurping the separation of powers:

> [r]ather than lead to a breakdown of the relationship between the judiciary and the executive, the structural interdict should be viewed as promoting a dynamic dialogue between these two branches. This dialogue is on the intricacies of implementing court orders and actualising constitutional rights.[110]

The use of the declaratory interdict (with no structural supervision in terms of compliance) in the *Grootboom* case may well have undermined the order granted in favour of Mrs Grootboom and others. However, Justice Cameron suggests that the policy implications implemented in response to the judgment will have a direct material impact for many other South Africans. He argues that '[t]he decision therefore had a direct material impact on many people's lives – perhaps many millions of lives. The nub of the judgment was to require the state to take active steps to create access to social services and economic resources for the most vulnerable'.[111]

So whilst the decision did not result in any directly enforceable right for the claimants, the executive action taken in response to the judgment has incrementally improved access to housing in accordance with the state's constitutional obligations. Incrementalism, deference and judicial restraint can therefore still result in substantive outcomes: '[t]he clear implication is that without Mrs Grootboom's rights-directed litigation, and without the Court's declaratory order, the country's housing programme would have continued to omit provision for the emergency needs of the poorest and most vulnerable'.[112]

This decision was to act as the 'seedbed' for future socio-economic jurisprudence.[113] Judicial restraint, deference and incrementalism continue to inform the court's theoretical approach to ESR adjudication. An incremental development in respect of the right to access housing can be seen in cases such

---

109 Ibid. Mbazira sets out the following remedies available in relation to ESR: declaratory orders (no inherent remedial action defined), mandatory order (confers positive obligations but does not supervise compliance – risk of non-compliance) and the structural interdict (allows the court to supervise implementation of its order, or, an interim structural order as employed in *Olivia Road* case, *Occupiers of 51 Olivia Road, Berea Township and 197 Main Street, Johannesburg v City of Johannesburg, Rand Properties (Pty) Ltd, Minister of Trade and Industry, and the President of the Republic of South Africa with the Centre on Housing Rights and Evictions and the Community Law Centre, University of the Western Cape as amici curiae.* CCT 24/07 [2008] ZACC 1.
110 Mbazira, n 108 at 11.
111 Cameron, n 104 para.31.
112 Ibid. para.35.
113 Ibid. para.31.

as Olivia *Road*[114] and *Moonlight Properties*.[115] Incrementalism in terms of the theoretical approach itself can be seen in the court's dicta on minimum core entitlement and in the types of remedies that the court can enforce – leaving the door open to potentially immediately enforceable positive entitlements and a more supervisory form of remedy in the future if necessary. This is evident, for example in the subsequent *TAC*[116] judgment that had far-reaching consequences in relation to addressing the AIDS epidemic.

The *TAC* judgment that followed *Grootboom* reaffirmed the court's approach to progressive realisation was to be achieved through a review on grounds of reasonableness. This case concerned administration of the antiretroviral drug nevirapine in order to reduce the risk of HIV-positive mothers transmitting the disease to their babies at birth. The court held that the state's policy to only administer the drug within specified treatment centres was unreasonable and that access to the drug should be extended to all expectant mothers who seek it.

The judgment went on to make some further clarifications and distinctions about the court's role under the constitution. The minimum core arguments were once again explored, however, the court was reluctant to depart from the *Grootboom* judgment.[117] Nevertheless, there is a 'latent notion of minimum core entitlement' in the *TAC* decision based on Grootboom reasonableness standard.[118] Pieterse argues that this latent and flexible notion of minimum entitlement has much potential in guiding a more entitlement based and need-focused jurisprudence.[119] This could be envisaged, for example, where on a reasonableness review the failure of the state to consider the minimum core is considered itself unreasonable. In other words:

> even though the Constitutional Court has rejected minimum core terminology, there may still be cases where a remedy requiring the satisfaction of needs akin to those represented by a minimum core approach would qualify as appropriate relief. This conclusion seems in line with statements in both *Grootboom* and *TAC* that the notion of minimum core may sometimes be relevant to an INQUIRY of reasonableness.[120]

---

114 *Occupiers of 51 Olivia Road, Berea Township and 197 Main Street, Johannesburg v City of Johannesburg and Others* CCT 24/07 Medium Neutral Citation [2008] ZACC 1 – meaningful engagement and participation is required by the constitution before an eviction order can be served (no forced eviction without notice).

115 *City of Johannesburg Metropolitan Municipality v Blue Moonlight Properties 39 (Pty) Ltd and Another* (CCT 37/11) [2011] ZACC 33 (1 December 2011) – the obligation to make emergency provision to those who are to be evicted extended to those being evicted by private landlords.

116 *Minister of Health v Treatment Action Campaign (no 2) (TAC)* 2002 (5) SA 721 (CC).

117 *TAC* ibid. para.29.

118 Pieterse, n 76 see also para.28 and 34 of *TAC* ibid.

119 Pieterse, ibid. at 475.

120 Pieterse, ibid. at 478.

The deferential and cautious approach of the judiciary in the *Grootboom* and *TAC* decisions is reflected in the court's approach to dealing with matters of polycentricity, and this too informs the kind of remedies imposed:

> Courts are ill-suited to adjudicate upon issues where court orders could have multiple social and economic consequences for the community. The Constitution contemplates rather a restrained and focused role for the courts, namely, to require the state to take measures to meet its constitutional obligations and to subject the reasonableness of these measures to evaluation. Such determinations of reasonableness may in fact have budgetary implications, but are not in themselves directed at rearranging budgets. In this way the judicial, legislative and executive functions achieve appropriate constitutional balance.[121]

However, The *TAC* judgment also clarified that remedies under the constitution are flexible and wide ranging. Whilst the court did not deem it necessary to issue a structural interdict in the *TAC* case, it did quite clearly reserve the right to do this in future cases if the circumstances required.[122] This in itself was significant in terms of understanding the court's approach to polycentric socio-economic right matters. As Pieterse highlights, '[a]rguably the TAC judgment's greatest contribution is its unequivocal dismissal of the government's argument that courts were not empowered to issue any order other than a declaration of rights in polycentric socio-economic rights matters, which has done more to affirm the justiciability of these rights than has been achieved in all of its previous declarations to that effect'.[123] Essentially, the court will take a deferential approach, however, a more structured and supervisory role is constitutionally available should the court require to implement one.[124] Likewise in the case of *Daniels v Scribante* the

---

121 *TAC*, n 116 para.38.
122 On an examination of other jurisdictions the court stated – 'What this brief survey makes clear is that in none of the jurisdictions surveyed is there any suggestion that the granting of injunctive relief breaches the separation of powers. The various courts adopt different attitudes to when such remedies should be granted, but all accept that within the separation of powers they have the power to make use of such remedies – particularly when the state's obligations are not performed diligently and without delay. South African courts have a wide range of powers at their disposal to ensure that the Constitution is upheld. These include mandatory and structural interdicts. How they should exercise those powers depends on the circumstances of each particular case. Here due regard must be paid to the roles of the legislature and the executive in a democracy. What must be made clear, however, is that when it is appropriate to do so, courts may – and if need be must – use their wide powers to make orders that affect policy as well as legislation.' *TAC*, ibid. para.112–113.
123 Pieterse, n 76 at 894.
124 Mbazira refers to the interim structural order in the Olivia Road case in which the court sought to build consensus between the parties to encourage dialogue and to create a favourable environment for ensuring enforcement of its final order (that the state must secure access to housing for those in desperate need) with minimum judicial involvement, Mbazira, n 108 at 17.

court established the possibility of widening the impact of ESR protection through a horizontal application of constitutional rights.[125] In this case, the court recognised the lasting impact of colonial rule and systemic discrimination granting relief to a tenant that was prohibited from maintaining the upkeep of her home on rented land. As noted by Nolan, the court:

> rejected the argument that constitutionally an owner bears no positive obligation to ensure that an occupier lives under conditions that afford her or him human dignity. In doing so, it recognised the possibility of the direct horizontality of positive obligations imposed by constitutional ESR.[126]

Pillay has argued that the judicial approach to ESR adjudication in South Africa and the UK[127] already share a strong theoretical framework.[128] In this sense, there is the possibility that the judiciary could take significant steps in the realm of ESR adjudication should it explore all the means of review and remedies at its disposal. Pillay suggests that indeterminate resource or policy implications tend to outweigh any other consideration for a court deciding on how rigorously it will scrutinise governmental action and what remedy it will hand down when considering ESR adjudication.[129] This, she argues, can be best managed through a theory of deference but with the opportunity to explore imaginative solutions and remedies when necessary (so not a strict theory of judicial deference but a flexible theory of judicial deference). In fact, according to Pillay, flexibility already plays an important role in how judges respond to ESR adjudication in the UK and South Africa. She argues that:

> judges in South Africa and the United Kingdom employ a range of factors to determine how closely to interrogate governmental action in cases with significant social and economic repercussions. This variability of the

---

125 *Daniels v Scribante and Another* (CCT50/16) [2017] ZACC 13 (11 May 2017).

126 Aoife Nolan, 'Daniels v. Scribante: South Africa Pushes the Boundaries of Horizontality and Social Rights', Int'l J. Const. L. Blog (27 June 2017), available at: www.iconnectblog.com/ 2017/06/daniels-v-scribante-south-africa-pushes-the-boundaries-of-horizontality-and-social-rights

127 Pillay refers to case law relating to ESR adjudication where Parliament has indicated its intention to be bound by ESR (welfare legislation), to interpretation of socio-economic rights through the common law and to case law relating to the adjudication of ESR through CP (through the ECHR). Whilst the South African courts employ reasonableness as a form of review, reviewability in the UK can occur on the grounds of reasonableness, proportionality, relevancy, procedural unfairness, bias *inter alia*. Anashri Pillay, 'Economic and Social Rights Adjudication: Developing Principles of Judicial Restraint in South Africa and the United Kingdom' (2013) *Public Law* 599.

128 Ibid.

129 Pillay also identifies other factors influencing the judicial approach if resources and policy implications are not severe such as the severity of the impact of the governmental action and state conduct. Ibid. at 616.

intensity of review is a flexibility device that allows judges to take a host of concerns into account. Naturally, this entails a degree of uncertainty. The idea of a theory of deference that would manage judicial action and account for judicial decisions is, therefore, attractive.[130]

The degree of 'interrogation' into governmental action in cases will depend to a large extent on the impact of polycentric issues and budgetary allocation and in the need to retain the appropriate separation of powers:

> [D]ue to limited resources and the sheer enormity of the task of redistributing wealth and services in the country, the legislature and executive are the ultimate architects of long-term socio-economic policy. In determining the appropriate balance of powers, UK courts will look to Parliamentary intent as an important concern whereas South African courts will look to the Constitution.[131]

In Pillay's analysis there is an underlying indication that the approach of the judiciary in the UK is of a much more conservative nature than that of South Africa.[132] Pillay refers to *Limbuela*[133] as the case in which the UK judiciary would go so far as to enforce positive obligations upon the state with cost implications under Article 3 ECHR 'because government policy could leave people destitute for an indefinite period of time'.[134] Whilst *Limbuela* does in some way resemble more closely the decisions of *Grootboom* and *TAC* in so far as addressing the needs of those in desperate need as a matter of priority, it is critical to note that *Limbuela* does not stand to set a precedent in the way South African jurisprudence has done so. As discussed in more detail below in Chapter 5, *Limbuela* would have been decided differently if there had not been a qualification in section 55(5) of the Nationality, Immigration and Asylum Act 2002 that imposed an obligation on the Secretary of State to act compatibility with Convention rights when carrying out the duties imposed by the 2002 Act. If this provision had been missing the Secretary of State would not have been able to arrange support for the asylum seekers under the Human Rights Act 1998, nor would the court have been able to offer them an effective remedy, 'however dire their plight'.[135] Pillay states that:

---

130 Pillay, ibid. at 600.
131 Pillay, ibid. at 602.
132 Many of the more conservative decisions are more clearly aligned than that of the more transformative.
133 *Regina v Secretary of State for the Home Department (Appellant) ex parte Adam (FC) (Respondent) Regina v Secretary of State for the Home Department (Appellant) ex parte Limbuela (FC) (Respondent) Regina v Secretary of State for the Home Department (Appellant) ex parte Tesema (FC) (Respondent) (Conjoined Appeals)* 2005 UKHL 66.
134 Pillay, n 127 at 610.
135 *Limbuela*, n 133 as per Lord Bingham para.4–5.

in any event, following the decision in *Limbuela*, it would be very difficult for a government agency to claim that it has no obligation purely on the basis that such an obligation would entail positive action, such as the provision of social welfare benefits to a particular group or class of people.[136]

However, such a precedent has not been followed as a matter of course. In the case where primary legislation cannot be read in a way that is compatible with Convention rights, it is not open to the court to issue an order that the state complies – the only remedy available to the UK court is to issue a declaration of incompatibility.[137] This declaration does not affect the operation of the incompatible legislation or any provision within it, nor does it confer any right upon the claimant. And herein lies the crucial difference. Whilst judges in South Africa and the UK may both approach ESR adjudication using principles of judicial restraint, it is only to the South African judges that a range of possible remedies are available in those cases that require a more interventionist approach in order to hold the state to account for non-compliance with fundamental constitutional rights. This is as a direct result of the framework model of constitutionalism to which the South African constitution pertains. The UK process model does not guarantee the same level of protection as there is no overarching constitutional structure.

Colombia

The Colombian Constitution divides human rights into three groups: fundamental rights, ESC rights and collective and environmental rights (Chapters 1, 2 and 3). The Constitution also places international treaties on a domestic constitutional footing (articles 44 and 93). The ESC rights included in the constitution relate to health, housing, work and education, among others. The Constitution also protects vulnerable and disadvantaged groups within society with particular measures for children, women, the elderly and persons with disabilities (articles 46–47). Responsibility for safeguarding the Constitution is assigned to the Constitutional Court (article 241). The constitutionalisation of ESR has caused a 'profound change' in the legal culture in Colombia with considerable advancements made in the judicial enforcement of ESR.[138] The main mechanism for the judicial protection under the constitution is the *tutela* device (article 86). The *tutela* enables a person to file a writ of protection before any court or tribunal for the immediate protection of her or his 'fundamental constitutional rights'. All decisions by ordinary judges on a writ of protection are sent to the Constitutional Court and are susceptible to review. Magistrates in the

---

136 Pillay, n 127 at 610.
137 Under section 4 of the Human Rights Act 1998.
138 Magdalena Sepúlveda, 'Colombia, The Constitutional Court's Role in Addressing Social Injustice' in Malcolm Langford (ed.), *Social Rights Jurisprudence, Emerging Trends in International and Comparative Law*, 144.

Constitutional Court can review *tutelas*, and where appropriate, will group cases together in order to address structural problems such as for example if an issue emerges that applies to a large group of vulnerable people the cases will be merged together and the court will issue a collective remedy.

The *tutela* device[139] is a fast-track remedial process whereby applicants can seek to enforce constitutional rights, including ESR, if they require immediate protection. In the context of social security, the Colombian Constitutional Court has developed the concept of *mínimo vital* (based on the Gerrman *existenz minimum*). Although the *mínimo vital* is not explicitly mentioned in the constitution it has been interpreted (teleologically and dynamically) as implicit to the right to life, the right to health, the right to work and the right to social security.[140] As explained by Sepúlveda:

> in cases of extreme urgency in which the basic subsistence of the individual and her family is in jeopardy, it is possible to file a writ of protection [*acion tutela*] as a fast-track emergency measure for the enforcement of ESC rights.[141]

The courts have intervened to ensure that those in desperate need have access to a remedy as quickly as possible. For example, an elderly man living in absolute poverty requested that the state provide him with economic assistance so that he could undergo an eye operation that would allow him to recover his sight. The court found that the legislature had not complied with its duty to adopt a law to address the situation of such persons and ordered the social security system to provide the treatment.[142] In another case, a poor elderly man who had not received a State subsidy was given access to a remedy because when he had initially applied he had been told the wrong information from the relevant administrative authority about the procedures necessary to obtain his benefit.[143] The tutela device cannot be used if there are other procedures available to remedy the situation – it is essentially a last resort in the case of absolute emergencies. For example, if the minimum conditions for a dignified life of a mother and new born depends on the payment of maternity benefits this right becomes a fundamental right that is immediately enforceable under the tutela device.[144] However, if the need is not immediate and there are other means of seeking a remedy then the tutela will not be necessary.

Since 1997, the Colombian Constitutional Court has handed down structural remedies in relation to the social security system,[145] massive prison

---

139 Article 86.
140 Sepúlveda, n 138.
141 Sepúlveda, ibid. at 150.
142 T-533/92.
143 T-149/02.
144 Sepulveda, n 138 at 151, see See T-568/96 – T-707/02.
145 SU-090/00;T-535/99; T-068/98; SU-559/97.

overcrowding,[146] lack of protection for human rights defenders[147] and failures in the healthcare system.[148] In 2004, the court combined 1150 tutela cases of internally displaced people (IDP) and issued a structural remedy[149] in three parts:

> First, it mandated that the government formulate a coherent plan of action to tackle the IDPs' humanitarian emergency and to overcome the unconstitutional state of affairs. Second, it ordered the administration to calculate the budget that was needed to implement such a plan of action and to explore all possible avenues to actually invest the amount calculated on programs for IDPs. Third, it instructed the government to guarantee the protection of at least the survival-level content (mínimo vital) of the most basic rights – food, education, healthcare, land, and housing. All of these orders were directed to all relevant public agencies, including national governmental entities and local authorities.[150]

In 2018, the Colombian Constitutional Court issued a structural remedy on the right to a healthy environment and the protection of future generations (Article 79). The court ordered the government to undertake a participative process to develop an 'intergenerational pact for the life of the Colombian Amazon' (PIVAC) to reverse the damage caused by deforestation of the Amazon. The tutela device and the operation of structural remedies such as this are embedded in participative and deliberative processes that seek to include those impacted by the decision. In this case, the court required coordination with the actors of the National Environmental System and the participation of the applicants (25 children and young people), the affected communities and interested population in general, to formulate a short, medium and long-term action plan to counteract the deforestation rate in the Amazon, tackling climate change and engaging directly with protecting the rights to water, air and health.[151]

Landau persuasively argues that the approach to structural remedies in Colombia helps to counteract the pro-hegemonic tendency of the court to act as a pro-majoritarian exercise of power when dealing with individual cases.[152]

---

146 T-153/98.
147 T-590/98.
148 T-760/08.
149 T-025/04.
150 César Rodríguez-Garavito, 'Beyond the Courtroom: The Impact of Judicial Activism on Socioeconomic Rights in Latin America' (2011) 89 *Texas Law Review* 1669–1698 at 1682.
151 STC4360-2018; No: 11001-22-03-000-2018-00319-01 (Approved in session on April 4th, 2018) Bogotá, D.C., (5 April 2018) For a discussion on the case see here: www.dejusticia.org/en/climate-change-and-future-generations-lawsuit-in-colombia-key-excerpts-from-the-supreme-courts-decision/
152 David Landau, 'The Reality of Social Rights Enforcement, Harvard Journal', (2012) 53 *Harvard International Law Journal* 189–247 at 235.

This unique and innovative remedial process of grouping systemic issues together helps deliver real change in a way that impacts the most vulnerable.[153]

Garavito further identifies that the benefits of this approach to ESR are far-reaching:

> [t]he effects includes – in addition to governmental action specifically mandated by the court – the reframing of socio-economic issues as human rights problems, the strengthening of state institutional capacities to deal with such problems, the forming of advocacy coalitions to participate in the implementation process, and the promoting of public deliberation and a collective search for solutions on the complex distributional issues underlying structural cases on [economic and social rights].[154]

One of the necessary components of a structural remedy is the role played by civil society as part of a participative and deliberative process where the court listens to evidence on the particular systemic issue and is open to issuing remedies that address the issue, compel the duty-bearer to act, supervise compliance and include those impacted in the post-judgment decision-making and compliance processes. This approach is embedded in the principles of participation and deliberation, as well as the remedial and counter-majoritarian principles as an ESR accountability mechanism.

Argentina

The use of structural remedies is also evident in the jurisprudence emerging from Argentina. The Argentinian Constitution was amended in 1994 and a number of international treaties were explicitly incorporated into the Constitution, including the International Covenant on Economic, Social and Cultural Rights.[155] This is a 'rights-affirmative' constitutional framework where the compliance with international human rights and constitutional rights is the default position, which, can be denounced by the executive if two-thirds of each chamber of the parliament approve (creating a rights-affirmative framework with the option for parliamentary derogation).[156] The distribution of powers in Argentina is separated into both federal and sub-national provincial autonomy (national and devolved). In addition to the changes to the national constitution

---

153 Landau notes that there are difficulties in the use of structural remedies in Colombia in terms of the costs as well as the willingness and ingenuity of the judiciary. The use of these remedies are underdeveloped. Landau references their origin having developed in India with *the People's Union for Civil Liberties v Union of India & Others* Writ Petition (Civil) No. 196 of 2001, (8 May 2002) (India) where the court started issuing structural orders to initiate food programmes, available at www.righttofoodindia.org/orders/may8.html

154 César Rodríguez-Garavito, n 150 at 1676.

155 Article 25 Constitution of Argentina.

156 Article 75 of the Constitution of Argentina 1853 (reinst. 1938, rev. 1994).

there were also a number of changes at the provincial level with individual states adopting constitutional amendments with better protection for ESR. One of the difficulties faced in Argentina was coherently delineating the distribution of responsibilities between the federal and provincial level. For example, sometimes disparities can exist between federal and provincial responsibilities as well as between public and private responsibilities in areas that engage with human rights.[157] Interestingly, parallels can be drawn with the complexity of devolved v reserved distribution of power in the UK context in terms of identifying who is responsible for what in the enforcement of ESR.

International human rights law has been directly incorporated into the national (Article 25) and subnational constitutions. Several cases have seen ESR enforced through the judiciary with reference to these international standards. For example, in *Saavedra* the court referenced UN General Comments 4 and 7 in interpreting the right to housing.[158] In *Gianelli*, a trial court declared that if tenants with children were threatened with forced eviction the government authority must assure alternative housing.[159] In *Delfino*,[160] the court considered the conditions of government funded private hostels did not meet habitability conditions and ordered the city administration to adopt measures to provide adequate housing – the courts also imposed fines on public officials for failing to comply with a court agreement that involved ensuring adequate housing conditions of a number of families included in an emergency housing plan.[161]

The court in Argentina has also gone so far as to offer structural remedies where the local authority has failed in implementing ESR, such as the right to housing. This has included wide-ranging structural remedies for collective cases involving multiple families (like a class action). In *Agüero*, a collective injunction involved 86 families living in irregular conditions on state-owned land.[162] Initially the case was settled and the administration agreed to design a specific housing plan for the families – the administration's failure to comply led to a new injunction and to a court-ordered seizure of public monies to secure funding for the promised plan. The administration adopted a plan to build 91 dwellings giving priority in the legal tender to enterprises offering jobs to residents. The administration was to offer residents access to a special line of credit

---

157 Christian Courtis, 'Argentina' in Malcom Langford (ed.), *Social Rights Jurisprudence, Emerging Trends in International and Comparative Law* (Cambridge University Press, 2008), 163–182 at 165.

158 Buenos Aires Supreme Court, Comisión Municipal de la Vivienda v Saavedra, Felisa Alicia y otros s/Desalojo s/Recurso de Inconstitucionalidad Concedido 7 October 2002.

159 Buenos Aires Administrative Trial Court No.3 Comisión Municipal de la Vivienda v Gianelli, Alberto Luis y otros s/Desalojo 12 September 2002.

160 Buenos Aires Adminsitarative Court of Appeals, Chamber I, Delfino, Jorge Alberto y otros v GCBA s/amparo 11 June 2004.

161 Buenos Aires Adminstrative Appelate Court, Chamber II, Ramallo, Beatriz v Ciudad de Buenos Aires, 30 September 2004.

162 Buenos Aires Administrative Trial Court No.5 *Agüero*, Aurelio E. v GCBA S/AMPARO, friendly settlement, Dec 2003.

where payments were not to exceed 20% of monthly income. This structural approach ensured budget, policy and outcome were all embedded in international human rights law.[163]

Similarly in a case involving the right to a healthy environment (Article 41) the court issued a structural remedy that required the state to produce and disseminating public information; control industrial pollution; clean up waste; expand water supply, sewer and drainage works; develop an emergency sanitation plan and adopt a monitoring system to assess compliance with the plans.[164]

Germany

The German constitution recognises the right to human dignity.[165] Whilst there is no specific or explicit guarantee to far-reaching ESR the courts have interpreted the right to human dignity, read together with the establishment of a 'social state', as requiring a minimum level of social assistance. In the *Hartz IV* case, the German constitutional court found that there is a fundamental right to the guarantee of a subsistence minimum that is in line with human dignity and the right to the enjoyment of a minimum subsistence level is not simply a facet of the right to human dignity but a stand-alone right of autonomous value.[166] The court declared the social security system unlawful when it failed to comply with the right to human dignity and when the means of calculating minimum subsistence (*existenz minimum*) were fundamentally flawed. The court found that 'it is the socio-economic right of every needy person to be provided, via statutory law, with material conditions that are indispensable for his or her physical existence and for a minimum participation in social, cultural, and political life'.[167]

The judgment stresses that there is a fundamental guarantee to a constitutional minimum that covers the material conditions that are indispensable for a person's physical existence (for example, housing, food, and clothing), for a minimum

---

163 For a discussion on this see Courtis, n 157 at 165.

164 *Beatriz Silvia Mendoza v National Government and Others* (2008) (Damages stemming from contamination of the Matanza-Riachuelo River) M. 1569, 8 July 2008 (Argentina, Supreme Court).

165 Article 1.

166 BVerfGE 125, 175 (*Hartz IV*), at par.133. See Trilsch, Mirjal, 'Constitutional protection of social rights through the backdoor: What does the "Social state" principle, the right to human dignity and the right to equality have to offer?', available at www.jus.uio.no/eng lish/research/news-and-events/events/conferences/2014/wccl-cmdc/wccl/papers/ws4/w4-trilsch.pdf. See also BVerfGE 132 where in 2012 the court went beyond the procedural protection in the previous case and recognised a substantive element to an adequate level of subsistence for asylum seekers relying on Article 9 ICESCR.

167 Case note – Human Dignity as a Matter of Legislative Consistency in an Ideal World: The Fundamental Right to Guarantee a Subsistence Minimum in the German Federal Constitutional Court's Judgment of 9 February 2010 By Claudia Bittner, 12 (11) *German Law Journal* (2011), 1950.

participation in human interaction (for example, telephone costs), and for a minimum participation in social, cultural, and political life (for example, membership in sport clubs, and going to the cinema).[168]

The *Hartz IV* case in Germany has provided an innovative approach to the right to social security that sets out a substantive standard as well as a procedural right. The court directly referenced Germany's obligation to comply with Article 9 ICESCR when assessing the minimum subsistence in a subsequent case dealing with asylum seekers.[169] The court has since taken a more restrictive approach to the doctrine established in the initial *Hartz IV* case law with the court upholding strict sanctions on the enjoyment of social protection for failure to comply with job seeker criteria, indicating the court's reluctance to over-reach.[170]

Conclusion: An Incoherent Legal Framework for ESR in the UK

The UK lacks a coherent overarching framework for ESR, and this in turn means that ESR do not form part of everyday governance. As noted at the start of this chapter, the devolved constitutional arrangements follow a framework model of constitutionalism (pertaining to a foundation) and at the UK level the constitution follows a process model (pertaining to fair processes). This causes constitutional incoherence when engaging with models of rights enforcement. As will become increasingly evident in the following chapter, although there is a constitutional resistance to ESR, adjudication of these rights occurs as part of the everyday practice of courts. So whilst there is no coherent overarching framework for ESR justiciability, it happens and will continue to happen. This book proposes potential ways forward to address the incoherent human rights framework, including adopting a renewed constitutional framework that better embeds ESR on the same terms as CPR. The devolved jurisdictions have already demonstrated the potential of a foundation-based framework model. It is not beyond the bounds of possibility that the Westminster model could learn from the devolved experience and other comparative examples, particularly in connection with the status afforded to human rights under the devolved framework and in relation to ESR constitutionalisation elsewhere. Ultimately, the style of UK political constitutionalism that can side line rights as matters of political bargaining risks becoming so far removed from a substantive rights-based conceptualisation of the rule of law that it is, in this era, no longer fit for purpose. This is particularly true within the post-devolved quasi-federal UK where progressive reform at the devolved level may ultimately risk fragmentation of the nation state.

---

168   *Hartz IV* case note Bittner, ibid. at 1952.
169   BVerfGE 132.
170   *Hartz IV*, BVerfGE L 7 AS 987/19 B ER, 17 July 2019.

5 Models of ESR Justiciability
Existing Mechanisms and Future Options

This chapter sets out models for ESR justiciability some of which are already under operation (existing mechanisms) and some of which could be developed in the future (future mechanisms for implementation). Much of this chapter draws on jurisprudence from the UK as well as comparatively. Navigating the existing justiciability mechanisms provides a much deeper understanding of how ESR adjudication already occurs in the UK – providing some light on an often misunderstood area. The future mechanisms help set out how ESR adjudication might develop in the future. Each model is examined in terms of the principles of adjudication developed in Chapter 1 and placed within a wider discussion on safeguards and recommendations in terms of democratic legitimacy. A detailed exposition is set out following a summary of the models for ease of reference:

An Introduction to the Models

Existing Mechanisms

Model 1: A Statutory Framework Providing for ESR That Is Subject to Judicial Remedies

This model explores the way through which ESR may become legally enforceable under the operation of parliamentary supremacy and the passage of legislation. This is the preferred approach under the existing constitutional framework in the UK. This model allows parliament to introduce legislation to account for ESR according to the prevailing circumstances and political will of the time. This model strongly supports a framework in which parliament holds supremacy. Problems with this model relate to the lack of safeguards in ensuring parliament introduces legislation which meets international legally binding standards without facing any accountability for retrogression or failure to comply. In other words, it does not necessarily amount to incorporation of international standards. For example, the National Minimum Wage Act 1998 sets a minimum wage to ensure fair pay at work. However, measured against international standards this 'ESR' mechanism has been deemed 'manifestly unfair'. So what appears as an ESR protection mechanism at the domestic level falls short of the normative standard in international human rights law. The theoretical considerations include whether the existing constitutional framework is fit for purpose and what other safeguards could be legitimately introduced, if any, to account for 'gaps' in the parliamentary supremacy constitutional model.

Model 2: A Judicial Remedy for Non-Compliance with Substantive Equality and Non-Discrimination Provisions

This model explores the way through which ESR are adjudicated on within the aegis of equality law. Through a comparative lens with other jurisdictions, such as Canada, it is evident that socio-economic rights protection occurs under equality provisions to a certain degree.

So for example, the UK public sector equality duty (s149 Equality Act 2010) requires public bodies to have due regard to various protected characteristics when implementing public policy decisions and in the allocation of budgets. Failure to do so can result in a judicial remedy issued by the court which renders the new policy or budget *ultra vires*. For example, in the case where Birmingham City Council made changes to allocation of their budget without considering the adverse impact on those with disabilities the court intervened and quashed the changes the council was trying to introduce.[1] This is a strong procedural protection to ensure that public bodies have due regard to vulnerable groups in the allocation of resources, however, it does not provide for substantive protection of ESR *per se* and does not meet the threshold of the substantive fairness principle.

On the other hand, the socio-economic equality duty (section 1 Equality Act 2010) would allow more substantive protection of ESR whereby a duty imposed on public bodies requires them to take into consideration socio-economic disadvantage. Section 1 of the Act was never commenced England, Scotland or Wales after passage of the legislation. The provision has now been devolved to Scotland and Wales and a new form of socio-economic protection has been implemented in Scotland under the Fairer Scotland Duty. Comparisons are drawn with jurisdictions such as the Northwest Territories in Canada that has implemented an expansive socio-economic equality duty.

The Equality Act 2010 does not apply in Northern Ireland which has a separate equality framework. Breaches of equality law in Northern Ireland tend not to be adjudicated in the court which raises concerns around the accessibility and remedial value of the existing structures. This means equality legislation protects socio-economic rights to different degrees across the UK with better protection in some parts compared to others. This has continuously been raised as an issue at UN Committee level where the UK has been called on to consolidate equality law.

---

1 *On the Application of W,M,G & H v Birmingham City Council*, [2011] EWHC 1147 Admin.

Model 3: The Judicial Interpretation of Civil and Political Rights According to the Principle of Indivisibility

Courts in the UK, Europe and internationally have adopted interpretations of civil and political rights in a manner that recognises socio-economic rights within the rubric of other rights. In the case of *Airey v Ireland*,[2] the European Court of Human Rights held that there is no water tight division between the spheres of civil and political rights and social and economic rights. Under the European Convention on Human Rights (ECHR) system rights relating to housing, health and basic subsistence have been developed under Articles 2, 3 and 8 of the European Convention of Human Rights. This trend is not unique to the ECHR and comparisons are drawn with other international and domestic examples of the expansion of civil and political rights to include socio-economic rights or dimensions of these rights (India, Germany, Latvia, European Union [EU], ECHR).

This interpretation of rights is referred to in the literature as the evolutive or dynamic interpretation of rights. Arguably, it is a natural evolution of interpretation when considered under the narrative that all rights were deemed indivisible at their original inception in the International Bill of Rights. The principle of indivisibility and the historical narrative of the erroneous bifurcation of rights are examined in detail in Chapter 2 This contextualisation helps explain why an evolutive approach is arguably teleological in nature – i.e. that the original purpose and design of the human rights legal framework would inevitably result in the judiciary interpreting civil and political rights as dependent on the enforcement of economic, social and cultural rights. On the other hand, it is argued that this type of 'dynamic' interpretation risks a juridification of rights and the judiciary stepping beyond its competence. Limitations of the model therefore include the limits that are placed on judges interpreting a text which is theoretically insufficient to account for the principle of indivisibility, such as the ECHR – the core human rights regime applicable in the UK. This raises concerns in terms of the deliberative quality of interpretation under a limited treaty framework and the balancing act between rights where CP rights are enforceable to the potential detriment of ESR meaning the counter-majoritarian principle is undermined. For example, the right to property under ECHR A1P1 may overshadow communitarian rights to land under a treaty structure that does not formally recognise economic and social rights, and indeed, cultural rights.

Model 4: The Common Law Application of (Customary) International Law

This model considers the common law interpretation of domestic law which incorporates international legal standards relating to ESR. Under the operation of parliamentary supremacy, unincorporated international treaties may not be adjudicated upon unless the domestic law has afforded recognition to the particular right in question. The UK judiciary has at times demonstrated competing views

---

2 32 Eur Ct HR Ser A (1979): [1979] 2 E.H.R.R. 305.

and polarised positions on this principle. In so far as the state has agreed to international human rights law without full incorporation there have been two competing understandings of the judiciary's role. Lady Hale, for example, has leaned towards an interpretation of domestic law which may partially incorporate international standards where appropriate (see, for example, *ZH Tanzania*[3] and dissenting judgment in the *SG*[4] case). This view was first articulated by Lord Steyn in the *McKerr* case where he argued international human rights law ought to be treated as a *sui generis* form of international law requiring deviation from the traditional rules of parliamentary supremacy.[5] However, the prevailing view, enunciated by Lord Reed in a case considering the accumulative impact of benefit caps on women and children,[6] is that without domestic incorporation of international standards through legislation the court cannot intervene and apply unincorporated international law as to do so would be stepping beyond its competence. Both strands of judicial theory are examined in relation to ESR and the model is framed in terms of the principles of adjudication.

Future Mechanisms for Implementation

Model 5: An International Complaints Mechanism

The UK is a party to the Council of Europe and the ECHR and so is already subject to a supranational complaints mechanism (the ECtHR in Strasbourg) to monitor human rights compliance (namely civil and political rights and limited socio-economic recognition subject to the evolutive interpretative approach). Likewise, until such time as the UK leaves the EU, the UK's membership of the EU entails both domestic and supranational remedies (in the Court of Justice of the European Union [CJEU]) through the existing limited recognition of ESR in the EU legal order. The UK has also acceded to other international complaints mechanisms that deal with ESR under the Optional Protocol to the Convention on the Elimination of All Forms of Discrimination against Women 1979 and under the Optional Protocol to the Convention on the Rights of Persons with Disabilities 2006. A more holistic approach to supranational adjudication on ESR could be achieved, for example, by signing and ratifying the Optional Protocol to the International Convention on Economic, Social and Cultural Rights (ICESCR) or through signing and ratifying the Additional Protocol Providing for a System of Collective Complaints to the European Social Charter. This model is therefore examined under the existing frameworks and in terms of what future options may be implemented to secure ESR through expanded access to international

---

3 *ZH (Tanzania) v Secretary of State for the Home Department* [2011] UKSC 4.
4 *R (on the application of SG and others (previously JS and others)) (Appellants) v Secretary of State for Work and Pensions (Respondent)* [2015] UKSC 16.
5 *Re McKerr* [2004] 1 WLR 807.
6 *SG* [2015] UKSC 16 para.90.

complaints mechanisms. It is also considered in the context of democratic legitimacy and wider considerations relating to viability in terms of supra-national judicial intervention on domestic issues and the often negative manner in which this is viewed in public discourse. The model engages with the principle of deliberation in terms of discourse across institutions from national to supranational. Legitimacy in such an approach can be derived from the opportunity to deliberate on the content of rights across institutions, and in so doing, helping to address the indeterminacy critique.

Model 6: A Constitutional Model

Any state seeking to embed social rights across areas of governance must create an overarching theoretical, conceptual, normative legal framework against which other implementation mechanisms can be measured. This is the constitutional model that provides constitutional recognition of ESR. The model proposed is identified as the most robust and democratically legitimate way of ensuring adjudication of ESR according to best practice. This model supports a multi-institutional approach to ESR adjudication that enables and facilitates the development of the other five models in a transparent environment. The multi-institutional approach framed within deliberative democracy theory considers the relationship and safeguards operating between different arms of power within the state – i.e. legislative, executive, adjudicative and constitutional. The constitutional model can set a foundation for the operation of the institutions of government – legislative, executive and adjudicative – each of which is bound to comply with the same legal framework embedded in the constitution, including the recognition of ESR.

There is a developing trend towards affording constitutional status to ESR in other states. The UK is in a peculiar position because the constitution is uncodified, limiting the way in which ESR could be constitutionalised. They cannot be constitutionalised through an amendment to an existing constitutional text so the options available are either to codify a constitution including ESR, or enact a 'constitutional statute' providing for their protection – i.e. something akin to the Human Rights Act incorporating ICESCR and/or the revised European Social Charter, an Economic and Social Rights Act or a Bill of Rights providing for ESR (as well as civil and political rights).

Options for constitutionalisation are considered at both the national and devolved level. This is placed within a comparative discussion on other constitutional models that provide explicit protection for ESR such as Finland, South Africa, Colombia and Argentina. This examination includes a discussion of both the attributes and potential weaknesses of this model as well as the lessons that can be learned from other jurisdictions.

The justiciability mechanisms are critically examined according to the principles of adjudication. Recommendations and safeguards are therefore proposed in order to ensure a democratic approach to ESR justiciability. The conclusion offered is that in order to secure the full recognition and substantive enjoyment of ESR a paradigmatic shift is required in terms of adopting a substantive human rights culture through the operation of a myriad of legal protection mechanisms and in a multi-institutional approach. The research also indicates that the most appropriate and democratically legitimate system is underpinned by a constitutional recognition of the status of human rights. Only then will accountability for the full realisation of all human rights be a possibility within a system that firmly secures their protection beyond the reach of retrogressive legislation or administrative policies that undermine ESR. Each of the mechanisms explored are measured in terms of this standard.

The preference for Model 6 as a foundationalist standard is based on a theoretical understanding of ESR in the context of a multi-institutional approach to rights adjudication.[7] Under the devolved frameworks there is a semi-foundationalist constitutional arrangement[8] and at the national level constitutionalism is based on parliamentary supremacy with a reluctance to recognise fundamental rights.[9] The latter of these two approaches to constitutionalism, i.e. Feldman's process model (political constitutionalism), means that rights protection is completely reliant on the will of the legislature to provide adequate protection mechanisms.[10] Legalisation of ESR can help address the significant accountability gap at the national level. This can be achieved in a way that allows for the sensible balancing of rights and resources and the balancing of decisions between different institutions of government without a wholesale transfer of power to the judiciary. The principles of adjudication help guide a state adapting to ESR adjudication as part of a multi-institutional deliberative framework.

An Examination of Existing and Future Justiciability Mechanisms

Model 1: A Statutory Framework Providing for ESR that is Subject to Judicial Remedies

As discussed above, the concept of democratic legitimacy within the context of the UK is based on the doctrine of parliamentary sovereignty. The theoretical framework upon which this doctrine is based is founded in the Diceyan concept of democratic legitimacy and is described by Hunt as amounting to a positivist foundational concept of sovereignty.[11] From this perspective, the sole responsibility in attaining, retaining and/or retrogressing from mechanisms for human rights protection belongs to the legislature. Without a paradigmatic shift in the constitutional framework of the UK, or its relationship with unincorporated

---

7 Ibid. This is developed further under Chapter 4.
8 Under the Northern Ireland Act 1998 and under the terms of the peace agreement and British-Irish Agreement of 1998.
9 See Chapter 4.
10 See Chapter 4 and David Feldman, 'Constitutionalism, Deliberative Democracy and Human Rights' in John Morison et al. (eds.), *Judges, Transitions and Human Rights* (Oxford University Press, 2007), 447–453.
11 Murray Hunt, 'Reshaping Constitutionalism' in John Morison et al. (eds.), ibid. at 468.

international law, the status of human rights protection will remain in the hands of those who are elected representatives in parliament through the legislative process. This approach is the preferred approach of theorists such as Waldron and Bellinger discussed below. The approach identified and the arguments posited here recognise that democratic legitimacy is best secured through a multi-institutional approach to ESR and that adjudication ought to be available based on a culture of legal accountability.

On examining the theoretical ideology which underpins this model of democratic legitimacy King opines that 'the best argument in favour of the presumptive legitimacy of legislation in a democratic society is based on the concept of political equality'.[12] The purpose of this approach is to afford 'equal respect to the moral claims of each citizen'[13] through a democratically representative legislature. In this respect, each citizen transfers authority to an elected representative to best represent their views, the result of which produces legislation that best represents the people as a whole. King criticises the idealistic view presented by those who avidly follow the 'rosy-picture' version of legislative supremacy in so far as majoritarian rule can often be displaced or driven by the 'priorities of a few at the top of a party which enjoy less than majority support, than by free votes taken after a good-faith parliamentary debate between persons of open minds'.[14]

The influence of lobbying within the parliamentary framework in the UK is also cited by King as undermining the principles of political equality within the representative framework.[15] This has, for example, come under scrutiny in the UK with the Prime Minister facing challenges of policy amendment based on tobacco lobbying[16] with other Members of Parliament and the House of Lords also being drawn into lobbying scandals on a number of issues.[17] This, as King notes, is particularly problematic within the context of social rights as a strong welfare state employing safety mechanisms for those who are vulnerable or

---

12 Jeff King, *Judging Social Rights* (Cambridge University Press, 2011), 154.

13 Amy Gutman and Dennis Thompson, *Democracy and Disagreement* (Cambridge, MA: Belknap Press, 1996), 26.

14 King, n 12 at 157. In particular, King cites the party whips system in Westminster that discourages departure from the central party policy, with the executive in some (or most) cases dominating the legislature.

15 King, n 12 at 157. King dismantles Jeremy Waldron's theory of formal voting equality posited in Jeremy Waldron, 'The Core of the Case against Judicial Review' (2006) 115 *Yale Law Journal* 1347. For a fuller explanation of Waldron's book see also Jeremy Waldron, *Law and Disagreement* (Oxford: Clarendon Press, 1999). Note, however, that lobbying in Scotland is a regulated activity under the Lobbying (Scotland) Act 2016.

16 Nicholas Winning, 'UK PM's Election Strategist Denies Lobbying on Tobacco Packaging', *The Wall Street Journal*, 23 July 2013, available at http://online.wsj.com/article/BT-CO-20130723-708955.html

17 See, for example, Newell, Calvert and Krause, Insight: 'I'm Like a Cab for Hire, at £5000 Pounds a Day', *The Sunday Times*, 21 March 2010, pp.6–7, as referenced in King, n 12 at 157 and Claire Newell, 'House of Lords Drawn into Lobbying Scandal', *The Telegraph*, 2 June 2013, available at www.telegraph.co.uk/news/politics/10093806/House-of-Lords-drawn-into-lobbying-scandal.html

marginalised 'is *diametrically opposed*, to the interests of the wealthy and is therefore precisely the target of the well-resourced lobbying interests'.[18] The introduction of the Lobbying Act 2014 may have gone some way to create greater transparency around lobbying, however, reports suggest it has a chilling effect on charities and NGOs whilst business interests continue to operate under an aegis of secrecy.[19]

On a critical analysis of the emerging 'democratic norm' thesis in international law (which pertains to the doctrine of legislative supremacy), Wheatley argues that the narrow interpretation of majoritarian deliberative democracy focuses too heavily on the institutional arrangements and holding of competitive elections without regard for the role of minority groups.[20] He submits that this approach conceives of:

> a thin model of democracy, whereby the function of government is to aggregate the preferences of individuals to find the decision that will be acceptable to most. In extreme versions, the role of the citizen is simply to determine who will hold power. The people do not actually rule in any obvious sense of the terms "people" and "rule", and democratic government becomes the rule of the elected politician.

This aggregative model Wheatley argues:

> is not conducive to realizing the interests and preferences of those minority groups with a high degree of solidarity and shared outlook, which find themselves permanently outvoted by the majority population. Even if they are represented in decision-making processes, there is nothing to prevent the more powerful and numerous participants from ignoring them. And for this reason, 'a more inclusive model must then be conceived, one in which decisions are based not only on the counting of votes, but also on the sharing of reasons'.[21]

With increased participation for minority communities the deliberative element of democratic governance could also arguably be undermined by ossifying or entrenching competing nationalisms/ethnicities and so voting on social policy according to ethnic/national status as opposed to political persuasion, such as is the case in some parts of the UK, most notably in Northern Ireland, and to

---

18 King, n 12 at 157.
19 Oliver Wright, 'Revealed: The Loophole That Lets Lobbying Companies Keep Their Clients a Secret', *The Independent*, 10 April 2016, available at www.independent.co.uk/news/uk/politics/revealed-the-loophole-that-lets-lobbying-companies-keep-their-clients-a-secret-a6977931.html
20 Steven Wheatley, 'Deliberative Democracy and Minorities' (2003) 14 *European Journal of International Law* 507.
21 Wheatley, ibid. at 509–510.

some degree on issues of independence in Scotland.[22] Feldman has argued that for the consociational model to work in Northern Ireland the electoral system ought to reward those people who express preference for candidates that represent policies resonant across the ethnic spectrum, and in so doing, force parties to obtain support from all groups or a range of groups in society forcing them towards moderation in their ethnic or nationalist policies.[23] Otherwise, there is a danger of entrenching divisions rather than producing a common commitment to the welfare of the *demos* as a whole.[24]

Without a constitutional arrangement for the protection of human rights, the legislative process is the most 'democratically sound' mechanism available under the democratic positivist process model. In other words, legitimate and viable ESR justiciability can occur if legislation provides for it and cannot occur if it does not. However, it must be noted that this model poses several difficulties. Before examining the problems posed let us consider the options available under this model/justiciable mechanism.

The Human Rights Act 1998 and its relationship with the devolved Acts offer a quasi-constitutional protection of the rights contained in the ECHR. The UN Committee on Economic Social and Cultural Rights has recommended that ESR ought to be protected in the same manner as civil and political rights.[25]

In this regard, it would be an option to extend the protection of rights under the Human Rights Act to ESR. An Act, for example, which incorporates the International Covenant on Economic, Social and Cultural Rights would be a mechanism open to the UK Parliament and would not infringe on the narrowest reading of the separation of powers and parliamentary sovereignty. Likewise, the devolved legislatures could, within their respective legislative competencies, enact legislation which observes or implements international obligations.[26] This holistic

---

22 See, for example, arguments posed by critics of consociationalism referenced by Bell et al. 'Justice Discourses in Transition' (2004) 13 *Social & Legal Studies* 305, 316.

23 David Feldman, 'Constitutionalism, Deliberative Democracy and Human Rights' in John Morison et al. (eds.), n 10 at 454.

24 Feldman, ibid. at 453.

25 UN Committee on Economic, Social and Cultural Rights (CESCR), General Comment No. 9: The domestic application of the Covenant, 3 December 1998, E/C.12/1998/24, para.7.

26 Under paragraph 3 of Schedule 2 of the Northern Ireland Act 1998 International relations, including relations with territories outside the UK, the European Communities (and their institutions) and other international organisations and extradition, and international development assistance and co-operation are excepted matters (i.e. beyond the legislative competence of the NI Assembly). However, an exemption to this excepted matter is the competence to observe and implement international obligations, obligations under the Human Rights Convention and obligations under Community law. Under Section 98 of the NI Act 'international obligations' are defined as 'any international obligations of the UK other than obligations to observe and implement Community law or the Convention rights'. Similar conditions apply in Wales and Scotland. Schedule 7A para.10(3)(a) Government of Wales Act 2006 exempts 'observing and implementing international obligations' from reserved matter of international relations and foreign affairs. Schedule 5 para.7(2)(a) of Scotland Act 1998 exempts 'observing and implementing international obligations' from foreign affairs reservation.

approach through a form of constitutional statute is discussed in more detail under Model 6 below (A Constitutional Model). Without a holistic approach the alternative legislative solution is through a piecemeal or sectoral protection of ESR.

THE PIECEMEAL APPROACH

In practice, ESR are provided for in some respects through the Acts which form the basis of the welfare state (enactments relating to education, housing, health, employment rights etc.). This is a sectoral approach, and if the rights are provided for in accordance with international legal standards can amount to sectoral incorporation of ESR. The UK Parliament has also enacted legislation to meet ESR recognised in international law such as Apprenticeships, Skills, Children and Learning Act 2009, which provided for a statutory right to education for detained young offenders in accordance with Article 28 of the UN Convention on the Rights of the Child and the Child Poverty Act 2010 in connection with the progressive realisation of an adequate standard of living under Article 27 of the UN Convention on the Rights of the Child.[27] Similarly, the Welsh Assembly has enacted the Rights of Children and Young Persons (Wales) Measure 2011, which imposes a duty on Welsh Ministers to have due regard to the UN Convention on the Rights of the Child. In Scotland there are numerous Acts of the Scottish Parliament referencing international treaties.[28] The Land Reform (Scotland) Act calls for the observance of international human rights, including the International Covenant on Economic, Social and Cultural Rights.[29] The Social Security (Scotland) Act 2018 also draws on ICESCR as a relevant international legal framework and declares the right to social security as a human right 'essential to the realisation of other human rights'.[30] In Northern Ireland, the Assembly has passed Commissioner for Older People (Northern Ireland) Act 2011. This Act requires the Commissioner for Older People to have regard to the United Nations Principles for Older Persons when performing his/her functions.[31] These legislative steps are indicative of important strides towards the realisation of international human rights law, however there are inherent limitations in relation to how far they go in providing an effective remedy for violations of such rights.

The current approach is limited through its piecemeal and incremental nature. First, there is no holistic legislative measure which deals with a full account of

---

27 For which the Government accepted a role for the court in ensuring the Secretary of State meets the obligations provided for in attaining poverty eradication targets. For further discussion on the role of the Joint Committee on Human Rights enhancing parliament's role in relation to international human rights obligations see Murray Hunt, 'Enhancing Parliament's Role in Relation to Economic and Social Rights' (2010) 3 *European Human Rights Law Review* 242 and chapter four.

28 See, for example, section 94(1)(a)(i) of the Public Health etc. (Scotland) Act 2008 and the Land Reform (Scotland) Act 2016.

29 Section 1 (6)(b) Land Reform (Scotland) Act 2016.

30 Social Security (Scotland) Act 2018 ss.1(b) and 22(5)(d).

31 Section 2(3).

ESR. Secondly, the legislation in place does not necessarily extend across the full jurisdiction of the UK. For example, section 48 of the Apprenticeships, Skills, Children and Learning Act 2009, the operative section providing for the educational measure for detained young offenders applies to England and Wales only. The duties contained in the piecemeal legislation may not fully encompass all of the duties conferred on the state by international law, nor do they extend to the full jurisdiction in every case. Incorporation of international standards through a piecemeal approach can act as an impediment to the indivisibility of rights and risks the dilution of international standards. They tend to impose procedural, as opposed to substantive duties, on the state and judicial review is only available to ensure the procedural aspects of the substantive rights are being fulfilled meaning non-compliant outcomes can still prevail. For example, the duty to have due regard to international obligations, does not in itself guarantee a justiciable right to the substantive realisation of a right. Rather, judicial review is only available to scrutinise whether the decision maker took the right into consideration during the decision-making process. This raises concerns for the remedial principle (where access to effective remedies may be limited or unavailable). It must also be noted that legislative protection of human rights, whilst laudable, is not free from interference with the threat of repeal or retrogressive measures. Again, this raises concerns under the counter-majoritarian principle and fairness principle where, under times of economic hardship, the greatest burden may be carried by the poorest and most marginalised communities with the least political power.

Through the legislative framework there are different degrees of transparency, accountability, acknowledgement of rights and substantive enjoyment of rights. The absence of a holistic approach undermines the state's commitment to ensure human rights are equally accessible to all people within the state's jurisdiction. As it currently stands there is a risk that human rights, particularly ESR, are subject to different degrees of protection in the UK depending on where the individual lives. There is also no certainty on the continuous development of protection as parliament can introduce retrogressive legislation which repeals current protection or undermines the status of rights. Finally, whilst it is within the gift of both the Westminster Parliament and the devolved legislatures to provide for the enactment of holistic legislation that confers an effective remedy on an individual for the violation of ESR there has been no legislation to address this gap holistically as yet. This presents as an accountability gap for the state at both the national and devolved level.

CAN WE RELY ON LEGISLATION TO FULFIL RIGHTS?

A constitutional solution is the most robust mechanism through which a comprehensive approach to rights adjudication can be legitimately secured. That is not to undermine the approaches identified under any of the other models. As such, a constitutional solution is identified as a mechanism required to secure the effective implementation of the other models and the other models are required to successfully implement what the constitutional model has set as a normative standard. This approach ought to be viewed in the context of a multi-institutional approach, i.e. legislative, executive, adjudicative and constitutional.[32]

As such the preference for a constitutional solution draws on a foundationalist framework based on a theoretical understanding of ESR in the context of a multi-institutional approach to rights adjudication.[33] Under the devolved framework of Northern Ireland, Scotland and Wales there are already semi-foundationalist constitutional arrangements in place[34] and at the national level constitutionalism is based on parliamentary supremacy with a reluctance to recognise fundamental rights.[35] The latter of these two approaches to constitutionalism means that rights protection is completely reliant on the will of the legislature to provide adequate protection mechanisms.[36]

The principle of agency is central to arguments in support of human rights as standards developed and adopted by political representatives through the operation of representative democracy.[37] Waldron in his book, *Law and Disagreement*,[38] argues that democratic legitimacy is ensured through the operation of political representation[39] and that the substance of rights should be realised through political consensus rather than through the courts. This is based on the concept that there is good-faith disagreement between persons about rights and the meaning of rights. This disagreement ought to be resolved by representative legislatures, after reasoned debate, through majority voting. His thesis is premised on the argument that the legislature is the most appropriate forum through which deliberation can occur to resolve substantive disagreements on the form and substance of rights and how they ought to be protected.[40] In response to this position King highlights some gaps in the operation of the principles of agency and political equality alone to secure substantive rights protection. Namely, the gap between preference and outcome (political representatives do not always give equal weight to each voter's preference) and equality and outcome-based departures from formal voting equality (strict voting equality is departed from as a matter of course).[41]

---

32 See Chapter 2 (IV) King, n 12.
33 Ibid. This is developed further under Chapter 6 'Democratic Legitimacy' King, n 12.
34 Under the Northern Ireland Act 1998 and under the terms of the peace agreement and British-Irish Agreement of 1998.
35 See Chapter 4.
36 See Chapter 4 and Feldman, n 23 at 447–453.
37 For a discussion on the concept of agency and rights as a construction of human reason within the political forum see Seyla Benhabib, 'Reason-Giving and Rights-Bearing: Constructing the Subject of Rights' (2013) 20 *Constellations* 38.
38 Waldron, *Law and Disagreement* n 15.
39 Based on political equality in participation in the system.
40 Ibid. at Chapter 5.
41 King, n 12 1 at 156 and 159.

The argument, or gap identified by King, in Waldron's thesis is that strict equality voting is departed from as a matter of course meaning that there are a number of 'blind spots' in relying on legislative supremacy to ensure adequate rights protection.[42] These blind spots can be categorised under (i) marginalisation (or majoritarian neglect) and (ii) lack of legislative focus.

First, the marginalisation of particularly vulnerable groups essentially means that representative democracy does not represent everyone. The principle of agency is undermined – i.e. the right to participate in politics to resolve disputes over substance and form of right cannot be accessed by those who are excluded from the majoritarian system.[43] Waldron and Bellamy – both critics of judicial review – concede that this issue is 'a real limitation to the argument for the legitimacy of legislation'.[44] This is particularly problematic in the conflicted democracy context in Northern Ireland where consociational politics and historic injustices can place minorities particularly vulnerable to potential human rights violations.[45] Affording constitutional status to substantive human rights can help bridge the gap in ensuring substantive change for vulnerable minorities.

Second, the lack of legislative focus simply accounts for the fact that the legislature may well not have envisaged that a provision of legislation would engage with a human rights issue at the time of drafting.[46] This is problematic because (a) the legislature may have had no overarching guidance to the focus the minds of the political representatives as to what kind of rights issues should be considered before passing legislation and (b) through the passage of time moral and normative claims over rights can change meaning that legislation can become problematic.[47]

---

42 Rosalind Dixon, 'Creating Dialogue about Socioeconomic Rights: Strong-Form versus Weak-Form Judicial Review Revisited' (2007) 5 *International Journal of Constitutional Law* 391.

43 For a discussion on the liberal theories of rights construction through 'the right to self-government' see Benhabib, n 37 at 46.

44 King, n 12 at 165. R. Bellamy, *Political Constitutionalism: A Republican Defence of the Constitutionality of Democracy* (Cambridge University Press, 2007), 26–48 and Waldron, 'The Core of the Case against Judicial Review' n 15 at 1404.

45 As was the case in Northern Ireland.

46 For example, in *Bellinger v Bellinger* [2003] UKHL 21 a post-operative male-to-female transsexual challenged s11 of the Matrimonial Causes Act 1973 for its failure to provide for the possibility of marriage by transgender persons post operation. It could not have been seriously considered by the legislature at this time that this would be a rights dispute. Likewise, in *McR's Application for Judicial Review* [2003] NI 1 Lord Justice Kerr found that section 62 of the Offences Against the Persons Act 1861 criminalising homosexual intercourse (buggery) was an unlawful interference with Article 8 ECHR. The normative moral claims had changed over time and the court was able, through the guidance of the ECHR, to refocus legislation around substantive rights claims where the legislature had not done so.

47 In relation to this last point, it does not necessarily stand to ground that problematic legislation ought to be remedied by the court – the legislature is capable of performing this task alone. However, unless there is a forum to legitimately challenge the legislation then representative democracy might not necessarily revisit the problematic legislation. I.e. at the very least the courts can play an important role through judicial review of drawing the legislature's attention to problematic legislation through deference at a minimum.

King develops a theory of democratic legitimacy based on the principles of elite deliberative democracy (deliberation between institutions)[48] that ensures legislative focus on rights and the protection of marginalised groups under an overarching constitutional framework.[49]

Benhabib argues that there is a place for the principles of democratic legitimacy argued by Waldron (through the legislature) and King (through the constitution and the court) and that each can co-exist. Without the right to self-government we cannot justify the range of variation in the content of basic human rights as being legitimate.[50] However, at the same time, self-government cannot be meaningfully exercised without the actualisation of human rights themselves:[51]

> Just as, without the actualisation of human rights themselves self-government cannot be meaningfully exercised, so too, without the right to self-government, human rights cannot be contextualised as justiciable entitlements[52]

Benhabib identifies that representative democracy and formulation of rights through deliberation in the legislature complements a substantive rights-based foundationalist approach to constitutionalism affording legally enforceable justiciable rights – and in the same vein a constitutional arrangement complements and benefits from a legislative system which engages with contextualising rights as justiciable entitlements.[53] Without the basic foundation creating an environment for political agency a person or collective cannot exercise self-governance.

Whilst a legislative model is useful, it is not enough to adopt one on a piecemeal basis if ESR are to be sufficiently protected. The basic constitutional foundation provides, at the very least, an overarching framework for the minimum of ESR protection (as well as CPR) in order to legitimately fulfil the other roles of autonomy required in a democracy.

Model 2: A Judicial Remedy for Non-compliance with Substantive Equality and Non-discrimination Provisions

Nolan et al. note the strong relationship between the violation of ESR and systemic inequalities that results in ESR adjudication under the rubric of equality legislation:

---

48 Stephen Tierney, *Constitutional Republicanism* (Oxford University Press, 2012), 3–4.
49 King, n 12 Chapter 6.
50 Benhabib, n 37 at 46.
51 Ibid.
52 Ibid.
53 This formulation is based on Habermas' theory of co-originatlity of public and private autonomy see Jürgen Habermas, *Between Facts and Norms: Contributions to a Discourse Theory of Law and Democracy*, Trans. William Rehg (Cambridge, MA: MIT Press, 1996), 84–104. See Benhabib, n 37 FN 42.

The relationship between the right to equality and non-discrimination and social and economic rights is of central importance to the adjudication of social and economic rights. Violations of most social and economic rights are directly linked to systemic inequalities and may, in many cases, be challenged as such. Thus, in jurisdictions lacking explicit protections of social and economic rights, the right to equality can serve as a critical vehicle for disadvantaged groups seeking to enforce their social and economic rights.[54]

The second justiciability mechanisms for ESR is through the rubric of equality legislation. The literature demonstrates that equality and non-discrimination measures are used as a vehicle to secure ESR.[55] Likewise, there are examples of both domestic and international case law through which equality legislation acts as a vehicle for socio-economic rights.[56]

In England, Scotland and Wales (Great Britain, or GB for short) all equality provisions are consolidated in one piece of legislation – the Equality Act 2010 (which does not extend to Northern Ireland). In Northern Ireland equality measures are dealt with under a series of legislative measures and underpinned by the equality provisions found in the Northern Ireland Act 1998 (this is discussed in more detail in chapter six in the section dealing with Northern Ireland).[57] McKeever and Ní Aoláin have documented the development of

---

54 Nolan et al., *The Justiciability of Social and Economic Rights: An Updated Appraisal* (Human Rights Consortium, March 2007) para.3.3.1.
55 Nolan et al., ibid. See also Grainne McKeever and Fionnuala Ní Aoláin, 'Thinking Globally, Acting Locally: Enforcing Socio Economic Rights in Northern Ireland' (2004) 2 *European Human Rights Law Review* 158; Mónica Feria Tinta, 'Justiciability of Economic, Social, and Cultural Rights in the Inter-American System of Protection of Human Rights: Beyond Traditional Paradigms and Notions' (2007) 29 *Human Rights Quarterly* 431. Equal protection and non-discrimination can also be construed in light of economic, social and cultural rights – including the conditions at work, the right to social security, the right to a healthy environment and the right to have access to basic public services. Tinta also identifies clusters of contentious cases – so most frequently adjudicated case types with ESR relate to children, indigenous population, workers rights and vulnerable and disadvantaged groups in Latin American society such as street children, children in institutions, indigenous populations, displaced peoples, migrants, manual workers and prison populations.
56 Domestic examples: *Harjula v London Borough Council supra Harjula v London Borough Council* [2011] EWHC 151 (QB); *on the Application of W,M,G & H v Birmingham City Council,* [2011] EWHC 1147 Admin. International examples: *Eldridge v. British Columbia (Attorney General)* [1997] 3 S.C.R.; *Awas Tingi v Nicaragua* Inter-Am Ct HR, August 31 2001; *Shelter Corporation v. Ontario Human Rights Commission* (2001) 143 OAC 54; also *Klickovic Pasalic and Karanovic v Bosnia and Herzegovina, the Federation of Bosnia and Herzegovina and the Republika Sprska,* CH/02/8923, CH/02/8924, CH/02/9364, 10 January 2003; *Khosa v Minister of Social Development,* 2004 (6) SA 505 (CC).
57 Section 75 and Schedule 9 of the Northern Ireland Act provides for the statutory equality framework in Northern Ireland. See also – the Equality Pay Act (NI) (as amended) 1970, which provided equality in employment between men and women; Sex Discrimination (NI) Order (as amended) 1976; Fair Employment Act 1976, which provided equality in employment between those of different religious beliefs; Fair Employment (NI) Act 1989; Disability

equality legislation within the Northern Irish jurisdiction and encouraged a move beyond a programmatic protection of socio-economic rights to a more inclusive and substantive enforcement model coupled with judicial remedies.[58] They argue that ESR protection would be better facilitated in Northern Ireland by amending section 75 to include 'socio-economic status' as part of the procedural duty to have due regard to encouraging equality of opportunity.[59]

A SOCIO-ECONOMIC EQUALITY DUTY

The socio-economic duty in the Equality Act 2010 imposes a public sector duty on public authorities regarding socio-economic equalities (this provision has not been commenced across GB as discussed below). Section 1 of the Act provides that a public authority must, when making decisions of a strategic nature about how to exercise its functions, have due regard to the desirability of exercising them in a way that is designed to reduce the inequalities of outcome which result from socio-economic disadvantage. The purpose of the provision was to reduce inequalities in education, health, housing, crime rates or other matters associated with socio-economic disadvantage.[60] Before the Act was commenced there was a change in administration in the UK Government. The Act was a product of the New Labour administration and when the Lib-Con Coalition Government came into power in 2010 the socio-economic provision was scrapped.[61] Theresa May, then Minister for Women and Equalities announced the move describing the provision as 'ridiculous':

> Just look at the socio-economic duty. It was meant to force public authorities to take into account inequality of outcome when making decisions about their policies. In reality, it would have been just another bureaucratic box to be ticked. It would have meant more time filling in forms and less time focusing on policies that will make a real difference to people's life

Act (UK wide) 1995; Race Relations (NI) Order 1997; Fair Employment and Treatment (NI) Order 1998; Police (NI) Act 2000; Equality (Disability etc) (NI) Order 2000; Employment Equality (Sexual Orientation) (NI) Regulations 2003; European Framework Directive on Equal Treatment 2004.

58 McKeever and Ní Aoláin, n 55.
59 McKeever and Ní Aoláin, ibid. at 172.
60 Explanatory Notes to the Equality Act 2010, available at www.legislation.gov.uk/ukpga/2010/15/notes/division/3/1/1 para.23. The explanatory notes also offer example scenarios in how the application of this provision was envisaged: 'The Department of Health decides to improve the provision of primary care services. They find evidence that people suffering socio-economic disadvantage are less likely to access such services during working hours, due to their conditions of employment. The Department therefore advises that such services should be available at other times of the day'.
61 Amelia Gentleman, 'Theresa May Scraps Legal Requirement to Reduce Inequality', *The Guardian*, 17 November 2010, available at www.guardian.co.uk/society/2010/nov/17/theresa-may-scraps-legal-requirement-inequality

chances. But at its worst, it could have meant public spending permanently skewed towards certain parts of the country. Valued public services meant to benefit everyone in the community closed down in some areas and reopened in others. Council services like bin collections and bus routes designed not on the basis of practical need but on this one politically-motivated target. You can't solve a problem as complex as inequality in one legal clause. You can't make people's lives better by simply passing a law saying that they should be made better. That was as ridiculous as it was simplistic and that is why I am announcing today that we are scrapping the socio-economic duty for good.[62]

Monaghan notes that there is an important constitutional question as to whether the executive can lawfully announce that it will not ever bring into force a provision of an Act of Parliament that has contained within it commencement powers anticipating its entry into force (as it usurps parliamentary supremacy).[63] Without parliament repealing the provision it ought to be beyond the competence of the executive to unilaterally declare the provision as unworkable without first seeking the approval of the legislature. There is now a civil society campaign in place urging MPs to pressure the Government to commence the provision in order to address the socio-economic equality gap.[64] This campaign, of course, should have been unnecessary from the outset, given parliament already passed the provision. As noted by Monaghan, the executive failing to commence this provision could be called into question as the executive is essentially usurping the role of the legislature.

The UK Government's reluctance to commence on a GB wide basis means there is a significant gap in addressing the role poverty plays in further entrenching social exclusion.[65] Nolan et al. cite comparative case law whereby the correlation between poverty and social exclusion is recognised and discrimination on a socio-economic basis declared unlawful.[66] Mullally draws upon the potential

62 Speech delivered by Theresa May, Minister for Women and Equality, on 17 November 2010, available at http://sta.geo.useconnect.co.uk/ministers/speeches-1/equalities_strategy_speech.aspx
63 Karon Monaghan, *On Equality Law* (Oxford University Press, 2012), 19, see also *Padfield v Minister of Agriculture, Fisheries and Food* [1968] 1 AC 997 as cited in Monaghan.
64 See, for example, the campaign run by Just Fair and the Equality Trust https://1forequality.com/
65 For a discussion on the correlation between poverty and social exclusion see, for example, Scottish Human Rights Commission National Action Plan, Getting it Right? Human Rights in Scotland, para.2.5.2 entitled 'Poverty and Equality' available at www.scottishhumanrights.com/actionplan/home; Carey Oppenheim and Lisa Harker, *Poverty: The Facts* (3rd Rev. ed., London: Child Poverty Action Group, 1996); and Monaghan, n 65 Chapter 1, 'There is a close relationship – indeed almost a direct correlation – between the level of inequality and the prevalence of social problems'. para.1.24, 10.
66 Nolan et al., n 54 draw attention to the decision of the Ontario Board of Inquiry which was upheld by the Division Court in *Shelter Corporation v. Ontario Human Rights Commission*

of addressing socio-economic disadvantage through equality law referring to the Canadian example of the Northwestern Territories Human Rights Act 2002.[67] This, Mullally contends, would bring legislation 'beyond the confines of traditional anti-discrimination measures, to combine a concern with group-based disadvantage and a politics of redistribution'.[68]

The duty has now been partially devolved. In Scotland, the there is a newly devolved power to enforce the socio-economic equality duty in relation to devolved matters. The new duty, now called the Fairer Scotland Duty came into force in April 2018.[69] The same power has now been devolved to Wales under section 45 of the Wales Act 2017. It is not yet clear to what extent this will give rise to litigious protection on the grounds of socio-economic disadvantage, if any. At the very least,

---

(2001) 143 OAC 54 where denials of housing on the ground of poverty or low income level was found to constitute discrimination on a number of grounds, including race, sex, marital status, age, citizenship status and receipt of public assistance. See also *Klickovic Pasalic and Karanovic v Bosnia and Herzegovina, the Federation of Bosnia and Herzegovina and the Republika Sprska*, CH/02/8923, CH/02/8924, CH/02/9364, 10 January 2003 where the Human Rights Chamber for Bosnia and Herzegovina decided that the disparity in pension payments given to pensioners returning to Bosnia and Herzegovina, versus those pensioners who remained in Bosnia and Herzegovina during the armed conflict, amounted to discrimination regarding the right to social security on the basis of the applicants' status as internally displaced persons and in direct connection with their socio-economic status.

67 Siobhán Mullally, 'Substantive Equality and Positive Duties in Ireland', (2007) 23 *South African Journal of Human Rights* 291, 309. The Human Rights Act 2002 of the Northwest territories, defines socio-economic status as a 'social condition' with regard to 'the condition of inclusion of the individual, other than on a temporary basis, in a socially identifiable group that suffers from social or economic disadvantage resulting from poverty, source of income, illiteracy, level of education or any other similar circumstance'. (section 1 of the 2002 Act).

68 Ibid. Kilcommins et al. conducted a comparative analysis of the use of socio-economic status as a grounds of discrimination in employment legislation across a number of jurisdictions, Shane Kilcommins, Siobhán Mullally, Emma McClean, Maeve McDonagh, Darius Whelan, 'Extending the Scope of Employment Legislation: Comparative Perspectives on the Prohibited Grounds of Discrimination', Report Commissioned by the Department of Justice, Equality and Reform (Government of Ireland, 2004). This comparative analysis reveals that socio-economic status as a ground for discrimination can help relieve ESR violations that occur as a result of social origin/socio-economic disadvantage, where poverty, social exclusion and social deprivation operate as constraints on an individual's social mobility (sometimes across generations). For example, in addition to the Northwest territories legislation other jurisdictions have employed related grounds of discrimination such as 'being in receipt of public assistance', or 'social income' to combat socio-economic disadvantage in other parts of Canada (Saskatchewan, Manitoba and Ontario) and case law in New Zealand has developed to include discrimination on the grounds of employment status (albeit in a more restrictive approach than socio-economic status *per se*). Kilcommins et al. propose a definition that takes into account level of education; level of literacy; homelessness; geographical location; source of income; level of income; type of work or profession; and employment status.

69 Scotland Act 2016, section 38. The Scottish Government completed a consultation on bringing the power into operation in November 2017, see Scottish Government, Consultation on the Socio-economic Duty: Analysis of Responses (November 2017), available at www.gov. scot/Resource/0052/00527914.pdf . The duty was first established under the Equality Act 2010, section 1 but was never commenced.

the duty confers an obligation on public bodies, including local authorities, to have due regard to reducing inequality of outcome caused by socio-economic disadvantage. The duty is procedural and not outcome based, nonetheless the duty does encourage decision makers to reach a particular outcome. Marrying this duty with a broader theoretical and conceptual framework that addresses poverty, social exclusion and socio-economic disadvantage within an ESR paradigm would help duty-bearers better understand how to achieve the socio-economic duty where it has been commenced. However, it is important to note that the duty alone does not go so far as to ensure substantive equality, falling short of the substantive fairness principle as any adjudication arising would be based on the principle of procedural, as opposed to substantive fairness. This also falls short of the substantive requirements of equality under the international legal framework.[70]

THE PUBLIC SECTOR EQUALITY DUTY

Despite the refusal to commence the socio-economic status provision on a GB wide basis, the Equality Act 2010 has nonetheless transformed the legal landscape in GB whereby adjudication on socio-economic rights occurs under the auspice of legislative measures providing for equality.[71] In this sense equality measures can act as a vehicle for the protection of ESR. The judiciary, particularly in England, saw a plethora of cases under the public sector equality duty following its commencement in so far as public bodies were under a duty to have due regard to equality needs in the decision-making process.[72] The judiciary quashed

---

70 The international legal framework requires states to take positive steps to address the substantive inequality between different groups. This requires steps to achieve equality of outcome as opposed to equality of opportunity. For a discussion on substantive equality see Sandra Fredman, 'Substantive Equality Revisited' (2016) 14(3) *International Journal of Constitutional Law* 712–738 and Catharine A. MacKinnon, 'Substantive Equality Revisited: A Reply to Sandra Fredman' (2016) 14(3) *International Journal of Constitutional Law* 739–746.

71 Prior to 6 April 2011 the relevant equality duties were contained in the Race Relations Act 1976 s.71; Sex Discrimination Act 1975 s.76A(1); and the Disability Discrimination Act 1995 s.49A(1). Section 149 of the Equality Act 2010 is now in force. The public sector equality duty extends to all the protected characteristics namely age, disability, gender reassignment, marriage and civil partnership, pregnancy and maternity, race, religion or belief, sex and sexual orientation. For a fuller discussion on the impact of the Equality Act 2010 see Sandra Fredman, 'Positive Duties and Socio-economic Disadvantage: Bringing Disadvantage onto the Equality Agenda' (2010) *European Human Rights Law Review* 290.

72 BBC, 'Birmingham City Council Care Funding Cuts Unlawful', 20 April 2011, available at www.bbc.co.uk/news/uk-england-birmingham-13147675, Helen Carter, 'Birmingham Council's Plan to Cut Care for Disabled Ruled Unlawful', *The Guardian*, 19 May 2011, available at www.guardian.co.uk/society/2011/may/19/birmingham-council-cut-disabled-care-unlawful; Tim Ross, 'High Court: Council Must Not Axe Care for Elderly', *The Telegraph*, 19 May 2011, available at www.telegraph.co.uk/news/politics/8524591/High-Court-Council-must-not-axe-care-for-elderly.html; Nicholas Timmins, 'Curb on Disabled Care Ruled Unlawful', *The Financial Times*, 19 May 2011, available at www.ft.com/cms/s/0/704f5a6a-8249-11e0-961e-00144feabdc0

decisions of public authorities that did not have due regard to this obligation and so, redistributive justice finds a way into the common law through the adjudication of equality of opportunity at a procedural level. The Equality Act 2010 therefore provides a mechanism through which individuals may seek to remedy a violation of an international human right not protected by the ECHR, EU law or domestic legislation. However, it amounts to a procedural protection to have due regard, rather than to ensure substantive outcomes. Whilst this may well impact on mainstreaming equality in the decision-making process and encourage the fulfilment of positive duties by the state, it is not a mechanism through which substantive outcomes can be guaranteed.

In relation to those provisions in force across GB the 2010 Act does not introduce the right to sue for a breach of an equality provision *per se*, nevertheless, decisions of public bodies are subject to judicial review (section 156). The explanatory notes to section 156 gives an example of how these rights are enforceable:

> A local council fails to give due regard to the requirements of the public sector equality duty when deciding to stop funding a local women's refuge. An individual would not be able to sue the local council as a result and claim compensation. She would need to consider whether to pursue judicial review proceedings.
>
> Equality Act 2010 Explanatory Notes, Section 156, para.508

This renders particular vulnerable groups that fall under the definition of a 'protected characteristic'[73] within the legal parameters of accessible justiciable remedies. The public sector equality duty in section 149 of the Act imposes a duty on public bodies to have due regard to the need to:

a   eliminate discrimination, harassment, victimisation and any other conduct that is prohibited by or under the Act;

b   advance equality of opportunity between persons who share a relevant protected characteristic and persons who do not share it; and

c   foster good relations between persons who share a relevant protected characteristic and persons who do not share it.

The judiciary has quashed economic decisions where equality impact assessments have not been carried out correctly under the public sector equality duty, i.e. where

---

73 The protected characteristics are listed in section 4 of the Equality Act 2010, namely age; disability; gender reassignment; marriage and civil partnership; pregnancy and maternity; race; religion or belief; sex; and sexual orientation. Section 75 of the Northern Ireland Act 1998 imposes an obligation to have due regard to the promotion of equality of opportunity between persons of different religious belief, political opinion, racial group, age, marital status or sexual orientation; between men and women generally; between persons with a disability and persons without; and between persons with dependants and persons without.

due regard has not been exercised.[74] This is a procedural safeguard to take into consideration the impact of measures on protected groups as opposed to imposing a duty to secure substantive equality. It closely adheres to the principles of adjudication associated with accessibility and procedural fairness but falls short on wider participation and counter-majoritarian principles (in relation to collective cases) and remedies are restricted to process-based outcomes (revisiting decision-making processes) rather than substantive-based outcomes (reaching a different outcome).

Procedural protection means that there is an obligation on the local authority to carry out an equality impact assessment (a process) before making a decision that might adversely impact on a protected group. If it does not do this then it is in breach of the duty under section 149 of the 2010 Act. However, the local authority can carry out an equality impact assessment and still make a decision which adversely impacts a protected group. In this sense, the protection is only procedural as there is no remedy available for a substantive breach if the due regard duty has been complied with. It is a right to a process, not a right to an outcome.

Furthermore, the development of jurisprudence is dependent on cases being raised and so violations of ESR are therefore being deliberated and adjudicated upon by the courts on an incremental basis. For example, there are more cases being raised in England than in Wales or Scotland[75] and the 2010 Act does not apply to Northern Ireland, meaning the case law in England is effectively revealing an equality divide between the various jurisdictions and in so doing, perhaps revealing a UK-wide ESR deficit with different degrees of judicial protection.

In terms of the principles of adjudication, the equality model presents similar problems to the legislative model. The protection afforded to ESR through the rubric of equality provisions is both piecemeal and incremental. The duties under the Equality Act 2010 are procedural rather than substantive and there are serious jurisdictional gaps in so far as judicial remedies are available to individuals in the rest of the UK that do not extend to Northern Ireland. Access to

---

74 For example, see the case of *Harjula v London Borough Council* [2011] EWHC 151 (QB) in which the judge quashed the decision of the council for failing to consider its obligations under s71 Race Relations Act 1976, section 76A Sex Discrimination Act 1976 and section 49A Disability Discrimination Act 1995 (these provisions have been replaced by section 149 of the Equality Act 2010). See also the 2011 case against Birmingham Council for failing to have due regard to equality duties by failing to consult. Held: the budgetary re-allocation of funds was declared unlawful, *on the Application of W,M,G & H v Birmingham City Council*, [2011] EWHC 1147 Admin.

75 This may be to do with the historic rules regarding standing in Scotland which had, prior to the decision of the Supreme Court in *Axa General Insurance Ltd v the Lord Advocate* [2011] UKSC 46, required an individual to establish 'title and interest' to take a case – a much higher threshold than the standing requirement in England and Wales. For a full discussion on this see the *Axa* case in which the judiciary amended the common law rule on title and interest in Scotland to mirror the standing requirement in England and Wales. See Chris Himsworth, 'The Supreme Court reviews the Review of Acts of the Scottish Parliament' [2012] *Public Law* 205.

effective judicial remedies for the potential violation of an equality provision currently depends on where you live. Whilst the UK Parliament would be able to
rectify the jurisdictional problem by extending protections afforded under the
Equality Act to Northern Ireland, the legislative competence of the Northern
Ireland Assembly may not be able to replicate the same protection under the
existing devolved framework – rendering any potential legislation beyond the
competence of the Assembly and open to a declaration by the court that it is
ultra vires.[76] The Northern Ireland context is discussed in more detail below.

Ultimately, whilst there are very positive aspects under the existing statutory
equality framework there is more scope to develop substantive equality protection
across the protected characteristics and on socio-economic grounds. MacKinnon,
for example, proposes a social hierarchy approach that addresses systemic and structural inequality beyond the paradigm of equal opportunity for substantive equality
to be achieved.[77] And Fredman argues that addressing poverty must feature as
a component of substantive equality in a multidimensional framework that recognises and addresses the distributional, recognition, structural and exclusive wrongs
experienced by disadvantaged groups.[78] Substantive equality measures would
require more proactive duties that seek to ensure equality of outcome for protected
groups, rather than equality of opportunity. A substantive approach to equality
would embrace the broader conceptualisation of the counter-majoritarian and
remedial principles of adjudication that recognise the systemic nature of ESR
violations.

Model 3: The Judicial Interpretation of Civil and Political Rights According to the Principle of Indivisibility

The third justiciability model for ESR is adjudication through the ambit of civil
and political rights. According to the principle of indivisibility ESR can form an
integral part of the realisation of a civil or political right and courts have found
that an ESR right can be implied, or derived from, a civil or political right. This
approach is referred to as the dynamic, or evolutive, approach to human rights
interpretation. For example, Tinta outlines the parameters of interpretation
available to the Inter-American Court that has enabled an evolutive approach in
so far as the judiciary may take into account the prevailing domestic system as
well as other international instruments or conventions which also constitute the
system of law in the relevant jurisdiction:[79]

> This evolutive interpretation is consequent with the general rules of the
> interpretation of treaties embodied in the 1969 Vienna Convention. Both

76 Under section 6(2)(b) of the Northern Ireland Act 1998.
77 MacKinnon, n 70 at 740.
78 Fredman, n 70 at 738.
79 Tinta, n 55 at 444.

this Court ... and the European Court ... have indicated that human rights treaties are living instruments, the interpretation of which must evolve over time in view of existing circumstances.[80]

As Tinta observes, 'the right to life or right to humane treatment appears inter-woven with the right to health, the right to livelihood, the right to food, or the right to education'.[81] In the case of *Villagran Morales* et al.[82] the court held that the right to life:

> includes, not only the right of every human being not to be deprived of his life arbitrarily, but also the right that he will not be prevented from having access to the conditions that guarantee a dignified existence. States have the obligation to guarantee the creation of the conditions required in order that violations of this basic right do not occur and, in particular, the duty to prevent its agents from violating it.[83]

The Colombian Constitutional Court has also found that a failure to provide health-care services may entail a violation of the right to life.[84] The judiciary in India has similarly extended a broad interpretation to the right to life in Article 21 of the Constitution as including, amongst other rights the right to food, the right to healthcare, the right to clothing, the right to a decent environment and an education.[85]

---

80 The Right to Information on Consular Assistance in the Framework of the Guarantees of Due Process of Law. Advisory Opinion OC -16/99, Inter-Am. Ct HR (ser A) No. 16 (1 Oct) 1999 cited in *Villagran Morales* et al. Inter-Am. Ct. HR No. 63 (19 November 1999).

81 Tinta, n 55 at 437.

82 *Villagran Morales* et al. n 81.

83 *Villagran Morales* et al. ibid. Tinta also cites the case of *Moiwana Village v Suriname* Int-Am CT hr Series C No.124 (15 June 2005) where, following forced eviction, the court recog-nised the indigenous cultural rights of the N'djuka community to its traditional land which was of 'vital spiritual, cultural and material importance'.

84 See, for example, cases T-484/1992, 11 August 1992; T-328/1993, 12 August 1993, T494/93, 28 October 1993, T-597/93, 15 December 1993, T-217/95, 23 June 1995.

85 *Shantistar Builders v. Narayan Khimatal Tomtame, Supreme Court of India*, Civil Appeal No. 2598/1989, 31 January 1990. At paragraph 9 the court stated, 'Basic needs of man have traditionally been accepted to the three – food, clothing and shelter. The right to life is guar-anteed in any civilized society. That would take within its sweep the right to food, the right to clothing, the right to decent environment and a reasonable accommodation to live in. The difference between the need of an animal and a human being for shelter has to be kept in view. For the animal it is the bare protection of the body; for a human being it has to be a suitable accommodation which would allow him to grow in every aspect – physical, mental and intellectual'. See also *Francis Coralie Mullin v. The Administrator, Union Territory of Delhi*, [1981] 2 SCR 516 and *Mohini Jain v state of Karnataka* 1992 AIR 1858, 30 July 1992 where the Supreme Court derived the right to education from the right to life under Article 21 of the Constitution – 'Right to life' is the compendious expression for all those rights which the court must enforce because they are basic to the dignified enjoyment of life. It extends to the full range of conduct which the individual is free to pursue. The right

Within a regional human rights context the European Court of Human Rights has likewise to some extent exercised a dynamic interpretation of civil and political rights. As discussed above, the purpose of the ECHR and the complaints mechanism was not originally devised to take into account the full range of human rights, preferring to leave aside the issue of ESR until a later date (which eventually transpired to be the European Social Charter). Hence, according to the *travaux préparatoires*, the Convention was an interim solution.[86]

Nonetheless, apparent in the jurisprudence of the court is a dynamic approach to interpretation of Article 8 (right to private and family life). This includes acknowledgement of the right to adequate housing respecting the cultural dimensions in the case of nomadic travellers (*Connors*);[87] or protection from unlawful eviction when makeshift houses were built to form an unlawful Roma settlement.[88] In the latter case, the court recognised a positive duty on the state to ensure that eviction must be proportionate and necessary in a democratic society.[89] The court specifically referred to various international standards,[90] including the standard set by the International Covenant on Economic, Social and Cultural Rights in connection with the right to adequate housing and the corollary positive duties incumbent on the state to respect this right:

to education flows directly from right to life. The right to life under Article 21 and the dignity of an individual cannot be assured unless it is accompanied by the right to education'. para.1.07. See also *Paschim Banga Khet Majoor Samity and other s state of West Bangal and another* (1996) 4 SCC 37, AIR 1996 Supreme Court 2426 5 June 1996, where the Supreme Court held that the right to life encompasses access to primary health care at least in cases of emergency.

86 Council of Europe, Seventeenth Sitting, 7 September 1949, Presentation of Report No. 77, Mr Teitgen, 'Certainly, professional freedoms and social rights, which have themselves an intrinsic value, must also, in the future, be defined and protected. Everyone will, however, understand that it is necessary to begin at the beginning and to guarantee political democracy in the European Union and then to co-ordinate our economies, before undertaking the generalisation of social democracy'.

87 *Connors v. UK*, European Court of Human Rights, Application no. 66746/01, 27 May 2004. The court noted that, 'the eviction of the applicant and his family from the local authority site was not attended by the requisite procedural safeguards, namely the requirement to establish proper justification for the serious interference with his rights and consequently cannot be regarded as justified by a "pressing social need" or proportionate to the legitimate aim being pursued. There has, accordingly, been a violation of Article 8 of the Convention'. para.95.

88 *Yordanova and Others v Bulgaria*, Application no. 25446/06, 12 April 2012.

89 Held: it was not demonstrated that it was necessary in a democratic society in this case and so the eviction order was unlawful.

90 The ECtHR referenced 'relevant international material' including the European Social Charter; a decision of the European Committee of Social Rights (*European Roma Rights Centre v Bulgaria* Complaint No 31/2005, 25 May 2005); the UN International Covenant on Economic, Social and Cultural Rights; and the Committee on Economic, Social and Cultural Rights (CESCR)'s General Comment No 7 on forced evictions. UN Committee on Economic, Social and Cultural Rights (CESCR), General Comment No. 7: The right to adequate housing (Art.11.1): forced evictions, 20 May 1997, E/1998/22.

[E]victions must meet a number of conditions, such as prior consultation with the persons to be evicted, the giving of adequate and reasonable notice as to when the eviction will take place and the availability of judicial remedies. If those evicted cannot provide for themselves, states should take all reasonable measures, utilising all available resources, to ensure the provision of adequate alternative housing.[91]

Although the decision of the court was not in itself based on the ICESCR provisions, there was, at the very least, reference within the judgment to the standard stipulated in international law and an implication that this influenced the outcome. The case saw the extension of Article 8 beyond respect for a family home to include the right to adequate housing indicative of the interdependence of all human rights.[92] As Remiche submits:

> the Court did not explicitly mobilise [the international instruments] in its assessment of the merits of the case. This lack of explicit mobilisation should nevertheless not lead to the conclusion that the principles they encapsulated were disregarded. On the contrary, that *Yordanova* demonstrates that the Article 8 right to respect for one's home is not interpreted in isolation from the right to adequate housing, protected by the ICESCR and the ESC [European Social Charter]'.[93]

In the case of *Watts v UK*,[94] the court also considered ESR arising from Article 2 (right to life), Article 3 (respect from inhumane or degrading treatment) and Article 8 (right to private and family life) in connection with an elderly care resident who was being transferred involuntarily between care homes. Whilst the application was considered inadmissible (on the grounds that the local authority had ensured appropriate safeguards), the court indicated that inherent within the right to life, and the right to respect of private and family life, are implicit positive obligations on the state to ensure that the operation of the transfer minimised the risk of impacting the individual's life, health and well-being. The court stipulated that execution of the positive duties could be performed through a carefully planned transfer taking into account the views of the individual, ensuring that they were not moved too far from family and friends, ensuring that there are appropriate facilities in the new home, and by moving residents within their friendship groups. Again, this case is indicative of the inalienable nature of rights and the interdependence of civil and political rights on the

---

91 *Yordanova and Others v Bulgaria*, Application no. 25446/06, 12 April 2012, para.83.
92 Adélaïde Remiche, 'Yordanova and Others v Bulgaria: The Influence of the Social Right to Adequate Housing on the Interpretation of the Civil Right to Respect for One's Home' (2012) 12 *Human Rights Law Review* 787.
93 Remiche, ibid. at 794.
94 *Watts v UK*, ECtHR, 4 May 2010, Application no. 53586/09.

fulfilment and protection of ESR. Furthermore, it demonstrates the ECtHR's willingness to adjudicate on ESR.[95]

It is also an example of how a human rights-based approach to areas such as social care need not always necessarily be heavily focused purely on the allocation of resources. The local authority in the *Watts* case exercised a considerate and sensible transfer by adopting a human rights-based approach to its procedural practice. There was no indication within the judgment that the procedure itself amounted to a disproportionate allocation of resources – certainly this was not a point argued by the respondents. The budgetary constraints concerned the closing of the home which necessitated the transfer. The local authority had an opportunity to demonstrate to the court (a deliberative accountability mechanism) that they had acted lawfully and proportionately in delivering care (and executing the transfer proportionately) under the constraints of budgetary cuts. The human rights-centred approach to the procedure in itself was sufficient to satisfy the court that the local authority had acted lawfully. This is an example of the adjudication of ESR whereby the court deliberates upon the substantive issues of a case and the state is offered the opportunity to defend and justify its actions. It therefore falls within Hunt's culture of justification as lending legitimacy to the deliberative democratic framework.[96] It is difficult to see why those opposed to the justiciability of ESR would view this deliberative process as damaging to the traditional concept of democracy. It demonstrates a dialogue between different institutions, namely the state and in this case a supranational court, which facilitates a transparent and accountable human rights forum enhancing the deliberative and remedial principles of adjudication. In respect of the ECtHR, this is done within the context of the margin of appreciation, to which the court has been keen to recognise the wide discretion afforded to the domestic institutions to deal with matters of socio-economic policy:

> Of further relevance in conducting the balancing act required by Article 8 § 2 is the wide margin of appreciation afforded to states in issues of general policy, including social, economic and health-care policies ... It should be recalled that national authorities have direct democratic legitimation and are, as the

---

95 For a further discussion on the widening scope of Article 2(the right to life) ECHR, see Carol Brennan, 'One More Step in the Expansion of "The Right to Life", Case Comment' (2012) 28 *Professional Negligence* 149.

96 Hunt, n 11 at 471, 'the proportionality principle is properly understood and applied by both decision makers and reviewing courts wherever Convention rights are in play'. Hunt argues that the operation of review through an examination of proportionality increases democratic accountability within the institutions exercising public power and in the adjudication of the court. Proportionality as a ground for review leads to a more substantive examination of the issues, more so than Wednesbury. This method of review 'preserves the very basis on which the legitimacy of both constitutional and administrative review depend in a democratic state: the recognition by judges that on judicial review they do not have primary responsibility, but a secondary responsibility to ensure that the primary decision-maker has acted in accordance with the requirements of legality'.

Court has held on many occasions, in principle better placed than an international court to evaluate local needs and conditions ... Accordingly, the role
of the domestic policy-maker – in this case the Council – should be given special weight.[97]

The dynamic interpretative approach to civil and political rights is also apparent in domestic jurisprudence. In the UK, ESR have also to some extent been
made justiciable under the ambit of civil and political rights. The courts have
therefore accepted the justiciable nature of ESR derived from civil and political
rights. There tends to be a crucial interplay between the Human Rights Act,
the Convention, rights engaged under EU law and the legislation in question,
or act of a public body under challenge in this type of adjudication and in
some cases, there has been extensive review of socio-economic rights. Even
where the applicant fails in establishing a violation of an ESR through civil
and political rights, the substantive consideration of the case by the court in
itself demonstrates that the ESR are subject to judicial review and justiciable
in nature.[98]

In the case of *Condliff*,[99] the applicant challenged the decision of the local
authority to deny life-saving treatment as a breach of Article 8. The application
failed, however, the court did not reject the argument on the grounds that Article 8 was not engaged. Rather, the court considered that the local authority
had performed its duties proportionately and in accordance with the law by creating an eligibility policy to administer access to health. Mr Condliff did not
meet the eligibility criteria. The court did not have difficulty in scrutinising how
the local authority justified its distribution of scarce resources and accepted that
the eligibility policy was lawful. If, however, the local authority had failed to act
with procedural proprietary, the case would still have been amenable to judicial
review and the decision potentially quashed on the grounds of a breach of Article 8 (if for example the justification of eligibility criteria was unfair or discriminatory, or proper procedure had not been followed, the decision could be
declared unlawful).

---

97 *Watts v UK* n 95 para.100.
98 See, for example, *Condliff v North Staffordshire Primary Care Trust*, [2011] EWCA Civ 910
where the court examined the lawfulness of the local authority's decision not to provide life
saving treatment and the alleged interference with Article 8. The court held that the local
authority had ensured appropriate safeguards were in place to ensure the fair distribution of
resources in healthcare and no violation was found. See also the case of *McDonald v Royal
Borough of Kensington*, [2011] UKSC 33 where the Supreme Court held that adequate safeguards were in place to ensure Ms McDonald's home care provision did not breach Article 8
following the withdrawal of a night nurse to assist the severely disabled applicant going to the
toilet at night. The ECtHR agreed and held that although an interference with Article 8 was
engaged the withdrawal of the night time service sought to pursue a legitimate aim: 'namely
the economic well-being of the State and the interests of the other care-users' para.53, *McDonald v UK*, Application No. 4241/12, 20 May 2014.
99 *Condliff* ibid.

The judiciary in the UK has gone as far as to declare an act of the Secretary of State as unlawful in connection with a breach of Article 3 (freedom from inhuman or degrading treatment) and associated ESR.

In the case of *Limbuela*[100] the House of Lords held that, contrary to section 55(1) of the Nationality, Immigration and Asylum Act 2002, the Secretary of State for Home Department was under a positive obligation to ensure that asylum seekers who had not applied for asylum 'as soon as reasonably practicable' ought to be provided for before their destitution reached the threshold of Article 3 engagement. Section 55(1) of the 2002 Act provides that the Secretary of State may not provide for the provision of support to a person who has made a claim for asylum if the claim was not made as soon as reasonably practicable after the asylum seeker arrived in the UK. Section 55(5) provides that subsection (1) shall not prevent the exercise of a power by the Secretary of State to the extent necessary for the purpose of avoiding a breach of the Convention. The Secretary of State had refused support to the applicants under section 55(1) and had thereafter argued that it was not within the remit of the court to quash this decision as it would interfere with socio-economic policy.

The Lords interpreted section 55(5) together with section 6 of the Human Rights Act and found that this imposed a positive socio-economic obligation upon the state. Lord Scott elaborated:

> The point has been made on behalf of the Secretary of State that the policy that state benefits should not be provided to asylum seekers who do not promptly on arrival in this country make their asylum applications is a lawful policy that should not be frustrated by over-indulgent judicial decisions. The policy in question, however, is only a lawful policy if it does not lead to breaches of Article 3 rights of asylum seekers. If and to the extent that it does lead to those breaches it is not a lawful policy. The legislative policy to which expression is given in section 55 requires subsections (1) and (5) to be read together. It was not the legislative policy that the regime imposed on asylum seekers should lead to breaches of their human rights.

Similarly, Lord Bingham noted:

> Each of the three respondents made recorded claims for asylum on the day of arrival in the UK or the day after, but the Secretary of State was not satisfied that any of them had made the claim as soon as practicable, and his conclusions on that point give rise to no live issue. If the legislation ended there, it would be plain that the Secretary of State could not provide or arrange for support of the respondents, even if he wished, and however

---

100 *Regina v Secretary of State for the Home Department (Appellant) ex parte Adam (FC) (Respondent) Regina v Secretary of State for the Home Department (Appellant) ex parte Limbuela (FC) (Respondent) Regina v Secretary of State for the Home Department (Appellant) ex parte Tesema (FC) (Respondent) (Conjoined Appeals)* 2005 UKHL 66.

dire their plight. But the legislation does not end there. The prohibition in section 55(1) is qualified by section 55(5).[101]

Hence, the court exercises legitimate jurisdiction in relation to ESR if the law confers on them an obligation to scrutinise and protect human rights, including ESR. The *Limbuela* case offered a degree of protection according to the 'minimum core' typology – i.e. that in consideration of the applicants' rights under Article 3 there was a threshold of destitution below which the state had an obligation to ensure the applicants did not fall. Lord Bingham was keen to stress however that an examination of this obligation was only made possible by the legislative qualification that the Secretary of State was under a duty to comply with Convention rights under section 55(5). If that qualification had not been available in the 2002 Act, then the court would not have been able to enforce the positive obligation contrary to section 55(1). This would lead to the conclusion that the mechanisms available under the Human Rights Act 1998 to interpret legislation in compliance with Convention rights in so far as it is possible to do so (section 3 of the Human Rights Act 1998) would not have been operational in this case and the only option available to the court would have therefore been a declaration of incompatibility under section 4 of the 1998 Act. The only remedy then available would have been to seek recourse in Strasbourg and the possibility of damages – there would be no remedy available that would strike down the offending provision in the legislation.

This case is indicative of the precarious nature of human rights protection in the UK and the restrictive grounds upon which an applicant can rely on protection at a domestic level. Whilst protection was afforded in this case it does not set a precedent in respect of future cases brought under Article 3 – unless the legislation in question offers a possibility of compliant interpretation or explicit human rights qualifications in the content of the legislation itself. This approach is in accordance with the doctrine of legislative supremacy and reaffirms the problems relating to applicability and possible retrogressive legislative measures.

Although the dynamic interpretation of civil and political rights opens the door to ESR justiciability, it brings with it problems in relation to applicability. First, the application of the ECHR is limited in the UK. If it is not possible to interpret legislation as compatible then the court can only issue a declaration of incompatibility undermining the remedial principle (there is no effective remedy as the declaration does not affect the application of the offending legislation). Second, judicial interpretation of civil and political rights according to the principle of indivisibility (giving effect to economic, social and cultural rights) will not be possible if the legislation qualifies the applicability of Convention rights and restricts a wider interpretation – limiting the deliberative quality and substantive fairness principles of ESR adjudication. Third, it is arguably a less transparent way of introducing ESR into jurisprudence, effectively through the back door. This undermines democratic legitimacy and again the deliberative quality of the adjudication is bound to

---

101 *Limbuela* ibid. para.4–5.

a framework that does not expand to the full international human rights regime. It would be more appropriate to explicitly recognise the indivisibility of human rights and pave the way with a transparent, accountable and deliberative forum with explicit and regulated recognition together with effective remedies.

Relying on the dynamic interpretation of CP rights without a broader framework for ESR means that court adjudication will marginalise ESR issues. In other words, CPR adjudication is not sufficiently broad to facilitate an adjudication culture that is accessible, participative, deliberative, fair, counter-majoritarian or remedial according to the principles of social rights adjudication.

Model 4: The Common Law Application of (Customary) International Law

Enforcing ESR as part of the common law tradition is not completely unfamiliar territory in the UK. For example, in the *UNISON* case the court found the imposition of fees in the Employment Tribunal as an unlawful impediment to the common law right to access justice (as well as the right to access justice derived from EU law) and discriminatory against women who were at higher risk of incurring them and thus in contravention of the Equality Act 2010. The court declared the fees unlawful because they were prohibitively high and examined this in the context of the 'minimum necessary to meet the essentials of life'.[102] This adjudication assessed a contextualisation of the social minimum with reference to the Joseph Rowntree Foundation definition of minimum income standards.[103] It is an example of the court addressing a multidimensional and complex ESR through the common law by engaging with minimum income standards, affordability of accessing justice and enforcement of employment rights derived from EU law and statutory law. It is also an example of the court drawing on various sources of expertise to better understand the socio-economic dimensions of human rights and equality and it is indicative of the court's capacity to achieve substantive change, at least in the form of recognising the importance of the procedural right to access justice.

Of course, human rights protections within the UK derive from both statutory and common law provisions. Rights emanating from the common law primarily concern civil rights and liberties such as the freedoms of expression and assembly, along with the rights to life, liberty and of access to justice. The fourth justiciability model for ESR is adjudication through the incorporation of customary international law or through judicial recognition of international human rights obligations to which the state has agreed to be bound when developing the common law. The former pertains to the recognition of *jus cogen* norms, that when acknowledged, ought to form part of the domestic application of the rule of law. The latter is concerned with obligations that may not hold customary

---

102 *R (on the application of UNISON) (Appellant) v Lord Chancellor (Respondent)* [2017] UKSC 51, para.90.
103 Unison, ibid. para.51.

status but are obligations to which the state has agreed to be bound nonetheless. When states sign and ratify international human rights treaties the state agrees to legally binding obligations. Within the dualist framework, under which the UK operates, international treaties that do not in themselves provide for legal redress if a violation occurs are dependent on the domestic state incorporating the obligations and providing a legal remedy through domestic legislation.

The question of domestic implementation of international obligations through the courts has been adjudicated upon and rejected by the UK courts and the leading *International Tin Council* case[104] is still authoritative law from a domestic perspective. The case adheres to the dualist principle of implementation in so far as international obligations are beyond the competence of the court unless they have been incorporated through domestic legislation. In the wake of human rights cases being adjudicated in the domestic courts following the enactment of the Human Rights Act, the implementation of international human rights law has been reconsidered to some extent. In the case of *McKerr*,[105] Lord Steyn considered that the dualist approach to international obligations may no longer be the most appropriate system of adjudication on human rights issues. He cited numerous sources[106] in support of this argument and concluded that, although it was not applicable to the circumstances in the *McKerr* case, the impact of customary international law in the domestic legal system is a subject of increasing importance and may have to be reconsidered in the foreseeable future.[107] This would mean the judiciary diluting the dualist approach by deliberating on international human rights standards once the state has indicated at an international level that it intends to comply with them,[108] even when such rights have not yet been incorporated through domestic legislation.[109]

---

104 *Re J.H. Rayner (Mincing Lane) Ltd. Appellants v Department of Trade and Industry and Others*, [1989] 3 W.L.R. 969.

105 *Re McKerr* [2004] 1 WLR 807.

106 Sir Robert Jennings in his 1989 F A Mann lecture 'An International Lawyer Takes Stock' (1990) 39 *International Comparative Law Quarterly* 513, 524–526; and Dame Rosalyn Higgins, 'The Relationship between International and Regional Human Rights Norms and Domestic Law', *Developing Human Rights Jurisprudence* (vol. 5, The Commonwealth, 1993). – see: https://www.squire.law.cam.ac.uk/eminent-scholars-archivedame-rosalyn-higgins/bibliography-dame-rosalyn-higgins; Murray Hunt, *Using Human Rights Law in English Courts* (Oxford: Hart Publishing, 1998); Lawrence Collins, 'Foreign Relations and the Judiciary' (2002) 51 *International Comparative Law Quarterly* 485; Andrew J. Cunningham, 'The European Convention on Human Rights, Customary International Law and the Constitution' (1994) 43 *International Comparative Law Quarterly* 537.

107 *Re McKerr* n 106 Lord Steyn at para.52.

108 This would mean overturning the decision in the *International Tin Council Case* in which the House of Lords found that agreement by way of international treaty was made by the Royal Prerogative and did not extend to altering domestic law or rights of individuals without the intervention of parliament and so was not a part of domestic law until it had been incorporated into it by domestic legislation, *Re J.H. Rayner (Mincing Lane) Ltd. Appellants v Department of Trade and Industry and Others*, [1989] 3 W.L.R. 969. Affirmed by *R v Secretary of State for the Home Department, Ex p Brind* [1991] 1 AC 696 and *R v Lyons* [2003] 1 AC 976.

109 *Re McKerr* (n 100) Lord Steyn at para.50.

This issue is not unique to human rights law. The operation of direct effect in EU law confers rights on the individual which are enforceable in the domestic courts without implementation through domestic legislation.[110] The application of this principle goes as far as to supersede domestic legislation which is incompatible with EU law[111] and the evolving nature of EU law encompasses rights featuring socio-economic characteristics such as the right to equal pay for equal work.[112] As discussed in detail above, the renewed legal EU constitutional framework provides a more robust and comprehensive approach to ESR justiciability than that available under the Council of Europe system. Of course, the impact of Brexit means that this body of law and the remedies attached to it will be largely lost in the domestic UK context.

There is scope within adjudication to recognise international obligations arising out of treaty ratification or the operation of *jus cogens norms* in respect of human rights. Craven has identified this as a model for the potential justiciability of ESR.[113] As with the other mechanisms presented, justiciability is already underway to some extent in the UK and the common law is in a state of flux as to whether it is appropriate to refer to, or to rely on, international obligations in this respect. There are also current discrepancies across the different jurisdictions in the UK with an underdeveloped justiciability existing in the devolved regions, revealing once again a potential deficit in substantive ESR realisation.

The UN Committee on Economic, Social and Cultural Rights has indicated that the judiciary ought to have regard to the rights enshrined in the Covenant when deciding whether a state's conduct is compatible with the Covenant.[114] In fact, the Committee has gone so far as to argue that a failure to do so is incompatible with the rule of law: 'within the limits of the appropriate exercise of their functions of judicial review, courts should take account of Covenant rights where this is necessary to ensure that the state's conduct is consistent with its obligations under the Covenant. Neglect by the courts of this responsibility is incompatible with the principle of the rule of law, which must always be taken to include

---

110 See the leading cases of *Costa v Enel* [1964] ECR 585 (6/64) and *Van Gend en Loos v Nederlandse Administratie der Belastingen* (1963) Case 26/62. For further discussion on direct effect see Paul Craig and Gráinne De Búrca, *The Evolution of EC Law* (Oxford University Press, 1999).

111 See the leading case of *R v Secretary of State for Transport, ex parte Factortame Ltd* [1990] 2 AC 85 & [1991] (No.2) 1 AC 603.

112 *Defrenne II* – Case 43/75 (1976) ECR455 - equal pay for equal work – equality between sexes – not only state obliged – employers required to comply. This case is indicative of the evolution of direct effect. The EU position and the opportunity to protect and enforce ESR under the EU constitutional framework is examined in chapter one.

113 'The second manner in which the Covenant could have significance in domestic law is if its terms were considered to be expressive of rules of customary international law'. Antonio Cassesse, 'Modern Constitutions and International Law' (1985) 192 *Hague Receuil* 335, 368–370.

114 UN Committee on Economic, Social and Cultural Rights (CESCR), General Comment No. 9: The domestic application of the Covenant, 3 December 1998, E/C.12/1998/24, para.14.

respect for international human rights obligations'.[115] Furthermore, the UN Committee on Economic Social and Cultural Rights has stipulated that a state cannot invoke the provisions of domestic law as a justification for its failure to comply with international obligations.[116] This, it argues, is in accordance with the application of public international law as stipulated in Article 27 of the Vienna Convention on the Law of Treaties which provides 'a party may not invoke the provisions of its internal law as justification for its failure to perform a treaty'.

In terms of international judicial standards the Bangalore Principles[117] stipulate that the judiciary is under a duty to keep informed of international human rights law.[118] However, the commentary which accompanies the Principles points out that judges are only required to take into account international human rights law in exercise of their power in so far as the domestic law permits.[119] This is of particular importance within the context of a dualist system. The dualist system is characterised by the Judicial Integrity Group as follows:

> Where the dualist theory is favoured, international law and municipal law are regarded as two separate systems of law, regulating different subject matter. They are mutually exclusive, and the former has no effect on the latter unless and until incorporation takes place through domestic legislation. One reason for this view is because the making of a treaty is an executive act, while the performance of its obligations, if they entail alteration of the existing domestic law, requires legislative action. However, in many of those states in which the dualist theory is preferred, the recognition and observance of fundamental human rights and freedoms is nevertheless now generally accepted as obligatory, or certainly as influential in the ascertainment and expression of domestic law.[120]

There is therefore recognition in terms of international best practice that unincorporated international human rights law may not be adjudicated upon unless the domestic law has afforded recognition to the particular right in question. This approach is consonant with the doctrine of parliamentary supremacy. However, the Judicial Integrity Group also recognises that fundamental rights and freedoms are generally accepted as obligatory or influential in the ascertainment of domestic

---

115 Ibid.
116 Ibid.
117 The Bangladore Principles are the international ethical standards recognised by the Judicial Integrity Group, which comprises of eminent Chief Justices and Superior Court Judges from around the world. Bangladore Principles, Judicial Integrity Group, Economic and Social Council document, ECOSOC 2006/23, available at www.judicialintegritygroup. org/resources/documents/ECOSOC_2006_23_Engl.pdf
118 Bangladore Principles ibid. para.6.4.
119 Commentary on Bangladore Principles of Conduct, Judicial Integrity Group, March 2006, available at www.judicialintegritygroup.org/resources/documents/BP_Commentary_Engl. pdf, 126.
120 Commentary on Bangladore Principles ibid. 21.

law. So the relevant question is where on this spectrum does the adjudication of international human rights norms, either through customary international law or applicable human rights treaties, fall in the constituent parts of the UK.

The judiciary in the UK have to some extent recognised that there is a requirement to give effect to international human rights law where there has been direct incorporation or the legislature have indicated that they intend to incorporate an international obligation.[121] This might be established for example if the legislature were to use similar wording as a treaty provision after the treaty has been incorporated.[122] In the case of *ZH Tanzania*,[123] Lady Hale had regard to a number of international human rights standards[124] and held that section 55 of the Borders, Citizenship and Immigration Act 2009 should be read in light of the duty to take into consideration the best interests of the child as provided for in Article 3(1) of the UN Convention on the Rights of the Child. It was held that this consideration ought to be of 'primary' importance in considering the welfare of the child in matters regarding immigration. As Lady Hale explained:

> This is a binding obligation in international law, and the spirit, if not the precise language, has also been translated into our national law. Section 11 of the Children Act 2004 places a duty upon a wide range of public bodies to carry out their functions having regard to the need to safeguard and promote the welfare of children. The immigration authorities were at first excused from this duty, because the UK had entered a general reservation to the UNCRC concerning immigration matters. But that reservation was lifted in 2008 and, as a result, section 55 of the Borders, Citizenship and Immigration Act 2009 now provides that, in relation among other things to immigration, asylum or nationality, the Secretary of State must make arrangements for ensuring that those functions "are discharged having regard to the need to safeguard and promote the welfare of children who are in the UK".[125]

The judiciary were therefore in a position to legitimately make justiciable the welfare of the child as a matter of primary consideration. This arguably went beyond the wording of section 55 which placed a duty on the Secretary of State to have regard to the 'need to safeguard and promote the welfare of children who are in the UK'. The duty was interpreted as being one of primary

---

121 For a discussion of the extent to which the Law Lords have engaged with international human rights law, including *jus cogens* and unincorporated treaties see Brice Dickson, 'Safe in Their Hands? Britain's Law Lords and Human Rights' (2006) 26 *Legal Studies* 329.

122 See, for example, *Belmarsh* No. 2, *A v Secretary of State for the Home Department (No 2)*, [2005] 3 WLR 1249 at para.27 'the words of a UK statute, passed after the date of a treaty and dealing with the same subject matter, are to be construed, if they are reasonably capable of bearing such a meaning, as intended to carry out the treaty obligation and not to be inconsistent with it'. para.27.

123 *ZH Tanzania v SSHD* [2011] UKSC 4.

124 Ibid. para.22.

125 Ibid. para.23.

importance in accordance with the wording of Article 3(1) of the UNCRC. In so doing, the judiciary gave effect to an international human rights obligation that was not explicitly incorporated but was implicit, or derived, from the wording of the legislation and should be interpreted in that light in the context of giving meaning to Article 8 ECHR as part of an obligation to interpret Convention rights 'in harmony with the general principles of international law'.[126] The onus placed on the Secretary of State was therefore greater than it would have been on a direct reading of section 55 of the 2009 Act. The result of this decision meant that immigration officials were required to place at the forefront of the decision-making process the adverse impact that removal might impose on a child's welfare,[127] the consequences of which impacted on the child's enjoyment of the full array of human rights: civil, political, economic, social and cultural. Dickson has previously noted that Lady Hale has taken an innovative approach to determining rights in connection with women and children in that 'she is resolutely in favour of enhancing the rights of women and children and ... she is prepared to adopt an innovative approach to statutory interpretation in order to achieve that goal'.[128] The judicial lineage of the *ZH Tanzania* case has seen the development of a principle whereby rights engaged under the ECHR, including Article 8 and Article 14, must be interpreted in light of international human rights obligations including ICESCR and UNCRC.[129]

There are obvious constraints on relying on this approach. Practitioners who seek to take cases directly relating to ESR are often forced to shoehorn breaches of ICESCR and UNCRC, for example, in to a legal structure that does not accommodate international human rights law. This is evident in the lineage of *ZH Tanzania*, where, for example, the application of a disproportionate benefit cap on lone parents in *DS and Others v SSWP* was found lawful based on a weak form of review (questioning whether the government's actions were manifestly without reasonable foundation, i.e. irrationality). The dissenting judgment of Lord Kerr urged the court to apply proportionality which would have led to a more intense review of the

---

126 Ibid. para.21 see also *Neulinger v Switzerland* (2010) 28 BHRC 706, para 131.
127 The decision was to be based on the broadest reading of section 55 of the 2009 Act, coupled with the exercise of the proportionality principle under Article 8 of the ECHR. In order to give effect to the duty the authorities would have to establish and consider the child's point of view. 'In making the proportionality assessment under article 8, the best interests of the child must be a primary consideration. This means that they must be considered first. They can, of course, be outweighed by the cumulative effect of other considerations'. Ibid. para.33.
128 Dickson, n 121 at 344.
129 *McLaughlin, Re Judicial Review (Northern Ireland) (Rev 1)* [2018] UKSC 48 (30 August 2018); *H (H) v Deputy Prosecutor of the Italian Republic, Genoa (Official Solicitor intervening)* [2013] 1 AC 838, *Stevens v Secretary of State for Communities and Local Government* [2013] JPL 1383, approved in *Collins v Secretary for Communities and Local Government* [2013] PTSR 1594. "See also *SG & Ors, R (on the application of) v Secretary of State for Work and Pensions (SSWP)* [2015] UKSC 16 and *DA & Ors, R (on the application of) v Secretary of State for Work and Pensions* [2019] UKSC 21 for a more restrictive interpretation of the reach of *ZH Tanzania*."

government's decision to prioritise the incentivisation of work over the devastating impact of leaving lone parent families in poverty. In the case of *SG and Others v SSWP* the court recognised that there had been a breach of an international treaty, however, the majority opinion found that without incorporation of this treaty there was no means of enforcing it. In other words while important strides have been made by the judiciary in an examination of UNCRC under the rubric of Articles 8 and 14 of the ECHR, this approach is not sufficient for a proper examination of compliance with ESR as they are defined in international law, meaning those who experience the burden of ESR violations are very much left without recourse to legal protection. Having said this, *ZH Tanzania* and the associated case law is indicative of an innovative approach and perhaps there is more scope for innovation elsewhere in jurisprudence and in other areas of rights protection.

The judiciary at the devolved level have been reluctant to afford any recognition to international human rights standards that have not yet been incorporated through domestic legislation. In Scotland, the judiciary has clearly stipulated that international human rights obligations will not form part of domestic law unless explicitly incorporated.[130] Likewise, in Wales the administrative court has indicated the 'provisions of an international treaty are not themselves enforceable in the domestic courts unless the treaty has been incorporated into domestic law'.[131] However, the administrative court of Wales has also recognised that international human rights law can take on an important interpretative role in determining the scope of domestic rights whether derived from the ECHR or common law.[132] In Northern Ireland, the judiciary has been reluctant to go beyond statutory and common law rights.[133] In relation to judicial review in Northern Ireland Anthony submits that:

> [u]nincorporated international treaties can, for instance, have some impact where the courts are open to arguments about parallelism in the common law and the need to interpret legislation in the light of international obligations [such as the ECHR]. However, where the courts are not open to such arguments for reasons of constitutional dualism, unincorporated international law may be deemed irrelevant.[134]

In the case of *JR 47's Application*[135] the High Court in Northern Ireland held that the applicant could not rely upon the UN Convention on Persons with Disabilities in

---

130 *Lord Hodge, Moohan & Anor v The Lord Advocate* [2014] UKSC 67 (17 December 2014), para.30.
131 *Tilley, R (on the application of) v The Vale of Glamorgan Council* [2016] EWHC 2272 (QB) (13 September 2016), as per Mr Justice Lewis at para.75.
132 *Calver, R (On the Application Of) v The Adjudication Panel for Wales* (Rev 2) [2012] EWHC 1172 (Admin) (3 May 2012), Mr Justice Beatson at para.41. See also *Heesom v Public Services Ombudsman for Wales* [2014] EWHC 1504 (Admin) (15 May 2014).
133 See *RE Adams* [2001] NI 1 and *Re Northern Ireland Commissioner for Children and Young People* [2004] NIQB 40.
134 Gordon Anthony, *Judicial Review in Northern Ireland* (Hart Publishing, 2008) para.1.23.
135 *JR 47's Application* [2011] NIQB 42.

determining a right to independent living because the Convention had not been incorporated into domestic law.[136] McCloksey J held that the basis for this was that the accession or ratification of an international treaty is an act of the executive government and not of the legislature and so whilst it remains unincorporated, the UNCRPD cannot be the source of rights or obligations in domestic law.[137]

A similar outcome was determined *In the matter of an Application by Caoimhín MacGiolla Catháin* in respect of Irish language rights and obligations emanating from the Council of Europe Charter for Regional or Minority Languages.[138] The court rejected the applicant's reliance on the Charter to support the use of the Irish language in the court system. The court considered this to be contrary to a ban on Irish language imposed by the Administration of Justice (Language) Act (Ireland) 1737, and, in any event an international treaty can have no effect unless incorporated into domestic law:

> Given the constitutional position the ratification of an international treaty by the Executive cannot, in the UK, be viewed as creating a legitimate expectation that the treaty should then be enforceable directly in domestic law. In my view the position is quite the contrary. The expectation, if any, will in light of the well-established constitutional position be that the treaty will not be enforceable in domestic law.[139]

In the case of *T's Application*,[140] the High Court in Northern Ireland rejected arguments that the applicant had a legitimate expectation that the Secretary of State would make a decision in respect of the applicant's immigration status with regard to the UN Convention on the Rights of the Child. The court rejected the application on the grounds that to recognise a legitimate expectation in this case would amount to 'incorporation through the back door'.[141] The court emphasised 'the constitutional importance of the principle that international conventions do not alter domestic law except to the extent that they are incorporated into domestic law by legislation'.[142] This case predates the enactment of the Borders, Citizenship and Immigration Act 2009 and so it merely serves to point out the

136 *JR 47's Application* ibid. para.23–24. McCloskey J relied on the well recited case law pertaining to the dualist theory of international law. Relying on *the International Tin Council* case [1987] 1 CH 419; *R v Secretary of State for the Home Department, ex parte Brind* [1991] 1 AC 692; *R – v- Lyons* [2003]; *Briggs v Baptiste* [2000] 2 AC 40; *Thomas v Baptiste* [2000] 2 AC 1.
137 *JR 47's Application* ibid. para.23–24.
138 *In the matter of an Application by Caoimhín MacGiolla Catháin* for Judicial Review, [2009] NIQB 66 regarding the status of the cultural right to use the Irish language in the court system (contrary to a ban imposed by the Administration of Justice (Language) Act (Ireland) 1737).
139 Ibid. para.36.
140 *T's Application* [2000] NI 516.
141 *T's Application* ibid. See also Anthony n 135 para.1.23.
142 *T's Application* ibid. 537.

reluctance of the Northern Ireland judiciary to rely on international human rights law prior to Lady Hale's judgment.[143] In August 2013, the High Court of Northern Ireland later refused to return a Sudanese family to the direct provision system operating in Ireland based on the welfare of the child test introduced by Lady Hale, indicating the NI judiciary embracing a change in step when the higher courts in the UK have paved the way.[144]

In Scotland, a similar cautious approach is evident. Whilst the courts may have regard to international treaties and reports of international organisations as an interpretative source of law they are not deemed to form part of the domestic legal system and are not binding on the court unless otherwise instructed by the legislature.[145] The Scottish Courts when faced with implementing international obligations through the common law do not consider ratified treaties binding unless the legislature has already incorporated the treaty into domestic legislation.[146] However, the judiciary has also indicated that observing and implementing international obligations falls within the devolved competence of the Scottish Parliament.[147] The court has pointed out that the Scottish Parliament can introduce legislation that implements

143 It should be noted that in the case of *E's Application* [2006] NICA 37, the trial judge, the Court of Appeal and the House of Lords acknowledged the best interests of the child consideration provided for in Article 3 of the UNCHR. Lord Hoffman stated that '[t]he Convention … has not been incorporated into domestic law. The requirement is nevertheless a consideration which should properly be taken into account by the state and its emanations in determining upon their actions. It is accordingly a matter which may be relevant in determining whether the actions of the police satisfied the obligations placed upon them by article 3 of the Convention'. At para.60 [2008] UKHL 66.

144 *ALJ and A, B and C's Application* for Judicial Review [2013] NIQB 88 – highlighting a serious gap in the commitment to ensure an equivalence of rights across the island of Ireland under the terms of the peace agreement and B-IA.

145 International treaties do not form part of the law of Scotland unless they are incorporated into domestic law through legislation – this was confirmed by Lord Brodie in *Whaley & Anor v. Lord Advocate* [2003] ScotCS 178 (20 June 2003) para.44. However, courts are free to give effect to international obligations when domestic law does not prohibit it as Lord Goff of Chieveley said in *Attorney General v Guardian Newspapers Ltd (No 2)* [1990] 1 AC 109, 283: 'I conceive it to be my duty, when I am free to do so, to interpret the law in accordance with the obligations of the Crown under [the Convention]'. The Supreme Court has treated this approach both tentatively and embraced it. In *Jones v Ministry of Interior of the Kingdom of Saudi Arabia* [2006] UKHL 26 Lord Bingham describes the legal authority of the decisions of the Committee Against Torture as 'slight'. However, in *ZH (Tanzania) v Secretary of State for the Home Department* [2011] UKSC 4, [2011] 2 AC 166 Lady Hale interprets section 55 Borders, Citizenship and Immigration Act 2009 in light of the UNCRC stating at para.23 '[t]his is a binding obligation in international law, and the spirit, if not the precise language, has also been translated into our national law. Lady Hale cites UN General Comments as part of the interpretation process.

146 Lord Hodge, *Moohan & Anor v The Lord Advocate* [2014] UKSC 67 (17 December 2014), para.30.

147 Paragraph 7(1)-(2) implementation of international obligations is an exception to the reservation of 'Foreign Affairs' to Westminster.

international obligations, including incorporating international human rights standards into the devolved framework of governance, should it choose to do so.[148]

Each of the devolved jurisdictions affords international obligations a particularly high status.[149] If the Secretary of State of a devolved jurisdiction considers that any action proposed by a Minister or public body would be incompatible with international obligations then the Secretary of State may, by public order, direct that the proposed action not be taken.[150] Likewise, if the Secretary of State considers that an action of a Minister or devolved department requires to be taken to give effect to international obligations the Secretary of State may direct that the action be taken. Finally, if subordinate legislation is incompatible with international obligations then the Secretary of State may revoke the legislation. There is therefore a great deal of power afforded to the Secretary of State of each devolved jurisdiction in the exercise of executive functions in relation to compliance with human rights. There is no reason why the exercise of this executive power ought not to be amenable to judicial review.

Dickson has suggested that there is perhaps a need to revisit the current constitutional position to better protect a substantive human rights culture:

> [T]he Law Lords need to appreciate that the challenge they face is really a larger constitutional one, namely to broaden and deepen the human rights culture within our legal system. This is not to say that human rights should be absolute, or that they should always trump every other value. But it is to say that the long-established international standards which the UK has agreed to abide by in treaties and lesser documents should be seen by our top judges as part and parcel of our legal heritage, deserving of careful scrutiny and application. We need further constitutional change to make that judicial approach a reality.[151]

A proposed mechanism to achieve this aim would be to introduce an obligation that the judiciary have due regard to international human rights obligations when interpreting domestic law. This duty could be introduced through legislation in order to inform the development of the common law. Section 2 of the Human Rights Act imposes a duty on the judiciary to take into account jurisprudence from Strasbourg when deciding matters relating to Convention rights. A similar legislative provision could be introduced to take into account other international treaties and the decisions and recommendations of the various UN and Council of Europe bodies responsible for scrutinising compliance with

---

148 *Whaley & Anor* n 145 Lord Brodie, para.44.
149 Section 26 of the Northern Ireland Act 1998; section 35 Scotland Act 1998; and section 82 of the Government of Wales Act 2006.
150 International obligations include international human right obligations.
151 Dickson, n 121 at 347.

human rights obligations. There is nothing to impede either the UK Parliament or devolved legislature from enacting such a provision should they so choose.

One way of safeguarding the separation of powers argument would be to ensure parliament has an opportunity to veto accession to a treaty, rather than it solely being the exercise of an executive prerogative power. In the UK there is now a requirement to lay treaties before parliament before ratification. Under the Constitutional Reform and Governance Act 2010 treaties are laid before parliament 21 days before ratification and parliament has the power to block ratification indefinitely by way of resolution (there is no requirement for a debate or vote). This somewhat limited approach affords parliament more power than previously existed. Does this mean the judiciary could take a more proactive approach to interpret international obligations through adjudication following endorsement by the legislature? It is a stretch given that there is no pre-ratification scrutiny or ability to amend the treaty laid before the legislature. If more robust procedures were developed arguably international ESR obligations and standards could thereafter filter down through domestic adjudication (admittedly, this would be somewhat more complex for existing treaty obligations as there would be no retrospective application through this mechanism).

Problems facing this mechanism relate to democratic legitimacy. Within the democratic positivist perception of constitutionalism any role assigned to the judiciary in this respect would usurp the legislative supremacy of parliament. On the other hand, the reluctance of the judiciary to engage with international human rights obligations also potentially undermines the rule of law and amounts to the judiciary abdicating their role in holding the executive to account. Furthermore, given the assignment of a great deal of executive power under the devolved statutes to oversee the implementation of international obligations there would appear to be an important democratic role to be played by the court in ensuring observance of these powers by way of judicial review.

Model 5: An International Complaints Mechanism

The fifth justiciability model takes its form when the state accedes to an existing international complaints mechanism dealing with ESR.[152] The UK is a party to the

---

152 There are a number of complaints mechanisms available for ESR. For example, under the UN General Assembly, Optional Protocol to the Convention on the Elimination of All Forms of Discrimination against Women: resolution/adopted by the General Assembly, 15 October 1999, A/RES/54/4 (the UK acceded to the OP on 17 December 2004 – see decision of the Committee *N.S.F. v. UK of Great Britain and Northern Ireland*, 10/2005 available at http://dac cess-dds-ny.un.org/doc/UNDOC/GEN/N07/379/48/PDF/N0737948.pdf?OpenElement (asylum seeker – fear of domestic violence if removed – inadmissible – did not exhaust domestic remedies); by way of declaration under Article 14 of the Convention on the Elimination of Racial Discrimination 1965, UN General Assembly, 21 December 1965, United Nations, Treaty Series, vol. 660, p. 195 (the UK has not made such a declaration); under the Optional Protocol to the Convention on the Rights of Persons with Disabilities 2006, UN General

Council of Europe and the Convention and so is already subject to a supranational complaints mechanism (the ECtHR in Strasbourg) to monitor human rights compliance (namely civil and political rights subject to the evolutive interpretative approach discussed above). Likewise, whilst the UK remains a member of the EU this entails both domestic and supranational remedies (CJEU) through the existing limited recognition of ESR in the EU legal order. The EU Charter offers a potentially more promising future than is available under the more restrictive bifurcated approach in the ECHR, and many ESR are already protected under the general principles of EU law. As discussed above, this body of law and its force in the UK will be potentially irrevocably lost as the UK leaves the European Union.

The UK has also acceded to other international complaints mechanisms that deal with ESR under the Optional Protocol to the Convention on the Elimination of All Forms of Discrimination against Women 1979 and under the Optional Protocol to the Convention on the Rights of Persons with Disabilities 2006. A more holistic approach to supranational adjudication on ESR could be achieved by signing and ratifying the Optional Protocol to ICESCR[153] or through signing and ratifying the Additional Protocol Providing for a System of Collective Complaints to the ESC.[154] The former offers an international ESR complaints mechanism for individuals and the latter offers the same to designated collective groups.[155] It is difficult to envisage how this would materialise

Assembly, 13 December 2006, A/RES/61/106, Annex II (the UK signed the Optional Protocol to the Convention on the Rights of Persons with Disabilities on 26 February 2009 and ratified the Protocol on 7 August 2009 – see list of jurisprudence available at www.ohchr.org/EN/HRBodies/CRPD/Pages/Jurisprudence.aspx in particular *Kenneth McAlpine v UK*, CRPD/C/8/D/6/2011 (inadmissible – alleged violation occurred before Convention in force); and under Article 24 of the Constitution of the International Labour Organisation (ILO), 1 April 1919, Adopted by the Peace Conference in April 1919, the ILO Constitution became Part XIII of the Treaty of Versailles (28 June 1919) (for case law relating to UK see www.ilo.org/dyn/normlex/en/f?p=1000:20060:0:FIND:NO:20060:P20060_COUNTRY_IDP20060_COMPLAINT_STATU_ID:1026511495812).

153 The UN General Assembly Optional Protocol to the International Covenant on Economic, Social and Cultural Rights: resolution/adopted by the General Assembly, 5 March 2009, A/RES/63/117 provides for a complaints system under ICESCR. It was opened for signature on 24 September 2009. It entered into force on 5 May 2013. The UK has not yet signed or ratified the Optional Protocol.
154 Additional Protocol providing for a system of Collective Complaints to the European Social Committee entered into force in 1998. Additional Protocol to the European Social Charter or the Additional Protocol Providing for a System of Collective Complaints, Council of Europe, 9 November 1995, ETS 158. The UK has not ratified the Additional Protocol.
155 For a full discussion of the merits and problems with the ESC Collective Complaints System see Robin Churchill and Urfan Khaliq, 'The Collective Complaints System of the European Social Charter: An Effective Mechanism for Ensuring Compliance with Economic and Social Rights?' (2004) 15 *European Journal of International Law* 417 and on the Optional Protocol to ICESCR see Martin Scheinin, 'The Proposed Optional Protocol to the Covenant on Economic, Social and Cultural Rights: A Blueprint for UN Human Rights Treaty Body Reform – Without Amending the Existing Treaties' (2006) 6 *Human Rights Law Review* 131. For a critical perspective on the Optional Protocol to ICESCR see Michael

in the near future given the current antipathy in the UK in prevailing politics towards the existing international complaints framework.[156] It is not an option open to any of the devolved legislatures or executives to sign up to either of the complaints mechanisms as an entity as entry as a ratifying member of an international treaty is consigned to sovereign states. In any event, the devolved executive governments do not have the devolved competence to exercise such a right as international relations is a reserved matter across the UK.

Dennis and Stewart have argued that adjudicating ESR through an international complaints mechanism presents more problems than it solves. In respect of the Optional Protocol to ICESCR they assert that 'much of the arguments in support of an optional protocol merely contends there is no reason not to establish a complaints mechanism, rather than demonstrating good reason to do so – for example, by establishing what tangible benefits would flow therefrom'.[157] They posit that the call for formal, binding case adjudication is an example of 'overreaching legal positivism, borne of the myth that judicial, or quasi-judicial processes intrinsically produce better, more insightful policy choices than, for example, their legislative counterparts'.[158]

Their dismissal of an international complaints mechanism rests on a rejection of the justiciability of ESR in itself, rather than a rejection of this particular mechanism. This rejection of the legitimacy of ESR justiciability is, they argue, based on a fear that by empowering a supranational (quasi-)court, such as the UN Committee ESCR, to adjudicate on ESR is a step toward establishing a judicially controlled 'command economy' and that this is fundamentally undemocratic.[159] However, they also recognise, despite not being persuaded, that their vantage point is based on an anti-Kelsenian view.[160] In turn, it is critical to place these arguments within the constitutional paradox particular to the UK and the debate as to whether there should be recognition of fundamental norms comprising of constitutional human rights, or not. The recognition of fundamental human rights norms (Kelsen's *grundnorm*), would in turn facilitate a Kelsenian-based theory of constitutional structure, and this would overcome Dennis and Stewarts' rejection of justiciability.

However, they also raise important fundamental questions in relation to viability. First, there is a concern that the ESCR Committee does not have the appropriate resources to take on an adjudicative role on top of an already demanding remit in respect of the existing reporting procedure. Second, they argue adjudication at the supranational level could undermine ESR adjudication at the micro level leading to inconsistencies and conflict in interpretation.

Dennis and David Stewart, Justiciability of Economic, Social and Cultural Rights: Should There Be an International Complaints Mechanism to Adjudicate the Rights to Food, Water, Housing and Health?' (2004) 98 *The American Journal of International Law* 462.

156 Theresa May, 'Tories to Consider Leaving European Convention on Human Rights', *BBC News Online*, 9 March 2013, available at www.bbc.co.uk/news/uk-politics-21726612

157 Dennis and Stewart, n 155 at 465.

158 Ibid. at 466.

159 Ibid.

160 Ibid.

These barriers could be addressed in the UK through domestic legislation similar to the Human Rights Act and the operation of the Ullah principle[161] where the domestic courts ought to have regard to Committee jurisprudence (section 2 of the Human Rights Act). In this sense the Committee could help give substance to the meaning of the rights in ICESCR, and the courts could be compelled to take this jurisprudence into account when interpreting ESR at the domestic level.

Craven has stipulated that:

> the justiciability of a particular issue depends, not on the quality of the decision, but rather on the authority of the body to make the decision. Prima facie then, in so far as the Committee is given the authority to assume a quasi-judicial role over the rights in the Covenant, those rights will be justiciable.[162]

In this respect, the UK Parliament could legislate for the adjudication of ESR through ratification of the Optional Protocol and/or European Committee of Social Rights Collective Complaints mechanism complemented by domestic legislation directing the domestic judiciary as to interpretation.

The complaints mechanism under ICESCR is still very much in its infancy, and of the 16 cases assessed by the Committee to date, only four have been deemed admissible with decisions on the merits.[163] For those cases deemed admissible the approach of the Committee is to consider the substantive evidence and, where a violation is established, to issue conclusions and recommendations. This is a deferential approach where ultimate responsibility for an effective remedy rests with the state. It enables the vertical application of the deliberative principle (deliberation between institutions on a vertical supranational to national scale) helping to address the indeterminacy critique by giving substance to rights by subject experts. It can also act as an important accountability mechanism, whilst enforceable remedies may not be available under the complaints system itself, the jurisprudence of the Committee can help highlight existing gaps in any given context. Indeed, the Spanish Supreme court has recently recognised the binding nature of UN treaty body

---

161 *R (on the application of Ullah) v Special Adjudicator; Do v Immigration Appeal Tribunal* [2004] UKHL 26. The Ullah principle was developed by the House of Lords in the aforementioned case. When taking Strasbourg jurisprudence into account under section 2 of the Human Rights Act the court held that the domestic UK courts are under a duty to act in compliance with the ECHR under section 6. However, this duty is to 'keep pace' with Strasbourg jurisprudence, rather than interpret Convention rights to give greater protection than the ECtHR has determined. As per Lord Bingham, 'The duty of national courts is to keep pace with the Strasbourg jurisprudence as it evolves over time: no more, but certainly no less'., para.20.

162 Craven, n 60 at 102.

163 *Jaime Efraín Arellano Medina v Ecuador* CESCR Communication No. 7/2015, UN Doc. E/C.12/63/D/7/2015 (14 November 2018); *Mohamed Ben Djazia and Naouel Bellili v. Spain*, CESCR Communication No. 5/2015, UN Doc. E/C.12/61/D/5/2015 (20 June 2017); *I.D.G. v Spain*, CESCR Communication No. 2/2014, UN Doc. E/C.12/55/D/2/2014 (17 June 2015); *López Rodríguez v Spain* CESCR Communication No. 1/2013, UN Doc. E/C.12/57/D/1/2013.

decisions in relation to ESR meaning an effective remedy ought to be enabled at the domestic level.[164]

Ratification of the Additional Protocol providing for a system of Collective Complaints to the European Social Committee would enhance the remedial and counter-majoritarian principles as well as the principles of accessibility, participation and deliberation of social rights adjudication. Of the 47 Council of Europe states only 15 are members of the collective complaints mechanism including France, Finland, Ireland, Italy, Norway and Sweden. Despite the small numbers, the jurisprudence and decision-making of the Council is advanced in terms of both the procedural and substantive principles of ESR adjudication. The Committee of Social Rights in the Council of Europe has recommended that states 'recognise, at national level, an individual universal and enforceable right to the satisfaction of basic material needs (as a minimum: food, clothing, shelter and basic medical care) for persons in situations of extreme hardship'.[165] For example, with respect to the adequacy of the level of social assistance the Committee has stipulated that the provisions given must make it 'possible to live a decent life to cover the individual's basic needs'. In order to assess the level of assistance the Committee considers multiple factors including basic benefits, additional benefits and the poverty threshold in the country which is set at the median equivalised disposable income and calculated on the basis of the Eurostat at risk-of-poverty threshold.[166] In the absence of the Eurostat indicator the Committee can instead refer to nationally defined thresholds such as the monetary cost of the 'the household basket containing the minimum quantity of food and non-food items which is necessary for the individual to maintain a decent living standard and be in good health'.[167] There are both procedural and substantive components to the assessment of a minimum threshold as well as absolute and relative components (covering both basic needs as well as a level of assistance to address poverty relative to a country's wealth). Facilitating access to the collective complaints framework could help the UK address the ESR accountability gap and assist in making the shift to a more ESR compliant national framework. It would also help address the indeterminacy critique by aligning domestic jurisprudence with already established standards and procedures that give substance to ESR across multiple European states. In addition,

---

164 *Angela González Carreño v. Spain*, Communication No. 47/20 12, UN Doc. CEDAW/ C/58/D/47/2012 (2014) was deemed binding on the Spanish state by the Spanish Supreme Court in 2018, Angela González Carreño Judgment 1263/2018, of 17 July 2018, available at www.womenslinkworldwide.org/files/3045/sentencia-angela-tribunal-supremo.pdf – it is not yet clear to what degree compliance post-judgment is realised.

165 Council of Europe in its Recommendation No. R(2000)3 (Adopted on 19 January 2000 at the 694th meeting of the Ministers' Deputies), has recommended that Member States.

166 *Finnish Society of Social Rights v. Finland*, Complaint No. 88/2012, decision on the merits of 9 September 2014, §112.

167 European Social Charter, European Committee of Social Rights Conclusions 2015, January 2016, p.26, https://rm.coe.int/1680593904

ratification of the revised treaty would bring the UK in line with the 34 states that have ratified the 1996 revised Charter that adopts a broader approach to ESR than its predecessor.[168]

Model 6: A Constitutional Solution

The sixth model is a constitutional recognition of ESR. As discussed in the introduction to this chapter, a constitutional solution is the most robust and democratically legitimate way of incorporating international human rights. It facilitates enables a coherent and holistic approach by establishing a normative frame of reference rather than a piecemeal or incremental adoption of ESR under the rubric of other mechanisms. This model supports a multi-institutional approach to ESR adjudication that facilitates the development of the other five models meaning multiple routes to remedy can be available under a holistic environment. There is a developing trend towards affording constitutional status to ESR in other states.[169] The UK is in a peculiar position because the constitution is uncodified, limiting the way in which ESR could be constitutionalised. Under the current framework they cannot be constitutionalised through an amendment to an existing constitutional text so the options available are either to codify a constitution including ESR, or enact a 'constitutional statute' providing for their protection such as through amendment to the Human Rights, through a dedicated Economic and Social Rights Act, or through a renewed, more expansive, Bill of Rights. Implementing a Bill of Rights at either the national or devolved level could enhance the way rights are protected in the UK. In relation to ESR, domestic legislation could seek to incorporate international human rights law, in the same way that there is already partial incorporation of the ECHR under the Human Rights Act 1998 and the devolved statutes.

Incorporation of international law into domestic law means embedding legal standards as set out in international law and making them enforceable at the domestic level. Direct incorporation of international treaties into domestic law is what is required within the UK constitution if international law is to acquire binding status domestically. However, it is worth noting that the concept of incorporation can be much further reaching than a direct reference to an international instrument. Incorporation can take many different forms and here I use the broadest definition of what that might mean. In other words, incorporation is referred to as a means of internalising international law into domestic law, whether explicit or implicit, whether directly or indirectly, or whether through means of an 'incorporating provision' or by means of growing a domestic-based constitutional model inspired by and derived from international human rights law. Constitutions all over the world internalise international human rights standards without necessarily

---

168 The UK is only one of nine states out of the 47 members that has not ratified the revised 1996 Charter, available at www.coe.int/en/web/turin-european-social-charter/signatures-ratifications

169 King, n 12. This is discussed in some detail in Chapter 4.

directly referencing the treaty and so a wider definition of incorporation recognises that fact and includes a domestication of treaty provisions in a way that is completely contextualised within the specific constitutional setting it springs from. Compliance with international human rights treaties can therefore occur through domestic internalisation of international norms by way of a variety of means.[170] Constitutional theory tells us the most appropriate way to incorporate and enforce ESR is through a multi-institutional approach: legislative, executive, judicial and constitutional.[171] Ultimately, the most robust form of incorporation is to grant a direct or indirect form of domestic recognition to international human rights law that is enforceable and coupled with effective remedies.[172] Constitutional recognition can help facilitate a more coherent conceptual, theoretical, normative and democratic approach to human rights, including ESR.

The United Nations human rights monitoring bodies have advised that the fulfilment of human rights requires states to take action at the domestic level in order to create the necessary legal structures, processes and substantive outcomes for human rights protection. Several UN Committees have recommended that the UK both incorporates international human rights law as well ensure effective justiciable remedies are made available for non-compliance.[173] For example, the Committee on the Rights of the Child suggests that fulfilment of international obligations should be secured through incorporation of international obligations[174] and by ensuring effective remedies, including justiciable

---

170 Oona A. Hathaway, 'Do Human Rights Treaties Make a Difference?' (2002). Faculty Scholarship Series. (1961) Paper 839.

171 King, n 12 at 41–57.

172 Katie Boyle, Models of Incorporation and Justiciability of Economic, Social and Cultural Rights, Scottish Human Rights Commission, (2018) at 14. See also UN Committee on Economic, Social and Cultural Rights (CESCR), General Comment No. 19: The right to social security (Art. 9 of the Covenant), 4 February 2008, E/C.12/GC/19. Para.77–80; UN General Assembly, Basic Principles and Guidelines on the Right to a Remedy and Reparation for Victims of Gross Violations of International Human Rights Law and Serious Violations of International Humanitarian Law: resolution/adopted by the General Assembly, 21 March 2006, A/RES/60/147. See also UN Committee on Economic, Social and Cultural Rights (CESCR), General Comment No. 9: The domestic application of the Covenant, 3 December 1998, E/C.12/1998/24, para.4.

173 Treaty bodies recommending incorporation: CEDAW/C/UK/CO/6 (CEDAW, 2009) Committee on the Elimination of Discrimination against Women; CAT/C/GBR/CO/5 (CAT, 2013) Committee against Torture; CRC/C/GBR/CO/4 (CRC, 2008) Committee on the Rights of the Child. Treaty bodies recommending justiciable enforcement and effective remedies: CRC/C/GBR/CO/5 (CRC, 2016) Committee on the Rights of the Child; E/C.12/GBR/CO/5 (CESCR, 2009) Committee on Economic, Social and Cultural Rights; E/C.12/GBR/CO/6 (CESCR, 2016) Committee on Economic, Social and Cultural Rights.

174 UN General Comment No. 5: General Measures of Implementation for the Convention on the Rights of the child, (2003), CRC/GC/2003/5, para 20; Concluding Observations of the United Nations Committee on the Rights of the Child on the United Kingdom (2002), CRC/C/15/Add.188, paras 8 and 9 and Concluding Observations of the United Nations Committee on the Rights of the Child on the United Kingdom (2008), CRC/C/GBR/CO/4, para 7; CAT/C/GBR/CO/5 (CAT, 2013) Committee against Torture, para.7;

remedies are made available domestically.[175] The UN Committee on Economic, Social and Cultural Rights has called for justiciable remedies for violations of economic and social rights.[176] The Committee also indicates that a blanket refusal to recognise the justiciable nature of ESR is considered arbitrary and that, ideally, ESR should be protected in the same way as CP rights within the domestic legal order.[177] This could mean, for example, expanding the scope of rights protection under the Human Rights Act, the devolved statutes, the common law and specific policy-based legislation to include those rights not currently protected (a sectoral approach).

The adoption of international human rights norms at both the national and devolved level is also considered a component of good governance.[178] Human rights compliance with international human rights has positive effects.[179] Simmons make the case that democracies are the natural allies of human rights and the expansion of democratic accountability has been associated with the expansion of the domestic protection of international norms.[180]

At the UK national level there is an increasingly regressive human rights trajectory at play. Both in relation to withdrawal from the European Union, meaning the irrevocable loss of many rights and remedies deriving from EU law (a 'fundamental change in the constitution' according to the Supreme Court[181]), as well as the continuing to and fro on whether the UK will repeal and replace the Human Rights Act 1998. These are seismic constitutional shifts with a chilling effect on human rights protection. In 2012 the Commission on a Bill of Rights explored the possibility of a UK Bill of Rights but did not recommend the implementation of one and recommendations for ESR did not feature as enforceable rights should such a Bill be implemented at a later date.[182] Indeed, as discussed above, the Bill of Rights debate at the UK level has become a discussion about regression v the status quo rather than a discussion about progressively improving rights protection, including the expansion of protection to ESR.

CEDAW/C/UK/CO/6 (CEDAW, 2009) Committee on the Elimination of Discrimination against Women; E/C.12/GBR/CO/5 (CESCR, 2009) Committee on Economic, Social and Cultural Rights para.13.

175 E/C.12/GBR/CO/6 (CESCR, 2016) Committee on Economic, Social and Cultural Rights, para.5; CRC/C/GBR/CO/5 (CRC, 2016) Committee on the Rights of the Child para.7.

176 UN Committee on Economic, Social and Cultural Rights (CESCR), General Comment No. 9: The domestic application of the Covenant, 3 December 1998, E/C.12/1998/24, para.10; E/C.12/GBR/CO/5 (CESCR, 2009) Committee on Economic, Social and Cultural Rights para.13.

177 General Comment No. 9, ibid.

178 Martha F. Davis, 'Upstairs, Downstairs: Subnational Incorporation of International Human Rights Law at the End of an Era', (2008) 77 *Fordham Law Review* 411–438 at 417.

179 Beth Simmons, *Mobilising Human Rights* (Cambridge University Press, 2009), 20.

180 Simmons, ibid at 25.

181 the *R (Miller) v. Secretary of State for Exiting the European Union*, [2017] UKSC 5, [2017] 2 W.L.R. 583, para.78.

182 Commission on a Bill of Rights, a UK Bill of Rights? The Choice Before Us, Volume 1 (December 2012) para.8.28.

184 *Models of ESR Justiciability*

At the devolved level, however, there are very different trajectories at play. In Scotland the First Ministers Advisory Group on Human Rights Leadership has recommended a Human Rights Act for Scotland that incorporates economic, social, cultural and environmental rights.[183] In Wales, the Welsh Assembly has increased protection of international human rights through the Rights of Children and Young Persons (Wales) Measure 2011 placing a duty on devolved bodies to have due regard to the UN Convention on the Rights of the Child and is now considering a similar approach to the UN on the Rights of Persons with Disabilities. In both Scotland and Wales, the socio-economic equality duty has now been devolved and has been commenced in Scotland as the Fairer Scotland Duty[184] – meaning designated devolved bodies, including the Scottish Ministers, must have due regard to addressing socio-economic inequality when undertaking their duties. With increased devolution Scotland has also passed the Social Security (Scotland) Act 2018 and whilst the legislative scheme does not fully incorporate or enshrine the right to social security as recognised in international law (it does not directly incorporate Article 9 ICESCR) it does declare social security as a human right required for the realisation of other rights. The Social Security Commission established under the 2018 Act is responsible for oversight of the scheme and may take international human rights instruments into consideration, in particular ICESCR and associated UN General Comments.[185]

The UK constitutional canvas upon which human rights protection mechanisms are legislatively drawn is changing. Devolved trajectories are moving beyond the national structure and diverging human rights frameworks will continue to emerge. Incorporation and justiciability of ESR is part of mainstream political and civil society discussions on constitutional change in Scotland and Wales and is emerging in civil society discussions across the UK.[186] The progress in Northern Ireland on a Bill of Rights following the 1998 peace agreement very much paved the way for the national and devolved discourse that followed, and yet now, it is Northern Ireland that has seen the least material benefit (because of political stalemate/unionist dissent) whilst the other devolved nations take up the mantle of progressive change. Comparative constitutional models, including the NIHRC Bill of Rights, are very much featuring as part of these discussions on progressive change.[187]

---

183 Alan Miller, Recommendations for a new human rights framework to improve people's lives, Report to the First Minister, First Minister Advisory Group on Human Rights Leadership, December 2018, available at http://humanrightsleadership.scot/wp-content/uploads/2018/12/First-Ministers-Advisory-Group-post-10th-December-update.pdf

184 The Equality Act 2010 (Authorities subject to the Socio-economic Inequality Duty) (Scotland) Regulations 2018 SSI No.101.

185 Social Security (Scotland) Act 2018.

186 See, for example, the work of Just Fair, Sustain UK, Nourish Scotland and the work of the Northern Ireland Human Rights Consortium and Scottish Human Rights Consortium as well as all of the national human rights institutions, in particular the Scottish Human Rights Commission's programme of work on economic, social and cultural rights: www.scottish humanrights.com/economic-social-cultural-rights/

187 The following constitutional models feature in the SHRC paper: Katie Boyle, Models of Incorporation and Justiciability of Economic, Social and Cultural Rights (SHRC 2018).

Lessons can be learned from comparative experience in terms of how different countries constitutionalise ESR. Constitutions should go further than guiding principles, whereby, if justiciable and enforceable CP rights are constitutionalised then so too should ESR.[188] In some cases the judiciary have developed justiciable rights through a wide interpretative analysis (such as in Canada through equality provisions, or in India through dynamic interpretation of CP rights). Other constitutions have directly enforceable ESR protection (such as in South Africa, Colombia and Argentina). Some constitutions place a strong emphasis on pre-legislative scrutiny (such as Finland and Sweden). More recently some countries are in the process of considering affording ESR justiciable constitutional status such as in Ireland and New Zealand.

A Brief Overview of Sample Constitutions Engaging with ESR (discussed in more detail in Chapter 4)

Argentina

The Argentinian Constitution was amended in 1994 and a number of international treaties were explicitly incorporated into the Constitution, including the International Covenant on Economic, Social and Cultural Rights.[189] This is a 'rights-affirmative' constitutional framework where the compliance with international human rights and constitutional rights is the default position, which, can be denounced by the executive if two-thirds of each chamber of the parliament approve (creating a rights-affirmative framework with the option for parliamentary derogation).[190] The distribution of powers in Argentina is separated into both federal and provincial autonomy (national and devolved). In addition to the changes to the national constitution there were also a number of changes at the provincial level with individual states adopting constitutional amendments with better protection for ESR.

Finland

In Finland, ESR receive constitutional protection. The constitutional provisions dealing with ESR in the Finnish model are directed at the legislature: the right to citizenship (article 5); the right to equality before the law (article 6); educational rights (article 16); the right to language and culture (article 17); the right to work (article 18); and the right to social security (article 19) are all required to be given effect to through subsequent legislation.[191] The constitutional mandate to fulfil the ESR obligations is therefore directly addressed

---

188 King, ibid. at 53.
189 Article 25 Constitution of Argentina.
190 Article 75 of the Constitution of Argentina 1853 (reinst. 1938, rev. 1994).
191 The constitutional provisions stipulate that the details of how the rights will be guaranteed require to be 'provided by an Act'.

to the legislature. In this sense, the constitution imposes a mandatory obligation on the legislature to legislate for the protection and fulfilment of ESR rights. The court ought to be available as a means of last resort to ensure executive and legislative compliance.[192] The UN Committee on Economic, Social and Cultural Rights has raised concerns that the Finish constitutional arrangements do not adequately facilitate access to justiciable remedies for violations of ESR potentially meaning that *ex post* judicial review is not yet sufficiently developed.[193]

Switzerland

In Switzerland, the default position is that responsibility to implement international obligations is at cantonal level.[194] It is therefore the responsibility of the devolved legislatures to implement international human rights law, including ESR. Some cantons go further than the federal level in introducing more extensive human rights protections.[195] However, as with Sweden and Finland the UN Committee on Economic, Social and Cultural Rights has raised concerns that some provisions of ICESCR cannot be directly invoked before the courts in Switzerland creating an accountability gap in terms of justiciable remedies.[196]

Colombia

The Constitution divides human rights into three groups: fundamental rights, ESC rights and collective and environmental rights (chapters 1, 2 and 3 of the constitution). The Constitution also places international treaties on a domestic constitutional footing (articles 44 and 93). The ESC rights included in the constitution relate to health, housing, work and education, among others. The Constitution also protects vulnerable and disadvantaged groups within society with particular measures for children, women, the elderly and disabled people (articles 46–47). Responsibility for safeguarding the Constitution is assigned to the Constitutional Court (Article 241). As a result, there has been a 'profound change' in the legal culture of the country with considerable advancements made in the judicial enforcement of ESC rights.[197]

---

192 See Kaarlo Tuori for a discussion of the Finnish system, Rights, Democracy and Local Self Governance: Social Rights in the Constitution of Finland www.juridicainternational.eu/?id=12700

193 Committee on Economic, Social and Cultural Rights, Concluding observations on the sixth periodic report of Finland, E/C.12/FIN/CO/6, 17 December 2014, para.6.

194 Sovereignty rests with the cantonal legislatures under the Swiss constitution (Article 3).

195 such as in Geneva and Vaud.

196 UN Committee on Economic, Social and Cultural Rights (CESCR), *Consideration of reports submitted by States parties under articles 16 and 17 of the Covenant: concluding observations of the Committee on Economic, Social and Cultural Rights: Switzerland*, 26 November 2010, E/C.12/CHE/CO/2–3, para.5.

197 Magdalena Sepúlveda, 'Colombia, The Constitutional Court's Role in Addressing Social Injustice', in Malcolm Langford (ed.), *Social Rights Jurisprudence, Emerging Trends in International and Comparative Law*, (2008, CUP) 144–162, at 144.

The main mechanism for the judicial protection under the constitution is the *tutela* device (Article 86). The *tutela* enables a person to file a writ of protection before any court or tribunal for the immediate protection of her or his 'fundamental constitutional rights'. All decisions by ordinary judges on a writ of protection are sent to the Constitutional Court and are susceptible to review. Magistrates in the Constitutional Court can review *tutelas*, and where appropriate, will group cases together in order to address structural problems such as for example if an issue emerges that applies to a large group of vulnerable people the cases will be merged together and the court will issue a collective remedy.

Germany

In Germany, human rights take on constitutional status. Constitutional rights do not include all economic and social rights, however the constitution does provide for a right to dignity (Article 1.1 Basic Law) that the court has interpreted as constituting minimum standards (*existenz minimum*) across particular social rights.[198] Governance responsibilities are divided between the federal level (Bund) and the devolved level (Länder) including compliance with human rights obligations.[199] The court has interpreted the constitution to include minimum obligations in the context of ESR.[200]

Ireland

The constitutional arrangements in Ireland take on a special significance in terms of a cross-border all-Ireland approach to an equivalence of rights as envisaged in the peace agreements. For the UK it is critical to be cognisant of the Irish constitutional framework in relation to the joint-responsibility exercised by both states for rights in Northern Ireland. Human rights are protected in Ireland through a variety of mechanisms – constitutional; legislative; administrative and judicial. The Constitution protects rights that fall predominantly within the civil and political category such as the right to life (art 40.3.3°), the right to freedom of expression of opinion (art 40.6.1°) and the rights of citizens to form associations and unions (art 40.6.3°). The right to education (art 42) and the right to private property (art 43) are examples of socio-economic rights explicitly protected in the Irish Constitution. Under Article 45 of the Constitution the directive principles of social policy, although referring to socio-economic duties, are not enforceable in court.[201] Some of the rights protected in the Constitution are explicitly mentioned and others are implicit, or derived from other rights (enumerated v unenumerated distinction).[202]

---

198 Article 1.1 Basic Law Germany 1949 (rev. 2014).
199 BVerfGE 125, 175 (Hartz IV).
200 Ibid.
201 Aoife Nolan, 'Holding Non-State Actors to Account for Constitutional Economic and Social Rights Violations: Experiences and Lessons from South Africa and Ireland' (2014) 12 *International Journal of Constitutional Law* 61 at 68.
202 The judiciary in Ireland have developed a number of unenumerated rights in the Irish Constitution. For a discussion on these rights see Elaine Dewhurst et al., *Principles of Irish Human Rights Law* (Clarus Press, 2013).

Economic and social rights are open to interpretation under the Irish Constitution as 'unenumerated' personal rights, which are primarily guaranteed under Article 40.3.1° of the Constitution. That provision states that: '[t]he State guarantees in its laws to respect, and, as far as practicable by its laws to defend and vindicate the personal rights of the citizen'. Nolan and Whyte argue that this provision imposes a duty on the State to take positive action in appropriate circumstances.[203] Through the jurisprudence of the Supreme Court it has become clear that there is a reluctance to recognise judicially enforceable socio-economic rights entailing positive duties as implicit within the explicit enumerated rights of the Irish Constitution.[204] The reluctance to extend protection to ESR rests on the premise first articulated by Costello J in *O'Reilly* that the separation of powers precludes the Irish Courts from intervening to enforce claims based on distributive justice (the sole responsibility of the legislature and executive), as opposed to commutative justice (which falls within the realm of the court's competence).[205] This reluctance was later reinforced in the decisions of *TD v Minister for Education*[206] and *Sinnott v Minister of Education*.[207] Whilst Nolan has highlighted that ESR are not entirely excluded from constitutional protection,[208] this is caveated with a warning that the courts are adopting an ever-more restrictive approach towards the definition of positive obligations imposed by constitutional economic and social rights.[209]

---

203 Nolan, n 201 and Gerry Whyte, Social Inclusion and the Legal System – Public Interest Law in Ireland 19 (2002).

204 See the cases of *O'Reilly v Limerick Corporation* [1989] ILRM 181, *TD v Minister for Education* [2001] 4 IR 259 and *Sinnott v Minister for Education* [2001] 2 IR 545. For an example of a somewhat limited departure from the views expressed by the Supreme Court in *TD*, see the Supreme Court decision in *In re Article 26 and the Health (Amendment) (No.2) Bill* [2005] IESC 7.

205 *O'Reilly* ibid.

206 [2001] 4 IR 259.

207 [2001] 2 IR 545.

208 Nolan, n 201. For example, Nolan notes that the Irish Courts have been prepared to recognize that the Constitution protects unenumerated economic and social rights under Article 40.3.1° including various rights of the child (*FN v. Minister for Education* [1995] 1 IR 409); the right to bodily integrity (*Ryan [1965]* IR at 313) – including the right not to have health endangered by the state (*The State (C) v. Frawley* [1976] IR 365); and the right to work or to earn a livelihood (*Murtagh Properties v. Cleary* [1972] IR 330 discussed infra; *Murphy v. Stewart* [1973] IR 97); and *Minister for Posts and Telegraphs v. Paperlink* [1984] ILRM 373). However, as Nolan acknowledges – it is only the first two of these rights mentioned above that have been held to give rise to a positive obligation on the state. See also the important discussions led by Liam Thornton on the recent partial judicial recognition of ESR in relation to right to housing for traveller community and the right to work for asylum seekers: Liam Thornton, 'Socio-Economic Rights, the Constitution & the ECHR Act 2003: O'Donnell v SDCC in the Supreme Court', Human Rigths in Ireland March 2015; Liam Thornton, 'February 2018: Asylum, Refugee and Immigration Law in Ireland', Exploring Law, Exploring Rights, 21 March 2018.

209 Nolan, ibid. at 69. This is evident, for example, in the context of the judicial identification of the level of service provision which the State is constitutionally obliged to provide under

Moving beyond the Constitution, the State has also legislated to protect human rights through the enactment of the European Convention of Human Rights Act 2003 ('the 2003 Act'). As discussed above, in some cases, the jurisprudence of the ECtHR has followed what can be described as an 'evolutive' or 'dynamic' approach to interpretation and this has resulted in an interpretation of CP rights that implicitly recognises ESR through the underlying indivisible nature of the human rights framework.[210] Under the 2003 Act, if the domestic court finds a violation of a Convention right through the act or omission of a public body (organ of the State) it can declare that the public body acted unlawfully and provide a remedy to the citizen (section 3 of the 2003 Act). In the same vein, if legislation is open to interpretation then the courts must interpret it in a way which ensures compliance with Convention rights (section 2 of the 2003 Act). These mechanisms further extend the protection of human rights, including some ESR, in Ireland within a 'rights-affirmative' interpretative framework.[211] However, if a public body acts in accordance with an obligation conferred on it by domestic legislation that is impossible to interpret in a way that is compatible with human rights, the court can only declare that the legislation is incompatible – meaning no direct remedy for the citizen.[212] Ireland is also subject to EU law, including compatibility with the EU Charter of Fundamental Rights.[213] The EU Charter has provided a new mechanism

Article 42.4 in the context of education (contrast – *O'Donoghue v. Minister for Health* [1996] 2 IR 20 (Ir.) and *O'Carolan v. Minister for Education* [2005] IEHC 296).

210 Compare for example the cases of *Chapman v UK* (2001) 33 E.H.R.R. 18 ECtHR and *Airey* v. *Ireland* 32 Eur Ct HR Ser A (1979): [1979] 2 E.H.R.R. 305. In the latter, the ECtHR recognised that there is no water-tight division separating CP rights from the sphere of ESC rights and the interpretation of CP may lead to the protection of ESC rights. On the other hand, in the former case the ECtHR refused to extend the right to housing to the realm of the court preferring instead to leave this to the political sphere. For a discussion on ECHR protection of CP and ESC rights see Liam Thornton, *'Seasca Bliain Faoi Bhláth: Socio-economic rights and the European Convention on Human Rights'*, Draft Paper, UCD School of Law & UCD Human Rights Network.

211 Meaning there is a presumption in favour of interpreting provisions in such a way as to ensure compliance in so far as it is possible to do so.

212 Section 5 of the 2003 Act – this is akin to the declaration of compatibility under section 4 of the UK Human Rights Act 1998.

213 For example, the following cases extended ESC protection in Ireland: *J. Mc. B. v L. E., Case C-400/10 5 October 2010* (father's rights of custody relating to family rights [Art 7] and the best interests of the child [Art 24.2]); *M. M. v Minister for Justice, Equality and Law Reform, C-277/11, 22 November 2012* (greater procedural protection for those seeking asylum [Art 41 Right to good administration]); Joined Cases C-411/10 and C-493/10 *N. S.* and *M.E.* ibid. (held: Article 3(2) of Council Regulation (EC) No 343/2003 of 18 February 2003 falls within the scope of EU law and indivisible approach to those seeking asylum in EU, removal to another member state and the right to freedom from inhuman and degrading treatment [Art 3 ECHR and Art 4 EU Charter]), 'Article 4 of the Charter of Fundamental Rights of the European Union must be interpreted as meaning that the Member States, including the national courts, may not transfer an asylum seeker to the "Member State responsible" within the meaning of Regulation No 343/2003 where they cannot be unaware that systemic deficiencies in the asylum procedure and in the reception

through which ESR can be more robustly protected in Ireland.[214] However, as discussed above, there are limitations associated with the Charter such as the rights v principles distinction that has yet to be clarified.

For those rights following within the ambit of the Constitution there are robust remedies in place with a potential ultra vires declaration if any law or action is incompatible with the Constitution. However, the Constitution, whilst offering robust remedies, is limited in the scope of rights it protects, meaning a restrictive framework model of constitutionalism.[215] In 2014, the Constitutional Convention voted in favour of strengthening the protection of economic social and cultural rights in the Irish Constitution.[216] As part of this recommendation there was strong support for the better protection of rights relating to housing (84% in favour); social security (78%); essential health care (87%); rights of people with disabilities (90%); linguistic and cultural rights (75%); and rights covered in the International Covenant on Economic, Social and Cultural Rights2 (80%). In addition, only 24% of voters preferred an update of the socio-economic issues contained in Article 45 of the Convention (which deals with non-justiciable social principles) and instead the majority of the Constitutional Convention (59%) voted in favour of inserting a provision 'that the State shall progressively realise ESC rights, subject to maximum available resources and that this duty is cognisable by the Courts'. This vote marks a potential paradigmatic shift in the potential framework of the Irish Constitution and marks the beginning of a critical discussion on how ESR ought to be better protected within the jurisdiction of Ireland.

Under the heading Rights, Safeguards and Equality of Opportunity of the 1998 multi-party peace agreement, there is a requirement that the Irish Government undertake to ensure at least an 'equivalence' of rights protection in the Irish jurisdiction as exists in Northern Ireland.[217] The duty is to ensure Irish

---

conditions of asylum seekers in that Member State amount to substantial grounds for believing that the asylum seeker would face a real risk of being subjected to inhuman or degrading treatment within the meaning of that provision'. At para.106.

214 For a discussion on this see Michael Farrell, 'Protecting Human Rights Another Way – Using the EU Charter of Fundamental Rights', *PILA Bulletin*, 23 April 2014, available at www.pila.ie/bulletin/april-2014/23-april/guest-article-by-flac-s-michael-farrell-protecting-human-rights-another-way-using-the-eu-charter-of-fundamental-rights/

215 This model of constitutionalism is discussed in more detail in chapter four.

216 Constitutional Convention press release, 85% of voters voted in favour of strengthening the protection of economic, social and cultural rights, 23 February 2014, 1 www.constitution.ie/AttachmentDownload.ashx?mid=adc4c56a-a09c-e311-a7ce-005056a32ee4

217 Section 9 – 'The measures brought forward would ensure *at least* an *equivalent* level of protection of human rights as will pertain in Northern Ireland'. (emphasis added). For a discussion on this see Suzanne Egan and Rachel Murray, 'A Charter of Rights for the Island of Ireland: An Unknown Quantity in the Good Friday/Belfast Agreement' (2007) 56 *International and Comparative Law Quarterly* 797; Siobhán Mullally, 'Substantive Equality and Positive Duties in Ireland' (2007) 23 *South African Journal on Human Rights* 291; and Colm O'Cinneide, *'Equivalence in Promoting Equality – The Implications of the Multi-Party Agreement for the Further Development of Equality Measures for Northern Ireland and Ireland'*, Equality Commission for Northern Ireland & Equality Authority (Ireland 2005).

mechanisms 'at least' reflect the same level of human rights protection available in Northern Ireland. This in itself does not mean that the UK Government are under a similar obligation to ensure that Northern Ireland mechanisms are equivalent to those available in Ireland. With the potential legal deficit of Brexit it is important to consider to what extent human rights protections might diverge in a post-Brexit landscape and so place the 'equivalence' obligation and the state of ESR across the island of Ireland in context. This is particularly pertinent given indications in the literature that Ireland is not yet in compliance with this duty and hence in breach of the terms of the peace agreement.[218] In a similar vein, Northern Ireland lacks some of the human rights protections better protected in Ireland, most notably and of recent significance the diverging practice in access to abortion and reproductive rights as well as the potential developments relating to the constitutionalisation of ESR in Ireland.[219]

South Africa

The South African model also adopts a mixture of substantive rights recognition, together with safeguards and limitation clauses contained in the Constitution. Rights are also afforded protection to different degrees along the respect, protect, promote, fulfil axis.[220] Some 'negative' rights enjoy immediate protection such as the right not to be evicted without fair procedure.[221] Some rights are afforded non-derogable status, such as rights relating to children.[222] Other rights are considered to be subject to progressive realisation such as the right to access adequate

---

218 For example, Mullally (ibid.) has highlighted that Ireland has not yet secured the equivalent level of protection in relation to positive equality obligations such as those available in Northern Ireland under section 75 of the Northern Ireland Act 1998. See also the recent case of *ALJ and A, B and C's Application for Judicial Review* [2013] NIQB 88 highlighting a serious accountability gap in the protection of the best interests of the child under the direct provision system in Ireland and a failure to ensure an equivalence of rights protection.

219 Ireland held a referendum repealing the Eighth Amendment to the Irish Constitution which prohibited access to an abortion. In Northern Ireland, the Offences Against the Persons Act 1861 and the Criminal Justice Act (NI) 1945 criminalise abortion. The Supreme Court in the UK has determined that this constitutes a breach of Art 8 ECHR. See *Human Rights Commission for Judicial Review (Northern Ireland: Abortion) (Rev 1)* [2018] UKSC 27 (7 June 2018). At the time of writing, there is an Economic, Social and Cultural Rights Bill passing through the Oireachtas that seeks to amend the constitution to incorporate ICESCR by way of a referendum.

220 Section 7 of the Constitution.

221 See, for example, *Occupiers of 51 Olivia Road, Berea Township and 197 Main Street, Johannesburg v City of Johannesburg and Others* CCT 24/07 Medium Neutral Citation [2008] ZACC 1 – meaningful engagement and participation is required by the constitution before an eviction order can be served (no forced eviction without notice).

222 Such as the right to be protected from maltreatment, neglect, abuse or degradation; and the right to be protected from exploitative labour practices (section 28(1)(d) and (e)). See section 37(5)(c) for a table listing non-derogable rights in the South African Constitution. For a discussion on the rights of the child (particularly girls' ESC rights) in the South African Constitution see Ann Skelton, 'Girls' Socio-Economic Rights in South Africa' (2010) 26 *South African Journal of Human Rights* 141.

housing and the right to access health care, food, water and social security.[223] There is a general limitation clause under section 36 whereby rights may be limited if reasonable and justifiable in an open and democratic society.[224] The South African Constitutional Court has adjudicated upon and enforced ESC rights employing a 'reasonableness' review in assessing state compliance.

Sweden

Sweden has recently taken a significant step in partially incorporating the UN Convention of the Rights of the Child into domestic law.[225] The legislation passed in June 2018 will come into force in January 2020. The new UNCRC Act clarifies that courts and legal practitioners must 'consider the rights contained in the Convention on the Rights of the Child and that [t]he rights of the child must be considered in deliberations and assessments made in decision-making processes in cases and matters that concern children'.[226] It is not yet clear to what degree UNCRC rights will be enforceable by the court. There is a tripartite process underway where the UNCRC implementation process will be supported through capacity building, a legal audit of where change is required to comply with the UNCRC (mapping the gaps and how to address them) and the development of extensive guidance to assist decision makers in compliance once the UNCRC is incorporated.

Comparatively the UK measures as one of the weakest constitutional models for ESR protection.

A Constitutional Model for the UK

It is of course open to the UK Parliament to take steps to 'constitutionalise' ESR in so far as it is possible to do so within the UK constitutional framework. This could occur through an extension of the Human Rights Act and devolved statutes, or could be achieved by signing up to an international complaints mechanism and affording the decisions binding status. Likewise, the UK Parliament could introduce a new legislative regime for ESR under an Economic and Social Rights Act to work in conjunction with the Human Rights Act. The UK Parliament could go further and grant international human rights law supremacy

---

223 For example, section 26 of the South African Constitution provides for the right to have access to adequate housing and section 27 provides for the right to have access to health care, food, water and social security. The constitution further provides that the State must take reasonable legislative and other measures, within its available resources, to achieve the progressive realisation of each of these rights (Sections 26(2) and 27(2) respectively).

224 The South African judiciary review compliance with the progressive realisation of sections 26 and 27 based on a reasonableness test as developed in *Government of the Republic of South Africa v Grootboom* 2001 (1) SA 46 (CC) and *Minister of Health v. Treatment Action Campaign (no 2) (TAC)*, 2002 (5) SA 721 (CC).

225 www.government.se/articles/2018/03/new-legislative-proposal-on-the-convention-on-the-rights-of-the-child/

226 Ibid.

Table 5.1 Constitutional Models for ESR

Country	Means of incorporation	Role of legislature/ executive	Role of court	ESR outcome
Argentina	Constitutional text and direct incorporation	Strong	Strong	Strong
Finland	Constitutional text	Strong	Weak	Strong
Switzerland	Devolved competence	Strong	Weak	Moderate
Colombia	Constitutional text and reference to international law	Strong	Strong	Strong
Germany	Social minimum – human dignity – limited in scope	Strong	Strong	Moderate
Ireland	Constitutional text and Human Rights Act	Strong for CPR but not ESR	Strong for CP but not for ESR	Weak
South Africa	Constitutional Text	Strong	Strong review/weak remedies	Moderate
Sweden	Legislation incorporating UNCRC	Strong	Not yet clear but may be weak if procedural duty to consider	Moderate
UK	None	Non-binding recommendations of JCHR may involve pre-legislative scrutiny	Only if under rubric of something else	Weak
Devolved	None	None	Only if under rubric of something else	Weak

over national law.[227] Under a system of parliamentary supremacy such an approach would not bind the parliament indefinitely but could remain in force until such time as the parliament chose to later repeal the binding provision (a 'self-regulatory' approach).[228] This is not far removed from the way that the

227 This is the approach adopted in Norway, for example, under the Human Rights Act 1999.
228 Katie Boyle and Edel Hughes, 'Identifying Routes to Remedy for Violations of Economic, Social and Cultural Rights' (2018) 22 *International Journal of Human Rights* 43–69.

Table 5.2 Constitutional Models for the UK

Constitutional model	Detail	Role of legislature/ executive	Role of court	ESR outcome
Codified Constitution	A single constitutional document enumerating the rights and binding the parliament, executive and legislature.	Strong	Strong	Strong
Rights enabling Act (holistic/ sectoral or both)	Direct incorporation or implicit incorporation through a 'constitutional statute' with the potential of granting IHRL supremacy over national law.	Strong	Strong	Strong
Amending devolved legislation, for e.g. Scotland Act	ss.29/101/57 amended to include ICESCR.	Strong	Strong (ultra vires remedy)	Strong
Amending Human Rights Act 1998	s.1 amended to include ICESCR and s.2 to include jurisprudence of international ESR courts.	Strong	Moderate (declaration of incompatibility)	Moderate depending on whether legislature/executive responds
International Complaints mechanisms	Sign up to Optional Protocol ICESCR/ ESC Collective Complaints Mechanism.	Strong (if admissable)	Weak/None – Moderate (depending on whether domestic courts must consider/follow)	Moderate depending on whether legislature/executive responds
Common law	Implementation of international human rights standards through the common law.	Weak	Strong but on a case-by-case basis	Weak – Strong depending on degree of enforcement

European Communities Act 1972 has operated in the UK. EU law superseded national law whilst the Act was in force, and will no longer have binding status because parliament has repealed the Act in line with EU departure. These are the options for constitutionalisation under the operation of parliamentary supremacy. The other approach open to the UK is to create a codified constitution which enumerates rights and binds the parliament, the judiciary and the executive to a pre-negotiated set of foundational norms, including ESR. Whilst this is the prevalent

Table 5.3 UK Economic and Social Rights Act

Preamble	Foundation of dignity underpinning all other rights
Incorporation	Either explicit or implicit ESR derived from international human rights law
Indicative Content of rights	Employment Housing Health Food Water Social Security Adequate Standard of Living Freedom from Poverty Healthy Environment Procedural and Substantive Equality Rights of Persons with Disabilities Rights of Children Rights of Women Rights of LGBT Rights of Older Persons Rights of Ethnic Minorities Right to an Effective Remedy
Interpretation	Interpret in accordance with international law and with regard to comparative law
Interpretation Remedies	Interpret as compatible in so far as it is possible to do so Must be effective – declaration of incompatibility or strike down power and development of structural remedies
Limitations	Rights can be limited according to principles of legality, legitimacy and proportionality
Standing	Expanded standing facilitating collective (multi-party) complaints and public interest litigation
Pre-legislative Scrutiny	Role of Parliament JCHR or another in systematically reviewing legislation for compliance with CPESCE rights

approach in many constitutions across the globe it would mean a paradigmatic shift in the operation of constitutionalism from political to legal in the UK.

The proposal to revisit the future of human rights as part of a Bill of Rights debate in the post-Brexit landscape need not be viewed entirely negatively. There is the possibility of increasing the accessibility and public understanding of UK human rights law by opening the debate for genuine informed, evidence-led, participative and inclusive deliberation on potential reform creating a space for ownership of human rights amongst the UK public. Brexit, whilst hugely problematic for rights protection and future regression, also presents an opportunity to re-imagine a constitutional settlement for rights across the UK with existing substantive rights acting as a minimum threshold (an 'ECHR-EU +' model).[229] In other words – leaving the EU and reforming the human rights structure should not, as a matter of principle and a matter of law, result in the diminishing of rights. In this sense the UK departure from the EU could be seen as a constitutional moment that compels the UK to address the constitutional rights gap left by Brexit. The challenge ahead for the UK constitutional settlement is to re-imagine a coherent framework that better protects rights rather than dimin-ishe them. A written constitution embedding civil, political, economic, social and cultural rights coupled with effective remedies for violations is one potential route of achieving this. Another option is to enhance the legislative regime by creating an Economic and Social Rights Act.

A Codified Constitution

The devolved settlements discussed in detail below clarify that parts of the UK operate under a framework model of constitutionalism. Morison and Lynch make the case that the Northern Ireland constitution, much like the frameworks of Scotland and Wales, offer a new way forward for the UK as a whole.[230] In other words, the devolved settlements present as a challenge to the whole of the British style of constitutionalism.[231] The UK constitution is in transition. As part of this journey the post-devolved UK state has taken on a form of quasi-federalism whilst at the same time removing some of the key pillars forming the nation state (EU and ECHR). Should the UK choose to embrace a framework model of constitutionalism to bridge the gaps emer-ging on its transitional journey it would require a codification of the various strands of the UK constitution. Indeed, the seismic changes occurring through the processes of Brexit and potential repeal of the Human Rights Act 1998, arguably compel the UK to take seriously the requirement that citizens must have an opportunity to re-forge the relationship between citizen and state. This could include revisiting the rights and remedies that should be available for violations of (constitutional) rights.

Process for Constitutional Reform

One means through which to revisit the constitution, and consider its potential codification, would be through the operation of a constitutional convention.[232]

---

229 Katie Boyle and Leanne Cochrane The complexities of human rights and constitutional reform in the United Kingdom: 'Brexit and a Delayed Bill of Rights: Informing (on) the Process' (2018) 16(1) *Journal of Human Rights* 23–46.

230 John Morison and Marie Lynch, 'Litigating the Agreement: Towards a New Judicial Consti-tutionalism for the UK from Northern Ireland', in John Morison et al. (eds.), *Judges, Tran-sitions and Human Rights* (Oxford University Press, 2007), 468 at 142.

231 Ibid.

232 See, for example, the campaign for a constitutional convention led by the Electoral Reform Society, available at www.electoral-reform.org.uk/campaigns/democratic-innovations/con stitutional-convention/

Constitutional convention processes have operated in British Colombia, Ontario, the Netherlands, Ireland, Iceland and in Scotland – each of which offer lessons for a UK process.[233] Making decisions around the future constitutional structure of the UK would require informed, participative and inclusive deliberation within a specific remit most likely followed by a referendum seeking to approve the proposed changes. According to principles of deliberative democracy a number of key benchmarks are required to ensure legitimacy in such a process, namely:

- popular participation (in which the informed citizen is able to make an informed decision);
- public reasoning (whereby the electorate is able to participate meaningfully in a deliberative process);
- inclusion and parity of esteem (whereby the process is inclusive and minorities are given an opportunity to participate fully); and
- consent in collective decision-making (whereby the process has been fair and inclusive, allowing for all participants to accept the outcome as a legitimate exercise of collective decision-making).[234]

Should any such process be undertaken, a codification of ESR ought to form part of evidence-led deliberations as part of any future rights framework model. Importantly, this discussion should be framed with reference to the principles of social rights adjudication when considering the role of the judiciary. Noting, in particular, that the historical arguments repudiating the possibility of ESR are now both outdated and most certainly surmountable.

Lessons could be learned from the Scottish, Welsh and Northern Irish processes, each of which managed to engage with international human rights law in a way that the 2012 Commission on a UK Bill of Rights did not.

---

233 See Stephen Tierney, *Constitutional Referendums: The Theory and Practice of Republican Deliberation* (Oxford University Press, 2012); David Farrell, 'The 2013 Irish Constitutional Convention: A Bold Step or a Damp Squib?' in Giuseppe Franco Ferrari and John O'Dowd (eds.), *75 Years of the Constitution of Ireland: An Irish-Italian Dialogue* (Clarus, 2014), 292–305; Amy Lang, 'But Is It for Real? The British Columbia Citizens' Assembly as a Model of State-Sponsored Citizen Empowerment' (2007) 35 *Politics and Society* 35–69; Lawrence LeDuc, 'Electoral Reform and Direct Democracy in Canada: When Citizens Become Involved' (2011) 34 *West European Politics* 551–567; Bergsson, B.T., and Blokker, P., 'The Constitutional Experiment in Iceland' in Kálmán Pocza (ed.), *Verfassunggebung in konsolidierten Demokratien: Neubeginn oder Verfall eines Systems?* (Nomos Verlag, 2014).

234 Tierney (2012); see also Stephen Tierney and Katie Boyle, 'Yes or No, Scotland's Referendum Carries Significant Constitutional Implications', Scottish Constitutional Futures Forum, 4 November 2013, available at www.scottishconstitutionalfutures.org/Opinionan dAnalysis/ViewBlogPost/tabid/1767/articleType/ArticleView/articleId/2550/Stephen-Tierney-and-Katie-Boyle-Yes-or-No-Scotlands-Referendum-Carries-Significant-Constitu tional-Implications.aspx

Conclusion

This chapter set out the ways in which justiciability occurs and can occur in the future. It is closely connected to the different means of constitutionalising rights, or the different means through which rights are incorporated into domestic law. Categorising the different models of justiciability helps assess to what extent any particular right is protected at any given time along the respect, protect, fulfil axis and in relation to both procedural and substantive enforcement. Rather than offer a 'one-size-fits-all' approach to ESR justiciability, the mechanisms are complementary and enable a more in-depth review of the status of rights (i.e. to what degree they can be protected in any given jurisdiction) by creating a new axis on which to measure enforcement.

The constitutional model is proposed as the means through which to secure the most comprehensive, robust and democratically legitimate model for ESR adjudication. It is not a 'preferred' model as such but rather a core component of a multi-institutional approach, and the other models are more effective when this model is implemented as a foundationalist framework.

6 ESR and Devolution

There is no comprehensive holistic framework that currently exists across the whole of the UK in relation to human rights and equality protections and in particular ESR. There are many different levels of protection and substantial jurisdictional gaps already exist. The framework of the jurisdictional hierarchy is 'patchy' and the domestic implementation of international norms is piecemeal with substantial discrepancies between jurisdictions – it is an insidious and rugged landscape in need of reform. Whereas in some areas there are clear paths and strong footing for right-holders, in other places there are unexpected steep declines in protection mechanisms, regressive measures, or simply nothing at all upon which an individual can rely.

These gaps and inconsistencies could be addressed by a levelling up of human rights and there is no reason why the local devolved level could not lead in this as an example of best practice. One of the key lessons emerging from this book is the importance of understanding the operation of human rights at the sub-national devolved level in order to better understand the UK national human rights landscape. Indeed, it is a key argument of this book that human rights reform emanating from the devolved legislatures may ultimately compel the UK to revisit what has been until now a regressive national discourse. This discourse sits in stark contrast to the more progressive human rights outlook at the devolved level that reframes what is legally possible in connection with ESR.

This chapter reflects on to what extent the improvement of ESR protection is within the competence of the respective devolved legislature and to what extent this competence has been exercised. This reflection is considered in relation to the principles of adjudication under a multi-institutional deliberative framework and potential future reforms are proposed in accordance with the distinctive devolved framework. It invites the reader to reflect on what lessons can be learned from the devolved experience and what pathways are open in terms of future development within the UK and comparatively. Each of the devolved legislatures has the legislative competence to observe and implement international human rights obligations, however, each also faces legislative restrictions in relation to areas such as equality, employment, social security and the justice system itself. In addition, these legislative and executive competence issues do not apply across the devolved domains. In other words, what is within devolved competence in one jurisdiction is not necessarily within devolved competence in another. Each of the jurisdictions is discussed in turn below.

Of course, ESR and human rights more broadly take on a special significance in Northern Ireland because of the peace process. The attention to rights as part of this process has in many respects set the scene and paved the way for the other devolved legislatures to expand and explore their engagement with the international human rights framework. Whilst Northern Ireland is now in limbo with a delayed Bill of Rights and long periods of no functioning devolved governance, Wales and Scotland have taken significant steps in improving rights protections, including in relation to the incorporation and justiciaibility of ESR. One jurisdiction therefore acts as a catalyst for change in another.

Ultimately, the devolved jurisdictions have each gone further and faster with ESR than the UK as a whole since the onset of devolution. And the most significant gap to emerge has been the potential lack of rights and remedies available in England compared to the devolved jurisdictions where the legislatures have exercised more ambitious rights development in devolved areas. It is an under-explored area ripe for further research. Viewing human rights through the devolved lens helps illuminate gaps and inconsistencies at the national level and offers potential routes forward on progressive reform.

Wales

Human Rights in Wales

For a variety of reasons, a distinct approach to human rights did not take hold in Wales until after devolution. Prior to devolution there had been a tendency for civil society to occupy a space across England and Wales as the relevant legal jurisdiction when engaging with rights-based issues. This, in turn, was not conducive to the development of a human rights legal agenda responsive to particular Welsh needs and priorities.[1] In fact, Sherlock notes the absence of a pre-devolution deliberative process in Wales meant that the region was generally unprepared for the onset of devolution.[2] This could be contrasted to the national deliberative processes pre-devolution in both Scotland through the constitutional convention and in Northern Ireland through the peace process.[3] This is not to say that human rights issues did not feature at all. Indeed, Butler and Drakeford make the case that the post-devolution Assembly's 'rights-perspective has deep roots in an established collectivist and non-conformist political tradition', and in the case of children's rights, was inspired by activists who had a long history of involvement

---

1 Ann Sherlock, 'Human Rights in Post-Devolution Wales: For Wales', See Wales (2006) 57 *Northern Ireland Legal Quarterly* 138 at 139.
2 Sherlock, ibid. at 138.
3 Ibid.

with NGOs prior to the onset of devolution.[4] However, the legal profession in Wales lacked a strong public law stream meaning an underdeveloped litigation culture focussing on rights or equality.[5] The court structure in Wales forms part of the jurisdiction of England and Wales and so there is no separate indigenous judicial body of law as is the case in both Scotland and Northern Ireland. The Welsh devolved settlement has also historically been the weakest framework in terms of the powers exercisable by the Assembly in the area of human rights. Until April 2018, the Welsh Assembly operated under a conferred powers model that did not include a general competence on human rights. However, since April 2018, the Welsh constitutional arrangement has transferred to a reserved powers model.[6] The Welsh Assembly has the same limitations placed on it as in Northern Ireland and Scotland in so far as it cannot legislate incompatibly with ECHR rights or EU law.[7]

Since devolution the human rights culture has flourished in devolved areas with engagement on child rights, older persons and consideration of broader ESR. The legal community, civil society, government Ministers and the Welsh Assembly have participated in broad deliberative and participative processes connected to rights-based policy formation.[8] Further to this, the Welsh Assembly has made one of the most significant moves in progressing on international human rights compared to any other part of the UK in passing the Rights of Children and Young Persons (Wales) Measure 2011. The Measure introduced a duty on Ministers to have due regard to the UN Convention on the Rights of the Child (UNCRC).[9] The Welsh Ministers are also under a duty to respond to recommendations of the UN Committee on the Rights of the Child as part of the duty to create a general scheme that sets out the arrangements they have made, or propose to make, for the purposes of securing compliance with the duty to have due regard.[10] Once the scheme is made there is a duty to have regard to the reports and General Comments issued by the Committee and a requirement to promote knowledge and understanding of the rights contained

---

4 Ian Butler and Mark Drakeford, 'Children's Rights as a Policy Framework in Wales' in Jane Williams (ed.), *The Rights of the Child in Wales* (Cardiff: University of Wales Press, 2013), Chp.1, 9–20, at 12.

5 Sherlock, n 1 at 139 and Richard Rawlings, *Delineating Wales: Constitutional, Legal and Administrative Aspects of National Devolution* (Politics & Society in Wales, 2003), 462 and 477; Richard Rawlings, 'Taking Wales Seriously' in Tom Campbell, Keith D. Ewing and Adam Tomkins (eds.) *Sceptical Essays on Human Rights* (Oxford University Press, 2001), 180.

6 For the conferred powers model, see the Government of Wales Act 2006, section 108. For the coming into force of section 3(1) of the Wales Act 2017, see The Wales Act 2017 (Commencement No. 4) Regulations 2017.

7 Section 3 Wales Act and section 108A of Government of Wales Act 2006.

8 For a discussion on this see Simon Hoffman, 'The UN Convention on the Rights of the Child, Decentralisation and Legislative Integration: A Case Study from Wales, International Journal of Human Rights' (Published online: 16 January 2019).

9 Section 1 Rights of Children and Young Persons (Wales) Measure 2011.

10 Section 2.

in the Convention.[11] Hoffman notes that the Measure and the use of Child Rights Impact Assessments has resulted in increased visibility and awareness of the UNCRC within the Welsh government and has resulted in some better policy outcomes for children and young people.[12] The Welsh Assembly has indeed established itself as a progressive human rights legislator with duties to have due regard to relevant international treaties, including ESR protections, introduced under the Social Services and Well-being (Wales) Act 2014, the Additional Learning Needs and Education Tribunal (Wales) Act 2018 and the Well-being of Future Generations (Wales) Act 2015. The Welsh Assembly is now preparing to engage with legislation on the right to adequate housing. This is a legislature alive to the international human rights framework.

In 2017 and 2018, the Equality, Local Government and Communities Committee in the Welsh Assembly heard evidence on the future of human rights in Wales. As part of this evidence it has become clear that there is now a space, and the devolved competence, to develop a distinct human rights framework for Wales with the possibility of continuing to enhance human rights protections pushing against the regressive tide at the national level. As Hoffman observes, it is now within the competence of the Welsh Assembly to 'observe and implement' international human rights obligations,[13] as is the case in both Scotland and Northern Ireland. This could mean that Wales take further legislative steps to integrate (or fully incorporate) other international human rights treaties into domestic law, such as the International Covenant of Economic, Social and Cultural Rights (ICESCR) and the UN Convention on the Rights of Persons with Disabilities (UNCRPD). In addition, the Wales Act 2017 devolves section 1 of the Equality Act to the Welsh Assembly.[14] This means that the Welsh Assembly can introduce a socio-economic equality duty, similar to the Fairer Scotland duty, that places an obligation on Ministers and other public bodies to have regard to socio-economic disadvantage when making decisions on public policy. As discussed in more detail in the justiciability mechanisms above, a socio-economic duty to have due regard is a procedural duty that creates a right to a process (to have due regard) rather than to an outcome (to eliminate socio-economic disadvantage). There is more scope in Wales to move duties beyond the procedural to more substantive and outcome-based duties of compliance with international human rights law.

Likewise, there is scope to ensure the important measures taken by the Welsh Assembly to improve the protection of rights and to ensure their full potential. This relates to the accessibility of law, rights and remedies under the Welsh system. Lord Lloyd Jones UK Supreme Court judge has said that 'the complexity

---

11 Section 3 and Section 5.
12 Hoffman, n 8.
13 Simon Hoffman, National Assembly for Wales, Equality, Local Government and Communities Committee, Human Rights Inquiry 2017, available at http://senedd.assembly.wales/documents/s59272/HR%2010%20-%20Dr%20Simon%20Hoffman.pdf para.14.
14 Section 45 of the Wales Act 2017.

of [Welsh law] is now a huge problem'.[15] In addition, and potentially related, there has been and under-engagement with new ESR protection mechanisms by the legal community and judicial review remains under-utilised.[16] Hoffman concludes that this is in part due to funding restrictions (undermining the accessibility and participation principles of adjudication), but also 'lack of familiarity with the legalisation, and a belief that public law remedies are ineffective or difficult to obtain, as reasons for practitioner reluctance to bring a cases to judicial review using the Child Rights Measure'[17] (meaning the deliberative, counter-majoritarian and remedial principles ought to inform future developments).

The potential of Welsh law is underdeveloped and the scope for increasing access to justice through judicial review has the potential to draw on the distinct approach the Welsh Assembly has taken to improving ESR protection. Hoffman argues '[t]he Welsh approach to regulation of public governance is distinctive; introducing new and unique duties on Welsh Ministers and public bodies... Social rights have been woven to the framework of public governance, with potential to ensure good governance, fairness and accountability'.[18]

The Legislation (Wales) Bill seeks to address some of the issues of accessibility through the consolidation and codification of Welsh law.[19] As part of the proposed legislation there is a duty to keep accessibility of Welsh law under review (Section 1). During the course of evidence hearings on the proposed Bill several stakeholders raised concern about the digitisation of law without appropriate support for citizens in accessing technology, and the lack of resources for advice bodies to support them.[20] Each of these issues engages, or rather highlights the absence of, the **principle of accessibility** for social rights adjudication.

Options for Enhancing ESR in Wales

The administrative court in Wales has taken a cautious approach to international human rights treaties when such treaties are invoked before the court.[21] Mr Justice

---

15 Lord Lloyd Jones, 'Codification of Welsh Law' Lecture delivered to the Association of London Welsh Lawyers on 8 March 2018, available at https://docs.wixstatic.com/ugd/ab7491_8c924cda0b7e4312b1e10fe9b8e7d501.pdf.

16 Submission to the Commission on Justice in Wales from Dr Simon Hoffman (Swansea University), available at https://beta.gov.wales/submission-justice-commission-dr-simonhoffman-swansea-university at para.7.

17 Ibid.

18 Ibid. at para. 3.

19 http://senedd.assembly.wales/mgIssueHistoryHome.aspx?IId=23311.

20 Constitutional and Legislative Affairs Committee, 29 January 2019, Legislation (Wales) Bill Evidence Session 5, Rob Sherrington, Citizen's Advice Cymru; Callum Higgins, Citizen's Advice Cymru Professor Richard Owen, Swansea Law Clinic; Tahmid Miah, Swansea Law Clinic, available at www.senedd.tv/Meeting/Archive/f11dc9ce-80a4-42a0-8c67-17c147448492?autostart=True#.

21 *Tilley, R (on the application of) v The Vale of Glamorgan Council* [2016] EWHC 2272 (QB) (13 September 2016). See also *J.H. Rayner (Mincing Lane) Ltd. v Department of Trade*

Lewis in a case before him declared that the 'provisions of an international treaty are not themselves enforceable in the domestic courts unless the treaty has been incorporated into domestic law'.[22] However, at the same time the court has also recognised the development of international human rights as an interpretative device that has enhanced the development of the common law.[23] There is a judicial recognition, at the very least, of the normative nature of international human rights law when interpreting domestic rights.

Interestingly, the new devolved settlement forged under the 2017 Act reserves the matter of the 'single jurisdiction of England and Wales' meaning that developing a distinct judicial approach to human rights would be restricted in the sense that the Welsh-based courts and the Welsh Assembly cannot alter the jurisdiction or create new courts/tribunals in Wales; cannot interfere with the appointment or role of the judiciary; cannot change the operation of civil proceedings (or criminal for that matter); and would be limited in terms of developing new remedies and unable to interfere with the operation of judicial review proceedings as they currently exist without further devolution of powers.[24] The judicial approach to ESR is therefore very much dependent on the framework employed in the jurisdiction of England and Wales. Pritchard on the subject of an emerging 'Legal Wales' highlights the 'fatal gap' of devolution to a jurisdiction that does not exercise control over its own administrative justice. He argues that whilst devolution might give Wales a distinct legal identity it does not allow 'for the Welsh Government to exercise justice functions or to develop a substantive justice policy suitable for the social or economic needs of Wales'.[25] Members of the judiciary have raised concerns that there is a dearth of knowledge on Welsh devolved law, meaning practitioners have come before the court without having realised that matters relating to English law do not apply in the jurisdiction of devolved Wales.[26] The devolved settlement comes with inherent limitations and without further devolution in administrative justice it will inevitably prove more difficult to initiate mechanisms that lead to transformative change. Nonetheless, Wales has taken some of the most significant steps to date, compared to any other UK jurisdiction,[27] and its ambition

[1990] 2 A.C. 418 (and see also *R (SG) v Secretary of State for Work and Pensions* [2015] UKSC 16, per Lord Reed at para. 82, Lord Carnwath at para. 115 and Lord Hughes at paras. 137–139 discussed above).

22　*Tilley* ibid. as per Mr Justice Lewis at para.75.

23　*Calver, R (On the Application Of) v The Adjudication Panel for Wales* (Rev 2) [2012] EWHC 1172 (Admin) (3 May 2012), Mr Justice Beatson at para.41.

24　Schedule 7A para.8 Government of Wales Act 2006 – with some minor exceptions in the case of family proceedings para.8(3).

25　Huw Pritchard, 'Revisiting Legal Wales', (2019) 23 *Edinburgh Law Review* 123–130 at 127.

26　Members of the Judiciary, Commission on Justice in Wales, Paper on Separation of Legal Professions, available at https://beta.gov.wales/sites/default/files/publications/2019-01/Submission%20to%20the%20Commission%20on%20Justice%20in%20Wales%20from%20members%20of%20the%20judiciary.pdf.

27　Hoffman, Commission on Justice, n 16.

continues to grow.[28] The Commission on Justice in Wales was established by the First Minister to review the operation of the justice system in Wales and in October 2019 reported its recommendations on a long-term vision for the future of the Welsh justice system. The Commission's recommendations include full devolution of justice to the Welsh Assembly , including the development of the law of Wales (distinct to the law of England) with a new separate tribunal and court system (distinct to that of England). Consideration of new remedies, and innovative means of collective litigation, would be key to the development of the **counter-majoritarian principle** in the adjudication of social rights under any renewed justice framework. No doubt innovative approaches will continue to flourish within the confines of the devolved settlement, which in and of itself may be subject to further change as Wales acquires, and grows in its status as, a distinct legal jurisdiction following the Commission's recommendations.

In the meantime, the judiciary should be equipped to respond to the Welsh legislature's attempts to better embed ESR – and at the very least, be prepared to respond to procedural due regard duties in respect of those rights thus enabling the **principles of accessibility, participation and deliberation**. Likewise, practitioners must be ready to invoke due regard procedural rights when the duty is not complied with. In terms of the future development of ESR in the Welsh context the Welsh Assembly could take further steps to incorporate (rather than implement/ integrate through due regard) international human rights obligations in devolved areas. Taking this step would enable better access to rights and remedies than currently exists under the weaker due regard duties. This is key to enabling the **accessibility, participative, deliberative and remedial principles** of social rights adjudication as well as the **principle of fairness** in both a procedural and substantive sense. Likewise, the Assembly could implement the socio-economic equality duty. There is also scope for the establishment of a Welsh Human Rights Commission, akin to the Scottish Human Rights Commission and Northern Ireland Human Rights Commission, each of which are the national human rights institution responsible for human rights in devolved areas. Whilst the Welsh Committee of the Equality and Human Rights Commission[29] could continue to advise and promote human rights and equality in reserved areas a distinct national human rights institution for Wales could help foster a human rights-based culture in newly devolved areas.[30] There is also scope in Wales to introduce more robust procedures around *ex ante* review of human rights as part of the work of the Welsh Assembly. In other words, a dedicated human rights and equality

---

28 Ibid., see also more broadly the work of the Commission on Justice in Wales https://beta. gov.wales/commission-justice-wales.

29 The EHRC is under a duty to establish a Welsh Committee with a Welsh EHRC Commissioner to oversee equality and human rights issues as they relate to Wales, Equality Act 2006 Schedule 1 para.24–31.

30 Hoffman recommends the implementation of a distinct WHRC in his evidence to the Welsh Assembly Simon Hoffman, National Assembly for Wales, Equality, Local Government and Communities Committee, Human Rights Inquiry 2017, available at http://senedd.assem bly.wales/documents/s59272/HR%2010%20-%20Dr%20Simon%20Hoffman.pdf para.19.

committee that regularly undertakes assessment of devolved legislation to ensure compliance with ESR and civil and political rights (CPR) before legislation is passed. This role could be performed within the existing remit of the Equality, Local Government and Communities Committee but would require additional resources to ensure that human rights scrutiny is embedded across the Assembly.[31]

The future development of ESR in Wales could draw on the multi-institutional approach across the legislative, executive and judicial sphere. Further devolution of the administrative justice system, and the development of a distinct legal jurisdiction, would allow for Wales to go further in reaching its ambitions on future human rights leadership.

Northern Ireland

The history of the conflict in Northern Ireland is a complicated and highly contested narrative where consensus on factual accounts of historical events is frequently elusive.[32] One pivotal point of consensus, however, is that the conflict in Northern Ireland occurred against a severely economically and socially deprived background.[33] Miller warns against the dismissal of the economic origins of conflict where 'apparent ethnic, racial or religious causes may mask the economic origins of conflict'.[34] If ESR violations were not root causes of the conflict, they certainly, at the very least, exacerbated the situation and acted as a catalyst for violence. It is not within the remit of this book to explore the history of the conflict. Nonetheless, it is imperative to note that a fragile peace prevails in Northern Ireland with remnants of the conflict continuing to shape everyday life, including continuing violations of ESR. McKeever and Ní Aoláin concur that the conflict in Northern Ireland was substantially triggered by the pervasive discrimination and disenfranchisement experienced by the minority Catholic community since the creation of the Northern Ireland sub-state in 1922.[35] This included systemic discrimination in relation to:

---

31 See, for example, the recommendations made to the Scottish Parliament Equality and Human Rights Committee (EHRiC) on enhancing *ex ante* review of legislation and introducing human rights rapporteurs across the parliament's work: www.parliament.scot/S5_Equal_Opps/Submission_from_Dr_Katie_Boyle.pdf and the report of EHRiC, 'Getting Rights Right: Human Rights and the Scottish Parliament', Scottish Parliament November 2018, available at https://sp-bpr-en-prod-cdnep.azureedge.net/published/EHRiC/2018/11/26/Getting-Rights-Right–Human-Rights-and-the-Scottish-Parliament-3/EHRiCS052018R6Rev.pdf.

32 This is described as a conflict about the conflict, or a 'meta-conflict', Bell et al., 'Justice Discourses in Transition' (2004) 13 *Social & Legal Studies* 305, 316.

33 Grainne McKeever and Fionnuala Ní Aoláin, 'Thinking Globally, Acting Locally: Enforcing Socio Economic Rights in Northern Ireland' (2004) 2 *European Human Rights Law Review* 158, 166 and Report by Lord Cameron (1969) Disturbances in Northern Ireland: Report of the Commission Appointed by the Governor of Northern Ireland; Chapter 16, (a)1 para.126–127.

34 Zinaida Miller, 'Effects of Invisibility: In Search of the "Economic" in Transitional Justice' (2008) 2 *International Journal of Transitional Justice* 266, 289.

35 McKeever and Ní Aoláin, n 33. See also Fionnuala Ní Aoláin, *Politics of Force* (Blackwell Press, 2000).

historical inequities in wealth accumulation and distribution; exclusionary political processes (including the artificial manipulation of electoral boundaries and the exclusion of the minority community for decades from political decision-making processes); and elite institutions such as the courts being unrepresentative of the community as a whole.[36]

Furthermore, relative to the rest of the UK, Northern Ireland was subject to higher levels of deprivation and both polarised communities (Catholic/Nationalist; Protestant/Unionist) suffered economic and social deprivation, with Catholics historically worse off than Protestants according to all the major social and economic indicators.[37] The 1998 peace agreement set Northern Ireland on a course that placed human rights at the heart of the constitutional framework. Nonetheless, following over 20 years of post-peace agreement governance Northern Ireland continues to be economically worse off relative to the rest of the UK.[38] This presents as a problem in terms of the state's international human rights obligations.

Historically, the border (and the geographical entity of Northern Ireland) came into being as a compromise between two seemingly irreconcilable positions on the sovereignty of the island of Ireland. Hayward explains that the line of inclusion and exclusion drawn in a territorial border has symbolic, social and economic as well as political importance, 'as the border became the locus and the focus of Irish/British differentiation after 1920, so nationalist/unionist disagreement as to the border's legitimacy became fundamental to individuals' political, economic and social identification'.[39] The shape and nuance of identity has continued to evolve in Northern Ireland with research indicating a growing trend towards identifying primarily as Northern Irish in the first instance, rather than British or Irish, or Protestant or Catholic, with the trend most prevalent among the younger demographic.[40] This is not forgetting those who by definition cannot belong to either of the polarised communities, who are often hidden or ignored by the contested political paradigm. Those minorities and vulnerable groups who pertain to other communities and characteristics face discrimination and hidden depths of inequality not yet fully captured in the Northern Irish context. Identity is forged by many factors and is a much more

36 Ibid.
37 McKeever and Ní Aoláin, ibid. See also 'Fair Employment for All', a submission by CAJ to the Standing Advisory Commission on Human Rights Employment Equality Review, Belfast, 1996. Findings on deprivation in 2003 also reflected that Catholics continued to experience greater levels of poverty than Protestants: Paddy Hillyard, Grace Kelly, Eithne McLaughlin, Demi Patsios and Mike Tomlinson, *Bare Necessities: Poverty and Social Exclusion in Northern Ireland-Key Findings* (Belfast: Democratic Dialogue, 2003).
38 Robin Wilson, The Northern Ireland Peace Monitoring Report, Number 4, September 2016, available at www.community-relations.org.uk/sites/crc/files/media-files/NIPMR-Final-2016.pdf, pp.69–70.
39 Katy Hayward, 'Reiterating National Identities: The European Union Concept of Conflict Resolution in Northern Ireland', (2006) 41 *Cooperation and Conflict* 261, 264.
40 Northern Ireland Life and Times Poll 2015, Community Relations, available at www.ark.ac.uk/nilt/2015/Community_Relations/NINATID.html.

nuanced picture than the binary categories associated with the conflict.[41] Citizenship and identity has become all the more complex and fraught as a result of Brexit, aspects of which run contrary to the principles of the peace agreement.[42] Human rights play a pivotal role in seeking to reconcile the fractured communities in Northern Ireland. Despite important strides made under the implementation of the peace agreement, including the drafting of a Bill of Rights for Northern Ireland, little progress has been made in embedding rights beyond those contained in the ECHR or EU law. This presents as an ESR accountability gap for the state (discussed further below).

The UK Government has acknowledged that grievances concerning social and economic discrimination had substantial foundation in Northern Ireland.[43] According to McKeever and Ní Aoláin, a failure to substantively protect ESR in Northern Ireland will result in a failure to address the systemic causes of the conflict.[44] The threat of a 'hard Brexit' where the UK crashes out of the EU has demonstrated the drastic consequences for the retrenchment of border controls that operated during the conflict. This backward step is hugely problematic for exacerbating the social and economic conditions that fuelled the conflict in the first place, and in so doing, destabilising an already fragile peace. As Northern Ireland is economically worse off relative to the rest of the UK there is also a danger that inequality in Northern Ireland becomes stuck in a 'sectarian time warp' focussing on remedying the inequality between polarised communities on a formal equality basis (where everyone might be equally poor) instead of addressing relative poverty across communities as a result of a 'market-oriented, conservative welfare system within a global context of rising inequality'[45] and a failure to embrace the full spectrum of international human rights law.

The consociational power-sharing arrangement in Stormont collapsed in January 2017 due to political impasse and Northern Ireland has operated without an executive or democratic accountability in devolved areas for a significant period of time. The democratic deficit this creates has led to significant political problems for resolving disputes around rights protection, including most recently on whether the UK Parliament should legislate in a devolved area to repeal and replace the legislation dating from 1861 criminalising abortion in Northern Ireland.[46] The Supreme Court has indicated that the law in Northern Ireland is incompatible with Article 8 of the ECHR.[47] Both Westminster and the Northern Ireland Assembly have the

---

41 Ibid.
42 Lisa O'Carroll, 'Derry Woman's US-born husband free to live in UK, court rules', *The Guardian*, 12 February 2018, available at www.theguardian.com/uk-news/2018/feb/12/derry-woman-us-born-husband-uk-emma-de-souza.
43 Report by Lord Cameron (1969) n 33.
44 McKeever and Ní Aoláin, n 33 at 163.
45 Wilson, Northern Ireland Peace Monitoring Report n 38 at 69.
46 *In the matter of an application by the Northern Ireland Human Rights Commission for Judicial Review (Northern Ireland)* [2018] UKSC 27.
47 Ibid. [2018] UKSC 27 para.2. The case was dismissed as inadmissible because the NIHRC could not establish standing. Nonetheless the court indicated that the law was incompatible *obiter dicta* despite being unable to issue a judgment to this effect.

legislative competence to make the changes but politically Westminster faces problems in doing so, because of a desire to withhold on trespassing into a devolved area
(by way of political convention[48]) but also because of the UK Government's reliance on the Democratic Unionist Party (DUP) as the political party that allowed
the Conservative government to retain power in Westminster during Theresa May's
term as Prime Minister.[49] These complexities place Northern Ireland in a very precarious constitutional position in terms of rights protections where vulnerable
people are left without access to rights or remedies whilst political instability ensues
during periods of dissolution. The power-sharing arrangements were restored in
January 2020 and at the time of writing an Ad-Hoc Committee on a Bill of Rights
has been established to re-open consideration of a Bill of Rights for Northern Ireland. The work of this Committee may be key in shaping the future of ESR in
Northern Ireland. Future research will be required to consider how that work com-
pares with devolved counterparts in terms of human rights leadership.

The Peace Agreement(s)[50]

The multilateral peace agreement reached in Northern Ireland in 1998 marked
a crucial turning point in the negotiations between non-state actors and two sovereign states (Britain and Ireland) in relation to the conflict. Peace agreements are
becoming more prevalent as the preferred way of resolving internal conflict[51] but
as Bell has noted, these agreements are often fragile instruments of soft law, thus
compliance is often difficult to enforce.[52] Furthermore, they do not necessarily
bring conflict to an end but often precipitate a 'no war, no peace' limbo.[53]

The 1998 Northern Ireland peace agreement is described by Bell as a 'partially
resolved, partially postponed' substantive or framework agreement.[54] It contains provisions on institutional reform (policing and criminal justice);[55] decommissioning of

---

48 As per the judgment in *Miller* [2017] UKSC 5, the Sewel Convention is a matter of politics
   and 'the policing of its scope and the manner of its operation does not lie within the constitutional remit of the judiciary, which is to protect the rule of law'. para.151.
49 Following a snap general election in 2017 the Conservative party entered into a coalition
   with the Northern Ireland DUP party in order to form a minority government.
50 The Belfast Agreement 1998/The Good Friday Agreement 1998, annexed to the Agreement
   between the Government of the United Kingdom of Great Britain and Northern Ireland and
   the Government of Ireland (with annexes), Belfast, 10 April 1998, Registration No. 1.36776
   UNTS 2114, Treaty series No.50 (2000) Cm 4705. Referred to as the 'peace agreement' or
   the 'multi-party peace agreement'. Other agreements relating to peace in Northern Ireland
   both preceded and proceeded the 1998 Agreement, including for example the St Andrews
   Agreement 2007 that sought to restore the power sharing arrangement in a devolved Northern Ireland Assembly.
51 Christine Bell, 'Dealing with the Past in Northern Ireland' (2002–2003) 26 *Fordham International Law Journal* 1095.
52 Christine Bell, 'Peace Agreements: Their Nature and Legal Status', (2006) 100 *American
   Journal of International Law* 373.
53 Bell, ibid. at 375.
54 Bell, ibid. at 378.
55 Peace agreement n 50 Strand One and Parts 9 and 10.

the paramilitary organisations;[56] demilitarisation through normalisation of the security arrangements;[57] human rights safeguards and reconciliation for victims of violence;[58] and self-determination on the unresolved future sovereignty of Northern Ireland.[59] On the surface, it would appear that the structure of the agreement is holistic. It is in fact skeletal in nature providing a framework for further engagement. The negotiations surrounding the agreement following the 1994 and 1998 ceasefires meant that it was constructed in a fragile political atmosphere where the parties to the agreement each had to compromise in order to reach consensus.[60]

One of the governing and most prevalent objectives of the peace agreement was the commitment of all parties to a human rights culture across the island of Ireland. The second paragraph of the Declaration of Support reads:

> The tragedies of the past have left a deep and profoundly regrettable legacy of suffering. We must never forget those who have died or been injured, and their families. But we can best honour them through a fresh start, in which we firmly dedicate ourselves to the achievement of reconciliation, tolerance, and mutual trust, and to the protection and vindication of the human rights of all.[61]

Hence, from the outset of proceedings, there has been a commitment to cultivate a human rights culture in post-conflict Northern Ireland. Paul Murphy, the then Northern Ireland Minister for European Affairs suggested that not only were human rights at the heart of the peace agreement but that the agreement was in fact inspired by the European principles of 'human rights, pluralist democracy and the rule of law'.[62]

If Northern Ireland is to adopt and retain a model that entrenches human rights then this requires all state actors to comply with fundamental norms. As Feldman acknowledges, 'the drafters of any constitution can decide that some provisions or values are too important, given the historical and social circumstances in which the constitution is being prepared, to be subject to amendment'.[63] Northern Ireland is required to pertain to a framework model of constitutionalism where the state is encompassed within the law rather than 'the state being simply the source of law'.[64] As part of this commitment human

---

56 Peace agreement ibid., Part 7.
57 Peace agreement, ibid., Part 8.
58 Peace agreement, ibid., Part 6: the establishment of the Northern Ireland Human Rights Commission hereinafter referred to as the NIHRC.
59 Peace agreement, ibid., Part 2, Constitutional Issues, para.1(i).
60 Bell, n 51.
61 Declaration of Support, section 1 of peace agreement n 50.
62 Paul Murphy, Northern Ireland Minister for European Affairs, quote published by Northern Ireland Office, Hermes database, 5 May 1998.
63 David Feldman, 'Constitutionalism, Deliberative Democracy and Human Rights' in John Morison et al. (eds.), *Judges, Transitions and Human Rights* (Oxford University Press, 2007), 463.
64 John Morison and Marie Lynch, 'Litigating the Agreement: Towards a New Judicial Constitutionalism for the UK from Northern Ireland' in John Morison et al. (eds.), ibid. at 142.

rights protections formed a pivotal normative source in the drafting of the peace agreement and subsequent devolved settlement.

Given the historical significance of the inclusion of human rights and equality in the Northern Ireland peace agreement and the devolved entrenchment of human rights in the subsequent Northern Ireland Act 1998, the pre-negotiated, pre-committed norms renders the NI settlement firmly within a model of constitutionalism under which the judiciary must play an active role in the democratic dialogue between institutions. Paradoxically, studies of jurisprudence in Northern Ireland and the rest of the UK demonstrate that the courts in Northern Ireland are less likely to interfere on matters relating to interpretation of what is perceived as a political peace agreement. The judiciary in Northern Ireland employ what Anthony describes as 'soft-edged review'[65] where there is a reluctance to interfere[66] in peace agreement litigation, and a tendency to employ a strict and literal approach to interpretation when any review does take place.[67] The Supreme Court (and previously the House of Lords) takes a much more progressive approach to interpreting legislation even when it engages the politics of peace – they have at least embraced the significance of the peace agreement.[68]

Northern Ireland as a Conflicted Democracy

Transitional justice is the legal and academic discipline in which conflict or post-conflict societies may address systematic human rights violations committed by a prior regime.[69] Northern Ireland is described as a 'conflicted democracy' within the transitional justice literature.[70] In this sense, it is an entity within a wider democratic state that is undergoing incremental transition in order to address historical systemic human rights abuses. The literature has identified that economic, social and cultural rights violations are often left unaddressed in the aftermath of conflict and that this oversight may undermine the transition from

65 Gordon Anthony, *Judicial Review in Northern Ireland* (Hart Publishing, 2008), 114.
66 *Re Williamson's Application* [2000] NI 281.
67 Compare, for example, the differing interpretations of the NI judiciary and the House of Lords in *Human Rights Commission* [2001] NI 271; [2002] UKHL 25 – no explicit power for HRC to intervene – NI court strict interpretation – could not allow intervention – HoL broad interpretation – held implicit right to intervene based on progressive, broad and purposive reading of Northern Ireland Act 1998.
68 Morison and Lynch, n 64 at 135.
69 Ruti Teitel, 'Transitional Justice Genealogy' (2003) 16 *Harvard Human Rights Journal* 69, 71–72.
70 Northern Ireland falls within the definition of a conflicted democracy as the state is a liberal democracy committed to international human rights at the macro level however, at the same time, a geographical entity within the state conformed to an illiberal regime subject to systemic human rights violations. For a further discussion on the 'paradigmatic transition' v 'conflicted democracy' see Fionnuala Ní Aoláin and Colm Campbell, 'The Paradox of Transition in Conflicted Democracies' (2003) 27 *Human Rights Quarterly* 172, 193.

war to peace with the vulnerable and marginalised remaining in a state of pre-conflict ESR violation.[71]

The conflict in Northern Ireland is unique in many respects as it is a partitioned section of a democratic state which has operated undemocratically in 'conflict' with the rest of the UK. Ní Aoláin and Campbell identify the paradoxical nature of Northern Ireland as a 'conflicted democracy'.[72] A conflicted democracy transition is different to a 'paradigmatic transition'. The latter of which occurs in societies emerging from authoritarian regimes on a journey to democracy. A 'conflicted democracy', on the other hand, is a transition from procedural to substantive democracy within a state that, overall, appears democratic on the surface. The term 'conflicted democracy' therefore refers to states undergoing transition that appear as legitimate democracies that are paradoxically faced with a program of change towards substantive democracy that, by the state's self-definition, should have been unnecessary from the outset, as was the case in Northern Ireland.[73]

A conflicted democracy can often lack the civic pressure required to push transitional societies towards reconciliation.[74] In a paradigmatic transition this civic pressure is normally obtained through a moral consensus which arises *ex post facto*.[75] Conversely, in the case of the conflicted democracy, no *ex post facto* situation exists as the transition has not yet reached an endpoint.[76] In other words, as Nino notes, recognition of an immoral state may be impossible until that state no longer exists.[77] In the 'paradigmatic transition', law can act as an important vehicle for reform. In the conflicted democracy, however, it can become a veil, whereby institutionalised state dysfunction continues under the aegis of 'procedural democracy'.[78] The move from war to peace does not necessarily correspond with a move from a dysfunctional regime to substantive democracy.

When discussing transition in post-apartheid South Africa (paradigmatic transition), Makau Mutua noted that the immediate transitional justice approach paradoxically froze 'the hierarchies of apartheid by preserving the social and economic status quo'.[79] The move towards justiciable ESR in South Africa is indicative of a state transitioning from ESR violation to ESR protection.[80] At the

---

71 Aoife Nolan and Evelyne Schmide, '"Do No Harm"? Exploring the Scope of Economic and Social Rights in Transitional Justice' (2014) 8(3) *International Journal of Transitional Justice* 362–382; Miller, n 34; Shirin M. Rai, 'Deliberative Democracy and the Politics of Redistribution: The Case of the Indian Panchayats' (2007) 22 *Hypatia* 65.

72 Ní Aoláin, n 35 at 179.

73 Ní Aoláin and Campbell, n 70.

74 Bell, n 51 at 1101.

75 Carlos Nino, *Radical Evil On Trial* (Yale University Press, 1996). As cited in Charlies Villa Vicencio, 'The Reek for Cruelty and the Quest for Healing – Where Retributive and Restorative Justice Meet' (1999–2000) 14 *Journal of Law and Religion* 165.

76 Ní Aoláin and Campbell, n 70.

77 Nino, n 75.

78 Bell, n 51.

79 Makau Mutua, 'Hope and Despair for a New South Africa: The Limits of Rights Discourse' (1997) 10 *Harvard Human Rights Journal* 68.

80 This adjudication is discussed in more detail in Chapter 4.

very least, this transition can be measured because ESR violations are now acknowledged through the constitutionalisation of ESR in post-apartheid South Africa (indicating a move from denial of ESR violations to acknowledgement of ESR violations). In the 'conflicted democracy' the dysfunctional state becomes democratic through a series of multisequential transitions.[81] This process has been described by Bell as the 'piecemeal'[82] approach and naturally faces great difficulty in reconciling transitional goals from the outset as there has effectively been no transformation (or acknowledgement) of state complicity. As a result, substantive transitions can be more difficult to identify and to measure and therefore take longer to address.

In Northern Ireland, civil and political rights violations can partially be legally addressed at the devolved and national level.[83] Even if violations persist, the transition to full protection can be assessed because there are legal mechanisms in place to acknowledge any failure of the state in this regard.[84] ESR, on the other hand, may be more difficult to realise, or to measure, as they have not, as yet, been afforded the same level of recognition. By way of example, there have been several significant cases that have been determined by the European Court of Human Rights (ECtHR) in relation to the conflict in Northern Ireland that reveal a systemic problem with human rights compatibility.[85] This jurisprudence has largely focused on addressing CPR violations. A number of cases illustrate violations of the European Convention of Human Rights (ECHR) in relation to UK's response to the conflict, particularly under Articles 2 and 3. In the case of *Ireland v UK*,[86] for example, the ECtHR held that the UK security forces' use of the 'five techniques': hooding; wall-standing; continuous white noise; sleep deprivation; and the bread and water diet, against detainees held in internment without trial amounted to inhuman and degrading treatment and a breach of Article 3 of the Convention.[87] In *McCann*

---

81 Ní Aoláin and Campbell, n 70 at 193.

82 Bell, n 51.

83 In the context of Northern Ireland this is evident in the recognition and acknowledgement of civil and political rights at the domestic level through the Northern Ireland Act 1998, at the national level through the Human Rights Act 1998, and at the regional level through the European Convention of Human Rights. At each of these levels civil and political rights can be adjudicated upon in court and protected by the judiciary.

84 For example, violations of civil and political rights in Northern Ireland continue in relation to the procedural element of posthumous investigations into deaths under Article 2 ECHR (the right to life). The ECtHR has adjudicated on the continuing failure of the state to remedy the non-compliant investigations into death by state forces in the context of the conflict. This is discussed in more detail below. See for example, *McCaughey and others v. UK* (Application no. 43098/09) 16 July 2013.

85 For an extensive discussion on the role of the ECHR in the Northern Ireland conflict see Brice Dickson, *The European Convention of Human Rights and the Conflict in Northern Ireland* (Oxford University Press, 2010).

86 *Ireland v UK* (1978) Series A No 25, 2 EHRR 25.

87 In 2018, the ECtHR declined to revisit the case in a plea to recognise the treatment as amounting to torture. The court took the view that the case was no longer admissible but did not come to a decision or set out whether or not the treatment did constitute torture as it is now conceived in more recent case law, *Ireland v. UK* (Application no. 5310/71) 20 March 2018.

v UK the court held that the inquest system in Northern Ireland failed as an accountability mechanism into deaths caused by the state in the context of the conflict.[88] In 2001, the conjoined cases of *Jordan, Kelly, McKerr and Shanaghan v UK*[89] extended the jurisprudence of the ECtHR towards a wider interpretation of Article 2 by imposing a positive obligation on the state to investigate a death (as a posthumous procedural element to the right to life) concerning killings by the security forces in Northern Ireland.[90] As the UK is bound by the decisions of the ECtHR it must implement any judgments immediately and effectively to avoid future human rights violations.[91] Following the above mentioned judgments, the reaction of the UK government was 'piecemeal',[92] i.e. there was no major transformation of the system. In July 2013, the ECtHR reiterated the obligation incumbent on the UK to carry out an effective investigation into killings by the security forces as part of the procedural requirements under Article 2.[93] In particular, the court noted that the UK was still in violation of the *Jordan* et al.[94] judgments made in 2001.[95] According to the court, delays into carrying out effective investigations into killings by the security forces, remains a serious and extensive problem in Northern Ireland. In 2014 the governments of the UK and Ireland committed to establishing an independent Historical Investigations Unit (HIU) and to support and provide resources for the continuation of legacy inquests in compliance with Article 2.[96] In 2017, the Committee of Ministers responsible for observing the execution of ECHR judgments has again highlighted its concerns regarding the lack of progress made with no HIU in place and insufficient resources to support effective legacy inquests.[97] In 2019 the Supreme Court found the UK in

---

88 *McCann v UK*, 21 Eur Ct HR Rep 97 (1996) para 130. The Director of Public Prosecutions failed to provide an explanation for his decision not to prosecute following an inquest and the emergence of new evidence. The breach of Art 2 therefore emanates not from the inquest itself but because it could 'play no effective role in the identification or prosecution of any criminal offences that could have occurred'. Fionnuala Ní Aoláin, 'Truth Telling, Accountability and the Right to Life' (2002) 5 *European Human Rights Law Review* 572, 585.

89 *Hugh Jordan v UK*, Application No. 24746/94; *McKerr v UK* 34 Eur Ct H.R. 553 (2002); *Kelly and Others v UK*, Application No.30054/96; *Shanaghan v UK*, Application No. 37715/97. Judgment was made in each of these cases by the European Court of Human Rights on 4 May 2001.

90 Bell, n 51 at 1133.

91 Under the Human Rights Act 1998 and also by virtue of Article 46 of the ECHR with execution of judgments being supervised by the Committee of Ministers of the Council of Europe.

92 Bell, n 51.

93 In the case of *McCaughey and others v. UK* (Application no. 43098/09) 16 July 2013.

94 *Jordan* et al. n 89.

95 *McCaughey* n 84 para.144.

96 The Stormont House Agreement between the Governments of the United Kingdom and Ireland, 23 December 2014, available at www.gov.uk/government/uploads/system/uploads/attachment_data/file/390672/Stormont_House_Agreement.pdf.

97 The committee noted that 'it considered it imperative that a way forward is found to enable effective investigations to be conducted particularly in light of the length of time that has already passed since these judgments became final, and the failure of previous initiatives to achieve effective,

violation of Article 2 (effective investigation) into the death of Pat Finucane in 1989.[98] This death is associated with the widespread collusive practice of the state during the conflict.[99] Jamieson and McEvoy contend that Northern Ireland provides an instructive example of a 'collusion continuum' where state crimes have been committed by serving members of the security force acting perfidiously; by special forces acting with de facto legal impunity; and through the use of both 'bad apple' collusion (where information on suspected Republican terrorists was passed on to Loyalist paramilitaries by individual officers sympathetic to the Loyalist cause) and 'institutional collusion' (where collusion with paramilitary groups has been organised, planned and bureaucratised implicating institutions, the criminal justice system and the political elite).[100] Whilst incorporation of ECHR was a positive step in securing the protection of CPR, jurisprudence of the court demonstrates that the UK continues to breach its human rights obligations in relation to dealing with the legacy of the conflict.[101] This evidence presents as 'an enormous accountability gap for the state'.[102] Whilst this CPR accountability gap can be 'seen' and therefore measured and assessed the ESR accountability gap remains largely hidden and unaddressed.

So what kind of ESR gap might continue to exist in Northern Ireland? Research suggests that the historical divide in areas such as employment have to some extent been addressed over time. For example, the employment gap has largely closed between Catholics and Protestants between the period 2001–2014 (with Protestants still comprising the majority of the workforce).[103]

expeditious investigations [and] deeply regretted that the necessary resources have not been provided to allow effective legacy inquests to be concluded within a reasonable time', CM/Notes/ 1294/H46-38, 1294th meeting (September 2017) (DH) – H46-38 McKerr group v. the United Kingdom (Application No. 28883/95), 22 September 2017, available at https://search. coe.int/cm/pages/result_details.aspx?objectid=0900001680739ed0.

98 *Finucane, Re Application for Judicial Review (Northern Ireland)* [2019] UKSC 7 (27 February 2019).

99 In 2007 Nuala O'Loan, then Police Commissioner for Northern Ireland, confirmed that collusive practices between state actors and loyalist paramilitaries were 'systemic' – Nuala O'Loan, Operation Ballast, Investigative Report, 22 January 2007, available at www.policeom budsman.org/publicationsuploads/BALLAST-PUBLIC-STATEMENT-22-01-07-FINAL-VERSION1.pdf. See also the Cory Reports – Canadian Supreme Court Judge Mr Peter Cory defined collusion as 'ignoring or turning a blind eye to the wrongful acts of their servants or agents or supplying information to assist them in wrongful acts or encouraging them to commit wrongful acts' Peter Cory, 'Cory Collusion Report Pat Finnucan' (2004) London, HMSO/The Stationary Office, 24 <www.cain.ulst.ac.uk/issues/collusion/cory/cory03finu cane.pdf>. The other reports conducted by Judge Cory into collusion in both Northern Ireland and the Republic of Ireland (Rosemary Nelson, Pat Finucane, Robert Hamill, Billy Wright, Chief Superintendent Breen and Superintendent Buchanan and Lord Justice and Lady Gibson) are available at <www.cain.ulst.ac.uk/issues/collusion/index.html>.

100 Ruth Jamieson and Kieran McEvoy, 'State crime by proxy and juridicial othering' (2005) 45 *British Journal of Criminology* 504, 511.

101 Ibid.

102 Bell, n 51 at 588.

103 Equality Commission for Northern Ireland, Fair Employment Monitoring Report No.25, An Overview of High Level Trends and Aggregated Monitored Returns (2014). The

In 1992, the unemployment rate was 9% for Protestants and 18% for Catholics; in 2016 these rates were 5% and 7% respectively.[104] However, at the same time areas such as housing and education continue to be segregated, and evidence suggests ESR gaps persist.[105] This can impact on different communities in different ways and is a hidden dimension of the Northern Ireland peace-building struggle.

There was recognition amongst those who framed the peace talks in Northern Ireland that social and economic inequalities ought to be addressed in order to bolster a more secure and stable society. The peace agreement designated a particular commitment to 'Social, Economic and Cultural Issues' under the heading 'Rights, Safeguards and Equality of Opportunity'. This commitment included a promise to sustained economic growth, social inclusion and various cultural protections, including the promotion of the Irish language, Ulster Scots and the languages of the various ethnic minorities. This acknowledgement of socio-economic and cultural inequalities opened a way forward for Northern Ireland which places it within unusual political and legal parameters. It has been the subject of deep political polarisation. For example, the Irish Language Act has been a consistent point upon which there is political stalemate, resulting in the Assembly's dissolution in January 2017 and remaining unresolved as part of the restoration agreement in January 2020.[106] Likewise, progress on a Bill of Rights for Northern Ireland remains contested with party–political consensus at a stalemate.

The ESR Accountability Gap

In 2009 and 2016 the Committee on Economic, Social and Cultural Rights has expressed its concern about the continuing levels of deprivation and inequality in Northern Ireland,[107] in particular with regard to the shortage of social housing for Catholic families in North Belfast.[108] The Committee recommended:

Protestant community continued to comprise the majority of the monitored workforce in 2014, members from the Roman Catholic community continued to increase their share (by around [0.4 pp] per annum) to [47.4%]. A gradual upward trend (averaging around [0.6 pp] per annum) in the share of members of the Roman Catholic community to the monitored workforce has been observed since 2001 (p.2).

104 Northern Ireland Executive, Labour Force Survey Religion Report 2016, available at www. executiveoffice-ni.gov.uk/sites/default/files/publications/execoffice/lfs-religion-report-2016.pdf.

105 The availability of housing for catholic communities continues to be a source of concern as highlighted by the Equality Commission and UN Committee ESCR.

106 Gerry Moriarty, 'Arlene Foster Will Not Accept Standalone Irish Language Act', *The Irish Times*, 1 August 2018, available at www.irishtimes.com/news/ireland/irish-news/arlene-foster-will-not-accept-standalone-irish-language-act-1.3582987.

107 UN Committee on Economic, Social and Cultural Rights (CESCR), Consideration of reports submitted by states parties in accordance with articles 16 and 17 of the Covenant: concluding observations of the Committee on Economic, Social and Cultural Rights: UK of Great Britain and Northern Ireland, the Crown Dependencies and the Overseas Dependent Territories, 12 June 2009, E/C.12/GBR/CO/5, para.31; and 14 July 2016, E/C.12/GBR/CO/6, para.49.

108 E/C.12/GBR/CO/5, ibid., para.29.

that the human rights framework, including the Equality Impact Assessment, be effectively implemented in Northern Ireland, particularly in the context of urban regeneration programmes by ensuring the participation of the affected populations and the development of adequate policies and targeted measures to promote substantive equality, provide for improved health care, as well as an increase in skills training and employment opportunities for young people and adequate housing programmes for the poor and, in particular, Catholic families.[109]

In 2015, the Equality Commission found that the Department for Social Development (DSD) had indeed failed in its statutory duty to promote equality of opportunity and have regard to good relations.[110] The DSD had strategic responsibility for urban regeneration, community and voluntary sector development, social legislation, housing, social security benefits, pensions and child support.[111] Following an investigation the Equality Commission found that the department had not been carrying out equality impact assessments before the development of housing policies indicating that the distribution of housing had occurred on a discriminatory basis.[112]

The current equality framework does not necessarily meet the equality of opportunity threshold that the legislation aims to achieve. Whilst section 75(1) of the Northern Ireland Act 1998 requires public bodies to have due regard to equality of opportunity, section 75(2) provides that further to the duty to promote equality of opportunity there is also a duty to promote good relations between the polarised communities (creating a potential imbalance in formal equality). In some cases, the realisation of equality of opportunity has been curtailed by a prioritisation of promoting good relations. This is evident in the long-standing issues relating to the collation, disaggregation and dissemination of data in the housing sector being misrepresentative of housing need.[113] As concluded by the Equality Commission for Northern Ireland (ECNI), the policies of

---

109 E/C.12/GBR/CO/5, ibid., para.31.
110 Equality Commission for Northern Ireland, Investigation Report under Schedule 9 of Northern Ireland Act1998, Department for Social Development: Housing Policy Proposals, November 2015, available at www.equalityni.org/ECNI/media/ECNI/Publications/ Employers%20and%20Service%20Providers/S75%20P%2011%20investigation%20reports/ HousingPolicyProposals-Investigation.pdf.
111 It has now been replaced by the Department for Communities.
112 The Commission concluded that, in regard to the 'Facing the Future: Housing Strategy for Northern Ireland 2012–2017, the Department failed to meet its screening and equality impact assessment (EQIA) commitments in a timely manner. The Commission also concluded that the Department failed to meet its Equality Scheme commitments in respect of screening and equality impact assessment when "Building Successful Communities"' was launched, specifically with respect to the selection of pilot areas (Section 75 Northern Ireland Act 1998).
113 Report of the Special Rapporteur on adequate housing as a component of the right to an adequate standard of living, and on the right to non-discrimination in this context, Raquel Rolnik, Mission to the United Kingdom of Great Britain and Northern Ireland, 30 December 2013, A/HRC/25/54/Add.2 para.73 'The Special Rapporteur recognizes the efforts of the Government to address these challenges. However, during her visit, she observed that long-standing issues related to inequality continue to require concerted efforts. She notes

the Northern Ireland Housing Executive have incorrectly prioritised shared housing schemes under section 75(2) in an effort to build good relations without fulfilling the immediate duty to address desperate need for those living in housing stress.[114]

Beirne and Knox have described these competing approaches as amounting to a false dichotomy between reconciliation and human rights.[115] Following a qualitative empirical study into the experience of human rights activists and reconciliation activists, they noted that there is a risk of undermining the transition to substantive peace unless both reconciliation (bottom-up fostering of good relations and the building of trust) and human rights (top-down legalistic framework substantively protecting rights) are sufficiently addressed. This requires a reconceptualisation of rights and reconciliation through a common understanding of shared 'humanity, poverty and political exclusion'.[116]

A Bill of Rights for Northern Ireland

The creation of the Northern Ireland Human Rights Commission (NIHRC) was a requirement of the peace agreement.[117] The body was created under section 68 of the Northern Ireland Act 1998 in compliance with the commitment set forth in the peace agreement and the St Andrews Agreement.[118] Paragraph 4 of the section entitled 'Rights, Safeguards and Equality of Opportunity' in the peace agreement reads as follows:

> The new NIHRC will be invited to consult and to advise on the scope for defining, in Westminster legislation, rights supplementary to those in the European Convention on Human Rights, to reflect the particular circumstances of Northern Ireland, drawing as appropriate on international instruments and experience. These additional rights to reflect the principles of mutual respect for the identity and ethos of both communities and parity of esteem, and – taken together with the ECHR – to constitute a Bill of Rights for Northern Ireland.

The NIHRC was tasked with consulting and advising on a Bill of Rights for Northern Ireland with specific reference to investigating rights supplementary to the ECHR and the Human Rights Act 'to reflect the particular circumstances of Northern

that concerns about differences in the way information is collected, disaggregated and presented have been raised'. para.22.

114 ECNI report n 110 and Equality Can't Wait, Participation in the Practice of Rights Project (2012), p.49, available at www.pprproject.org/sites/default/files/Equality%20Can%27t%20Wait.pdf.

115 Maggie Beirne and Colin Knox, 'Reconciliation and Human Rights in Northern Ireland: A False Dichotomy?' (2014) 6 *Journal of Human Rights Practice* 26.

116 Beirne and Knox, ibid. at 33.

117 Section 6 Rights, Safeguards and Equality of Opportunity, para.5.

118 Agreement at St Andrews 2006, Annex B, 'Human Rights, equality, victims and other issues'.

Ireland, drawing as appropriate on international instruments and experience'.[119] On the human rights v good relations spectrum, the Bill of Rights together with ECHR and EU protections offers the top-down legalistic framework required to substantively protecting rights.[120] In other words, a pre-requisite for the nurturing of good relations is a framework that ensure human rights and equality for all.

After a ten-year consultation process at grass roots level, at the macro level[121] and after seeking expert advice internationally[122] the NIHRC published the 189-page *Bill of Rights for Northern Ireland* – with more than 120 proposals detailing rights which they considered as supplementary to the ECHR and particular to the circumstances of Northern Ireland. The NIHRC adopted a structured legal methodology in undertaking the task of producing a Bill of Rights for Northern Ireland by looking at the particular circumstances of Northern Ireland whilst recognising the rights encompassed by the Human Rights Act, the ECHR and any supplementary rights which should be included according to best practice in international law.[123] The recommendations entail additional protection for women, children, vulnerable adults and victims of the conflict. Supplementary rights include the right to identity and culture, language rights, the right to health, the right to an adequate standard of living, the right to work, the right to accommodation and environmental rights.

119 Letter from the Secretary of State for Northern Ireland to the Commission, received 24 March 1999, p.8. The the peace agreement also included a mechanism to ensure better of protection of human rights in the Republic of Ireland, including rights supplementary to the Convention. As part of this commitment, representatives from the human rights Commissions in each jurisdiction (NIHRC and Irish Human Rights Commission) were to consider 'establishing a charter, open to signature by all democratic political parties, reflecting and endorsing agreed measures for the protection of the fundamental rights of everyone living in the island of Ireland'.(paragraph 10, Part 6). The Commissions reported on their recommendations in June 2011. The recommendations reflected those rights already protected in law based on a 'minimum protection structure'. This arguably reflects the mandate in the peace agreement and there was no explicit direction to make the charter legally binding. However, as part of the ongoing scrutiny of the Constitution in Ireland (through the Constitutional Convention for example, which is under a duty to comply with the peace agreement), there would be an option to examine further constitutional protection for rights, both in relation to Convention rights and those rights supplementary to the Convention (including economic, social and cultural rights) in the jurisdiction of Ireland.
120 A pre-requisite of good relations is a top down substantive legal rights framework according to Beirne and Knox, n 115.
121 During consultation process with NIO Commissioner Mr Duncan stated that the Commission consulted with 'NGOs, political parties within Northern Ireland, church leaders, human rights spokespersons from major parties at Westminster, Irish Government Officials, the Northern Ireland Office and various other interest groups', A Bill of Rights For Northern Ireland: An Interim statement, Sixth Report of Session 2009–2010, Report together with formal minutes, oral and written evidence, Ordered by the House of Commons to be printed 15 March 2010, at 13.
122 For example, Judge Albie Sachs who co-authored the South African Bill of Rights, A Bill of Rights For Northern Ireland: An Interim statement, Sixth Report of Session 2009–2010, Report together with formal minutes, oral and written evidence, Ordered by the House of Commons to be printed 15 March 2010, 13.
123 A Bill of Rights for Northern Ireland Report, December 2008, 15.

During the course of the consultation process there was cross-community support for the concept of such legislation with independent opinion surveys demonstrating 87% of Protestant respondents and 85% of Catholic respondents in agreement on the concept of a Bill of Rights.[124] However, as the consultation process unfolded, it became clear that there was a lack of consensus on what a Bill of Rights should actually entail in substance. This lack of consensus was evident in the conclusions of the Bill of Rights Forum[125] and in the eventual dissent of two unionist Commissioners from the final recommendations issued to the Secretary of State.[126]

The NIHRC submitted their recommendations to the British Government in 2008. The response of the Northern Ireland Office ('NIO' – i.e. the arm of the UK government operating in Northern Ireland) to the Commission's recommendations was published on 30 November 2009 in the form of a consultation paper entitled 'A Bill or Rights for Northern Ireland: Next Steps'.[127] ESR were dismissed by the NIO for two reasons. First, they were considered beyond the remit of the NIHRC's mandate, as not particular to the circumstances in Northern Ireland, because they were common to the whole of the UK and therefore at risk of creating an equality divide.[128] Second, the NIO considered ESR as outside the democratic mandate of the judiciary emphasising that the democratically elected government must retain full responsibility for the prioritisation of expenditure[129] and therefore they were not appropriate in an enforceable Bill of Rights. The NIO response argued that the UK's international obligations are met through a combination of entitlements in domestic legislation, policy schemes and administrative action.[130] Thereafter the NIO concluded that ESR fall within the ambit of a UK-wide debate and are not particular to the Northern Irish case.[131] It relied heavily upon the advancement of a UK Bill of Rights

124 NIHRC Opinion Survey, Market Research Northern Ireland, March 2004, first published in Progressing a Bill of Rights for Northern Ireland: An Update (2004) NIHRC, Belfast.
125 The Bill of Rights Forum was a consultation body established by the UK Government following the St Andrews Agreement whereby the government committed to establish a round-table with the opportunity for cross-political engagement on the issue of a Bill of Rights. The Forum comprised of 28 members: 14 from the five main political parties and 14 from sections of civil society and was chaired by Chris Sidoti. The Forum was tasked with delivering their conclusions to the Northern Ireland Human Rights Commission so that the Commission could take the recommendations into account before making recommendations to the Secretary of State on the Bill of Rights in accordance with the peace agreement. Bill of Rights Forum, Final Report, Recommendations to the Northern Ireland Human Rights Commission on a Bill of Rights for Northern Ireland, 31 March 2008.
126 Mr Jonathan Bell and Lady Daphne Trimble did not support the final recommendations issued to the Secretary of State, A Bill of Rights for Northern Ireland, Advice to the Secretary of State for Northern Ireland, Northern Ireland Human Rights Commission, 10 December 2008, 4.
127 Northern Ireland Office Consultation Paper, 'A Bill of Rights for Northern Ireland, Next Steps', November 2009.
128 NIO Next Steps ibid. para.3.15.
129 Ibid. para.3.20.
130 Ibid. para.3.15.
131 Ibid.

and Responsibilities referring to the 2009 Green Paper produced by the UK Government. The UK Government's Green Paper offered an even clearer and more explicit assertion with regard to ESR and the overall operation of a UK-wide Bill of Rights and Responsibilities:

> The Government does not consider a general model of directly legally enforceable rights or responsibilities to be the most appropriate for a future Bill of Rights and Responsibilities. In terms of economic, social and cultural rights, for example, this may not be the best mechanism for ensuring fair provision for society as a whole.[132]

It was clear that an enforceable ESR framework was not on the agenda in the UK. This predisposition was confirmed in the concluding recommendations of a majority of the members of the UK Bill of Rights Commission in 2012.[133] The argument advanced by successive UK Governments is that ESR have already been implemented through domestic legislation and do not require entrenchment through an inflexible Bill of Rights.[134] The Green Paper outlined the history of the social welfare system in the UK, the enactment of the Education Act 1944 and the National Health Service Act 1948. Of course, whilst the provision of services under the statutory framework engages with ESR, it does not necessarily mean that international standards are being complied with to the extent required by international law, creating an accountability gap for the state.

The national Bill of Rights discussion also failed to acknowledge that part of the UK is a sub-state emerging from protracted conflict where human rights violations were systemic. The Green Paper (upon which the NIO relied) reads, '[i]n its recent history, the UK has not had to struggle for self-determination or nationhood and has not been torn apart by civil strife in the same way as other countries'.[135] This is a demonstration of how far removed the particular circumstances of Northern Ireland are from the rest of the UK. Northern Ireland had undergone thirty years of protracted conflict followed by a very fragile peace since 1998. The Human Rights Consortium raised concerns about the NIO response and stated that it

> disregards the particular circumstances of the conflict that led to Northern Ireland politicians and people wanting to explore how a Bill of Rights could help in peace-building. Despite the relative peace we now enjoy, no-one can doubt that this is still very much a post-conflict society that had huge community and sectarian divisions at the heart of its conflict, and that the conflict continues to shape and influence this society today. The rest of the

---

132 Ministry of Justice, *Rights and Responsibilities: Developing our Constitutional Framework* Cm 7577 (March 2009), Cm.7577 (Green Paper) para.3, 10.
133 Ibid. para.8.28.
134 Ibid.
135 Ibid. para.1.10.

UK has no such context for ... a UK Bill of Rights and Responsibilities and can therefore not hope to seriously address the specific nuances of the Northern Ireland context within a much wider UK document.[136]

Ultimately neither the local or national Bill of Rights processes materialised into greater rights protections for the people of Northern Ireland.

Unionist Dissent and the Conservative Alliance

The lack of consensus on human rights in Northern Ireland is a significant barrier for future human rights reform. Whilst local level data demonstrated broad support for the inclusion of ESR in a NI Bill of Rights (93–97% of the population)[137] the party–political divide presented a different picture. Following the NIHRC recommendations on a Bill of Rights the DUP[138] issued a response to the NIO consultation paper indicating that the unionist community did not support the Bill of Rights and highly criticised the NIHRC in their draft proposals. The response stated that:

> [i]t has become clear at every stage lobbyists and those political parties intent on giving them cover are determined to foist an all-encompassing Bill of Rights including socio-economic rights on the people of Northern Ireland regardless of the views of their elected representatives ... They have wasted huge resources seeking to motivate a disinterested public rather than trying seriously to engage with unionists and seek a realistic agreed way forward. The pro-rights lobby has made no effort to build consensus. They seem perfectly happy to try to impose proposals over the heads of the majority opinion.[139]

The DUP Response further explained that the unionist community is the traditional guardian of human rights and democracy. The party position is therefore not against the concept of human rights fulfilment *per se*. This aspect of unionist ideology is absolutely crucial to understanding the fundamental opposition to enacting a Bill of Rights for Northern Ireland. Turner posits a useful theory on the unionist perspective, arguing that '[t]he increasing use of law to achieve political reform presents a challenge to traditional unionist conceptions of law's function. The absence of any sustained academic scrutiny of the unionist attitude

---

136 Submission from the Human Rights Consortium to the Consultation on A Bill of Rights for Northern Ireland: Next Steps (March 2009).
137 The Northern Ireland Omnibus Survey, Millward Brown Ulster, June 2009, available at www.billofrightsni.org.
138 The Democratic Unionist Party hold 8 of the 18 Member of Parliament (MP) seats for Northern Ireland in the UK Parliament (2018–2019) and hold 38 of the 108 Members of the Legislative Assembly (MLA) seats in the Northern Ireland Assembly. It is the party with the largest political representation for Northern Ireland in both legislatures.
139 DUP Response to NIO consultation paper, A Bill of Rights for Northern Ireland: Next Steps, Response by Democratic Unionist Party, 30 March 2010.

towards law and politics, coupled with the mass of literature that exists in favour of reform, has resulted in a one sided narrative of transition which has not yet fully acknowledged the deeper public law implications of some of the legal changes proposed for Northern Ireland'.[140] The unionist theory of law favours 'minimal interference by the state into the private lives of individuals'. Rather than perceive a Bill of Rights as a constitutional guarantee to the protection of fundamental freedoms, it is viewed with suspicion as an interference with liberty. Turner explains that the human rights movement and the idea of political reform undermines the tenants of law from a unionist perspective:

> Unionists view law as normative, in that it exists to facilitate a system of govern-ment rather than to create specific obligations in and of itself. Much of the law making that underpins political and legal reform in transitional contexts is what could be termed functionalist, in that its purpose it to bring about substantive change to a previous legal regime that has been deemed to be problematic.[141]

The unionist approach is normative: liberty free from interference from the law, whereas, the perceived nationalist approach is functionalist: liberty substantively protected through legal enforcement.

This became all the more complicated under Conservative DUP political alliance formed following the 2017 general election during which the DUP lended a majority to a minority Conservative Government on a confidence and supply demand. Whilst the DUP and the Conservative parties are firmly committed to reforming the human rights landscape in the UK (removing the UK from the EU and ECHR framework), as a Government they were bound to comply with the British-Irish Agreement 1998 and peace agreement (a deal the DUP opposed).

As above, the lack of consensus on human rights in Northern Ireland is a major barrier for reform. Although there is an indication that the consoci-ational party–political level may not represent the views at grass roots level, pro-ceeding without political consensus would undermine legitimacy in the process and there is no political support among unionist parties to support a Bill of Rights. This is an issue that remains to be resolved. One of the reasons for unionist dissent is that introducing a Bill of Rights for Northern Ireland that protects ESR without corresponding measures available in the rest of UK would create a substantial gap in the protection of human rights across the state. This arguably goes against the very principle of the universality of human rights.[142]

---

140 Catherine Turner, 'Political Representations of Law in Northern Ireland' (2010) July *Public Law* 453, 454.
141 Ibid. 454–455.
142 Brice Dickson, Written Evidence, House of Commons, Northern Ireland Affairs Committee, A Bill of Rights for Northern Ireland: an Interim statement, Sixth Report of Session 2009–2010, Report together with formal minutes, oral and written evidence, 15 March 2010, (NIAC Report), available at www.parliament.the-stationery-office.co.uk/pa/cm200910/cmselect/cmniaf/236/236.pdf at para.12 'If rights are inserted in the Bill in an attempt to

The dissenting voice of Lady Trimble in the NIHRC process raised concerns in relation to unequal access to rights across the UK:

> If you look at the proposals around the socio-economic rights, the areas that those are addressing are by and large common societal problems right across the UK; if you look at housing, that is a problem right across the UK, it is not specific to Northern Ireland; ditto the environment, and rights to social security. So it seems to me to be rather difficult to come up with a proposal that there should be rights around these areas in Northern Ireland when there are not similar rights in the rest of the UK, and I feel concerned that we may lead to rights tourists coming to Northern Ireland to avail of these proposed rights which are not necessarily going to be available to people in other parts of the UK, or even in other parts of Europe, because what is proposed goes so much beyond what is in the European Convention, and so much beyond what is in the Human Rights Act, that we would be in a very, very particular standalone bubble, if you like, and I just am not at all sure that the consequences of that would be particularly good.[143]

Lady Trimble's concerns were also echoed by Stephen Pound MP, a member of the Northern Ireland Affairs Committee (2007–2010), and whilst questioning the NIHRC on its mandate he stated:

> Lady Daphne Trimble has identified an issue that is of considerable concern to many of us and it can broadly be described as the question of whether you are moving away from the universality of human rights to the localism of human rights. There is an issue as to whether you are actually constructing a template for the future or a tool to address the issues of the past. For many of us there does seem to be a certain dichotomy in here where human rights stop and start between Larne and Stranraer and you have additional ones at one end of the ferry and not at the other, to put it crudely.[144]

Northern Ireland already sits apart from the UK in many respects. The equality framework is different. The ECHR takes on special significance in the devolved frameworks as a binding treaty. The universal v local argument that featured as part of the unionist rejection of a Northern Ireland Bill of Rights has largely been displaced with both Scotland and Wales having independently taken steps that seek to improve human rights protections in devolved areas. There is no comprehensive holistic framework that currently exists across the whole of the UK in relation to human rights and equality protections, and in particular ESR.

---

address the peculiarities of Northern Ireland's divided society, this will risk undermining the basic principle that human rights are universal norms'.

143 Lady Trimble, Oral Evidence, NIAC Report ibid., Ev.15.
144 Stephen Pound (MP), Oral Questioning, NIAC Report ibid., Ev.3.

As Beirne and Knox note, there is a danger that if the macro-political scene signals that human rights and equality protections in Northern Ireland are 'all sorted' the peace process could be substantially undermined.[145] They argue that poverty and human rights abuses remain an important legacy for all of the communities impacted by the conflict and until they are addressed the peace process will be undermined.[146] Dickson has argued that there is 'no plausible case to be made for saying that unless Northern Ireland obtains a comprehensive Bill of Rights the peace process there will fall apart'.[147] On the other hand, Ní Aoláin has commented on the failure to fully realise the peace agreement human rights commitments and describes this unwillingness as 'under-enforcement'. Whilst Ní Aoláin contends that the reasons for under-enforcement in post-conflict societies are complex and multiple, she makes a useful observation in relation to Northern Ireland in what can be deemed an ongoing threat to stabilised peace:

> Partial or non-implementation of human rights provisions can be correlated with what a state sees as necessary to achieve conflict resolution in the short term. Undoubtedly, some reform issues are difficult and their resolution has high political costs ... Sometimes immediate reform can seem too daunting or too much for a society to bear as it comes to terms with a transforming society. However, I contend that this short-sighted view operates in opposition to the goal of preventing a return to conflict in the long run. This is particularly true of societies where human rights violations have formed the basis for the underlying experience of communal violence in the first place. In those societies, meaningful and sometimes hurtful transformation is a necessary pre-condition to a stable and long-lasting peace.[148]

Any 'backslide' on human rights norms promised in the peace agreement does not merely violate the terms of the 1998 agreements, it dissipates the wider political peace process and further disenfranchises communities. State emanated control over the post-agreement process requires leadership for long-term peace over shorter-term political goals. Effectively, undermining the prevailing peace in any way escalates the possibility of a return to conflict. Perhaps then, the decision to put the process on hold by the UK Government is inadequate. If no decision could be reached due to political difficulties at the very least it would have been crucial to keep discussions open and to facilitate a move towards consensus. This is an obligation incumbent on both the British and Irish governments in accordance with the terms of the British-Irish Agreement[149] read together with the

145 Beirne and Knox, n 115 at 37.
146 Ibid.
147 Brice Dickson, NIAC Report n 142 Ev. 25, para.10.
148 Fionnuala Ní Aoláin, *The Peace Agreement, role of human rights in peace agreements*, International Council on Human Rights Policy, Review Meeting, Belfast, 7–8 March 2005, (International Council on Human Rights Policy 2005), para.45.
149 Agreement between the Government of the United Kingdom of Great Britain and Northern Ireland and the Government of Ireland (with annexes), Belfast, 10 April 1998, Registration No. 1.36776 UNTS 2114, Treaty series No.50 (2000) Cm4705 (the B-I A).

peace agreement. Rather than facilitate consensus building Northern Ireland has been without governance in devolved areas for significant periods of time. The UK Parliament has gone so far as to introduce legislation that would afford executive functions to civil servants to fill the political void on devolved issues during the political impasse.[150] As Tierney highlights, when the institutions of devolution remain suspended the administration of Northern Ireland is highly dysfunctional.[151] The Northern Ireland state was very much on a journey to back to direct rule, something that the peace agreements have continuously sought to avoid. At the time of writing, the Northern Ireland Assembly is functioning under a renewed power-sharing agreement. Legacy issues around the conflict remain outstanding, including the Bill of Rights process. As difficult as it may be to secure, the transitional justice literature suggests that consensus building around human rights reform is key to a prolonged and stable peace.

Options for Enhancing ESR in Northern Ireland

Enhancing Equality

There is scope to expand the way in which equality is addressed in the Northern Ireland context as part of a holistic approach to address ESR in relation to both procedural and substantive inequality.

How Does Equality Measure Up in Northern Ireland?

The reaction of the UK government in addressing socio-economic inequalities through procedural equality provisions does not support a system in which the substantive realisation of equality is the end result. As discussed above, the research also demonstrates that the current equality framework does not necessarily meet the equality of opportunity threshold that the legislation aims to achieve. Section 75(2) provides that further to the duty to promote equality of opportunity there is also a duty to promote good relations between the polarised communities. In some cases, the realisation of equality of opportunity can be curtailed by a prioritisation of promoting good relations. Concerted efforts must continue to ensure statutory equality duties are not displaced by good relations but work hand in hand with reconciliation. Furthermore, access to judicial review for a breach of equality is significantly undermined in the Northern Ireland system. In England, Wales and Scotland, a person can seek judicial review of a decision if there has been discrimination on equality grounds under the Equality Act 2010. The Equality Act 2010 does not extend to Northern Ireland. There is a distinct difference in the statutory bodies responsible for monitoring equality compliance in Northern Ireland and the rest of the UK.

---

150 Northern Ireland (Executive Formation and Exercise of Functions) Bill 2017–2019.
151 Stephen Tierney, 'Governing Northern Ireland without an Executive: Quick Fix or Constitutional Minefield?' U.K. Const. L. Blog (30 October 2018).

Historically, Northern Ireland was treated as a separate political entity to the rest of the UK by the UK Government when dealing with Northern Ireland's distinct political landscape. Equal opportunity policies and anti-discrimination legislation formed part of a reactionary attempt to quell civil unrest and to deal with the entrenched divide between the communities. Equality became a very explicit objective of the government prior to the peace agreement of 1998 and in 1991 the Targeting Social Need (TSN) programme was implemented. The programme was unique to Northern Ireland and was designed to tackle the significant differences in the socio-economic profiles of the polarised communities. Whilst this was a positive direction to assume, the policy lacked definition and failed to address the significant underlying factors in social exclusion.[152] In 1994, the Policy Appraisal and Fair Treatment (PAFT) guidelines were introduced to further bolster the move towards social inclusion. The PAFT initiative was to provide public bodies with recommendations on how to counter inequality within the public sector, the main objective was 'to ensure that issues of equality and equity inform policy making and action in all spheres and at all levels of Government activity, whether in regulatory and administrative functions or in the delivery of services to the public'.[153]

This initiative was a positive step towards equality of opportunity in Northern Ireland as government departments were required to submit implementation reports in accordance with the guidelines. However, without any legal enforcement measures or legislative status, the discretionary guidelines merely appeared democratic at a procedural level without any substantive implementation. Ní Aoláin and McKeever reference these failures as an indicator of the difficulty in 'actualising political will into meaningful action when the issue of poverty and exclusion need to be addressed'.[154]

Following the St Andrews Agreement in 2006 there was a duty on the UK government to introduce legislation to enhance the operation of the TSN policy. Section 16 of the Northern Ireland (St Andrews Agreement) Act 2006 added section 28E to the Northern Ireland Act, which requires the NI executive to adopt a strategy setting out how it proposes to tackle poverty, social exclusion and patterns of deprivation based on objective need. In 2015 the Committee on the Administration of Justice, an NGO, successfully challenged the NI Executive by way of judicial review for failing to adopt a strategy within the meaning of section 28E.[155] This adjudication is indicative of the potential reach of a right to a policy/strategy, as opposed to a right to a particular outcome. Whilst it did not guarantee compliance with outcome-based remedies it certainly facilitated a procedural obligation to ensure a strategy was in place and that the

---

152 McKeever and Ní Aoláin, n 33.
153 Policy Appraisal and Fair Treatment Annual Report 1995, Central Community Relations Unit (June 2006), para.1.1, available at www.ccruni.gov.uk/equality/docs/paft95.htm#back.
154 McKeever and Ní Aoláin, n 33 at 169.
155 *The Committee on the Administration of Justice (CAJ) and Brian Gormally's Application* [2015] NIQB 59.

strategy sought to address objective need with the court playing an important accountability mechanism in reviewing compliance with the duty.

In accordance with the commitment towards equality stipulated in the peace agreement the UK Parliament introduced a statutory equality framework (through section 75 of the Northern Ireland Act 1998) supported by a policy initiative (through a revised TSN initiative). The two were designed to work in tandem. The former crystallised the legal protection of equality of opportunity between persons of different religious belief, political opinion, racial group, age, marital status or sexual orientation; between men and women generally; between persons with a disability and persons without; and between persons with dependants and persons without. The latter was identified in the peace agreement as one of the government's key socio-economic commitments and operated on a discretionary basis. Formal (but not substantive) equality became a legal requirement through section 75, however, socio-economic disadvantage excluded from the definition of protected groups under the legislation. Social inclusion in the socio-economic sphere was delegated to the implementation framework of the New TSN which was an improved version of the 1991 TSN. Despite its shortfalls, this framework was progressive for its time – going much further than what existed in other parts of the UK when first introduced.

Socio-Economic Status

Under section 75 public bodies are required to carry out Equality Impact Assessments for submission to the Commission[156] to determine the impact of their policies on the promotion of equality across the designated groups. This equality requirement does not extend to socio-economic status. There was a sense of lost opportunity in this approach. Ní Aoláin and McKeever proposed that section 75 be extended to include a duty to promote equality on the grounds of socio-economic status, they note that this proposal would 'push the concept of equality of opportunity beyond its more formal and limited connotations and provides a more substantive understanding of equality which is already implicit in s.75'.[157] Amending section 75 to include socio-economic status could potentially be substantively transformative – encouraging equality of opportunity on the grounds of socio-economic disadvantage. This would be akin to how section 1 of the Equality Act 2010 is designed to operate.[158]

A more robust approach, and a step further towards substantive equality, would be to introduce socio-economic disadvantage as a protected characteristic. This is a different type of protection than a duty to have due regard to equality of

---

156 Equality Commission for Northern Ireland was established as the compliance monitoring body in accordance with schedule 9 of the Northern Ireland Act 1998.

157 McKeever and Ní Aoláin, n 33 at 171.

158 See, for example, the devolved status of section 1 of the Equality Act in Scotland under the newly enacted Fairer Scotland Duty. An amendment to section 75 NIA could operate in a similar way.

opportunity. Socio-economic disadvantage as a ground for non-discrimination would require duty-bearers to ensure that they did not discriminate against someone because of their social status. Anti-discrimination legislation in Northern Ireland, where discrimination is prohibited on grounds of a particular characteristic, is dealt with under a series of piecemeal legislation (i.e. there is no consolidated approach).[159]

Expanding Equality through a Consolidated Approach

The NIHRC has called for the development of a single equality instrument consolidating all legislative instruments, providing clarity and strengthening existing protections in Northern Ireland.[160] Various UN and Council of Europe bodies have echoed this concern urging the UK to extend the Equality Act 2010 to Northern Ireland. The Advisory Committee to the Framework Convention for the Protection of National Minorities has recommended a consolidated framework to combat discrepancies between jurisdictions.[161] The Advisory Committee has also highlighted that the political climate in NI has prevented progress on equality reform and that this has meant those from national minorities also fall between equality 'gaps'.[162] The UN Committee on Economic Social and Cultural Rights has likewise recommended the Equality Act 2010 be extended to Northern Ireland[163] and that the human rights framework, including the equality impact assessment be effectively implemented in the jurisdiction in order 'to promote substantive equality, provide for improved health care, as well as an increase in skills training and employment opportunities for young people and adequate

---

159 Equality Pay Act (NI) (as amended) 1970 provided equality in employment between men and women; Sex Discrimination (NI) Order (as amended) 1976; Fair Employment Act 1976 provided equality in employment between those of different religious beliefs; Fair Employment (NI) Act 1989; Disability Act 1995; Race Relations (NI) Order 1997; Fair Employment and Treatment (NI) Order 1998; Northern Ireland Act 1998; Police (NI) Act 2000; Equality (Disability etc) (NI) Order 2000; Employment Equality (Sexual Orientation) (NI) Regulations 2003; Employment Equality (Age) Regulations (Northern Ireland) 2006.

160 The 2012 Annual statement, Human Rights in Northern Ireland, Northern Ireland Human Rights Commission, available at www.nihrc.org/documents/advice-to-government/2012/HRC_Annual_statement%202012.pdf, 11.

161 For example, Advisory Committee to the Framework Convention for the Protection of National Minorities concluded: 'Existing legislation in NI remains complex and piecemeal. Consolidated legislation, such as that adopted in Great-Britain, is needed to put an end to the significant discrepancies and inconsistencies that exist between the different jurisdictions'. para.66, and 'Additional steps should be taken to develop a comprehensive and human rights-based antidiscrimination and equality legislation for Northern Ireland', p.2, FCNM, Third Opinion on the UK, adopted on 30 June 2011, ACFC/OP/III (2011) 006 www.coe.int/t/dghl/monitoring/minorities/3_FCNMdocs/PDF_3rd_OP_UK_en.pdf.

162 Council of Europe: Secretariat of the Framework Convention for the Protection of National Minorities, *Fourth Opinion on the United Kingdom adopted on 25 May 2016*, 27 February 2017, ACFC/OP/IV(2016)005 para.27.

163 UN CESCR 2009, E/C.12/GBR/CO/5 n 107 para.16–17.

housing programmes for the poor and, in particular, Catholic families'.[164] The Committee on the Elimination of Racial Discrimination has recommended that the state party should take immediate steps to ensure that a single equality law and a Bill of Rights are adopted in Northern Ireland or that the Equality Act 2010 is extended to Northern Ireland.[165] The UN Committee on the Rights of Persons with Disabilities together with the NIHRC and the ECNI identified concerns for disabled people who have less protection in Northern Ireland than in the rest of the UK in terms of access to remedies against perceived and associative discrimination and indirect discrimination.[166]

The ECNI itself has recommended that equality law in Northern Ireland should be harmonised, simplified and strengthened.[167] In 2014 the ECNI issued a report identifying equality law gaps between Northern Ireland and Great Britain. The main areas identified for immediate reform by the ECNI include race equality legislation, disability legislation and age discrimination legislation relating to the provision of goods and services.[168] The ECNI report identifies that Northern Ireland equality law contains 'a number of unjustifiable exceptions which limit the scope of the equality legislation, as well as unnecessary barriers that limit individuals' ability to exercise their rights under the legislation'.[169] The ECNI highlighted that the failure to keep pace with new and emerging forms of discrimination may leave individuals with limited or no protection against unlawful discrimination.[170] The range of gaps in equality law between NI and GB may impact on vulnerable and marginalised individuals who experience discrimination and who have less protection against unlawful discrimination, harassment and victimisation across a number of equality grounds.[171]

The Northern Ireland Assembly has the devolved power to legislate to improve and strength equality provisions in devolved areas on a piecemeal basis. Any modification, however, to the Northern Ireland Act 1998 and the overarching equality framework would require Westminster legislation. If Northern Ireland were to keep pace with devolution in both Wales and Scotland, then an amendment to section

---

164 E/C.12/GBR/CO/5 ibid. para.31.

165 UN Committee on the Elimination of Racial Discrimination (CERD), UN Committee on the Elimination of Racial Discrimination: Concluding Observations, UK of Great Britain and Northern Ireland, 14 September 2011, CERD/C/GBR/CO/18–20, para.19.

166 Disability rights in Northern Ireland, Supplementary submission to inform the CRPD List of Issues on the UK, Northern Ireland Human Rights Commission and Equality Commission for Northern Ireland, February 2017, available at www.equalityni.org/ECNI/media/ECNI/Publications/Delivering%20Equality/CRPD-NI-supplementary-submissionLOI.pdf.

167 See the discussion paper on Gaps in equality law between Great Britain and Northern Ireland, Equality Commission for Northern Ireland, March 2014, available at www.equalityni.org/ECNI/media/ECNI/Consultation%20Responses/2014/Gaps-in-Equality-Law-in-GB-and-NI-March-2014.pdf.

168 Ibid. at 1.

169 Ibid. at 5.

170 Ibid.

171 Ibid. at 7.

75 to include socio-economic status as a grounds for promoting equality of opportunity would bring Northern Ireland in line with the Fairer Scotland duty or newly devolved power in Wales. Going further, a consolidated approach could help to address existing gaps across a number of grounds. As part of any revised approach discrimination on the grounds of socio-economic disadvantage would go further than a requirement to have due regard to equality of opportunity. A more progressive approach to equality requires positive steps to substantive equality, this means leveling up across protected groups rather than establishing equality of opportunity without substantive thresholds (i.e. a concept of equality where everyone can be equally poor). There is an opportunity in Northern Ireland to develop a more robust substantive concept of equality. This would require ensuring disaggregated data is collected and positive steps taken to ensure leveling up across the conflicted groups in terms of ethnicity and religion, but also for those groups not categorised as part of the conflict, i.e. those marginalised because of race, gender, age, geographic location, health status, economic status and so on. Much more attention must be paid to substantive equality measures across the UK if equality of outcome is to be attained in accordance with international human rights law.

Making Equality Amenable to Judicial Review

The Equality and Human Rights Commission for England and Wales has a power under section 30 of the Equality Act 2006 to bring cases for judicial review on behalf of individuals. Under Part VII of the Northern Ireland Act 1998 the ECNI has no corollary right. Instead the Equality Commission in Northern Ireland is the main arbiter of complaints under paragraph 10 of Schedule 9 of the 1998 Act. The difference between the two Commissions therefore rests on the former acting as an advocate for individuals and the latter acting as a regulator for complaints in a quasi-tribunal forum.

If a complaint is brought before the ECNI the applicant will not normally have access to judicial review proceedings following on from a decision with which they are dissatisfied. The judiciary has relied on curial deference[172] as a means of placing a stop on cases decided by the Commission subsequently being the subject of judicial review. In the case of *Neill's Application*[173] the question before the court was whether the legality of the Anti-Social Behaviour (Northern Ireland) Order 2004 should be amenable to judicial review or whether the alleged breach ought to be remedied under the Northern Ireland Act 1998 (by the Equality Commission). The Order was challenged on the ground that it was made in breach of the NIO's equality obligations under the Northern Ireland Act 1998. The Court of Appeal considered that the case was more appropriately dealt

---

172 The application of curial deference is not unusual when dealing with specialist tribunals whereby a supervisory court will respect the authority and validity of a decision by a public body with specialist expertise rather than extend the decision amenable to judicial review. For a discussion on curial deference see Gerard Coffey, *Administrative Law* (Round Hall, 2010).

173 *Neill's Application* [2006] NICA 5.

with in accordance with the remedy already available under the statutory framework. This case has set a precedent in terms of access to judicial review following a decision of the Commission.[174] And the precedent is that access to judicial review is restricted and limited meaning review of equality decisions are not justiciable in the way they are in other parts of the UK. This undermines the social rights adjudication accessibility principle in Northern Ireland.

Anthony submits that the courts have through this case recognised that the statutory mechanism available under the Northern Ireland Act may provide for superior procedure and remedy without the need to revert to judicial remedies and that this approach is consonant with the doctrine of legislative supremacy.[175]

Limiting the administrative remedy to the sole jurisdiction of the quasi-tribunal nature of the Equality Commission also means that there is no judicial scrutiny of alleged statutory equality breaches in Northern Ireland. Given the particular circumstances of Northern Ireland, the scrutiny of compliance with equality obligations should at the very least match the mechanisms available in the rest of the UK. In other words, without transparent scrutiny measures through justiciable mechanisms (at least as a last resort) the current system represents a procedural, or administrative, process that could be veiling a substantive equality deficit – a pitfall identified in the conflicted democracy literature.[176]

The UN Committee on Economic, Social and Cultural Rights has welcomed the development of administrative remedies such as that offered by the Equality Commission to deal with potential violations of ESR. In the same respect, the Committee has also recognised that, whilst administrative measures may suffice as an effective remedy (without the need to resort to a judicial remedy), this is not always the case – particularly with reference to obligations concerning non-discrimination. Paragraph 9 of General Comment 9 of the Committee provides that:

> an ultimate right of judicial appeal from administrative procedures of this type would also often be appropriate. By the same token, there are some obligations, such as (but by no means limited to) those concerning non-discrimination, in relation to which the provision of some form of judicial remedy would seem indispensable in order to satisfy the requirements of the Covenant. In other words, whenever a Covenant right cannot be made fully effective without some role for the judiciary, judicial remedies are necessary.[177]

---

174 The court did not rule out judicial review in every circumstance, however, the case does set a high precedent from which to depart in order to reach the judicial review threshold.

175 Anthony, n 65 at 191.

176 The Special Rapporteur's concerns regarding the potential prioritisation of the promotion of good relations (under section 75(2) of the Northern Ireland Act 1998) over the need to address those in desperate need of housing in the Catholic community (under section 75(1) of the 1998 Act) is indicative of such an issue. Section 75(2) only applies once the duties under section 75(1) have been satisfied. Raquel Rolink Report A/HRC/25/54/Add.2 n 113 at para.73.

177 Also UN Committee on Economic, Social and Cultural Rights (CESCR), General Comment No. 9: The domestic application of the Covenant, 3 December 1998, E/C.12/1998/24 at para.9.

A Constitutional Model for Northern Ireland

As discussed above, the peace agreement conferred a duty on the newly established NIHRC to advise on a legislative mechanism to provide for rights supplementary to those in the Convention and to reflect the particular circumstances of Northern Ireland drawing on international instruments and treaties.[178] The NIHRC recommendations contained a comprehensive list of ESR. The NIO rejected the proposed Bill of Rights and was opposed to the inclusion of ESR.[179] The NIHRC have argued that the failure to properly consider the recommendations to the Secretary of State in relation to a Bill of Rights undermines the peace process. The UN Committee on Economic, Social and Cultural Rights has called for the enactment of a Bill of Rights for Northern Ireland, which includes justiciable ESR, without delay.[180] Political impasse that has ensued and the lack of consensus between political parties at the devolved level has brought the process to a standstill.

Whilst it would lack democratic legitimacy to enact legislation without political consensus, there is also a democratic failure at the national level to facilitate consensus at the devolved level. The enactment of a Bill of Rights that recognises the ESR deficit ought to at the very least be given due consideration. In a defence of the recommendations made to the Secretary of State on this issue Ms Hope (Commissioner) stated in evidence to the Northern Ireland Affairs Committee:

> It is officially acknowledged that grievances amongst large sections of the population in Northern Ireland in relation to discrimination, exclusion, poverty, particularly in the areas of employment and housing, were prime factors in the conflict in Northern Ireland. That relationship between social and economic grievances and the conflict was recognised by the Government at the outbreak of the conflict and Lord Cameron made specific reference to them in his Commission Report. If we were to look at the particular circumstances in Northern Ireland, remembering that this Bill of Rights is a Bill of Rights addressing issues in a society that is coming out of conflict, then, as far as we were concerned, social and economic rights had to be part of that. In fact, it is one of the confidence-building measures that would be contained in the Bill, not least to say the abuses that took place around those particular rights would not happen again, so they should be very much in a Bill of Rights.[181]

---

178 As per paragraph four of the section entitled 'Rights, Safeguards and Equality of Opportunity' in the 1998 peace agreement n 50.

179 The proposed Bill of Rights was presented by the Northern Ireland Human Rights to the Northern Ireland Office in 2008. The Northern Ireland Office rejected the proposed Bill on 30 November 2009 citing various reasons for the decision, including the perceived controversial inclusion of socio-economic rights, Northern Ireland Office Consultation Paper, 'A Bill of Rights for Northern Ireland, Next Steps', November 2009.

180 'The Committee notes the draft Bill of Rights for Northern Ireland, which includes economic, social and cultural rights which are justiciable, and calls for its enactment without delay', UN CESCR (2009) n 107 E/C.12/GBR/CO/5 at para.10.

181 NIAC Report n 142 Evidence Briefing, Ms Ann Hope, Commissioner, Ev1.

Given the commitments contained in the peace agreement on the continued enhancement of human rights protection in Northern Ireland (beyond ECHR) there is an arguable case that the avoidance of addressing the ESR human rights deficit undermines the transition to substantive peace.[182] The newly established Ad Hoc Bill of Rights Committee in Northern Ireland has an opportunity to address this gap and to make progress on a renewed progressive human rights framework for Northern Ireland, keeping in step with devolved counterparts in Scotland and Wales.

Now that a power-sharing agreement has been reached, then the Northern Ireland Assembly could take steps to progress human rights protections under the devolved framework. The Northern Ireland Assembly has already made progress in this area[183] and could continue to 'implement and observe' international human rights obligations in devolved areas.[184] This could be done on a piecemeal basis (right by right) or it could be achieved on a holistic basis through an overarching statutory framework that imposes subsequent duties on the legislature and executive to provide ESR coupled with effective remedies to protect ESR (this is similar to the Scottish approach discussed below).[185] This could also be complemented by a *ex ante* parliamentary review system whereby a specialised Committee in the Northern Ireland Assembly could be tasked with ensuring that legislation is compatible with human rights before enactment. This Committee could seek evidence from constitutional and human rights experts on the legal nature of rights rather than a political review. There could be a duty placed on the Assembly to comply with the recommendations of the Committee and the courts could act as a means of last resort for *ex post* judicial review of compatibility. It would be possible for the Assembly to create a Committee that acts as a pre-legislative scrutiny mechanism in the assessment of human rights, including ESR.[186] This is something that has been recommended by the NIHRC.[187] As discussed above in Chapter 5, this is a multi-institutional approach to ESR.

A Bill of Rights for Northern Ireland could be implemented by either the Northern Ireland Assembly or Westminster. In the case of the former, the rights covered and the remedies available may differ because the NI Assembly's competence is

---

182 Fionnuala Ní Aoláin, 'The Good Friday Agreement, Role of Human Rights in Peace Agreements', International Council on Human Rights Policy, Review Meeting, Belfast March 7–8 2005, International Council on Human Rights Policy, para.45.

183 Section 2(3)(b) of the Commissioner for Older People Act (Northern Ireland) 2011 requires the Commissioner to have regard to the United Nations Principles for Older Persons when carry out his/her functions and section 6(3)(b) of the Commissioner for Children and Young People (Northern Ireland) Order 2003 the Commissioner must have regard to the UN Convention on the Rights of the Child in exercising his/her functions.

184 Schedule 2 paragraph 3(c) NIA 1998 exempts observing and implementing international obligations from the 'international relations' exception.

185 Such as the approach under the Constitution of Finland discussed in Chapter 4.

186 Standing Order 53(1).

187 Northern Ireland Human Rights Commission, Bill of Rights for Northern Ireland, Advice for the Secretary of State (2008), available at www.nihrc.org/uploads/publications/bill-of-rights-for-northern-ireland-advice-to-secretary-state-2008.pdf at 170.

restricted to devolved areas (for example the right to social security would engage with a reserved area and strike down powers for devolved legislation may be restricted).[188] In the case of the latter, it is open to Westminster to legislate for a Bill of Rights in accordance with the recommendations of the NIHRC. The newly established Ad Hoc Committee on a Bill of Rights will require to weigh up these considerations for Northern Ireland.

Table 6.1 NIHRC Proposed Bill of Rights[189]

Preamble	Underpinned by civil, political, economic, social, cultural and environmental (CPESCE) rights, dignity and commitment to peace
Human rights – including supplementary rights and for the particular circumstances of Northern Ireland	Right to life and right to an effective investigation
	Freedom from torture
	Freedom from slavery
	Right to liberty and security
	Fair trial and no punishment without law
	Right to private and family life
	Freedom of thought, conscience and religion
	Freedom of expression
	Freedom of assembly and association
	Right to marriage and civil partnership
	Democratic Rights
	Property Rights
	Education Rights
	Freedom of Movement
	Freedom from violence, exploitation and harassment
	The right to identity and culture
	Language rights
	Rights of victims
	Right to civil and administrative justice
	Right to health
	Right to adequate standard of living
	Right to accommodation
	Environmental rights
	Social Security Rights
	Children's Rights

(Continued)

188 This reading is dependent on whether a self-regulatory devolved Bill of Rights was considered to 'modify' the Northern Ireland Act if the Northern Ireland Assembly sought to restrict its own competence in devolved areas to comply with ESR (with a strike down power for future non-compatible legislation). For a further discussion on this see 'Scotland' below. Either way declarations of incompatibility could be used.

189 This is a summary of the Bill as presented in the NIHRC Advice (2008) ibid.

Table 6.1 (Cont.)

Duties	Duty for public authorities, or any person or body performing public functions to comply with the Bill
Duties	Duty to pay due regard to the Bill and respect, protect, promote and fulfil rights
Duties	Minimum core and progressive realisation of rights
Remedies	Declarations of incompatibility for incompatible Westminster legislation and strike down powers for incompatible devolved legislation
Remedies	Courts must grant an effective remedy and for this purpose may grant such relief or remedy, including compensation, or make such order, as they consider just and appropriate
Pre-legislative scrutiny	Northern Ireland Assembly should establish Standing Committee on Human Rights and Equality, with a mandate to examine and report on all human rights and equality issues coming within the competence of the Northern Ireland Assembly, including the compatibility of Bills within relevant human rights standards; and the Committee should be empowered to conduct inquiries into human rights issues
Review	NIHRC should monitor compliance with the Bill
Interpretation	ust strive to achieve the purpose of the Bill Due regard to relevant international human rights law May consider comparative case law
Interpretation	In so far as it is possible to do so primary and subordinate legislation should be read as compatible with human rights in Act
Entrenchment	Entrenched in Westminster legislation and amendable only with cross-community approval in Northern Ireland
Limitations	Subject only to reasonable limits which are prescribed by law to the extent that the limits are necessary in a society based on the values of human dignity, democracy, liberty and equality, taking account of all relevant factors

(Continued)

Table 6.1 (Cont.)

Derogation	In times of emergency but not applicable to non-derogable rights
Standing	Sufficient interest test
Legal aid	Sufficient support through legal aid to ensure access to justice

Principles of Adjudication under the NIHRC Bill of Rights

The proposed NIHRC Bill facilitates the social rights adjudication principle of accessibility. The Bill seeks to ensure that there is sufficient support through legal aid to ensure access to justice and that standing can be established based on 'sufficient interest' in the outcome. This is a wider test than that of 'victim-hood'. In relation to public interest litigation the Court of Appeal has already set out a four-fold approach in Northern Ireland:

- That standing is a relative concept to be deployed according to the potency of the public interest content of the case;
- That the greater amount of public importance involved the more ready the court should be to hold the applicant has established standing;
- That the focus of the court should be to examine the 'wrong' committed by the public authority rather than uphold the personal right or interest of the applicant; and
- That the absence of another potential challenger is a significant factor and to ensure that a matter of public interest is therefore not left unexamined.[190]

This flexible approach to standing is designed to facilitate access to justice for public interest litigation, particularly when weight can be given to the public importance of the outcome without the need to establish a private interest in the case. Each of these approaches facilitates the **principle of accessibility** in social rights adjudication.

Whilst the NIHRC proposals facilitate access by recognising the importance of legal aid and standing there requires further work to enable genuine **participation** in adjudication. Empirical research conducted by McKeever on access to justice in Northern Ireland establishes the concept of legal participation as encompassing effective participation.[191] Effective participation implies the opportunity to have a voice within the proceedings that can influence the outcome. In the litigant in person domain McKeever proposes a model that facilitates substantive participation addressing three main barriers: intellectual, practical and emotional barriers.[192]

190 D, Re an Application for Judicial Review [2003] NICA 14 (10 April 2003).
191 Grainne McKeever, Litigants in person in Northern Ireland: barriers to legal participation, available at www.ulster.ac.uk/__data/assets/pdf_file/0003/309891/179367_NIHRC-Litigants-in-Person_BOOK___5_LOW.pdf.
192 McKeever, ibid. at 31.

Substantive participative experience requires (a) supporting users to navigate the process and communicate with the actors to understand everyone's role in the process; (b) collaboration between different court actors in ensuring that individuals are supported throughout their journey through the process and support in addressing difficulties as they arise; (c) enabling and equipping individuals with the ability to engage as equals with an element of self-determination.[193] Much can be learned from this work and applied to cases where litigants act autonomously or with representation. In other words, regardless of the approach litigants should be able to substantively participate in proceedings in which the outcome will impact them. The **principle of participation** is also supported through **deliberation** and **counter-majoritarian principles**. A key element of which is the facilitation of multi-party and structural cases.

The proposed NIHRC Bill adopts a multi-institutional approach to adjudication where the legislature, executive and judiciary each play a deliberative approach in an inter-institutional dialogue. For example, pre-legislative scrutiny facilitates the **principle of deliberation** on compliance before legislation is passed and ex post judicial review facilitates deliberation between the court and legislature after legislation is passed. In addition, the interpretative obligations allow for horizontal and vertical dialogue in relation to comparative case law and international human rights treaty decisions. The **principle of fairness** is engaged under the rights proposed (full spectrum of international human rights) as well as the degree of enforcement (both minimum core and progressive realisation). Ultimately, adjudication under this model could include both procedural and substantive review in terms of human rights compliance. One of the major barriers for ESR adjudication is its potential to act as an exercise of elite power. A key component of any framework that engages with ESR adjudication must include mechanisms to support the **counter-majoritarian principle**. One means through which to achieve this is to facilitate access to collective complaints/multi-party action and public interest litigation. Given the reluctance of the Northern Ireland court to engage in peace agreement adjudication to date much more attention should be given to consideration to how best to facilitate counter-majoritarian adjudication in a delicate political framework. This could include revisiting how best to deal with structural cases in housing, health, education and so on as these cases are not currently being adjudicated upon in relation to widespread structural issues (the ESR accountability gap discussed above). It could also include taking steps to ensure that the judiciary is representative of society as a whole – a key component of a conflicted democracy state.

The approach to remedies in the proposed Bill of Rights facilitates the **remedial principle** by suggesting the court may grant such relief or remedy, including compensation, or make such order, as they consider just and appropriate should a violation occur. A flexible approach to remedies is key to the remedial principle, however, identifying what type of remedy should be used and when requires further consideration.

---

193 Ibid. at 31.

The NIHRC Bill of Rights continues to provide a key opportunity for rights reform in Northern Ireland, with a view to bringing the devolved jurisdiction of Northern Ireland in line with ongoing developments in both Wales and Scotland, and importantly to keep pace with developments in Ireland, in relation to ESR. More research is required to fully understand the grass roots support (or lack thereof) for ESR. Better understanding the grass roots level might help alleviate political stalemate in what is seen has a highly politicised and nationalist agenda. When rights issues are depoliticised and treated as legal norms they can facilitate long-term peace and reconciliation. Rights and rights reform is key to building and sustaining peace. Both the UK and Irish governments must continue to facilitate dialogue and to support peace building. Addressing ESR must, one way or another, feature as part of this process.

Scotland

I am keen to see Scotland advance incorporation and justiciability of rights because it is the best way to realise economic, social and cultural rights for all, especially those most in need of protection by the state... These rights are everyday rights that are essential for people to live in dignity in everyday life. If Scotland wishes to honour its social justice commitments, it should pursue the incorporation debate without losing momentum and make economic, social and cultural rights justiciable in Scotland's courts. In the present context of Brexit, every day matters and every argument counts.[194]

Virginia Brás Gomes, Chair of UN Committee on Economic, Social and Cultural Rights

21 May 2018, Edinburgh

Scotland has been engaged in a long process over its constitutional future, the history of which is not fully captured here. Prior to devolution there was a lengthy constitutional convention comprised of political parties, churches and other civil society groups, the result of which proposed a devolved settlement framework for Scotland. This paved the way for Scotland Act 1998 and the opening of the Scottish Parliament in 1999. Deliberative processes have continued under the devolved jurisdiction most notably in relation to whether Scotland should become an independent country, the result of which marginally favoured to remain in the United Kingdom (55% voted no to independence).[195] In 2016, Scotland supported remaining in the European Union (62% voted in favour of remain), setting it apart from the UK along with a similar outcome in

---

194 Virginia Bras Gomez quoted in the National: 'Call for Scots Law to Incorporate Social and Economic Rights', *The National*, 21 May 2018, www.thenational.scot/news/16238234. call-for-scots-law-to-incorporate-social-and-economic-rights/.

195 55% of the electorate voted to remain part of the United Kingdom.

Northern Ireland (56% in favour of remain).[196] Constitutionally there is a 'special quality to Scotland's autonomy'.[197] Since the Act of Union 1707 Scotland has retained a distinct constitutional status.[198] The onset of devolution may have changed the place of Scotland within the broader 'union' state,[199] however, it is important to place this within the broader historical context of Scotland having always retained a separate legal jurisdiction with a distinct body of law that has set it apart since the formation of the state.

In January 2018 the First Minister, Nicola Sturgeon MP, stated a commitment to mitigate the risk to human rights posed by Brexit with a specific focus on the principles of non-regression, ensuring an equivalence of rights post-Brexit and providing leadership on the future of rights protection.[200] The First Minster established an Advisory Group tasked with considering how Scotland can continue to lead by example in human rights, including economic, social, cultural and environmental rights and potential incorporation of those rights into domestic law.[201] In December 2018, the First Minister's Advisory Group on Human Rights Leadership (FMAG) made recommendations to incorporate economic, social, cultural and environmental rights across Scotland's governance.[202] The means of incorporation is to be delivered through an Act of the Scottish Parliament with enhanced roles for the legislature, executive/administrative and judicial branches (a multi-institutional approach).[203] The proposed reform is to be

---

196 62% of Scotland voted to remain in the EU. This has strengthened the Scottish Government's resolve to forge an independent settlement deal for Scotland, Scottish Government White Paper, Scotland's Place in Europe (2016). 56% of Northern Ireland voted to remain. This has sparked the reemergence of support for a border poll on the potential reunification of Ireland with 46% (a lead of 51%) in favour of reunification in a recent poll condunted by Lord Ashcroft, Lord Ashcroft Polls, My Northern Ireland survey finds the Union of a knife-edge, Wednesday 11 September 2019, available at https://lordashcroftpolls.com/2019/09/my-northern-ireland-survey-finds-the-union-on-a-knife-edge/.

197 Ibid.

198 Chris Himsworth and Christine O'Neill, *Scotland's Constitution: Law and Practice* (Bloomsbury, 2015), 45.

199 Stephen Tierney, 'Scotland and the Union State' in Aileen McHarg and Tom Mullen (eds.), *Public Law in Scotland* (2006).

200 Ambition on human rights, Scottish Government, available at https://news.gov.scot/news/ambition-on-human-rights.

201 First Minister's Advisory Group on Human Rights Leadership (FMAG), available at https://beta.gov.scot/groups/first-ministers-advisory-group-on-human-rights-leadership/.

202 The author is a member of the First Minister's Advisory Group. The recommendations are available in the following report: Alan Miller (Chair), First Minister's Advisory Group on Human Rights Leadership, *Recommendations for a new human rights framework to improve people's lives*, Report to the First Minister (December 2018) at 6–7, available at http://humanrightsleadership.scot/wp-content/uploads/2018/12/First-Ministers-Advisory-Group-post-10th-December-update.pdf . See also Katie Boyle, 'The First Minister's Advisory Group on Human Rights Leadership: a new path forward on incorporation of economic, social, cultural and environmental rights' (2019) 4 *European Human Rights Law Review* 361–373 from which excerpts are gratefully drawn upon in this section.

203 Ibid. at 34–38.

preceded by a lengthy deliberative process that facilitates a bottom-up approach to incorporation that is inclusive and participative allowing the internalising of international norms to occur in a way that gives people ownership of rights and their means of implementation within their local context.[204] The method of incorporation includes implementation of rights and accountability mechanisms embedded across the public sector, including the regulatory framework, with the court as a means of last resort if other accountability mechanisms fail.[205] Access to effective remedies are stipulated as a requirement of the proposed future structure, including enabling structural remedies more appropriate for systemic issues (in accordance with the **remedial and counter-majoritarian principles**).[206] The report emphasises that there is inadequate 'everyday accountability' for violations of human rights and that it is in the space of practical implementation and everyday accountability that rights either stand or fall.[207] The recommendations of the First Minister's Group seek to address this accountability gap by transforming the human rights landscape in Scotland.

Scotland's Changing Constitution

The political rhetoric in Scotland often reflects progressive principles with a commitment to building an 'inclusive, fair, prosperous, innovative country, ready and willing to embrace the future'.[208] Arguably the political impetus to establish Scotland as a 'leader in human rights, including economic, social and environmental rights'[209] stems from a commitment to create the necessary constitutional building blocks to foster a renewed legal system that better protects these rights. This would reflect the upward trajectory of rights protection evident in, and emanating from, deliberative processes at the subnational level.[210]

---

204 Ibid. at 39–40.
205 Ibid. at 28–29.
206 Ibid. at 35.
207 Ibid. at 25.
208 See Programme for Government 2017–2018, available at https://news.gov.scot/speeches-and-briefings/2017-18-programme-for-government.
209 Ibid.
210 For example, in Scotland see the Children and Young People (Scotland) Act 2014 (2014 Act) requires specified public authorities, including all local authorities and health boards, to report every three years on the steps they have taken to secure better or further effect of the UNCRC and the Social Security (Scotland) Act 2018 stating that social security is a human rights and encouraging compliance with ICESCR; in Northern Ireland see Section 2(3)(b) of the Commissioner for Older People Act (Northern Ireland) 2011 requiring the Commissioner to have regard to the United Nations Principles for Older Persons when carry out his/her functions and section 6(3)(b) of the Commissioner for Children and Young People (Northern Ireland) Order 2003 requiring the Commissioner to have regard to the UN Convention on the Rights of the Child in exercising his/her functions; in Wales see Rights of Children and Young Persons (Wales) Measure 2011 imposing a duty on Welsh Ministers to have due regard to the UN Convention on the Rights of the Child (UNCRC) in performance of their functions.

Scotland's constitutional journey in recent years has arguably created a form of transformational constitutionalism that includes embedding ESR in the constitutional framework.[211] In this sense, Scotland is arguably seeking to pertain to a form of social constitutionalism[212] where the rule of law contains a social justice component. This moment arrives without necessarily having the appropriate legal building blocks in place to realise such a commitment. In other words, a shift in legal culture will undoubtedly be required if political will is to materialise into transformative change, and in turn, this will entail necessary disturbance to administrative, public and constitutional traditions.[213] As noted by Courtis, the judicial enforcement of social rights, as with any set of rights, 'requires the development of standards and criteria and a new litigation culture and practice, without which any application of abstract legal concepts is impossible'.[214]

Davis suggests that the adoption of human rights norms within subnational settings is good for devolved governance pointing to evidence that human rights compliance leads to health benefits of individuals, that human rights standards can lead to more stable and lasting conflict resolution and that ultimately human rights norms are intimately linked to good governance.[215] At the same time, Davis recognises that incorporation at the subnational level may also be a means of establishing autonomy and an intentionally subversive act:

> While inspiration may come from many sources, deliberate subnational adoption of international human rights standards is not always a neutral activity... [for] an activity that seems purely local in nature, subnational governments may in fact be making an outward looking statement to both the federal government and to the global community.[216]

That being said, compliance with and implementation of international human rights obligations at the sub-national level is considered best practice. In the

---

211 As early as 2015, First Minister Nicola Sturgeon committed to exploring how to incorporate international human rights into Scotland's laws. See press release from Scottish Human Rights Commission, available at www.scottishhumanrights.com/economic-social-cultural-rights/.

212 Social constitutionalism is adapted from liberal constitutionalism as the model developing in the Global South, in particular Latin America, Natalia Angel-Cabo and Domingo Lovera Parmo, 'Latin Amercian Social Constitutionalism: courts and popular participation' in Helena Alviar García, Karl Klare and Lucy A. Williams (eds.), *Social and Economic Rights in Theory and Practice, Critical Inquiries* (Routledge, 2015), 85–105.

213 Katie Boyle, 'The Future of Economic, Social and Cultural Rights in Scotland: Prospects for Meaningful Enforcement' (2019) 23 *Edinburgh Law Review* 110–116. I am grateful to Edinburgh Law Review for permission to reproduce minor excerpts from this article in this section.

214 Christian Courtis, 'Argentina, Some Promising Signs' in Malcolm Langford (ed.), *Social Rights Jurisprudence, Emerging Trends in International and Comparative Law* (Cambridge University Press, 2008), 181.

215 Martha F. Davis, 'Upstairs, Downstairs: Subnational Incorporation of International Human Rights Law at the End of an Era' (2008) 77 *Fordham Law Review* 411–438 at 417.

216 Davis, ibid. at 420.

context of subnational responsibility for international obligations the UN Committee on the Rights of the Child suggests that any process of devolution must ensure that devolved authorities have the necessary financial, human and other resources effectively to discharge responsibilities for the implementation of international human rights law.[217] The UN Special Rapporteur on Adequate Housing has called for increased engagement in complying with ESR at the devolved level and highlighted that the effective application of rights at the local and subnational levels is critical for enhanced accountability.[218] As above, compliance with international human rights law at the subnational level is considered best practice.[219]

Whilst there is political will for change in Scotland, the legislative approach to embracing international human rights norms has been both ambitious in its vision, whilst also tentative in its commitment to create any real substantive or legally enforceable rights. For example, in 2018 the Scottish Parliament introduced social security legislation that recognised the right to social security as a human right 'essential to the realisation of other human rights'.[220] The legislation also introduced an independent Commission that has an oversight function in reviewing the devolved social security system. As part of this review the Commission is under a duty to scrutinise and report on whether the expectations of the legislation are being met. As part of this oversight function it 'may' have regard to relevant international human rights standards, including the ICESCR.[221] During the committee stage of the Social Security (Scotland) Bill a proposed amendment to the Bill supported by the Scottish Human Rights Commission sought to introduce a duty to have 'due regard' to ICESCR. During the Committee stage of the Bill a number of concerns were raised in relation to introducing a duty to have 'due regard' to ICESCR when implementing the right to social security.[222]

These concerns reflected the often-cited legal rejection of ESR justiciability in UK discourse. They included, the indeterminacy critique (that social rights are too vague), the democratic legitimacy critique (that courts should not usurp the role of parliament), and challenged the authority of unelected UN Committees in setting international norms on domestic issues.[223] Although many of the

---

217 UN Committee on the Rights of the Child (CRC), *General comment no. 5 (2003): General measures of implementation of the Convention on the Rights of the Child*, 27 November 2003, CRC/GC/2003/5, para.41.

218 UN Human Rights Council, Report of the Special Rapporteur on adequate housing as a component of the right to an adequate standard of living, and on the right to non-discrimination in this context, 22 December 2014, A/HRC/28/62, para.43.

219 Ibid. Comparatively speaking it would not be unusual, subnational systems for human rights protection exist in Canada, Argentina and Switzerland for example.

220 Social Security (Scotland) Act 2018 ss.1(b) and 22(5)(d).

221 Section 22 Social Security (Scotland) Act 2018.

222 Amendments 116–117 Stage of the Social Security (Scotland) Bill available at www.parliament.scot/parliamentarybusiness/report.aspx?r=11360.

223 Stage 2 of the Social Security (Scotland) Bill, in particular see the interventions of Adam Tomkins MP, Ben Macpherson and Jeanne Freeman MP and Committee Convener.

concerns raised engage with democratic legitimacy concerns they are not insurmountable barriers. Nonetheless, the Social Security Committee chose to reject the amendment that would embed a procedural duty to have due regard to international human rights law. This suggests that there requires to be further engagement to ensure an informed legislature is in a position to make informed decisions on what is legally possible if political rhetoric is to materialise into substantive change on ESR incorporation. The Social Security Act 2018 is innovative, but it is not legally transformative.[224]

Incorporation and Justiciability at the Subnational Level

The Scottish courts when faced with implementing international obligations through the common law do not consider ratified treaties binding unless the legislature has already incorporated the treaty into domestic legislation.[225] Whilst the courts may have regard to international treaties and reports of international organisations as an interpretative source of law they are not deemed to form part of the domestic legal system and are not binding on the court unless otherwise instructed by the legislature.[226]

As with devolution in Northern Ireland and Wales, the Scottish constitutional framework is restricted in terms of legal competence along a reserved v devolved division of power.[227] Reserved matters remain the sole authority of Westminster legislation and devolved matters primarily fall within the remit of the devolved legislature and executive (Westminster retains power to legislate in devolved matters but by convention does not do so without seeking permission).[228]

Observing and implementing international obligations falls within the devolved competence of the Scottish Parliament.[229] The Scottish Parliament can introduce legislation that implements international obligations, including incorporating international human rights standards into the devolved framework of governance. As Lord Brodie observed:

> Section 29(2)(b) [of the Scotland Act 1998] provides that a provision is outside the competence of the Scottish Parliament so far as it relates to the

---

224 For a discussion on the weak enforcement mechanisms and the limited legal impact see Colm O'Cinneide, 'The Social Security (Scotland) Act 2018 – A Rights-Based Approach to Social Security?' (2019) 23 *Edinburgh Law Review* 117–123.
225 Lord Hodge, *Moohan & Anor v The Lord Advocate* [2014] UKSC 67 (17 December 2014), para.30.
226 International treaties do not form part of the law of Scotland unless they are incorporated into domestic law through legislation – this was confirmed by Lord Brodie in *Whaley & Anor v. Lord Advocate* [2003] ScotCS 178 (20 June 2003) para.44.
227 Schedule 5 Scotland Act 1998.
228 See Sewell Convention, Scotland Act 2016 s 2.
229 Schedule 5 para.7(1)-(2) Scotland Act 1998 implementation of international obligations is an exception to the reservation of 'Foreign Affairs' to Westminster.

matters which are reserved to the United Kingdom Parliament. Schedule 5, which is given effect by section 30, defines reserved matters. Paragraph 7 has the result of including among reserved matters, "international relations", but excludes from "international relations", observing and implementing international obligations. The Scottish Parliament therefore has the power to legislate with the object of observing and implementing international obligations.[230]

Social rights adjudication at the subnational level in Scotland therefore requires incorporation of rights if they are to take on legally binding status. This can occur by way of Westminster legislation or at the devolved level itself.

Scotland is already on a journey of incorporation in relation to a number of human rights. For example, it is following in the footsteps of other jurisdictions including Norway, Belgium, Spain and most recently Sweden[231] in its proposals to incorporate the UN Convention of the Rights of the Child.[232] In addition, the First Minster's Advisory Group was tasked with considering how Scotland can continue to lead by example in human rights, including economic, social, cultural and environmental rights and potential incorporation of those rights into domestic law.[233] The recommendations of the First Minister's Advisory Group on Human Rights Leadership included a form of incorporation through an Act of the Scottish Parliament as one model through which to achieve this aim (discussed below).

Models of Incorporation

As discussed in Chapter 5, incorporation of international human rights law in a dualist state can take many different forms.[234] It can be understood as means of internalising international law either directly, indirectly or on a sector-by-sector basis.[235] Another approach is to identify the gateway, or 'port' through which international law becomes domestically binding.[236] For example, is the international obligation imported via the constitution,

230 *Whaley & Anor v. Lord Advocate* n 226 para.44.
231 New legislation passed in Sweden will see the incorporation of UNCRC into Swedish law in January 2020.
232 Programme for Government 2018–2019, Scottish Government, September 2018, available at https://beta.gov.scot/programme-for-government/.
233 First Minister's Advisory Group on Human Rights Leadership (FMAG) n 201.
234 Katie Boyle and Edel Hughes, 'Identifying Routes to Remedy for Violations of Economic, Social and Cultural Rights' (2018) 22 *International Journal of Human Rights* 43–69. See also Rosalynd Higgins, *Problems and Process: International Law and How We Use It* (Oxford University Press, 1994).
235 Kasey McCall-Smith, Incorporating International Human Rights in a Devolved Context, *European Futures*, 17 September 2018, available at www.europeanfutures.ed.ac.uk/article-7114.
236 Judith Resnik, 'Law's Migration: American Exceptionalism, Silent Dialogues, and Federalism's Multiple Ports of Entry' (2006) 115 *Yale Law Journal* 1564.

legislation, the common law, or through opening a channel to an international complaints mechanism?[237] Social rights and constitutional theory tells us that incorporation of ESR can, or ought to, occur across different branches of government: legislative, executive, judicial and constitutional in a multi-institutional approach to ESR enforcement.[238] Regardless of the approach taken the key component that determines the difference between softer mechanisms of 'implementation' and stronger forms of 'incorporation' is that incorporation ought to ensure access to an effective remedy for a violation. Essentially domestic incorporation of international norms, be that direct, implicit or sectoral, should be both derived from and inspired by the international legal framework and should at all times be coupled with an effective remedy for a violation of a right.[239]

Options for Options for Enhancing ESR in Scotland

A Legislative 'Constitutional' Framework

The Scottish Parliament has the devolved competence to legislate for ESR. This could be a form of constitutionalisation in so far as it is possible to create such a framework.

In December 2014 James Wolffe, previously Dean of the Faculty of Advocates and now Lord Advocate for Scotland, considered a number of potential constitutional arrangements should Scotland choose to implement ESR in the future.[240] First, Wolffe suggests the option of using the existing Scotland Act 1998 framework and extending constitutional status to ESR in Scotland in the same way that the ECHR is currently protected through a section 29 type of clause.[241] This could be achieved through an amendment to the Scotland Act itself, which would require later the passage of legislation at Westminster.[242] Or,

---

237 Boyle and Hughes, n 234.
238 Jeff King, *Judging Social Rights* (Cambridge University Press, 2011).
239 Katie Boyle, Models of Incorporation and Justiciability of Economic, Social and Cultural Rights, Scottish Human Rights Commission, (2018) at 14. See also UN Committee on Economic, Social and Cultural Rights (CESCR), *General Comment No. 19: The right to social security (Art. 9 of the Covenant)*, 4 February 2008, E/C.12/GC/19. Para.77–80; UN General Assembly, *Basic Principles and Guidelines on the Right to a Remedy and Reparation for Victims of Gross Violations of International Human Rights Law and Serious Violations of International Humanitarian Law: resolution/adopted by the General Assembly*, 21 March 2006, A/RES/60/147. See also UN Committee on Economic, Social and Cultural Rights (CESCR), General Comment No. 9: The domestic application of the Covenant, 3 December 1998, E/C.12/1998/24, para.4.
240 'Economic and Social Rights in Scotland: Lessons from the Past; Options for the Future', A lecture for International Human Rights Day 2014 by W. James Wolffe QC, Dean of the Faculty of Advocates, Edinburgh School of Law, December 2014, available at www.scottish humanrights.com/media/1469/wolffe2014lecture.pdf.
241 Ibid.
242 The Scotland Act 1998 is the subject of reservation under the terms of the Act.

it could be a 'self-regulatory' Act introduced in the Scottish Parliament where the Scottish Parliament limits its own power and confers a power on the court to strike down incompatible legislation whilst the 'self-regulatory' provision is in force.[243] The power of the Scottish Parliament to do this is contested given that such an Act would arguably modify the Scotland Act (by further restricting the competence of the Scottish Parliament).[244] Notably the Supreme Court considered that the Scottish Parliament's attempt to retain the force of the EU Charter of Fundamental Rights post-Brexit (a self-regulatory competence provision with strike down powers for incompatible legislation) was within the competence of the Scottish Parliament when the EU (Legal Continuity) (Scotland) Bill was passed – suggesting at the very least it is within the power of the Scottish Parliament to enact such self-regulatory provisions.[245] The Bill's competence was challenged by the UK Government by way of reference by the UK Law Officers under section 33 of the Scotland Act 1998 – which meant the suspension of it becoming an Act of the Scottish Parliament. In the intervening period the UK Parliament passed the EU Withdrawal Act. The EU Withdrawal Act sought to remove the EU Charter from domestic law and provided for no right of action based on a failure to comply with general principles of EU law, with no power to quash any enactment or conduct on the basis of incompatibility. The court found, and the Scottish Government conceded, that section 5 of the Scottish Bill (retaining the Charter) constituted a modification of the subsequent UK EU Withdrawal Act, therefore rendering the provision beyond competence.[246] This case leaves the door ajar to a self-regulatory provision but within the narrow confines of devolved competence including ensuring it does not modify a protected Act. Limiting the competence of the Scottish Parliament by adding new rights to be protected could be argued to constitute a form of 'self-regulation' or self-imposed limitation on legislative power that would not 'modify' the Scotland Act because it does not amend or otherwise affect the continuing operation of devolved competence (it adds temporarily to it rather than modify or amend its affect).[247]

---

243 It is within the legislative competence of the Scottish Parliament under Paragraph 7(2)(a) of the Scotland Act 1998 to observe and implement international obligations. Arguably, there is a potential challenge to the Scottish Parliament's devolved competence on implementing ICESCR directly in so far as it relates to the reserved matter of Equal Opportunities (Reservation L2 Schedule 5). However, where such disputes arise the courts have regard to the nature and purpose of the legislation to determine whether the Act is outwith competence, meaning a presumption in favour of legislation that would seek to implement international obligations. Likewise, the Scotland Act 1998 is a reserved area and protected from modification.
244 Schedule 4 – enactments protected from modification.
245 Section 5 of the EU Continuity Bill.
246 The *UK Withdrawal from the European Union (Legal Continuity) (Scotland) (rev 2)* [2018] UKSC 64 (13 December 2018 para.102).
247 *Imperial Tobacco Ltd v The Lord Advocate (Scotland)* [2012] UKSC 61 para.44. See also EU Continuity Bill case ibid. para.46 and 51.

A second option would be to use the Human Rights Act 1998 structure, which encompasses different implementation mechanisms, including an interpretative clause; a duty imposed on public bodies to comply; and an option for the courts to make declarations of incompatibility.[248] Again, it is beyond the competence of the Scottish Parliament to amend the Human Rights Act,[249] but the devolved legislature could pass secondary legislation of a similar structure relating to the ICESCR as opposed to the ECHR.[250] The third option proposed by Wolffe is to implement ESR by imposing a duty to have due regard to the rights contained in an international treaty such as the ICESCR, similar to the approach of the Welsh Assembly when implementing a procedural duty to consider the United Nations Convention on the Rights of the Child in 2011, and once again, it would be within the power of the Scottish Parliament in connection with the observance or implementation of international obligations.[251] However, it should be noted that this is not incorporation but a form of legal integration in decision-making (there is no substantive remedy for a violation).

Options 1 or 2 could grant ESR a form of constitutional status through a Scottish Bill of Rights or Charter of Rights introduced by an Act of the Scottish Parliament. In fact, it would be open to the Scottish Parliament to legislate to meet international ESR standards in devolved areas within the Parliament's competence through specific legislation designed to address ESR. In the same way that devolved legislation is subject to repeal (by the Parliament itself) or challenge (by private legal persons or the Advocate General) each of these legislative options would also be open to repeal, such is the nature of an uncodified constitution. It is important to note, therefore, that any such mechanism does not entrench ESR *per se*, but would constitutionalise the rights in so far as it is possible to do so in a system that respects parliamentary supremacy. That is to say that it is open to both the Scottish Parliament and the UK Parliament to introduce a form of 'self-regulatory' legislation that imposes limits on the legislature, the executive (including all bodies exercising public functions) and the judiciary to comply with international human rights standards, as is already the case.[252]

---

248 Ibid.
249 Reserved under Schedule 4 para.4 of the Scotland Act 1998.
250 Again, this would fall within the competence of the Scottish Parliament under Paragraph 7(2)(a).
251 Children and Young Persons (Wales) Measure 2011.
252 Examples of self-regulatory constitutional legislation already exist in the form of constitutional statutes such as defined by Lord Justice Laws in *Thoburn v Sunderland City Council* [2002] QB 151. For example, section 2 of the European Communities Act 1972 gave the courts power to strike down legislation incompatible with EU law – *Factortame (No 2)* [1991] 1 AC 603, 658–659.

Table 6.2 Models of Incorporation for Scotland[253]

Constitutional Model for ESR	Details	Barriers to adopting this route	Constitutional safeguards	Outcome
MODEL A* Scottish Parliament legislative framework full incorporation (Human Rights Act for Scotland) * This could be based on a Scotland Act or Human Rights Act structure or something more like constitutional text with domestic formulation of rights	Parliament imposes 'self-regulatory' legislation, which incorporates international human rights including ICESCR or imposes domestically drafted form of ESR The model could also enshrine rights and leave further detail to be later defined and implemented by parliament (Finnish model) This model can go further than international human rights law where appropriate	This would need to comply with the current reserved v devolved framework and so consideration of reserved areas such as equality[254] would need to be considered in terms of devolved competence	Enhanced role of the Scottish Parliament in *ex ante* review of legislation Equality and Human Rights Committee to assess compliance with CPESCE rights before passage of subsequent legislation Court has power to oversee compliance with Act and offer remedies for non-compliance (including interpretative obligation, ultra vires remedy, declaration of incompatibility, compliance duties on parliament and executive, court can potentially strike down unlawful legislation)[255]	Positive enforcement of CPESCE with various options for constitutional safeguards Most comprehensive form of CPESCE protection with powers and responsibilities shared between institutions Does not cover reserved areas such as employment law and equality law

(Continued)

253 This table is developed from reports published by the Scottish Human Rights Commission: Katie Boyle, Economic, Social and Cultural Rights in Scotland (SHRC 2015); Boyle, Models of Incorporation (2018) n 239.
254 Reservation L2 Schedule 5 Scotland Act reserves, with some exceptions, the area of 'Equal Opportunities'.
255 This is contentious. Constitutionally, it is not clear whether the Scottish Parliament has the power to impose self-regulation by limiting its own competence, binding the Scottish

Table 6.2 (Cont.)

Constitutional Model for ESR	Details	Barriers to adopting this route	Constitutional safeguards	Outcome
MODEL B UK/Scottish Parliament legislative framework based on Human Rights Act structure	Either UK or Scottish Parliament could adopt a similar structure to Human Rights Act that extends to ESC/ICESCR	This would need to comply with the current reserved v devolved framework It is beyond the competence of the Scottish Parliament to amend the HRA	This option includes an interpretative clause; a duty on public bodies to comply and courts can issue declaration of incompatibility	This is a less robust constitutional framework in terms of judicial overview Declarations of incompatibility are not binding on Parliament and do not affect the application of the law There is a strong element of deference to the legislature
MODEL C UK Parliament legislative framework based on Scotland Act structure	UK Parliament could extend scope of section 29 of Scotland Act 1998 to include rights enshrined in the ICESCR	Requires political support by majority of UK Parliament – it is not within devolved competence of the SP to amend the Scotland Act 1998	This framework is how the ECHR is currently protected in Scotland The judiciary are tasked with the responsibility to review compatibility and can declare unlawful legislation ultra vires	Positive ESR enforcement Human rights-affirmative framework providing ESR with constitutional status in Scotland Under this model the judiciary play a role in scrutinising substantive compatibility

(Continued)

Parliament in relation to subsequent legislation unless expressly repealed (discussed above). The answer lies in the interpretation of 'modification'. The Scotland Act prohibits modification of the Scotland Act 1998 (Schedule 4). The Scotland Act sets out the Scottish Parliament's competence (section 29). Changing or adding to the list of areas that are beyond the competence of SP does not necessarily 'modify' s29. For a discussion on this see judgment by the Supreme Court EU Continuity Bill case [2018] UKSC 64 n 246 (13 December 2018) para.50–51 'the protected enactment has to be understood as having been in substance amended, superseded, disapplied or repealed by the later one'.

Table 6.2 (Cont.)

Constitutional Model for ESR	Details	Barriers to adopting this route	Constitutional safeguards	Outcome
MODEL D UK/Scottish Parliament legislative framework based on duty to have due regard to ICESCR (or other international treaties)	Similar to the Equality Act 2010 public sector equality duty or the duty imposed by the Welsh Assembly to have due regard to the UN Convention on the Rights of the Child	This would need to comply with the current reserved v devolved framework	This option requires that the judiciary play a supervisory role in ensuring compliance with the duty to have due regard. This is a procedural duty to take into consideration and does not necessarily result in a substantive human rights compliant outcome	Weaker type of enforcement Procedural protection of ESR May help with initial implementation of ESR as part of the decision-making process but does not constitute incorporation
MODEL E UK Parliament signs the UK and Scotland up to an international complaints mechanism	Optional Protocol to ICESCR or Collective Complaints Mechanism under European Social Charter. This would not be dissimilar to the way complaints can currently be raised with the ECtHR or the Court of Justice of the European Union	This would require implementation through Westminster	The decisions of the committees may not necessarily be made automatically binding giving legislature time to implement change in order to comply with any findings of non-compliance	Weaker type of enforcement unless decisions of committees made binding Improved scrutiny of ESR compliance and access to alternative remedies

The First Minister's Advisory Group has recommended that Scotland undergoes a lengthy participative process to deliberate on the means of incorporating economic, social, cultural and environmental rights and how to give domestic contextualisation to ESR norms derived from international law.[256] The Advisory Group recommended incorporation through a domestically conceived framework inspired by and derived from international human rights law (**Model A**).[257] In this sense, the proposed framework can go further than international human rights law where possible, for example, through enhancing rights protection for older persons, LGBTI communities as well as for protection against poverty and social exclusion.[258] As part of the recommendations the Advisory Group set out a skeletal framework[259] for an Act of the Scottish Parliament:

Table 6.3 FMAG Proposed Human Rights Act for Scotland[260]

Preamble	Human dignity underpins all rights
Competence	Act only applies within devolved competence
Human Rights – full framework: civil, political, economic, social, cultural, environmental [CPESCE], further specific rights	Act lists all rights belonging to everyone in Scotland in one place (including ECHR civil and political rights). Not all rights can be included in the Act as legally enforceable rights because of the limitations of devolved competence (employment rights for example are excluded as reserved matter)
Interpretation	When interpreting rights courts must have regard to international law and may have regard to comparative law
Interpretation	In so far as it is possible to do so primary and subordinate legislation should be read as compatible with human rights in Act
Duties	There is an initial duty placed on decision makers to have due regard to the rights and a subsequent duty to comply with rights set out in Act. The duty to comply will commence after specified period (sunrise clause)
Limitations	The Act recognises that limitations can be placed on rights where rights may be balanced with other considerations such as the general welfare in a democratic society. Limitations can be imposed when

(Continued)

256 Miller, FMAG Report, n 202 at 39.
257 Boyle, Models of Incorporation n 239 at 10.
258 Miller, FMAG Report, n 202 at 32.
259 Ibid. at 58–59.
260 Ibid.

Table 6.3 (Cont.)

	'provided for in law and carried out according to law, there is no other less restrictive alternative; and the measures are reasonable, non-discriminatory, based on evidence, subject to review, and of limited duration'[261]
Remedies	Act facilitates access to an effective remedy. Options for consideration include declarations of incompatibly (if consistently given effect to); strike down power; delayed remedies; development of structural remedies for systemic cases
Standing	Expanded definition of standing to facilitate both individual and collective complaints
Pre-legislative scrutiny	The Act should make provision for enhanced pre-legislative scrutiny including systematic scrutiny of proposed legislation to ensure compliance with CPESCE rights. This should include regularly calling on independent expertise of constitutional and human rights experts to assist. Decisions should be published and carry sufficient weight in legislative process

Enhanced Legislative Scrutiny

The legislature can play one of the most significant roles in ensuring that ESR rights are incorporated and enforced, including by designing and delivering legislation which sets out ESR as legal standards. Under the FMAG proposed incorporation model the legislature would continue to be responsible for fulfilling rights through subsequent legislation as well as scrutinising compliance with rights as a matter of course in the everyday legislative process ('pre-legislative scrutiny'). Effective human rights scrutiny by committees is a particularly important aspect of accountability in the Scottish Parliament because the legislature is unicameral. The United Nations Office of the High Commissioner on Human Rights and the Inter-Parliamentary Union has recommended that '[h]uman rights should thoroughly permeate parliamentary activity'.[262]

The model of incorporation proposed by the FMAG (Model A) coincided with a report of the Scottish Parliament Equality and Human Rights Committee

---

261 Ibid. at 59.
262 United Nations Office of the High Commissioner. Inter-Parliamentary Union, Human Rights, Handbook for Parliamentarians No.26 at 111.

(EHRiC) who sought to set out a road map[263] for a renewed human rights culture in the Scottish Parliament. The report recommends, *inter alia*, a role for the
Scottish Parliament as guarantor of human rights in both pre- and post-legislative
scrutiny of Acts engaging with human rights and equality;[264] engagement with
international treaty monitoring mechanisms (UPR +);[265] and the expansion of
human rights scrutiny across the parliamentary remit through deployment of
'human rights champions'.[266] The renewed approach proposes to include a 'pilot
systematic human rights scrutiny of Government Bills with a dedicated legal
adviser'[267] and enhanced disclosure of the Presiding Officer's statement on legislative competence.[268] The Committee does not explicitly recommend expansion of
the remit to ESR, however, the recommendations engage responding to the work
of the FM Advisory Group,[269] which, by extension includes further engagement
with economic, social, cultural and environmental rights.

The proposals set out by the EHRiC goes further and faster than any other
human rights committee established under the UK or devolved legislative systems.
Historically, pre- and post-legislative scrutiny of human rights has been weak under
the devolved frameworks. In Scotland, ex ante (pre-legislative) review of human
rights occurs to some extent (in accordance with the Scotland Act 1998)[270]
through non-disclosed assessments by the Executive and the Presiding Officer of
the Scottish Parliament before legislation is passed. There is a requirement for the
relevant Minster and the Presiding Officer to make a statement of compatibility in
relation to each Bill being considered. However, these limited reviews do not take
the full body of international human rights law into consideration meaning that
ESR, for example, are not regularly reviewed as part of the pre-legislative process.

Under the Finish constitution there is a process of pre-legislative scrutiny that
ensures any legislation passed by Parliament is fully compatible with constitutional
rights and international law, including ESR. This is a 'rights-affirmative' constitutional framework that operates on a presumption in favour of human rights compatibility rather than an ad hoc approach.[271] This constitutional model imposes
a duty on the legislature to introduce legislation to fulfil the right (one step further than the proposals under EHRiC and one step closer to the proposals of the
FM Advisory Group). However, under the Finnish model, there is only a limited

---

263 Scottish Parliament Equality and Human Rights Committee (SP EHRiC), Getting Rights
    Right: Human Rights and the Scottish Parliament, November 2018, available at https://
    sp-bpr-en-prod-cdnep.azureedge.net/published/EHRiC/2018/11/26/Getting-Rights-
    Right–Human-Rights-and-the-Scottish-Parliament-3/EHRiCS052018R6Rev.pdf.
264 Ibid. SP EHRiC Report Recommendations 19, 22, 31 and 32.
265 Ibid. SP EHRiC Report Recommendation 11 *inter alia*.
266 Ibid. SP EHRiC Report Recommendation 37.
267 Ibid. SP EHRiC Report Recommendation 29.
268 Ibid. SP EHRiC Report Recommendation 23.
269 Ibid. SP EHRiC Report Recommendation 17.
270 See evidence provided by Dr Boyle, Human Rights Inquiry, EHRiC, 29 March 2018, avail-
    able at www.parliament.scot/S5_Equal_Opps/Submission_from_Dr_Katie_Boyle.pdf.
271 For a discussion on this see Boyle (2015) n 253.

role for the court which can review legislation if it is found that it does not comply with the constitution.[272] Furthermore, in Finland, ex ante review is reactive rather than pro-active. For example, when parliament was reforming welfare legislation in 2003 the Finish Constitutional Law Committee (FCLC) declared the already in force provisions of the 'partial labour market subsidy' unconstitutional (those living with parents received only 60% of unemployment benefit). The provisions had formed part of the welfare state before the constitution was revised in 1995. It was not until the provisions came before the FCLC under the 2003 reform that the constitutionality of the existing legislation to be retained was scrutinised. The subsidy was transformed in to a means tested subsidy in order to comply with International Labour Organisation Convention 168 on Employment Promotion and Protection against Unemployment.[273] This would differ significantly from the model proposed by the FM Advisory Group in two respects. First, the recommendations include an overarching statute that proactively requires further legislation and statutory guidance to ensure fulfilment of a right. And second, an effective remedy in court should be available as a means of last resort (after all other accountability mechanisms exhausted).[274] The FM Advisory Group recommends that public body duty-bearers must be regarded as 'the first resort' and that building their capacity is 'key to the practical implementation of rights, to everyday accountability, and to the improvement of people's lives'.[275]

Nonetheless, important lessons can be drawn from the experience of the FCLC. The FCLC makes its decision on the compatibility of legislation after listening to constitutional and human rights experts. These decisions are not politically motivated but based on legal standards. The decisions of the Committee are not binding on Parliament but are considered to carry sufficient weight that by convention parliament complies with them. In Scotland, the EHRiC could draw from this experience. Ex ante review could be supported by a panel of human rights and constitutional experts (including expertise on ESR).[276] Compatibility decisions of the EHRiC and the expert advice received could be published to ensure transparency. The decisions of the Committee may not necessarily be binding but, similar to the FCLC, should carry sufficient weight in guiding the legislature on human rights compliance. A renewed remit for the

---

272 See Kaarlo Tuori for a discussion of the Finnish system, Rights, Democracy and Local Self Governance: Social Rights in the Constitution of Finland www.juridicainternational.eu/? id=12700.
273 PeVL 46/2002 vp, at 5.
274 Miller, FMAG Report, n 202 at 29.
275 Ibid.
276 SP EHRiC Report n 263 at 59 citing Draft Principles on Parliaments and Human Rights, Annex 1 to Report of the Office of the United Nations High Commissioner for Human Rights, Contribution of parliaments to the work of the Human Rights Council and its universal periodic review, Composition and Working Methods, Annex I, para 8, A/HRC/38/ 25 (17 May 2018).

EHRiC would therefore require sufficient support and resources to support these aims (something that the report recommends).[277]

The Scottish Parliament EHRiC has decided to pilot a model based on the Joint Committee on Human Rights for systematic scrutiny of all legislation. This will require a dedicated legal adviser with the necessary human rights expertise to scrutinise policy/human rights memorandums to highlight legislative areas 'where there is a need for further human rights information and where there are human rights matters of significance or opportunities to advance human rights'.[278] This approach is pro-active in identifying opportunities for human rights as well as potential legislative gaps.

If the Committee's recommendations are fully implemented it will place the Scottish Parliament as an example of best practice on pre-legislative scrutiny of human rights and within the Scottish context it will facilitate the multi-institutional approach to ESR envisaged under the theoretical framework proposed above.

Enhanced Role for the Executive

ESR should be streamlined as part of everyday decision-making in the same way that the executive is under a duty to comply with civil and political rights.[279] The FM Advisory Group that the incorporation model (Model A) create obligations on those exercising state authority to comply with international ESR norms.[280] This includes a duty to have due regard to the rights set out in a framework Act, as well as a duty to comply (creating both procedural and substantive obligations).[281]

This administrative space also includes an enhanced roll for regulators, meaning devolved inspectorates in housing, health, education and so on would require to assess compliance with reference to international human rights standards, creating more immediate accountability mechanisms than a court or tribunal.[282] It is within this regulatory space that the everyday accountability of rights can occur.[283] Barret and others have argued that sector specific enforcement can be greatly enhanced when bodies, such as the Equality and Human Rights Commission occupy more immediate enforcement space than that occupied by the court.[284] This approach can help facilitate a wider deliberative

277 SP EHRiC Report n 263 at 60.
278 Ibid.
279 Scotland Act 1998 and Human Rights Act 1998.
280 Miller, FMAG Report, n 202 at 28–29.
281 similar to that found in Human Rights Act 1998 s 6.
282 Miller, FMAG Report, n 202 at 40–41.
283 Ibid.
284 See David Barrett, 'The Regulatory Space of Equality and Human Rights Law in Britain: The Role of the Equality and Human Rights Commission' (2019) 39(2) *Legal Studies* 247–265.

model where the decision-making sphere of public bodies is regulated on a sectoral basis, with the potential for the relevant national human rights institution to take the lead in facilitating this dialogue and ensuring equality and human rights work permeates the role of other regulator in areas such as health, housing and education.[285]

The recommendations of the FMAG has suggested enhanced roles for the Scottish Government under the proposed human rights framework. This includes a distinct Scottish Government National mechanism for monitoring, reporting and implementation of human rights.[286] In addition, the report suggests that the national performance framework (NPF) includes human rights-based indicators to help the government recognise governance gaps in the enforcement of ESR as well as enabling the allocation of resources early on the budget process.[287] Finally, the government is ultimately responsible for the implementation of the recommendations by establishing a National Task Force, led by the Scottish Government, to take forward the proposed human rights reform.[288]

Enhanced Role for the Court

This brings us to the development of judicial review of ESR compliance under a potentially renewed constitutional framework. Recourse to judicial review must be a means of last resort when all other accountability mechanisms fail. However, a legal remedy remains a necessary component. Meaningful and justiciable incorporation of ESR must first address the first and second wave critiques of ESR (first wave: the 'anti-democratic critique', the 'indeterminacy critique', the 'incapacity critique'; and the second wave: the 'pro-hegemonic critique'). This requires us to consider the principles of adjudication as they apply to the Scottish context.

Access to justice is primary in any renewed framework that seeks to protect ESR. Issues relating to standing and legal aid require to be addressed as part of the **accessibility principle**.

For those seeking legal aid support, the Legal Aid (Scotland) Act 1986 sets out eligibility criteria including whether the Board is satisfied that the applicant has *probabilis causa litigandi* and whether it appears to the Scottish Legal Aid Board (SLAB) that it is reasonable in the particular circumstances of the case that the applicant should receive legal aid.[289] The subjective test of reasonableness by SLAB could result in some applicants struggling to secure the financial resources required to take a case – this would be particularly problematic in the sphere of ESR where the litigation culture is in its infancy. SLAB may, for

---

285 Barrett proposes various models for achieving this aim: neo-institutionalist; deliberative; pragmatic; and genetic approach, ibid.
286 Miller, FMAG Report, n 202 recommendation 4.
287 Miller, FMAG Report, n 202 recommendation 5.
288 Miller, FMAG Report, n 202 recommendation 6.
289 Section 14(1).

example, examine the likely costs of any case and balance these against the benefit an applicant will get from the proceedings.[290] Judicial review can be expensive, and should only be used as a means of last resort. In addition, when claiming ESR the financial implications may not necessarily be addressed as sufficiently significant in financial terms for support to be provided by the relevant legal aid board. A justice system that facilitates access to remedies for violations of ESR cannot be based on balancing whether or not the outcome will be of sufficient financial gain for the applicant, particularly when dealing with access to basic services such as welfare, housing or educational provision. This would suggest that the current restrictions on access to legal aid may require to be given careful consideration in order to facilitate ESR justiciability and access to an effective remedy for a violation of an ESR.

Currently in Scotland, an individual must be able to establish 'sufficient interest' in order to be able to seek judicial review of a decision.[291] In addition, when the case engages with human rights under the ECHR then the applicant must also establish victimhood.[292] This is a restrictive test and requires to be expanded if access to justice is to be fully enabled to meet the **principles of accessibility and participation**.

Public interest litigation has not been widely used in the different parts of the UK as a means of challenging societal issues on a wide scale basis.[293] Historically public interest litigation was not allowed and, although English courts began to hear interest group cases, this did not necessarily trickle down to devolved jurisdictions.[294] Holding the executive to account by means of judicial review has largely been based on a private rights model with a preference on focussing on individual concerns on a case-by-case basis.[295] Courts in applying the sufficient interest test will exclude applications made by 'cranks, busybodies or mischief makers'.[296] Public interest litigation facilitates the **principles of accessibility,**

---

290 Sarah Harvie-Clark, *Judicial Review*, Spice Briefing 16/62, 8 July 2016 at 35.

291 This has long been the test applied in England and Wales, see Supreme Court Act 1981 s.31(3). In Northern Ireland, the requirements for standing are found in the Judicature (Northern Ireland) Act 1978 s18(4). In Scotland, the test is still relatively new. Applicants must seek permission by establishing sufficient interest under 27B of the Court of Session Act 1988. Prior to the decision of the Supreme Court in *Axa General Insurance Ltd v the Lord Advocate* [2011] UKSC 46, standing could only be secured if an individual could establish 'title and interest' to take a case – a much higher threshold than the standing requirement in England and Wales. For a full discussion on this see the *Axa* case in which the judiciary amended the common law rule on 'title and interest' in Scotland to mirror the 'sufficient interest' standing requirement in England and Wales see Chris Himsworth, 'The Supreme Court reviews the Review of Acts of the Scottish Parliament' (2012) April *Public Law* 205.

292 Section 100 of the Scotland Act 1998 and section 7 of the Human Rights Act requires the applicant to be a victim in terms of Article 34 ECHR.

293 Tom Mullen 'Public Interest Litigation in Scotland' (2015) 4 *Juridical Review* 363–383 at 363.

294 For a discussion on the historical reluctance and a more recent leniency (in England) see Carol Harlow, 'Public Law and Popular Justice' (2002) 65 *The Modern Law Review* 1.

295 Mullen, n 293 at 367.

296 *R v Inland Revenue Commissioners, ex parte the National Federation of Self-Employed and Small Businesses Ltd* [1982] AC 617.

participation and the counter-majoritarian principle and historical conceptualisations around 'busybodies' or 'mischief makers' is simply insufficient to justify
restricting access to justice for public interest groups.

The expansion of standing in Scotland in 2012 was intended to facilitate
access to public interest litigation and enhance the protection of rights beyond
the private rights model.[297] However, when engaging with ECHR rights eligibility is still restricted by the victim test under devolved legislation[298] and the
Human Rights Act 1998.[299] This can make it difficult to establish standing in
public interest litigation, which in turn, is problematic for the application of the
principles of accessibility and participation. Seeking judicial review in a public
interest challenge should allow litigants to raise a public law issue which is of
general importance even if the claimant has no private interest in the outcome
of the case.[300] The additional threshold of establishing victim status in connection with an ECHR breach means that there is a restrictive interpretation of
standing for those who might wish to intervene on behalf of large groups.[301]
This may well undermine the justiciability of both CPR and ESR because it may
not always be possible for cases to be brought by individuals who meet the eligibility criteria in order to take a case. For example, if a housing charity wishes to
raise a public interest litigation case on behalf of social housing tenants the
restrictive application of standing may mean that they cannot take a case based
on Convention rights. If the enforcement of human rights is to extend to ESR
then the tests for establishing standing should be expanded to ensure public
interest cases are actionable in keeping with the principles of **accessibility and
participation**.

Scotland's legal system includes the possibility of seeking judicial review of
decisions made by those exercising power on behalf of the state. This includes
the well-developed grounds for review (**illegality, irrationality and procedural impropriety**) discussed in Chapter 1. Likewise, the court deploys varying
intensity of review depending on the circumstances (**reasonableness, proportionality, procedural fairness, anxious scrutiny, substantive fairness**) as discussed in Chapter 1. In relation to the **principle of fairness** social rights
adjudication requires both procedural and substantive review depending on
the circumstances. The book proposes adopting judicial review that assesses
human rights compliance relying on reasonableness and proportionality when
assessing whether states have taken sufficient steps to fulfil a right (reviewing
the processes and policies rather than outcomes). The book also proposes
adopting a normative threshold that can help facilitate substantive enforcement

---

297 Harvie-Clark, n 290 at 14.
298 Scotland Act 1998 (section 100); Northern Ireland Act 1998 (section 71); Government of
Wales Act 2006 (section 81).
299 section 7.
300 *R v Lord Chancellor ex p Child Poverty Action Group* [1999] 1 WLR 347 353G.
301 See *Christian Institute v Others* [2015] CSIH 64 – para.43–44 – standing established on EU
law grounds but not under s100 of Scotland Act because charities could not meet victim test.

should the circumstances require it, this can be viewed as a similar approach when dealing with the most vulnerable and in need under the Colombian *tutela* system. Under this system the court will intervene and enforce a substantive remedy where the threshold of an 'unconstitutional set of affairs' has occurred.[302] In Scotland, a substantive threshold is already something the court has been willing to enforce. For example, this can arise when legislation requires that a person's needs be assessed and if, following that assessment, services are required to meet human rights, including ESR, then there is a duty to provide those services.[303] This approach meets the **peremptory threshold** proposed in Chapter 1. For example, in the case of *McGregor v South Lanarkshire Council* the court held that a local authority was obliged to provide an elderly man with a place in a care home under the terms of the Social Work (Scotland) Act 1968 despite the local authority claiming they did not have the immediate funds to make the placement available.[304] The lack of resources was not considered a justifiable defence. According to the statutory framework, the duty to provide a place in a care home crystallised when an assessment of his needs determined he required one.[305] Lord Hardie reflected on what type of remedy would be most appropriate stating:

> I have given consideration to the appropriate remedy in this case. Although I have reached the conclusion that the respondents have acted ultra vires the question is whether I should simply pronounce a declarator to that effect or whether I should ordain the respondents to provide the petitioner with nursing home care immediately and, if so, whether that care should be in the residential home where he presently resides. While I agree with counsel for the respondents that normally it would be appropriate for the court to pronounce a declarator that the respondents had acted ultra vires and to remit the case back to the respondents for their reconsideration, I do not think that is an appropriate remedy in the present case where the respondents have determined that the petitioner should be provided with nursing home care. The only remaining issue for the respondents is to determine in which nursing home he should reside. I have, however, reached the conclusion that it would not be appropriate for me to pronounce an order of specific implement naming the nursing home in question. It should suffice for the petitioner's purposes that I pronounce a declarator that the respondents have acted ultra vires and to remit the case back to the respondents to make the necessary provision of residential nursing home care. This will

302 Magdalena Sepúlveda, Colombia, The Constitutional Court's Role in Addressing Social Injustice, in Malcolm Langford (ed.), *Social Rights Jurisprudence, Emerging Trends in International and Comparative Law* (Cambridge University Press, 2008), 144–163.
303 *Crossan v South Lanarkshire Council* 2006 CSOH 28, Lady Smith para.23–24.
304 *McGregor v South Lanarkshire Council* 2001 SC 502.
305 Ibid. para.7.

enable the respondents to consider what nursing home facilities are available for the care of the petitioner and to make urgent provision for his care.[306]

The court was therefore willing to enforce a substantive outcome through a declaratory remedy enforcing a substantive threshold, the only deference employed was to allow the local authority to choose the care home.[307] Enforcement exists on a spectrum and the court must be able to adopt a flexible approach depending on the circumstances in each case. This approach, enabled through a clear statutory obligation to meet a **peremptory threshold** should an assessment of needs demand an outcome, is indicative of an innovative and flexible approach to remedies in keeping with the **remedial principle**. It is also an example of judicial engagement with the **principle of fairness** in both a procedural as well as substantive sense.

Reflecting on existing remedies helps to highlight that the 'broad range of remedies already within our legal system should be available to be applied as appropriate' to meet the needs of ESR adjudication (reduction; declaratory; suspension and interdict; specific performance or specific implement; interim orders; damages).[308]

Further to existing remedies there is scope to consider further developing the range available remedies in the Scottish legal system.[309] This is something that FMAG has recommended suggesting that there should be the development of collective cases and structural interdicts.[310] Enhancing the availability of effective remedies is in and of itself an important aspect of the **remedial principle**. Further, the enhancement of multi-party actions and collective litigation supports both the **principles of accessibility, participation and deliberation** as well as the **remedial and counter-majoritarian principles** by facilitating access to justice and effective remedies for systemic issues.

Collective litigation is another means of challenging a breach of human rights where a group of individuals take a collective group case against the state (also known as a class action or a multi-party action). In England and Wales, multi-party actions tend to be engaged in relation to competition law, personal injury claims or pension disputes rather than in relation to human rights issues.[311] There is more scope across the breadth of the UK to challenge injustice and ESR violations through collective litigation.

Collective litigation has proved successful in dealing with systemic human rights violations under the Colombian *tutela* system where the court can group together

306 Ibid. para.12.
307 Ibid.
308 Miller, FMAG Report, n 202 at 35.
309 Ibid.
310 Ibid.
311 See Civil Procedure Rules and Practice Directions, as supplemented by statute (including the Senior Courts Act 1981). Also, the Competition Act 1998 and the Consumer Rights Act 2015 provide for certain competition law damages claims to be brought before the Competition Appeal Tribunal (CAT), for which the Competition Appeal Tribunal Rules 2015 (*SI 2015 No. 1648*) provide the requisite procedure.

cases in order to issue a structural remedy. The Colombian Constitutional Court has heard and decided 'structural' cases where it considers whether an 'unconstitutional set of affairs' requires to be remedied.[312] Usually this will involve multiple applicants (collective cases) and will allow the court to review whether the state can remedy a systemic problem engaging multiple stakeholders and multiple defendants.

This could be compared with the type of adjudication that saw a broad-based approach to human rights violations such as addressing slopping out in prisons in Scotland (where prisoners did not have access to toilets and required to defecate into buckets).[313] In this case, the court issued damages to the plaintiffs finding that slopping out amounted to inhuman and degrading treatment (a violation of Article 3 ECHR). The *Napier* case, for example, dealt with the petition of one prisoner claiming a breach of human rights as a result of slopping out. Several other cases were sisted (suspended) pending the outcome of *Napier*.[314] Following the *Napier* judgment, and in anticipation of the far-reaching implications, the court accepted a motion to determine the standard of proof for future cases.[315] The Scottish judiciary has demonstrated capacity to deal with systemic human rights violations. Nonetheless, remedies for systemic issues in the Scottish cases tends to favour compensation as a form of remedy rather than a structural injunction to correct a systemic violation. In the *Napier* case Mr Napier received damages for the violation of his rights but there was no order compelling the relevant authorities to end the practice of slopping out. Whilst this particular remedy did not amount to a structural order, it was sufficient to compel the Scottish Government to address the violation. In other words, the longer-term material impact of the judgment was the end of slopping out in Scottish prisons. This is a form of moderate review/moderate remedy materialising into long-term symbolic and material change.[316] There may be more scope to explore the possibilities of viewing alternative remedies as part of a cultural shift in addressing ESR violations. If structural issues arise in relation to ESR it would not be beyond the reach of the legislature, executive and judiciary

---

312 For an in-depth discussion on this see César Rodríguez-Garavito, 'Beyond the Courtroom: The Impact of Judicial Activism on Socioeconomic Rights in Latin America' (2011) 89 *Texas Law Review* 1669–1698.

313 *Napier v. The Scottish Ministers* [2005] ScotCS CSIH_16 (10 February 2005) in which the court accepted a motion to determine how future cases might be dealt with as a matter of public interest (setting out the standard of proof on a balance of probabilities) following the potentially wide-reaching decision of Lord Bonomy that slopping out in prison amounted to degrading treatment contrary to Art 3 ECHR in the single case of Robert Napier: Opinion of Lord Bonomy, *Napier (Ap) v. The Scottish Ministers* ScotCS CSOH P739/01 (26 April 2004).

314 *Alexander Maley v Scottish Ministers* A3898/03 Glasgow Sheriff Court (31 March 2004). See also the discussion led by the law firm leading the slopping out cases: Taylor & Kelly, Slopping Out in Scottish Prisons www.taylorkelly.co.uk/prison-law/slopping-out/.

315 *Napier* (2005) n 313 para.5–7.

316 César Rodríguez-Garavito and Diana Rodríguez-Franco, *Radical Deprivation on Trial, the Impact of Judicial Activism on Socioeconomic Rights in the Global South* (CUP 2015) at 10.

to work together to remedy the matter through **principle of deliberation**.[317] For example, if a systemic problem arises in relation to human rights protection then there could be a role for the court to supervise whether the legislature and/or executive could take steps to remedy this through a form of structural injunction. In many respects Scotland is well placed to develop the **deliberative dialogue** already underway with an executive committed to enhancing ESR,[318] a parliament ready to scrutinise this commitment[319] and a judiciary equipped to review and remedy as directed by any forthcoming reform.[320] Landau argues that addressing violations of social rights through a structural and deliberative approach to remedies facilitates a form of social rights adjudication that positively impacts on the lives of poorer citizens and prioritises the most vulnerable, a key component of the **counter-majoritarian principle**.[321]

In Scotland, multi-party actions have been addressed on ad hoc basis by identifying a lead case that can act as a test case and sisting (suspending) other cases whilst awaiting for the outcome of the lead case.[322] Following suggested reform recommended in reports of both the Scottish Law Commission (1996)[323] and the Scottish Civil Courts Review (2009)[324] the Court of Session rules were amended to facilitate the adoption of new procedures for multi-party cases to be initiated at the direction of the Lord President allowing more flexibility for case management by the nominated judge (Rule 2.2).[325] Multi-party procedures have been facilitated under Rule 2.2 on a number of occasions to deal with systemic issues, including claims under the Damages (Asbestos-related Conditions) (Scotland) Act 2009[326] and in response personal injury actions relating to the use of vaginal tape and mesh.[327] Rule 2.2 may offer a potential route to remedy

317 Such as the response by the executive and legislature to introduce emergency legislation to deal with the fall out of systemic human rights violations following the Cadder judmgment. See *Cadder v Her Majesty's Advocate* (Scotland) [2010] UKSC 43 (26 October 2010) and the Criminal Procedure (Legal Assistance, Detention and Appeals) (Scotland) Act 2010.
318 Scottish Government, New Task Force to lead on Human Rights, 10 December 2018 https://news.gov.scot/news/enhancing-human-rights.
319 SP EHRiC Report n 263.
320 Miller, FMAG Report, n 202 at 35. See also Wolffe n 240.
321 David Landau, 'The Reality of Social Rights Enforcement' (2012) 53 *Harvard International Law Journal* 189.
322 See Rule of Court 22.3(6), available at www.scotcourts.gov.uk/docs/default-source/rules-and-practice/rules-of-court/court-of-session/chap22.pdf?sfvrsn=8.
323 Scottish Law Commission, *Report No. 154, Multi-Party Actions* (1996), para.64.
324 Scottish Civil Court Review (2009), Volume 2, Chapter 13, pp.152–155, available at www.scotcourts.gov.uk/docs/default-source/civil-courts-reform/report-of-the-scottish-civil-courts-review-vol-1-chapt-1—9.pdf?sfvrsn=4.
325 See Rule of Court 2.2 available at www.scotcourts.gov.uk/docs/default-source/rules-and-practice/rules-of-court/court-of-session/chap02.pdf?sfvrsn=10.
326 Court of Session No.2 of 2012, www.scotcourts.gov.uk/rules-and-practice/practice-notes/court-of-session-directions.
327 Court of Sessions Directions No.2 of 2015 and No.2 of 2016, www.scotcourts.gov.uk/rules-and-practice/practice-notes/court-of-session-directions

for multi-party cases as part of a cultural shift in human rights adjudication around systemic ESR violations. Further reform under the Civil Litigation (Expenses and Group Proceedings) (Scotland) Act 2018 will provide for group litigation in the Court of Session. Further detail on the group procedure for judicial review will be set out in new rules of court to be developed by the Scottish Civil Justice Council.[328] Reform in this area will require to be cognisant of the social rights adjudication principles discussed here.

There is more scope for exploring the possibilities that multi-party actions or group cases can provide in terms of dealing with systemic ESR rights violations. Comparative experience indicates that courts must adapt procedures to deal with systemic ESR violations by facilitating access to a collective procedure with multiple stakeholders, multiple defenders and through the deployment of structural remedies.[329] Responding to this need in the deployment of effective remedies is something that the First Minister's Advisory Group has recommended.[330]

Outstanding issues relate to those cases which do not necessarily fall within the existing court procedures. For example, should it become clear that a number of cases are emerging at tribunal level new procedures might be considered to group the cases and 'refer up' to the Court of Session, or for the possibility to confer powers at the Tribunal level to hear systemic issues by using a multi-party approach (for example, where a systemic issue arises in the Housing and Property Chamber of the First Tier Tribunal (for private rental sector). Likewise, similar consideration must be given to cases arising in the Sheriff Court and what procedures can be used to facilitate multi-party action or grouping of cases when systemic issues arise, such as in relation to complaints on social housing provision currently within the domain of the Sheriff Court.

Process for Reform

The FMAG recommendations include significant space for participation in a deliberative process around what the constitutional future of Scotland should look like. This approach is not new to Scottish politics, with previous examples of a constitutional convention (prior to devolution) and deliberative referendum processes (in relation to independence and EU withdrawal) paving the way for future deliberative models. As discussed in Chapter 5, such deliberative models should ensure informed, inclusive, participative deliberation that seeks to ensure consensus in the outcome (engendered through legitimacy in the process). The FMAG recommendations propose that Scotland undertakes a participative process around the formation of a new Act of the Scottish Parliament where by different epistemic communities (rights-holders/practitioners/decision makers/

---

328 Policy Memorandum, Civil Litigation (Expenses And Group Proceedings) (Scotland) Bill, para.94.
329 Garavito and Franco, n 316 and Landau, n 321.
330 Miller, FMAG Report, n 202 at 29 & 35.

subject experts/citizens) have the opportunity to help give substance to the rights provided for in the Act. This is not to detract from or dilute the rights as provided for in international human rights law but to address the indeterminacy of what progressive realisation of some of those rights mean in any given context, including the rights to health, education, housing and so on. This participative process is an important part of building capacity and awareness of rights as well as allowing a sense of ownership to develop as a bottom-up model rather than imposing a top-down approach *per se*. Whilst the overarching statute will seek to acknowledge the broad array of rights to be protected, a normative elaboration of what those rights mean in practice should be set out in subsequent more detailed legislation (or amendments to existing legislation) and statutory guidance.

The proposed process therefore includes the establishment of a National Task Force in 2019; a participatory process, capacity-building and the development of the National Performance Framework from 2019–2020; and finally the passing of an Act of the Scottish Parliament that provides for the rights, introduces pre-legislative scrutiny, requires public bodies to have due regard to the rights with a sunrise clause for full compliance, and subsequent legislation and statutory guidance on how to implement the rights (and duties) in practice.

Scotland is on the precipice of significant constitutional change. A renewed human rights framework that embraces the full body of international human rights will require thought, imagination, innovation and courage. It will require actors across disciplines, sectors and institutions to work together and for political leadership to ensure political will materialises into long-term systemic change that seeks to improve people's lives. Closing the accountability gap on ESR is an important part of this journey.

ESR and Devolution Some Concluding Thoughts

This final chapter looks much more closely at how the devolved frameworks can enhance the protection of ESR under different constitutional frameworks. In Wales, significant steps have already been taken with the potential for future incorporation of rights – particularly if further devolution occurs in relation to administrative justice.

In Northern Ireland, the better protection of human rights, whilst contested, remains a significant objective of the post-conflict peace process. The conflicted democracy paradigm helps highlight how pre-conflict ESR violations can potentially continue under the aegis of procedural democracy unless addressed holistically. The chapter argues that there is a mandate to better protect ESR in Northern Ireland and sets out the potential means of achieving this, including reforming aspects of equality law and revisiting the indigenous Bill of Rights process.

In Scotland, the Scottish Government has promised to explore the constitutionalisation of ESR and the incorporation of UNCRC. In addition, the Scottish Parliament has sought to better embed rights protection as part of parliamentary processes, including both pre and post-legislative scrutiny. The judiciary has indicated a willingness to adjudicate on international human rights law, but only when such rights are incorporated into the domestic framework. The Scottish constitutional framework is emerging into a multi-institutional approach to human rights, including ESR. The future looking trajectory of human rights protection mechanisms sets Scotland apart, however, it remains to be seen if the political will manifests into transformative change.

Most importantly, the chapter demonstrates that the UK human rights canvas is much more complex than would first appear. Indeed, the devolved trajectories have been much more ambitious in seeking to address outstanding human rights claims in devolved areas engaging with ESR. This could present as hugely problematic should it lead to further fragmentation of a unitary state – potentially leaving England behind on access to rights and remedies compared to those derived from devolved legislation. On the other hand, a more progressive analysis might concede that the devolved trajectories, once better understood at the national level, could provide the catalyst for enhancing and progressing on rights reform across the UK and in doing so propel the national dialogue beyond the chilling discourse on rights regression into a more positive space on rights progression.

Conclusion: Incorporation, Justiciability and Principles of Adjudication

This section serves as the concluding paragraphs of the book. It retraces the contributions of each chapter looking at the ground traversed, the conclusions reached and reflecting upon where the research might go next.

It is time to move on from the old debates, stereotypes and myths that characterise the rejection of ESR as 'real rights' and that hold ESR adjudication as an affront to democracy. Of course, there are challenges to overcoming the democratic risks that come with adjudication of ESR, but these challenges are not insurmountable. The first chapter sets out safeguards to address the risks by facilitating an approach to ESR adjudication based on flexible principles of good practice derived from deliberative democracy theory. The book orientates arguments in favour of a substantive rights-based model of constitutionalism that reframes the roles of the different constitutional actors where the court, executive and the legislature each must comply with fundamental norms, including ESR. This is not to change the role of the court, or afford it more power, but to recognise it as the important accountability mechanism it already ought to be. Future research will require quarrying deeper into the different adjudication principles, exploring, for example the procedural and substantive components of review and enforcement as well as looking at what each of the principles mean in practice in any given context. What, for example, will participation and remedial action mean in different constitutional settings, how is accessibility to be conceived and facilitated, what kind of intra-state or supranational deliberative mechanisms exist/will develop and what supervisory roles might be played by different institutional actors? The development of collective litigation and structural remedies will be of particular interest to the social rights scholar.

The second chapter looked at the status of ESR in international law and concludes that access to an effective judicial remedy for a violation of ESR is indeed a component of a state's international obligations. The chapter highlights the danger and risks posed by a long-held misconception around the nature of rights: that they existed as a 'generational' hierarchy, when this was not the original intention as far back as the UDHR. Laying aside these long-held and systemic structural misunderstandings will no doubt be difficult, however, it is imperative that legal communities make the effort to address this. The lens of this historical legal error continues to frame the discourse in the UK and traps legal communities in an erroneously formed debate about whether or not justiciability of ESR is possible (let me say one more time, it is), much to the detriment of the people the legal system ought to protect. A failure to address the ESR accountability gap places the burden of ESR violations on the weakest and most vulnerable. Without the appropriate legal structures and institutional mechanisms in place to adequately address this gap we leave the burden and the brunt of ESR violations to be addressed by those at the front line who are essentially left without appropriate means to support those who need it most.

Chapter 3 highlights the (somewhat limited) role played by European regional systems in the protection of ESR, whilst at the same time concluding that the regional systems form integral parts of the UK constitution. Both the ECHR and EU law may not remain pillars of the UK constitution for long and this is hugely problematic for rights regression in a state with an uncodified constitution. The risks posed by Brexit have not yet fully been accounted for and there is a significant shortfall on constitutional rights moving forward. Chapter 4 addressed the constitutional resistance to human rights in the UK compared to other models of constitutionalism. It becomes clearer as the book delves further into the UK constitution that different models of constitutionalism already co-exist and that the devolved lens completely transforms the way in which rights can be understood as forming a substantive component of the rule of law. Looking to other comparative examples from South Africa, Colombia, Argentina, Finland and Germany, it becomes clear that the UK could develop an approach to ESR adjudication that is cognisant of parliamentary supremacy should it so wish.

Chapter 5 categorised models of justiciability with reference to the principles of adjudication. It evidences case law demonstrating a wealth of court experience in the adjudication of ESR in the UK. Whilst existing mechanisms are far from perfect, they certainly evidence that the justiciability of ESR is something that occurs in the everyday practice of court adjudication. The chapter suggests other ways forward for enhancing justiciability, including signing up to an international complaints mechanism or, through the development of a constitutional model – either by way of an Economic and Social Rights Act or a codified constitution. It is the latter of the models, the constitutional solution, that the book proposes as the most democratically sound. It offers access to justice for ESR (and CPR) in way that recognises the role of the legislature, executive and judiciary in a multi-institutional approach where each institutional actor is responsible for upholding human rights. It also provides an overarching framework in which all the other mechanisms can co-exist meaning multiple routes to remedy can be available for the rights-holder.

The final chapter in the book, Chapter 6, sets out the means through which ESR are developing in the devolved frameworks of Wales, Northern Ireland and Scotland. The book reveals that there is no universal human rights and equality framework that applies across the UK and that the trajectories of the devolved regions have completely transformed the way in which human rights are framed. One of the key contributions of the book highlights just how important it is to pay more attention to the devolved frameworks. Failure to do so could cause further fragmentation of state unity – where the devolved jurisdictions offer enhanced protection on ESR, compared to England, or to each other. If the UK seeks to undermine progressive change at the devolved level then it risks encouraging separatist tendencies, and more importantly risks undermining an international peace treaty in the case of Northern Ireland. The UK adopting a holistic approach could allow a levelling up of rights across the board, indeed the devolved trajectories might, in the end, compel the UK to address the national ESR accountability gap.

Overall, the book seeks to offer ways forward for ESR according to the principles of adjudication and the particular justiciability mechanisms available under different forms of incorporation (constitutionalisation) of rights. In particular, it gives practical examples of how the legislature, executive and judiciary can act as guarantors of rights and proposes that the court must act as an accountability mechanism, and a means of last resort, should other institutional mechanisms fail. In so doing, it seeks to propel the national discourse beyond discussions around regressive human rights reform and presents pathways to better protect ESR both within the UK and beyond.

Future research will require more attention to the practical implementation of access to justice on the ground for ESR and the principles of adjudication proposed here act as a theoretical framework for this endeavour. Ultimately, it is hoped the book will help guide future research that continues to close the ESR accountability gap in access to justice for violations of such rights. This requires revisiting our substantive conception of justice as well as the means of accessing and achieving it.

Index

Note: Page locators in **bold** refer to tables.